Can We Survive Our Origins?

Studies in Violence, Mimesis, and Culture

Can We Survive Our Origins?

READINGS IN RENÉ GIRARD'S THEORY
OF VIOLENCE AND THE SACRED

Edited by Pierpaolo Antonello
and Paul Gifford

Michigan State University Press · *East Lansing*

♾ The paper used in this publication meets the minimum requirements of ANSI/NISO Z39.48-1992 (R 1997) (Permanence of Paper).

 Michigan State University Press
East Lansing, Michigan 48823-5245

Printed and bound in the United States of America.

21 20 19 18 17 16 15   1 2 3 4 5 6 7 8 9 10

LIBRARY OF CONGRESS CONTROL NUMBER: 2014941652
ISBN: 978-1-61186-149-5 (pbk.)
ISBN: 978-1-60917-435-4 (ebook: PDF)
ISBN: 978-1-62895-035-9 (ebook: ePub)
ISBN: 978-1-62896-034-1 (ebook: Kindle)

Book design and composition by Charlie Sharp, Sharp Des!gns, Lansing, Michigan
Original front cover art and cover design by David Drummond, Salamander Design,
www.salamanderhill.com. Backcover image of pillars at the temple of Göbekli Tepe
(Anatolia, Turkey) is by Vincent J. Musi, National Geographic Creative and is used with
permission.

g green press INITIATIVE Michigan State University Press is a member of the Green Press Initiative
and is committed to developing and encouraging ecologically responsible
publishing practices. For more information about the Green Press Initiative and the use of
recycled paper in book publishing, please visit *www.greenpressinitiative.org*.

Visit Michigan State University Press at *www.msupress.org*

This book is dedicated to
the memory of Bob Hamerton-Kelly,
whose energy, enthusiasm and inspiration
were instrumental to the realization
of our project.

Contents

Foreword

Rowan Williams

In the English-speaking intellectual world, René Girard's work continues to inspire and exasperate in almost equal measure. But part of the difficulty in developing a systematic and properly critical reception of this extraordinary schema or set of schemata is that only very gradually have Girard's theories been systematically connected with the main currents of intellectual modernity as understood in the Anglo-American tradition—notably the natural sciences and the whole world of empirical social and anthropological studies.

The essays collected by Pierpaolo Antonello and Paul Gifford make a very significant contribution to this connectedness. In the light of these two new volumes exploring Girardian mimetic theory in a Darwinian frame, it will be that much harder to see (and dismiss) Girard as an exotic intellectual outlier, operating in a milieu where serious scientific research is generally bypassed.

This is not exclusively a matter of the scientific basis or lack of it for Girard's theories; in the nature of the case, speculations about the origins of culture are not going to be easily "proved" (Darwin's own "big picture theory," prior to the advent of the modern science of genetics, has, of course, something of the same flavor). There is always going to be, in such cases, a powerful element of heuristic myth, tested not by "discoveries" but by the resourcefulness of the narrative in making sense of where we are. And it should be clear that "myth"—here and later in these pages—is being used in the sense of a comprehensive shared schema for making sense of social experience, not in the popular sense of "fiction."

It is no derogation from Girard's genius to say that what he provides is something like a "novelistic" version of human origins—a bid for a narrative that will allow all of us to "read" our human experience differently and with greater honesty or truthfulness. And it is important to say—in the light of some critical comments in recent discussion—that, like a novel (indeed, arguably like Jewish-Christian scripture as well), this does not of itself endorse, let alone sacralize, what it narrates: it seeks to induce a kind of recognition that makes possible a different narrative. Girard provides not only a narrative of origins but also a narrative—the Christian narrative of a radically nonviolent deity—that equips us to recognize what we would rather not recognize because it simultaneously opens a new path.

Pulling together much of the diverse discussion presented in these essays, we might try to retrace and re-present the Girardian picture in terms something like these. The containment of the spiral of competitive desire by means of sacrificial/sacralized violence is a point of intersection between "nature" and "culture." We cannot understand the rituals of violent sacrifice (granted that not every ritual sacrifice is intrinsically violent, a point that Girard does not initially register) either by a fully naturalized explanation or by a simple story of cultural history (human speakers constructing a more or less arbitrary scheme of meanings designed both to explain and to avert disaster).

One of Girard's boldest claims is that sacral violence precedes and indeed *generates* culture; yet to say this is not to bind ourselves into a mechanistic account of what culture and language "really" are. It is more like saying that there is a moment in biological evolution when a convergence of new material (neuronal) patterns and new environmental circumstances produces a crisis whose (slow) resolution moves inexorably toward language and culture. The vocabulary we need here is hard to find, and Girard's own formulations are often far from precise. But the underlying idea is that on the one hand, enhanced cranial capacity and the evolution of mirror neurons clarifies and intensifies the mimetic capacity of human beings, and on the other hand, the extended period of extreme vulnerability and dependency in the human young requires means for protecting those young, and thus of limiting aggressive behavior in the group. In other words, the *cost* of violent behavior is increased (the possible loss of the vulnerable young of the species) at roughly the same time as the *occasions* for violent behavior are multiplied because we are better able to recognize and identify with the desire of the other and thus to see our desire "in" the other, and to see ourselves as competing for what the other desires.

Girard suggests that this is the crisis that is primordially resolved by acts of exclusionary violence, the projection of danger onto some member of the group who is eliminated and thus becomes the absent, sacred source of harmony. The repetition of this act becomes a key element in the development of properly symbolic behavior: an action is recalled by means of another action, an absent reality is represented in the present. The recognition that an action is effective prompts a repetition in another mode; and thus the belief gains traction that acts may stand for other acts, things may stand for other things. Language as we know it is being brought to birth—and brought to birth, ironically, in a strategy of avoidance, in the refusal to recognize the original sacral murder as arbitrary.

But the implication of this is that the origin of culture is irretrievably implicated in violence. We learn as humans how to behave "symbolically" as a result of the success of a strategy of exclusion and murder; the absent reality that language represents is the slaughtered victim, arbitrarily picked out to resolve our mimetic tensions. And this means (as several of the essays collected here indicate) that attempts to resolve current cultural crises without an understanding of the buried mechanism of culture will simply reproduce, in one way or another, the same absent reality—one or another form of exclusionary violence. In a society like that of Western modernity, in which the symbolic as such is so widely ignored or misunderstood, the risks are enormous. Our ability in technologically sophisticated mass killing is unprecedented. But if we have no symbolic equipment, we have no capacity to make sense of/contain violence; and if we have no symbolic *literacy* of the kind Girard is most concerned about, we remain prisoners of arbitrary murderousness, disguised as rationality.

Girard is thus pointing out a double sickness in our culture. We do not take symbolism seriously and so are inclined to ignore the fundamental cultural fact that our linguistic communication is rooted in the question of how we limit the destructive effects of imitative desire. At worst we speak and act as if there were no crisis of imitative desire, no problem of stopping the spiral of mimetic competition. We risk reverting literally to a pre-human state in which we have not yet worked out how to contain aggression. Equally, we have lost our familiarity with the myth that exposes the arbitrary and irrational nature of the primitive symbolic concordat—the myth of a voluntary and innocent death that unravels the exclusionary sacrificial illusion, the myth (and fact) of Christ's cross. We deal in discourses about war that pretend that technological advance makes war rational; but the analysis of what Mary Kaldor and others have called "new wars" shows how the pattern is actually one of vastly increased moral and social confusion, in which the question of legitimate authority in the public or political handling of violence has become worryingly obscure. The refusal to recognize the primitive symbolic character of modern conflict, the radical un-modernity of our warfare, is one of the most dangerous illusions of our time. And the equal unwillingness to see the symbolic workings of exclusion in an era of dramatic gaps between rich and poor, when unrestrained competition and unlimited "growth" are taken for granted as intelligible values, is no less of a time bomb.

It is as if we had gone back to that evolutionary turning point at which we first properly recognized each other as centers of desire and found that we had no means of negotiating it except by struggles for power. And of course unless we begin by acknowledging the need for symbolic resolution, we shall not come to the point of acknowledging the necessity of having our initial and brilliantly successful symbolic answer turned inside out by the counter-myth of divine nonviolence.

To make a slightly provocative point: I am aware that there is a distantly but distinctly Hegelian feel to this way of presenting Girard's argument—first the creative error, the "misrecognition," then the negation and reconstruction; but that is no bad thing, especially for those (supporters and opponents) who would like to see Girard as simply overthrowing an entire philosophical legacy. Girard—reasonably—mistrusts a mechanical, algorithmic version of Hegelian dialectic and insists on the conversation (absent in Hegel, for a variety of historical and intellectual reasons) with the sciences of human origins and development; but the point that the origin of culture itself is involved in a sort of symbolic original sin takes us beyond empirical science alone, requiring a phenomenology of some kind. Girard makes no sense unless the drastic transformation of the symbolic order offered by the Christian narrative is engaged with some sort of recognized symbolic order to start with. The contemporary mythology that presents the human subject as essentially a will in the void gives little purchase to any adequate grasp of a converting alternative to violence. And the labor of understanding this is one of the hardest and most interesting aspects of reading, let alone commending Girard today.

Girard uses the analysis of contemporary sociopolitical realities to help decipher the original drama of our becoming human, in a biologically and culturally speciated sense ("hominization"), and he uses the recognition of that—still remarkably little understood—evolutionary development to help us discern and confront prophetically the ethical perils of the modern age and of our human coming-to-be in historical time (our "humanization"). His "archeological" and cognitive project and his ethical challenge develop recip-rocally. Together they constitute a genuinely dialectical enquiry, faithfully reflected in these present volumes on Darwin and Girard (*Can We Survive Our Origins?* and its companion *How We Became Human*).

In respect of the latter volume, the notion of "heuristic myth" points, at least potentially, to an unsuspected filiation. As I am using it, this term connotes an imaginatively constructed paradigm, which serves to model and address something not (yet) visible, not (yet) fully known or compre-hended—a cast of the intellectual line, indicating a direction for genuine empirical work, but uncertain in advance of what will be drawn in. A heuris-tic myth of this type, if it receives consistent empirical confirmation (and so develops self-critically, acquiring further refinement and further reinforce-ment as it becomes more specific), begins to look and function increasingly like a working scientific hypothesis rather than simply a useful fiction.

And the bold question posed by *How We Became Human* is whether we have underestimated the degree of confirmation that might be available. The continuity of the phenomenon of victim identification and expulsion across the animal-human divide; the role of "religion" as the most basic cul-tural matrix, antedating settlement and domestication; the distinctions to be drawn between animal and human violence; the role of sacrifice in the earliest forms of "religion"—all these tell strongly in favor of something very like Girard's account as an empirically credible story of cultural origins. Once again, remember the history of Darwinism: a "big picture," inspiring and exasperating, gradually fleshed out by work in unexpectedly relevant fields.

That is why we so badly need careful work on the frontiers between Girardian theory and other currents of critical thought—biology and neuroscience, anthropology, war studies, economics, and, not least, the specific stories of conflict, scapegoating, self-recognition, and transformation that emerge from the conflicts of our time, from Northern Ireland, the Middle East, Sudan, and South Africa. As Girard indicates, the stakes are very high at present. But it is possible also to see—as he repeatedly points out—that the arbitrariness of "sacral" violence is harder and harder to conceal for those who reflect seriously about conflict in our world.

The Christian myth tells us that the most fundamental and generative subject or energy or resource we can imagine is beyond rivalry; it demonstrates this in the enactment of a human life in which arbitrary violence is both exposed for what it is and accepted without retaliation, so that we see that we do not need exclusionary sacrifice after all; and it thus establishes a form of human solidarity that does not depend on the identification of a scapegoat and the closing of boundaries against the stranger.

The importance of studies such as the ones contained in this book is that they both underline the urgency of the cultural crisis and open up impressive possibilities for conversation between Girardians and others in the mainstream of our discourse. If Girard and most of the contributors to this volume are right, such conversation is anything but a luxury.

Acknowledgments

This book originated in a series of conferences held between 2009 and 2011 at St John's College, Cambridge and at Stanford University. Our kindest thanks go to Imitatio, and in particular to Lindy Fishburne, for the outstanding financial support that made all our endeavors possible. We thank the Master and the Fellows of St John's College for their logistical and financial help. Our thanks go also to Jean-Pierre Dupuy for his invaluable advice on the organization of the Stanford event; and to Noah Burbank, Jimmy Kaltreider, Christopher Woods, and Brendon Flint for their contributions to resolving organizational, logistical, and graphic problems on both sides of the Atlantic. Our thanks go to National Geographic for permission to reproduce (back cover) the image of a T-Pillar at the world's oldest known temple of Gobekli Tepe (Anatolia), Turkey. Photo by Vincent J. Musi.

Introduction

René Girard's "mimetic theory" addresses the role of "sacred violence" in the constitution of human culture and social order. It has been increasingly acknowledged as one of the most striking breakthrough contributions to twentieth-century critical thinking: in particular, for its power to model and explain violent sacralities, ancient and modern, ranging from Crusade and pogrom to Dreyfus and the Holocaust; from gospel apocalyptic and environmental crisis to the religious wars, suicide bombers, and culture clashes of our fast-globalizing world.

The present volume sets this power of explanation into an evolutionary and Darwinian framework. It aims to observe and explore how Girardian insights modify our understanding of evolution, at a human and cultural level, first of all—but then ultimately also as a total phenomenon retracing life-on-earth within an open process of cosmic emergence.

It focuses on the questions: How and how well do we "survive our origins"? How may we best hope to do so? In Girardian perspective, these large questions can be specified more precisely. We are asking: How far do "cultural" mechanisms of controlling violence, which allowed humankind to cross the threshold of "hominization"—i.e., to survive and develop in evolutionary terms—still represent a "default setting" that threatens to destroy us? How may we transcend them and escape their field of gravity?

This central enquiry engages a number of subset questions. How far is violence biologically rooted in our human mimetic fabric; how far it is socially shaped and determined? How did proto-institutions emerge as regulatory principles of violence, both internal to the community or group and intercommunal? By which control mechanisms has it been kept at bay in prehistorical and historical times; how far has violence been a programmed part of the institutions of society and the structures of culture ever since?

How can recent world events be said to have reopened the whole area of questioning to which Girard points so insistently: the *obscure foundational link,* which he offers for the first time to decipher in fundamental and decisive terms, *between religion and violence?* And what crucial role in the understanding and remediation of this deep-laid complicity has, on his equally insistent submission, been provided by the Hebrew and Christian scriptures?

Are religions intrinsically violent (as is strenuously argued by the "new atheists")? Or, as Girard argues, have they been functionally "rational" instruments to *manage and cope with* the intrinsically violent runaway dynamic that characterizes human social organization in all periods of human history? Can we discern clear daylight, as Girard suggests—but here perhaps more controversially—between Christian and pre-Christian inspirations? Is violence decreasing in this time of secular modernity post-Christendom; or are we, rather, at increased—and even *apocalyptic*—risk from our enhanced powers of action and our decreased socio-symbolic protections?

It will be seen that the present volume enters a field of concern that, often enough, resembles a minefield—an area, at least, of "lively anthropological debate." Most recently, the debate has been relaunched by Steven Pinker's *The Better Angels of Our Nature: Why Violence Has Declined* (2011). This work retraces the "ascent of man" read as a function of a phenomenon statistically traceable in history: that of apparently *diminishing* human violence—thus giving grounds, so its author hopes, for moral optimism invested in civilizing progress and the intrinsic potential for good of human moral nature. It may usefully be set side by side with Girard's theory, which offers a different accountancy of violence, another interpretation of human nature and its violent sacralities, and, overall, an alternative and more radical vision of the way in which the theme of survival is related to that of "salvation."

◆ ◆ ◆

The contributions brought together in this study derive from a series of three interdisciplinary conferences: the first and last of them held at St John's College, Cambridge, the second at Stanford University (California). In the wake of the Darwin commemoration of 2009,[1] and in the context of the ongoing questions generated at the interface between science and religion, this series of events sought to assess the significant, yet still uncertainly charted, contribution made by Girardian "mimetic theory" (MT) to our understanding of human origins and its importance for social and fundamental anthropology.

Two companion volumes now bring this thinking to a wider public. *How We Became Human: Evolution at the Threshold of Cultural Invention* looks backwards, toward evolutionary origins, in dialogue with the latest findings of the relevant empirical sciences. Leading specialists from many disciplines (evolutionary biology and neuroscience, animal behavior studies, social anthropology, culture theory, philosophy, and theology) consider Girard's bold and very cogent scenario of "hominization" (i.e., the evolutionary passage from animal to human); they examine the socio-symbolic mechanisms of emissary victimization that, so Girard argues, were developed by our species to meet the all-important need—strangely invisible to, or at least discounted and minimized by, many evolutionary theorists—of *managing the threat of intraspecific conflict and violence;* and they assess the role of its symbolico-ritual prolongations in the development of language and religion, myth, moral codes, law, and institutions, etc. They finally evaluate the current standing of Girardian mimetic theory as a generative account of the origins of human culture as a whole.

The other volume, introduced here, moves forward from origins. It retraces and assesses the implications of Girardian insights for the most central problem that mimetic theory brings so sharply into focus: the fact that the enabling spring of human emergence and development was originally, and remains continuously, reciprocal to the human capacity to generate types and levels of violence that risk bringing humankind to self-destruction, both in its constituent communities, and—today, for the first time (Girard 2007, 47 [2010a, 35])[2]—as a *species.*

This challenging reciprocity is followed here in some of the variations it has displayed over historical time: passing from the archaic and ancient through the offer of redemption that Christianity makes, at the opening of our own "Common Era," in substituting, for the immanent evolutionary finality of *survival,* the offer of a transcendent *salvation* operating in-and-through the historical (and evolutionary) "here-and-now." Approaching the contemporary world, it visits the challenges of peace-making amid the violent reciprocities of our own time, and it concludes with a look at some "apocalyptic" scenarios that, more than ever, threaten to abridge and abort the human future.

The problem of origins, as appears most clearly in the present volume, is not to be divorced from the problem of meanings and ends. A pivotal role, accordingly, is given here also to "religion": *not* as understood in the manner of archaic-sacral "fundamentalisms"; nor yet as conceived, reactively, by the intellectually fashionable dismissal of "cognitivist" ("left brain") scientism; but rather, in the evolutionary ambiguity proper to it, of which Girard offers a fresh and highly illuminating account. "Religions" are the worst *and also*—insofar as they transcend their own origins *divinely*—the best of things human . . . Yet we also *regress,* or *fall back* into the archaic patterns that made us human in the first place.

Overall, the aim of both volumes is to set out clearly and strategically, for perhaps the first time, a poignant ambiguity defining the human condition. The selfsame mechanisms that allowed humankind to emerge, survive, and thrive biologically—and the very inventions that drove forward a new evolutionary phase, engaging the culture-programmed, civilizing social existence of *Homo sapiens*—are *also* the *default mechanisms* that mortgage human moral progress and threaten to foreclose the human future.

We thus walk the fine line between Progress and Abyss.

◆ ◆ ◆

Can we specify the wider antecedents of this agenda? The reader who has only nodding acquaintance with Girardian theory, or none at all, may well be grateful for some guidance in the leading ideas that bring this French American anthropologist and culture theorist to the particular point of insight and questioning at which we here meet him.

It is most economically provided by referring to his latest work, *Achever*

Clausewitz (translated under the English title *Battling to the End*). This book treats the crisis of the modern world, read in the perspective of evolutionary hominization—in particular, in relation to the changing character of modern warfare and the acceleration of history observable in the twentieth century of the Common Era.

Girard himself proclaims it to be a "peculiar sort of book." It presents, he says, "things never said before, with the violence and the clarity they require." It envisages "the possibility of an end to Europe, of the Western world and of the world as a whole." That these things should today be a real *possibility* makes it, he declares, "an apocalyptic book" (9 [ix]).

His readers, both those who write within the covers of the present volume, and their readers in turn, are left to judge whether such decided insistence is an aging theorist's fevered rant, parting company with reason, or a deep-seeing and far-flung prophetic vehemence, designed to awaken the sleeping—those who observe with complacency, but without joined-up understanding, the time of world wars, atomic weapons, multiple genocides, and imminent eco-catastrophe—and the globalizing and cosmic reach of an ever-accelerating and increasingly human-shaped and human-driven history.

We may retain from this work three crucial ideas that run through the present volume.

◆   ◆   ◆

The first is that of a *crisis of the modern world,* brought about by an accelerating rhythm of history, discernible in many aspects and dimensions of human life. The dimension principally considered here—the significantly alerting case, so to speak—is the transformation visible in the area of *human conflict and warfare.*

Girard reads this phenomenon in dialogue with Carl von Clausewitz, the nineteenth-century Prussian military theorist who thought and wrote out of an intense love-hate relationship to the genius of Napoleon Bonaparte. There is a hidden truth of Clausewitz, Girard argues: something Clausewitz glimpsed in terrible longing, but was shy of articulating, and which he hid away behind the lesser and perilous half-truth for which everyone today remembers him—namely, that "war is the continuation of diplomacy by other means."

Not really, not anymore, says Girard. It is true that warfare was once a way of *regulating* and thereby *limiting* the violence bred out of human rivalries and conflict. This was true in respect of its actors: only those of one sex, and of a certain age range, dressed in a certain uniform, and drawn from within a specialized professional category, were eligible to participate, and then only in restricted numbers. Similarly, its objectives, its permitted modalities and legitimate victims, its tactics, its intensity and extent: all these factors were, by tacit convention, controlled and managed. So it was in all the wars fought between European nations in the period of the rise of nation-states—i.e., in Europe: until the twentieth century. It was particularly so in the ballet-like, laced and frilled bloodlettings of the eighteenth century. Warfare in this period was violence domesticated, passion subject to calculation, and compatible with reason, admitting conventional limitation and the mitigating play of all contingencies that dilute its essential character of violence-to-the-death. This is what made it *usable* as an instrument of policy—and even as a tool for deciding, at *tolerable cost,* conflicted issues between nations and states.

Then came the post-Revolutionary conflict between Napoleon and his Continental adversaries. This was something little observed on the English-speaking side of the Channel or across the Atlantic; but von Clausewitz observed it closely and struggled to theorize what he intuited: namely, a deregulating modulation of warfare, aligning it ever more closely with its essence or principle of reciprocal violence.

This modulation affected the actors, the scale, and the intensity of warfare. The French Revolutionary Army began to be identified with the civil population of the French Republic; whereas bands of non-uniformed partisans sprang up in the countries *liberated* and/or *subdued* by them and became significant combatants, while the scale of warfare became continental, with epic displacements of armies. Above all, the passionate, ideologically charged ferocity of the military struggle introduced into warfare a new intensity. Warfare began to resemble its intrinsic logic or law, which Clausewitz identified as that of the *duel to the death:* an escalation of violence, according to a structure of tit-for-tat reciprocity, and its consequent pursuit toward the *extermination* of the adversary (rather than simply his reasonable and advantageous *submission*). The logic and the law became ever clearer in each of the three wars, which, between 1870 and

1945, engaged the Franco-German duelists, and increasingly, their continent-wide alliances. The savagery of the war on the Eastern Front from 1941 to 1945 between ideologically mobilized titans of Nazi Germany and Stalinist Russia is the case that unveils decisively the face of *de-restricted and unlimited warfare.*

The larger trouble is that today, violence *isn't any longer containable or predictable:* it overflows its supposed constraints; it overtakes and it takes over the soldiers who fight; it overruns the politicians and their political calculations. It no longer respects conventionally set bounds and patterns. So that "war" is more profoundly defined today as violence coinciding with its own intrinsic law of a *montée aux extrêmes*—an inherent dynamic of escalation to extremes, or crescendo toward paroxysm.

> We have therefore entered a time of generally unpredictable hostilities, where adversaries scorn each other and plot their mutual destruction: Bush and bin Laden; Palestinians and Israelis; Russians and Chechens; Indians and Pakistanis—the combat is the same. The fact that we speak of "rogue states" proves how far we have exited all codification. . . . Inter-state wars are fought under the cover of maintaining international security. The [younger] Bush administration did what it wanted in Afghanistan, as did the Russians in Chechnya. Reciprocally, Islamist terror strikes anywhere. (131 [67])

This character of unpredictable non-containability is, Girard considers, ever clearer in the era of ultimate—i.e., *global*—imitations and rivalries, the era of ultimate weapons: smart bombs, and the poor man's mimetic riposte to them, in point of "shock and awe," the suicide bomber. Not to mention H-bombs, ever with us and escaping the conventionally struck "balance of terror."

And—here is the message of his book—these developments constitute a *phase change in the long history of human violence,* and one that is properly *apocalyptic.* Not in the sense conceived by a "barmy army" of fundamentalists, i.e., as *divine retribution wrought in judgment* upon an errant humankind, but in the sense that claims the most sober authority of the gospels, sanely interpreted. The apocalypse is human violence escaping its culture-bound containments, obeying its intrinsic law of escalation, and dislocating the cosmos in its crescendo—thus, potentially, *destroying humankind itself.*

It is clear for Girard that we have to stop thinking in received post-Enlightenment patterns and begin to come to grips instead with the real—*nodal and originary*—character of human violence.

◆ ◆ ◆

For what undoes all modern thinking in the Hegelian mode, Girard considers, is the failure to grasp a second idea: namely, that the perilous dynamic of escalation to extremes is no merely modern aberration, still less an epiphenomenon or byproduct of civilizing progress. It is, on the contrary, in exacerbated modern form, *a repetition or replay of a drama played out at the threshold of hominization and programmed into the birth process of culture itself, as a "default mode" of human social functioning.* Before dashing off prescriptions for its remediation, we need to take the measure of this considerable "given."

What Girard reads in Clausewitz's notion of *Wechselwirkung*—the "reciprocal action" uniting adversaries in a tit-for-tat crescendo of retaliatory violence—is, indeed, continuous with the original drama of our becoming human in an evolutionary world. He sees the modern phenomenon as referring to a very primitive and very fundamental pattern of archaic group functioning, which he has described under the names of "mimetic crisis" and its "scapegoat resolution" through "sacrifice."

What *is* Clauswitzian "apocalypse," after all, but

> an abstract principle becoming real, reality catching up with a concept; and humankind, as we must be lucid enough to recognise, tends intrinsically toward the annihilation here envisaged. This is the relentless law of the duel-to-the death which Clausewitz reads in the primacy of defence over attack. (55 [19])

By starting from the ideas of "attack" and "aggression," we commonly *misthink* violence. In fact, violence is almost always-already caught in a structure of reciprocity between rivalrous and conflicted parties, and it is the *defensive function* that is primary (in the sense that it is what causes conflicts to endure and to escalate). One of the signs of this is that we never think of ourselves as "attacking" anyone except as a way of defending ourselves from some threat to which that structure of reciprocity exposes us. Another is that no conflict has an absolute beginning, but represents always, rather, a transformation, at some critical moment of their outworking, of increasingly conflicted rivalries. To know that much, indeed, we need only reflect that the same structural reciprocity is everywhere imprinted in ancient law and moral precept designed for the *controlling* of violence, e.g., the law of minimal or "just" reprisal ("an eye for an eye"), or the so-called "golden rule" ("do unto others as you would be done by").

Moreover:

> Men are distinct from animals, which manage to contain their violence within what animal behaviourists call dominance patterns. Humans, for their part, cannot contain the reciprocity between them because they imitate each other too much, and resemble each other more and more and ever-more quickly. (55 [19])

For Girard, mimesis—the power to replicate, copy, or imitate any behavior, pattern, or stimulus—is certainly to be observed in pre-human nature, especially in the higher primates; but it is not developed to the prodigious degree allowed by the much larger human brain. This is the secret of human divergence and development from animal antecedents, as mapped by Darwin's tree of life-forms, since it both enhances human group intelligence, particularly symbolic intelligence and language-learning, and constitutes therefore also the greatest single factor enabling social cooperation between humans.

But that superiority comes at a price, which Girard's previous work has already spelled out with rare consequence and cogency. Human mimetic capacity is *also* the power to imitate what other cospecifics desire; to model our desires upon theirs; but then also—since we now so vividly represent and desire the same objects as they do—to enter into *rivalry and hence also conflict* with these Others. Mimetic desire is always potentially acquisitive and rivalrous—always caught in a tissue of social relationships and reciprocities.

Moreover, from the earliest origins of humanity, it carries for the group the threat of self-annihilation, since mimetically vectored desire turns out to be the most contagious or "viral" thing there is. Our common experience today of "viral" mimetic phenomena—for instance, the sudden "crazes" and convergent Internet "hits" occurring within electronic cyberspace—will readily confirm this observation, as will the sudden mimetic movements registered by and between the world's stock exchanges. Acquisitive and rivalrous desire—active within a field of interlinked social relationships and creating conflictual reciprocities—leads, perilously, to generalized violence, increasing in intensity and extent and quickly assuming the gravity of an "apocalyptic" threat to group survival.

A propensity for *escalation to extremes,* in other words, is inscribed deep in the evolutionary experience and in the cultural DNA of *Homo sapiens.* We know that many human groups, both throughout recorded history and in prehistorical times, did in fact fail to survive. Classic rationalist ethnography and evolutionary anthropology have been reluctant to give this fact any very significant—i.e., *nodal and originary*—place in human development. These sciences have always invoked preferentially ecological and climate factors, together with deficient technologies or other failures to adapt to the challenges of environment. But an equally cogent and far less visible candidate in the causal order—a factor much closer to home, consistent with human singularity in nature, entirely inferable from the well-documented history of human conflict—is the *exceptional character of cospecific violence among humans,* which can indeed result in intra-group implosion, or intercommunity devastation or wipeout.

The very fact that we *have* "survived our origins" perhaps makes our survival all too "obvious"; it takes away from us the recognition of *what* we have survived, and thus also the perceived need to *explain how and why* we are indeed "survivors." Yet it is, at least, deductively clear that the *management of self-generated intra-specific violence* must have been, in respect of human origins, just as it remains today, the number one imperative of all evolving and evolved human societies everywhere. It is logically the case that hominid groups *could not* have crossed the threshold of hominization, or survived and progressed as humans in an evolutionary world, had they not devised some "soft-wired" (i.e., *cultural*) means of containing their own intrinsic capacity for self-destruction.

Girard's major thesis, brilliantly developed in *Violence and the Sacred* (original French edition, 1972) from the attesting documents supplied by world mythologies and by Greek tragedy, is that this number one condition is in fact met by the very mechanism that historically inaugurated and still, in part, secretly founds all social life, and everything we call "culture." This is the "victimary process" or "scapegoat mechanism."

We recognize the phenomenon of scapegoating elementarily from the many vestigial forms it still takes in the modern world: "taking it out on" the dog or the wife after a stressful day in the office; sacking the manager because the press are "howling for blood" after a run of poor performances by the national team. At the extreme limit of its virulence, we may even dare to recognize the paradigmatic instance-in-principle of this phenomenon, which is supplied, precisely, by "civilized" twentieth-century Europe: namely, the Holocaust of European Jews during the Second World War.

Girard asks us to attend, however, to scapegoat violence in its *archaic* form. Where the adversaries originally wanted diverse things—to appropriate the same woman, to seize the first place, to exact retributive justice, and so on—they end up polarized quite irrationally upon a single adversary, arbitrarily designated to the common fury by a single rage-modeling leader. In other words, any gathering crisis of generalized violence tends to simplify, at its apex, into a polarized and unanimous antagonism of the type "all-against-one." The collective blood-rage is at this point deflected outwards and discharged against a single, arbitrarily chosen—and consequently "innocent"—victim, who is expelled or killed.

The scapegoat, in fact, acts as a sort of *lightning conductor* to all the violently destructive energies gathered within the community. The mechanism of emissary victimage may here be compared to the disjunctor switch that breaks the circuit and prevents that gathering and perilous electricity of mimetic desire from consuming the human house. It also sets up the first and founding equation of collective identity-bonding: all are one ... against, and by virtue of, the scapegoated Other.

What then? Girard asks us to imagine the victim lying inert before the hushed group of hominids or primitive men. He or she appears simultaneously and contradictorily as (1) the guilty origin of the crisis: he must have been guilty or we wouldn't have killed him; (2) as the beneficent provider of the miracle of renewed peace and social harmony. This moment of conflicting persuasions and surpassing awe is the beginning of a process of *sacralization;* the dead victim will come to be seen as the potent bearer of a power of life and death, as the Power capable of reversing the current of life energies from negative to positive: such terrible wrath, such amazing beneficence!

The first perception will suggest in retrospect that the sacrificial victim must surely have willed his own death; the second, once the corpse has been disposed of, will come to suggest that this exceptional and departed Visitor must indeed have been a god in disguise. At which point, the god becomes the center and focus—indeed, the attributed origin—of all social and moral codes developed against the return of crisis and catastrophe.

No one, even belonging to our own "evolved" here-and-now, easily admits responsibility—least of all for acts of collective murder committed in hallucinatory states and belied, to all seeming, by the beneficial effects they appear to procure for the community. Primitive man did, and we still do, *offload guilt and shift the blame, disguising the inadmissible violence committed.* This is well known in the language of the tribe (or at least of our Western tribes):[3] it is called "maquiller le cadavre" (putting makeup on the corpse), "passing the buck" (cf. Fr: "le bouc émissaire"). The Sacred, with its entire logic of ambivalence and its transferred blame, its disguises and delegations—its *sacrificial logic*—starts here.

Girard's originality as an anthropologist, and his abiding claim to distinction, is to have shown how this neglected factor of self-generated or intrinsic scapegoat violence, together with the culture-founding response it generates, can be held to unlock all the "unresolved enigmas" of human origins as registered by post-Enlightenment anthropologists and ethnologists under the name of the "mimetic crisis"; together with its resolution in the mechanism of emissary victimage, it is shown to be the generative nerve point commanding the entire system of archaic (or "primitive" or *natural*) religion—and hence also of all culture (*Things Hidden,* original French edition, 1978).

His golden key is used first to prosecute decisively the "stalled" decipherments of nineteenth- and twentieth-century ethnography. Girard deciphers, in and through the panoply of its diverse forms, the *functional logic* of the principal components of the entire system of primitive religion-and-culture, namely: prohibition (*taboo, interdict*), something that evolves over time into moral codes and laws; ritual (in particular, *ritual sacrifice*), which evolves to give all the *institutions* of social government; and *myth* (or identity storytelling), which binds a community and its culture together, offering a narrativized rationale for its cohesion.

Prohibition tends essentially to deny access to all the objects at the origin of the rivalries that originally degenerated into the traumatizing-and-unnamable founding crisis. Basically, the entire system of taboos and interdicts prolongs the original movement of expelling the scapegoat, in the—illusory and ever-vain—hope of closing down all recurrences of the founding crisis.

The set of ritual behaviors and practices instituted by early man follows an inverse path, albeit one that is also pre-sketched in the inaugural crisis— this time in the identity-defining unanimity of the all-against-one by which the original crisis had found its resolution. Ritual sacrifice installs at the heart of the common life a reenactment or replay of the founding murder itself. The ritual slaughter of a surrogate victim replicates as exactly as possible (here is another brilliant Girardian leap of understanding) the original scapegoat murder—of course, with the *arrière-pensée* of re-creating its pacifying, reconciling, identity-bonding outcome. The victim is chosen—often from a purpose-specific reserve (as in the case of the Aztecs from among the marginal, the weak, or the vulnerable—e.g., children, the sick, prisoners of war).[4] This rite is triggered by the incipient signs of returning mimetic crisis; these are indeed solicited and prepared by a time of license (or "festival"), which, significantly, frames the sacrifice. The sacrificial climax of the festival "resolves" once more this staged renascence of contagion, or at least it exorcises the anguish of its feared return—but now *ritually,* which is to say, *repeatably.*

The rite's collective, strongly participatory, and essentially theatrical character comes to be ceremonially regulated and aesthetically enhanced over time, delivering a no doubt spellbinding potency of emotional charge—such as we readily still understand from the later homologies of theme and the affective echoes it finds in Greek tragedy. (We understand here, perhaps, how Greek tragedy became for Girard an echolocating Ear to the hearing of lost human origins. In the path of this discovery, he has had, of course, to lay, if not to slay, the ghosts of both Nietzsche and Freud (Girard 1972, 1978, 2008).

Myth, finally, is the telling of the Story—the story or collection of stories that fashions and undergirds the identity of the group or tribe by representing in epic narratives its own founding events, its provenance, traditions, and special character. What identifies myth for Girard—and gives this concept a rather singular inflection or signature proper to Girardian hermeneutics—is that the mythological story told indefinitely rehearses the founding mimetic crisis and scapegoat murder; yet it does so, crucially, in a disguised, allusive, artlessly artful way (it is, as the French version says, "mystifié-mystifiant" in its very pertinence).

The brief formula of this self-deceiving deceptiveness is "the story as seen from the perspective of the victimizers." For example: one South Sea island myth says: "the god flew away over the cliff toward the islands he had come from"; we have to learn to decipher the *real subtext:* "we advanced toward the scapegoat, cudgels in hand, no one daring to strike the first blow; but his distress was such that he threw himself over the cliff to his death on the rocks below."

If archaic culture can be deciphered thus—and the structural patterns Girard tirelessly adduces from mythologies all over the world bring impressive confirmation—then another strategic point of "anthropological" insight, much coveted and hugely seminal in its implications, lies within reach.

Is not the victimary process also the *missing link* that gives us access to the "lost" and forever invisible interface between the animal world and the human world: the principle that explains the "hominization" of the primates—and, more generally, the process of "humanization" (i.e., the development of self-cognizant human culture and civilization) as such? From *Things Hidden since the Foundation of the World* onwards (from 1978, date of the French original) Girard pursues this hypothesis with vigor.[5]

Is this entire evolutionary excursion an unnecessarily long way round when it comes to understanding contemporary violence and its risk of apocalypse? Not so, replies Girard in *Battling to the End:* it is the shortest way home. "We do have to go back several thousands of years. The discovery of a principle of violence is set at that price" (2007, 59 [2010a, 21]). And he insists: "Humanity was only able to come to birth and to progress, both these things in tandem, because religious prohibitions emerged early enough to ward off the risk of self-destruction" (122 [62]). "I think that the two great institutions of archaic religion, prohibitions and sacrifice, played an essential role in the passage of pre-human to human societies, precisely in preventing hominids from destroying themselves and each other" (123–24 [63]).

Pointing to human emergence as an outcome fraught with cognitive and moral ambiguities, he confirms and signs:

> They invented sacrifice without knowing it, unconsciously, by channeling their violence against an emissary victim, the arbitrary designation of which

was necessarily hidden from them. They had, each time, in order to effect an exit from crisis, to transform their mutual violence into a force emanating from all, polarized against one. Each time, an "external" appreciation (which sees reciprocity) had to coincide—while remaining distinct from it—with a perspective arising from within the group (which only wishes to see difference). At which point, all turned against the one. (56 [19])

Here, then, is the originating point of the long shadow cast by the "ascent of man." It follows that, for Girard, human history, in its nodal point of origin, and in its ongoing moral crux, is always, in some sense, an equation between that superiority and the darker shadow associated with human emergence.

◆　◆　◆

Girard's third—and undoubtedly most controversial—idea is that Christianity has deprived humankind of its "failsafe" survival mechanism, and offered it instead something more radical, but also still very equivocal in its effects: namely, the possibility of salvation. "Good in the absolute," this novelty is, he says, "bad relatively speaking" (9 [x]).

Its relative disadvantage is more immediately visible than the absolute good it represents in a more ultimate or comprehensive vision of things. If we follow Girard's account, humanity only "made it" over the threshold of hominization because it developed a *pharmacology of the containment of violence*—this containment being developed, but always also refracted, in all the rituals, institutions, laws, moral codes, and myths that make up its "culture." Its very *civilizational progress* is built on this foundation: more precisely, on this mechanism converting the greatest human peril into the major human possibility.

"Progress" represents, therefore, a direct expression of the outworking of the "threshold solution." Girard, it will be seen, would not wish to deny the validity of Pinker's *observational data* on the advancing gentle-kindness of our laws, morals, and manners. In his system of thinking, this is one proof among others that the "containment" of violence *does work* and *has worked*—up to a point, in the perspective of evolutionary survival and flourishing. What his theory calls into question, rather, is the adequacy of Pinker's basis for interpreting this phenomenon, and the conclusions to be drawn from it.

How does Christianity *deprive* us of the *default settings* that have allowed evolutionary humanity to survive and progress? Girard says: it *exposes the untruth or make-believe of the mythico-religious pharmacology* inherent in both our survival and our progress. It disarms the deepest spring of human self-deception, and with it our protection against our own violence. That is its "time-bomb effect" (47 [14]).

At this delicate point, it will be well to let Girard explain himself extensively. He is referring here to the notion, applying to archaic religions, of "the god" as a sacralized transcendence, emanating from, but immanent in, the social community (a notion often known by the Latin tag derived from it, *vox populi, vox dei*):

> It is with the biblical tradition and Christianity that the supremacy of the crowd is overthrown and violent unanimity is put into reverse; and it is with this tradition that the principle of reciprocity is clearly designated as such. The Christ, the last of the prophets, sets humanity before a terrible alternative: either to continue not seeing that the duel orders subterraneously the entire set of human activities, or to escape this hidden logic in favor of another, that of love and its positive reciprocity. It is striking to observe how much negative and positive reciprocity are [i.e., structurally] like each other: they tend toward almost the same type of non-differentiation, and yet, from the one to the other, the difference is the salvation of the world! (124 [63])

More precisely:

> Consenting to die crucified, Christ brings surging up to the light what had remained hidden "from the foundation of the world," in other words, that foundation itself, the unanimous murder which is revealed as such for the first time with the Cross. Archaic religions demand for their functioning that their own founding murder, rehearsed continually in the form of ritual sacrifices, and protecting human societies from their own violence, be covered up. By revealing the founding murder, Christianity destroys the ignorance and the superstition indispensable to these religions; it allows the rise of a [scientific] knowledge previously unimaginable. (16 [xiii–xiv])

Christ came to take the place of the victim. He placed himself at the heart of the system to reveal the hidden springs of the system. The "second Adam"—to pick up St Paul's expression—reveals to us how the "first" came about. The Passion teaches us that humankind comes out of sacrifice, that it was born with the religious. Only the religious order was capable of containing the conflicts which must otherwise have destroyed the first groups of humans. (19 [xv])

Here, then, is Christianity's claim to defy the assault upon it of the great and the wise of modern times:

The Christian revelation comes and confirms all religions in a relation to the divine denied by the modern world. It confirms what they glimpsed. In a certain way, it is because the Christ entered into the matrix of false resurrections that he is truly risen. The beneficiaries of archaic religions which bring back calm and order, stood in a relation to the divine that was real. There was something Christian in all myths. But in revealing the innocence of their victims, the Passion makes positive what in these myths was still negative . . . Satan becomes the name of a form of the sacred devalued by the role and action of Christ. For this reason, Vatican II, when it eliminated from Catholic doctrine the violence of God, but not the reality of evil, accomplished a decisive move. (20 [xvi])

And here is the wider evolutionary significance of Christianity:

Humankind, still in process of education, and not yet fully human, will only become so by measuring up to the divine. Comes the moment when God can fully reveal himself to them. It's understandable that Christ frightened his apostles. But he is also the only Model, the one who puts humans at the right distance from God. Christ came to reveal his Kingdom: not something of this world, but something allowing humankind, having once understood the mechanisms of its own violence, to have an accurate intuition of transcendence. We can all participate in Christ's divinity, on condition of renouncing our violence. Yet we know, in part thanks to Clausewitz, that men will not do so. The paradox is that we were beginning to grasp the gospel message at the very moment when the

escalation to extremes has caught up with us, imposing itself as the only law
of history. (19–20 [xv–xvi])

The alternative, for Girard, is thus clear and decidedly stark: either we undo
the crisis of the modern world by adopting Christ-like values and behavior;
or the escalation to extremes, developing precisely to those extremes, leads
logically to the extinction of life on this planet.

Through its liberation from sacrificial constraints, our society has
become the most creative and powerful that ever was, but it has become also
the most fragile and the most threatened. Girard explains more closely how
this happens:

> A scapegoat sacrifice is effective as long as we believe the victim guilty.
> Having a scapegoat implies that we don't know we have one. Learning that
> we do have one, is to lose it and to lose it forever; and it is to expose oneself
> to mimetic conflicts without possible resolution. Such is the implacable
> law of escalation to extremes. It is this protective system of scapegoating
> which the accounts of the Crucifixion end up destroying, by revealing the
> innocence of Jesus, and, little by little, of all analogous victims. The process
> of education without violent sacrifices is therefore happening, but very
> slowly, in an almost always unconscious way. (17 [xiv])

The "cloud cover" of primitive sacrality, with its false transcendence, is burned
away by our post-Christian—and post-Christendom—ultra-reflexive, ratio-
nalistic, and scientific modernity, leaving the defense mechanism of origins
enervated and useless. The fragile and crucial self-spun auto-protection
against man's intrinsic violence is "blown." Meanwhile, the cultural osmosis
of the values of actual Christian faith—for want of an entire faith-acceptance
of the Christic model (and the Kingdom "come on earth, as it is in heaven")—
is, if assuredly active and fruitful, still a very slow and fitful process; slower, to
all seeming, than the accelerating rhythm of secularized history.

All manner of confusions abound in the *clair-obscur* of this "in-between
time." They are generated by the free play between those two concepts of *survival* and *salvation*, and by the experienced gap by which they fail to coincide
in human time. (Girard also says: "Christianity is the only religion to have
foreseen its own failure. Its prescience is called the apocalypse" (10 [x]).

Thus, for instance, Christian cultures themselves are perfectly capable of *regressing to archaic patterns of violence.* Here is Girard's formula for the violence within medieval Christendom: the violence of Crusade and pogrom, Inquisition, and, later, witch-hunting—and of the religious civil wars that marked the ending of "Christendom" and the rise of "Europe." (We may note in passing that *all* today's "new atheists," rooted as they are in the Enlightenment, are centrally shaped by its *abreaction* to Europe's religious wars.) "Regression" is also, in the *contemporary* world, Girard's formula accounting for the fundamentals to which "fundamentalism" reverts, but also for all "empires of sacrifice," including the established, morally well-considered and trend-setting ones of today.

Moreover, ambiguities abounding, Christianity is mistaken for the "religion" it supplants and transcends:

> The trap into which rationalism falls is to confuse Christianity with all religions. But the God who rises up beside the consenting emissary [and Victim] is a complete unknown. God, the most external and the most internal to common humanity, the most God and the most Man . . . Foreign to the social community as ordered by the play of sacred difference. (104–5 [50])

The Christian faith is, indeed, "misrecognised by its enemies *and* its supporters." Whereas, all unobserved, "All demystification stems from Christianity. . . . [For] the only true form of the religious is that which demystifies archaic religion" (19 [xv]). Just as the only cogent offer of *salvation* is one that not only relays but also corrects-and-transcends the immanent program of "survival," there has to be continuity *and* breaking away.

We need some form of apocalypse-thinking, perhaps even a form of apocalyptic thinking. But Girard sees confusion even worse confounded, given that

> the only Christians who still speak about apocalypse are the fundamentalists, [and] they have an entirely mythical idea of it. They think that end-of-time violence will come from God himself; they can't manage without a nasty God. They don't, strange to say, recognize that the violence we are busy accumulating over our own heads is entirely sufficient to unleash the worst. They have no sense of humor. (21 [xvi])

The confusion of Christians, naturally enough, feeds the confusions of the new atheism. (We might, as an interesting test case of this contention, consider the *amalgams* practiced by Christopher Hitchens in his title *God Is Not Great: How Religion Poisons Everything.*)[6]

◆ ◆ ◆

Is it perhaps the confusions inherent in the "in-between time" that explain the "apocalyptic turn" of the modern age? Contemporary humanity has lost the simple art of *survival;* and it has "blown" its sacred cloud cover—while not yet grasping the offer of *salvation.* And it is, accordingly, frightened of its own Promethean and sacrificial shadow let loose upon the world.

Girard struggles against pessimism: "More than ever . . . history has a meaning; and this meaning is redoubtable; but where peril abounds, there also grows that which saves" (23 [xviii]). Accordingly, he does not make his own the "apocalypticism" of the progeny of Clausewitz and Hegel, whose *unthought-out* quality he has *rethought* and *thought out "to the end"*:

> Like Hölderlin, I think in turn that only Christ allows us to confront [our contemporary] reality without going mad. The apocalypse [in my language of thought] does not announce the end of the world; it founds a hope. He who suddenly sees reality is not in the absolute despair caused by modern un-thought-out-ness, but re-finds a world where things have a meaning. (16 [xiii])

It will be seen that Girard here explicates his own title (*Achever Clausewitz*), and even justifies his translator (*Battling to the End*). Almost certainly, he does so in testamentary mode.

◆ ◆ ◆

These are the figures of sense to which the diverse and multidisciplinary reflections of the present volume are addressed. Not all their authors are specialist Girardians. Not all Girardians understand Girard in the same way. Predictably, they do so *least* in relation to his "third idea"—in relation to which readers will hear many voices and detect a definite but fruitful tension of dialogue. None would wish to think of René Girard—most certainly, he does not think of himself—as in any way sacrosanct or incorrigible.

All are concerned to explore, evaluate, and, in some cases, build on the breakthrough account of violence and the sacred that he offers. They do so here in four movements.

Part 1 of our volume deals with the secretly "programming" origins of sacred violence and their legacy in our contemporary world. Paul Dumouchel, in dialogue with animal behaviorists, investigates the inaugural problem that Girardian theory converts into an immense possibility of strategic understanding: the specificity of human violence in relation to that of our nearest animal relatives. He shows that the latest empirical research in this area, when conscious of its own postulates and master of its own implications, points toward the foundational solution Girard offers us: an important demonstration reproblematizing an area of evolutionary theory where "phyletic gradualism" often reigns unchallenged. Pierpaolo Antonello then retraces, this time in dialogue with social anthropologists, the Girardian resolution of this key pointer to human difference. He examines the foundational link between violence management and emissary victimization; its role in the threshold emergence of the human (mind-made) cultural order, particularly in relation to the symbolicity that gives us both ritual and language; while also noting that what primes our human potentials, and enables our human survival, also programs into us default mechanisms for dealing with violence. On the one hand, these mortgage human freedom and ensure that we carry with us, as we evolve culturally, a violence we have contained, by dint of transactional self-mystification, but not yet recognized or addressed in ourselves. On the other, this invention sets up a space and creates a promise of self-fashioning creativity, which is here given its positive—and potentially prophetic—due. Harald Wydra picks up the story by examining the legacy of the victimary mechanism in all epochs of culture and civilization, and the considerable resonance of all its constituent themes for contemporary anthropology. Integrating human specificity into the Darwinian paradigm, Girard is seen to account for a legacy of peril and possibility not previously present in nature.

The detailed cartography of this ambivalent legacy, in all its diversity and range, might occupy many volumes. We here illustrate the perennial power of this evolutionary self-programming by reference to a single key example: that of supposedly Christian America, considered as an "Empire of Sacrifice." This exercise in Girardian culture analysis by Jon Pahl and Jim Wellman shows the reach of Girardian theory; in confounding all innocent simplisms functioning on the basis of labels and stereotypes ("religion," "Christian nation," "sacrifice"), it illustrates how deep, pervasive, and far-reaching, in all cultures, is the evolutionary programming of the foundational link between violence and the archaic sacred. It also represents a distinct challenge, specifically, to one very major "Christian culture." It might equally, for this latter reason, have figured in the following section as an example of a late prolongation into the modern world of the "regressions" more obviously visible within medieval Christendom.[7]

Is the Christian gospel, then, as Girard suggests, *crucial?* Does its coming mark a key point of inflection in the evolutionary history of human culture, human religion, and human violence? Part 2 is devoted to these questions-in-principle. Wolfgang Palaver explores this proposition in contrasting the identity-forming ethic of the gospels with that of previous mythologies. He shows that it is, decisively, the Christian gospels that chart humanity's passage from a parochial (hence: conflictual and violent) altruism to a universal (nonviolent and inclusive) one—something Girard himself calls "a new ethic . . . for these times of catastrophe, these times when catastrophe itself must, urgently, be taken into rational account" (64). Paul Gifford looks at the source of this "conversion" by reading the Christian Cross as a game-changing inversion of the "founding murder." This figure of symmetrical inversion, he thinks, attests the contribution made by Girard's fundamental anthropology to rebuilding understanding between secular intelligence and faith, and to naturalizing the evolutionary paradigm within theology itself. Robert Hamerton-Kelly (in this volume) spells out the strategic meaning of this game-change, using the Girardian notion of "novelistic truth" (*vérité romanesque*): he contrasts the notions of *survival* and its attendant *apocalypticism* (which he follows in contemporary expressions and in the ancient Babylonian *Epic of Gilgamesh*) with the Christian *salvation,* and its attendant "eschatological" hope, as caught up and projected in the thought of St. Paul. "Both evolutionism and Christianity are, in their different ways, approaches to the central fact of violence in nature; but how these approaches are reconcilable and complementary appears only in the light of mimetic theory."

Part 3 follows the fortunes of "violent reciprocities and peace-making in the contemporary world": both as a way of exploring how mimetic theory has in practice been used as a tool in defusing conflict and building peace, and, more theoretically, in exploring the Girardian ambiguities of the period "in between" the protections of archaic sacrality and the vital acceptance of a salvational model. Duncan Morrow looks at the inheritance of conflict in Northern Ireland, in terms of political context and in relation to mimetic theory. Derick Wilson shows how mimetic theory (MT) has been inspirational as an applied tool in modeling alternative community relations at the Corrymeela Community and beyond. Leon Marincowitz (on South Africa) and Mel Konner (on Israel/Palestine) then discuss how far these analyses are transposable to other contexts of sacred violence. Scott Atran (*Talking to the Enemy*) reviews all these essays and evaluates his own encounters with, and divergences from, Girard in respect of practice and theory. All are concerned with the Girardian conversion of negative ("bad") into positive ("good") mimesis. All render some echo to Girard's later thought: "We are obliged to remain within history, to act within the heart of violence, because we are gaining an ever better understanding of how it works. Does that however mean we can entirely foil its workings? I doubt it" (2007, 80 [2010a, 35]).

Part 4 ("Between Progress and Abyss") monitors the notion of apocalypse, envisaged as a key concept witnessing to our modernity and to Girard's "in-between time." Jean-Pierre Dupuy sees the balance of nuclear terror as a modern form of the archaic sacred. He goes on to commend the creative solution it brings to human violence, and to ask whether Girardian theory needs to be revised in the light of its apparent success: a conclusion entertained with reservations by Margo Boenig-Liptsin, but contested by Paul Dumouchel and Paul Gifford. Michael Northcott attempts to clarify the notion of apocalypse as applied to the phenomenon of climate change, a harbinger of apocalypse analyzed only from afar by Girard, but a prime revealer of his theory. Michael Kirwan makes a clarifying overall review of the "apocalyptic turn" in Girardian theory, by distinguishing the functional poetics of apocalypse in its secular (and "survivalist") acceptance, from its theological reinterpretation and Christian "salvational" meaning.

Our authors diverge on many things. They converge principally, however, in this: that Girard's rare combination of consequence and depth, precision and originality, prophetic pertinence and sheer intellectual brilliance, deserve a closer hearing and a more mature exploration than they have yet received in the English-speaking world.

Notes

Note: Contributors with native or professional language competence have been invited to quote from original French editions, making their own translations, which may significantly differ from standard published translations. Please see, for each chapter, the bibliography "Cited Texts and Further Reading." This notice particularly concerns three key works: *La violence et le sacré* (1972), *Des choses cachées* (1978), and *Achever Clausewitz* (2007).

1. The bicentenary of Darwin's birth (in 1809) coincided with the 150th anniversary of the publication (in 1859) of *On the Origin of Species.*

2. Quotations from *Achever Clausewitz* in this chapter refer to the French original and are translated by the authors. Corresponding pages of the English translation are given in square brackets. See, at the end of the present chapter: "Principal Texts by René Girard cited in this volume."

3. Girard discusses the difference between Western and Eastern cultures in *Des choses cachées* (1978: bk. 1, chap. 5). The crystallization of the concept of "scapegoat" in Europe and Japan is developed in an interview available at the Imitatio website, given for the first of our Darwin-Girard conferences in 2009.

4. See David Carrasco, *City of Sacrifice: The Aztec Empire and the Role of Violence in Civilization* (Boston: Beacon Press, 1999). As its title suggests, this example represents one paradigmatic expression (among innumerable and very diverse variations it is capable of assuming in space and time) of Girard's thesis on the origins of human culture and social functioning.

5. Girard's scenario of origins is taken up and evaluated in relation to contemporary scientific readings of these same processes in the introductory chapter of *How We Became Human.*

6. *All* "religion" is recognized from the undeclared archetype established by this *Islamic* formula, and in a context where the clear reference is to *Islamist fundamentalism.* It is said to poison *everything;* and this verdict is *without appeal,* since any attempt to *differentiate* or *specify* becomes an instance of rivalry, hence of violence—hence of the "poison" alleged.

7. Readers may wish to read this piece in resonance with the statement of Derick Wilson, speaking of Northern Ireland: "We always remind ourselves centrally that Girard envisages 'Christendom' and its offshoots and residues (of which Northern Ireland is one) as entirely capable of *regressing* to unchristian patterns of *archaic* religion, precisely under the persuasion of falsely sacralising mimetic rivalries" (Girard 2007, 149ff. [2011, 79–80ff.). See also Michael Northcott's section on "A late-modern return of the religious?"

Principal Texts by René Girard Cited in This Volume

Girard, René. 1966. *Deceit, Desire, and the Novel: Self and Other in Literary Structure.* Translated by Y. Freccero. Baltimore: Johns Hopkins University Press. Original edition, *Mensonge romantique, vérité romanesque* (Paris: Grasset, 1961).

——. 1977. *Violence and the Sacred.* Translated by P. Gregory. Baltimore: Johns Hopkins University Press. Original edition, *La violence et le sacré* (Paris: Grasset, 1972).

——. 1986. *The Scapegoat.* Translated by Y. Freccero. Baltimore: Johns Hopkins University Press. Original edition, *Le Bouc émissaire* (Paris: Grasset, 1982; Le Livre de Poche "Essais," 1986).

——. 1987a. *Job: The Victim of His People.* Translated by Y. Freccero. Stanford, CA: Stanford University Press. Original edition, *La route antique des hommes pervers* (Paris: Grasset, 1985).

——. 1987b. *Things Hidden since the Foundation of the World: Research undertaken in Collaboration with J.-M. Oughourlian and G. Lefort.* Translated by S. Bann and M. Metteer. Stanford, CA: Stanford University Press and London: Athlone Press. Original edition, *Des choses cachées depuis la fondation du monde* (Paris: Grasset, 1978; Le Livre de Poche "Essais," 1998).

———. 1991. *A Theater of Envy: William Shakespeare.* Oxford: Oxford University Press.

———. 1996. *The Girard Reader.* Edited by James Williams. New York: Crossroads.

———. 2001. *I See Satan Fall Like Lightning.* Translated by J. G. Williams. Maryknoll, NY: Orbis Books. Original edition, *Je vois Satan tomber comme l'éclair* (Paris: Grasset, 1999).

———. 2004. *Oedipus Unbound: Selected Writings on Rivalry and Desire.* Edited and with an introduction by Mark R. Anspach. Stanford, CA: Stanford University Press.

———. 2008a. "Apocalyptic Thinking after 9/11." Interview with Robert Doran, in *SubStance* 115, vol. 37, no. 1: 20–32.

———. 2008b. *Evolution and Conversion.* With Pierpaolo Antonello and João Cezar de Castro Rocha. New York: Continuum; London: Continuum, 2007.

———. 2010a. *Battling to the End: Conversations with Benoît Chantre.* Translated by M. Baker. Studies in Violence, Mimesis, and Culture. East Lansing: Michigan State University Press. Original edition, *Achever Clausewitz: Entretiens avec Benoît Chantre* (Paris: Éditions Nord, 2007).

———. 2010b. *Christianity, Truth, and Weakening Faith: A Dialogue.* Edited by Pierpaolo Antonello. Translated by William McCuaig. Cambridge: Cambridge University Press.

———. 2011a. "Mimesis, Sacrifice, and the Bible: A Conversation with Sandor Goodhart." In *Sacrifice, Scripture, and Substitution: Readings in Ancient Judaism and Christianity,* ed. Ann Astell and Sandor Goodhart, 39–69. Notre Dame, IN: University of Notre Dame Press.

———. 2011b. *Sacrifice.* East Lansing: Michigan State University Press.

PART ONE

The Programming of Origins: Sacred Violence and Its Legacy

A Covenant among Beasts

Human and Chimpanzee Violence
in Evolutionary Perspective

Paul Dumouchel

René Girard in *Violence and the Sacred* (1972) and again in *Things Hidden since the Foundation of the World* (1978) claims that in most animal species intraspecific violence is generally limited, and that instinctual inhibitions strongly reduce or totally exclude murder among conspecifics. He adds that the weakness of instinctual checks against murder among humans gave a special urgency to the problem of violence in our species. In this he partially followed Konrad Lorenz, who had argued, a few years earlier, that while most animal species had evolved mechanisms that rein in intraspecific aggression or divert it toward alternative targets, humans apparently lacked such mechanisms, or at least that modern technology had made these natural restraints obsolete (Lorenz 1969).

Girard, in fact, suggested an explanation for what Lorenz essentially presented as an empirical observation. Humans, he claimed, are characterized by a propensity for imitation that he called *mimesis,* which is many times stronger than what we find among other animals; and it is this greater capacity for imitation that came to override instinctual restraints against intraspecific murder. Implicit in Girard's proposal is an important, but usually unnoticed, change of outlook relative to Lorenz and to that of most primatologists or sociobiologists interested in the relationship between animal violence and human violence.

As indicated by the original title of Lorenz's book, the Austrian ethologist proposes a "natural history of aggression" in order to understand what we call "evil." He argues that from an evolutionary point of view, aggression is good and useful, and that in many species, animals have evolved characteristics that capitalize on the beneficial effects of aggression and reduce its negative consequences. Furthermore, Lorenz claims that it is the invention of modern weapons, which allow us to kill others easily and from a distance, that explains why such mechanisms seem unable to restrain our violent behavior toward each other. There is a clear Rousseauistic flavor to Lorenz's argument—i.e., nature is good while culture is bad—but principally, it implies a form of dualism according to which human violence is in some way "unnatural," and culture is called upon to explain this "unnaturalness."

Girard rejects this common prejudice and reverses the tenor of the explanation. While Lorenz views human aggression as unnatural in some way and calls upon culture to explain the particularity of human violence, Girard considers the higher propensity for intraspecific violence as a biological characteristic of our species, and uses this particular characteristic to build a naturalistic explanation of human culture. Nothing could be more different than these two points of view: Lorenz, like most sociobiologists, is looking for vestiges of the natural history of aggression in human behavior; Girard is trying to understand the appearance of culture as an adaptation to a novel situation created by the heightened propensity among humans for imitation and violence.

It might, however, be argued that an essential part of what Girard learned from Lorenz has turned out to be false. By far the major part of the observations that Lorenz reports are correct, but one of the specific claims on which Girard builds his argument—the absence of intraspecific murder among most animal species—today needs to be qualified in an important way. In the forty years that separate us from the original publication of *Violence and the Sacred,* extensive observation of chimpanzees both in the wild and in captivity has shown that our closest cousins regularly engage in the killing of conspecifics, and that the number of victims is far from negligible. In fact, Richard Wrangham et al. have even argued that death rates from violent aggression are similar among chimpanzees and hunter-gatherers (Wrangham, Wilson, and Muller 2006, 14–26).

Even if this particular claim is perhaps not entirely convincing, it seems that the difference between human violence and that of our closest relatives is not absolute, as Girard assumed it to be. More to the point: if it is the greater level of violence among humans that forced us to invent culture, why have chimpanzees failed to do so, if among them the level of intraspecific violence is more or less similar to that in *Homo sapiens?* Furthermore, according to Girard, the heightened violence of humans comes from their greater ability to imitate. Observation during those forty years partially supports that claim by showing that great apes, including chimpanzees, do not imitate, or imitate only very little, compared to humans. However, if such is the case, how can we account, from a Girardian point of view, for the high level of intraspecific violence among chimpanzees? What role does imitation, or mimesis, play in human violence?

My purpose in this chapter is to review, in the light of recent developments in primatology and in the study of imitation, Girard's claim of having provided a "naturalistic" explanation of the rise of culture. Far from falsifying Girard's central tenets, will I argue, these developments strengthen their claims, since they allow us to determine more precisely the difference between human and chimpanzee violence, and to pinpoint the role of mimesis in the humanization process. However, first a detour is necessary. It will take us from the way in which mainstream evolutionary biology conceives the relationship between cooperation and conflict to the meaning of social species.

Competition and Cooperation, Altruism and Conflict

Evolutionary biologists tend to view conflict and cooperation as polar opposites. They tend to consider that one excludes the other: when animals cooperate they are not in conflict, and vice versa. This impression may be due in part to the extensive use of evolutionary game theory, which induces us to represent animal behavior as composed of discrete, even mutually exclusive elements,[1] a persuasion that has led biologists, in the last forty years or so, to accord a central and strategic significance to the issue of "altruism." An action is said to be *altruistic* when it has a cost for the agent who performs it, but benefits a different organism. Conversely, an action is *selfish* if it benefits the agent; but this is true whether or not it also costs something to another. When it does, either directly or indirectly, the animals are in competition, and conflict can develop as a more extreme form of competition. Altruistic actions are Other-regarding, while selfish actions are Self-regarding. Animals who are in conflict, however, do seek to harm each other; so that conflict, like altruism, *must also be seen as Other-regarding.* Perhaps that is the exact and sufficient reason why conflict tends to appear to us not just as the opposite of altruism, but also—misleadingly—as incompatible with it.

According to our current understanding of evolutionary theory, altruistic actions should not, in principle, occur, because selection must be expected to act against altruists. Since, by definition, altruistic actions reduce the fitness of those who perform them, in favor of one or more other organisms, altruists should normally, under a regime of survival of the fittest, come to be replaced by the more selfish creatures that benefit from their generosity. Competition and conflict, on the other hand, are something we take for granted: given that everyone is assumed to act selfishly, in a finite environment organisms will inevitably become rivals and enemies. Nonetheless, it is clear that animals sometimes do cooperate and act at least *as if* they were incurring a cost in order to help others. Consequently, explaining the "anomaly" of altruism has been high on the agenda of biologists.

> There are two issues involved here; one is empirical and the other theoretical. The empirical issue is whether altruistic behaviours *really are* altruistic. Empirically it is not clear how much *true altruism* there is "out there," and it could be that much of what we consider as such may be better described as forms of competition, or of reliable signalling which involves a cost to the signaller. (Zahavi and Zahavi 1997)

However, the empirical issue has been overshadowed by the theoretical issue. The question here is to explain how altruistic behavior could have been selected for. Darwin appealed to group selection to explain the existence of moral altruism, arguing that groups that contain individuals who were willing to sacrifice themselves for the benefit of the group would win in a competition with groups composed of pure egoists.

However, until recently it was considered that group selection is too weak to counterbalance selection against altruism at the genetic or individual level. Today the received explanation rests on the notions of *kin selection,* and more generally, of *fitness correlation.* Organisms, it is argued, will generally tend to cooperate and to act altruistically toward one another to the extent that the fitness of one is correlated to the fitness of the other, whether this correlation is due to genetic causes, as is the case in kin selection, or to social or ecological factors. That is to say, altruism is possible (and consistent with evolutionary theory) whenever the fitness of the donor is related to the fitness of the recipient in such a way that the benefit accruing to the latter will ultimately also benefit the donor or his genes. Organisms that are naturally and necessarily selfish will only act generously toward each other if that generosity is also in some way beneficial to them; otherwise, natural selection will inexorably weed out the generous. As Joan Roughgarden says, such theories "take the altruism out of altruism" (Roughgarden 2009, 3).

In these explanations, fitness correlation plays the role of "particular circumstances." What is usually argued, in fact, is that there are certain particular circumstances—i.e., whenever the fitness of the donor organism and of the recipient are related in the right way—in which altruism and cooperation are possible or even likely. However, even in those circumstances, appearances notwithstanding, selfishness remains the rule, and conflict and competition should be expected as the *default behavior* most of the time.[2]

Yet conflict, as mentioned earlier—unlike competition, predation, or even aggression—is a relation where organisms seek to *harm each other.* It seems therefore that if naturally and necessarily selfish organisms will only cooperate and act altruistically when certain circumstances are satisfied, they will also only enter into conflict in specific circumstances; for conflict is expensive and dangerous. Animals will tend to minimize danger to themselves and will not—or at least they should not—choose conflict when walking (or running) away is a better deal. If selfishness can be expected to lead to a high rate of aggression—for example, in disputes over resources or territories—aggression will often lead to rather limited conflicts, with one of the adversaries rapidly fleeing. Conflicts will be more intense when the prize is more important and when walking away is not an option.

Social Animals, Group Intelligence

Interestingly enough, to my knowledge, there are few definitions of the "social animal" or of "social species" in biology. There is a generally received (and sometimes challenged) definition of "eusociality";[3] but it is, apparently and for the most part, assumed that *everyone knows* what the concept "social species" means and can recognize a "social animal" when he or she sees one. For example, searching the Internet, one can find the following examples of definitions: "A social animal is a loosely defined term for an organism that is highly interactive with other members of its species to the point of having a recognizable and distinct society."[4] Another rather unhelpful but common definition, also found on the Internet, is: "an animal that exhibits social behavior,"[5] while the *Encyclopedia Britannica* defines social behavior as "the suite of interactions that occur between two or more individual animals, usually of the same species, when they form simple aggregations, cooperate in sexual or parental behavior, engage in disputes over territory and access to mates, or simply communicate across space."[6] Unsatisfactory as these definitions may be, they all indicate that social animals spend a lot of time interacting with each other, and that these interactions play a fundamental role in the fitness of each individual. This suggests a rather straightforward definition of social species: a species is social to the extent that *the fitness of its members depends on their interactions with each other rather than on each individual's unmediated relationship to the environment.* This suggestion has the advantage of avoiding the circularity that plagues many definitions of social animals, which claim, as above, that social animals are animals that interact to the point of forming recognizable societies. Mostly it captures something that is biologically fundamental: *an animal's fitness,* and the extent to which it *depends on the actions*—and therefore the *fitness*—of *other conspecifics.*

Understood in this way, sociality is a question of degree; most (probably all) animal species are more or less social, and all sexually reproducing organisms are to that extent social. The more animals are social, the more their fitness is related to that of other members of their species. Sociality is an aspect of an organism's niche that can, in fact, be measured in at least two dimensions, its importance and its extension. How important is the contribution that interactions with conspecifics bring to an individual's biological success, and to how many conspecifics (to mate and family only, or also to others) does this codependence extend? Sociality is not just a question of living in close proximity or in groups, therefore; it depends, rather, on the relations that exist between the animals, and on the extent to which animals of the same species affect each other's fitness.[7]

If social animals are organisms whose fitness essentially depends on their interaction with their conspecifics, then we should expect that *highly social species will also exhibit high levels of intraspecific conflict and violence*. This is because there are essentially *two ways in which organisms can influence each other's fitness: cooperation and competition*. Exclusive competition will disperse individuals so that they will all face nature alone, while perfect cooperation will lead to a situation where individuals face external threats all together as one. The proportion of cooperation and competition will vary from species to species, but in more social species we should expect individual behavior to exhibit a greater mixture of affiliation and conflict. *Contrary to what common sense suggests,* among social animals, violence and cooperation, conflict and consensus are not polar opposites; they will tend to *grow together, in tandem*. As nature makes members of a species more and more dependent on each other for their survival, it simultaneously augments the occasions of conflict among them and raises the stakes involved in such disputes. This is an explosive mix; and consequently, as species become more social, *managing this difficulty will become more and more of a problem*. Humans, given the extent and complexity of the cooperation and interdependence that exists between them, are certainly the most social animals we know of.

There is some evidence from different parts of biology showing that cooperation and altruism tend to be greater among organisms that are genetically closely related. However, it does not follow from that evidence that the number of conflicts among organisms decreases automatically as an inverse function of their degree of relatedness—or, more generally, of fitness correlation. These are two logically independent hypotheses, and the second, though often taken as evident, rests on a rather simple-minded view of human psychology and of the world. Clearly, acts of altruism between two individuals do not preclude future conflicts between them, or even the existence of a profound disagreement when the altruistic act takes place. Furthermore, among humans at least, past altruism often constitutes a major cause of future disputes. Whatever good reasons we have to believe that higher levels of correlation between the fitness of organisms—whether brought about by close genetic relation, the structure of the group to which they belong, or in any other way—increases their tendency to cooperate and to engage in altruistic (or apparently altruistic) behavior. They cannot and should not make us assume that this increased cooperation will *also* lead to a reduction in the number of conflicts.

On the contrary, the more organisms interact, the more occasions of conflicts arise.[8] Cooperation, which makes the fitness of an organism partially dependent upon actions undertaken by another, diversifies and augments motives of disagreement and quarrels. With opponents, we compete for a prize that we cannot share. With collaborators, we can also disagree about how they are doing whatever we are doing together! The fact that among social animals violence and cooperation *grow together* rather than *exclude each other* is nothing strange or remarkable. It should be *the standard default hypothesis*. It is what we have every reason to *expect*.

Forms of Conflict and Violence

Conflicts, however, can take different forms. From a biological point of view, it is interesting and profitable to distinguish at least two different types of conflict. First, there are *contests that oppose near equals;* these, for evident biological reasons, will tend to be more guarded, even if they can also develop into conflicts of extreme violence. Secondly, there are *encounters between broadly mismatched opponents;* these tend to have *extreme consequences for only one of the parties.* The terms "equal" and "unequal" can be made more rigorous here. Two parties in a conflict are equal if the *cost* for the winner(s) is identical to the *cost* for the loser(s). Even in situations of perfect equality, it may be rational (i.e., worthwhile) for adversaries to enter into conflict if the benefit is superior to the cost. We can call *e-contests* those contests where the relation between the cost for the winner and the cost for the loser remains within a limited range of difference. Two parties in a conflict are perfectly unequal, on the other hand, if the cost for one is nil while it is maximal for the other. Therefore encounters between "unequals" are not really contests, and they can rapidly turn to extreme violence, even if the expected benefit for the certain winner is very small. We can call *u-encounters* episodes of violence where one party is liable to suffer extreme cost while the other is only exposed to minor damage. This distinction between *e-contests* and *u-encounters* is biologically relevant inasmuch as it refers to the cost and the benefits individuals can incur in different types of violent encounter.

Analytically there are good reasons to distinguish between these two types of behavior. Conflicts between equals depend on the size or importance of the gain.[9] The decision to resort to violence should reflect the expectation that the potential gain is worth the danger involved. Furthermore, in an *e-conflict* contestants, given their relative equality, will be uncertain of the issue.[10] This should further reduce the temptation to resort to violence, for individuals should weight the difference between cost and benefit by the probability of success, which, given their "equality," we should expect to be small. It seems, therefore, that in these cases the use of violence will tend to be "rational," that is to say, it will make sense in terms of a cost/benefit analysis.[11]

In encounters between "unequals," by contrast, the issue is certain, and danger for one of the parties all but disappears. The use of violence will from the beginning be independent of the importance of the gain, and the slightest show of resistance will be enough to unleash maximal violence. In fact, resistance is probably not even necessary, if we assume that the exercise of violence, in a situation where it is without danger to the violent party and assured of success, brings its own reward, something that seems likely in view both of anecdotal evidence and psychological research on violence. In *u-encounters*, resorting to violence is not a function of the expected gain, but results from the absence of cost, reinforced by the intrinsic pleasure of victory without danger or effort. In consequence, such violence *will tend to appear irrational*, as it escapes explanation in terms of cost/benefit analysis.

There are, therefore, good reasons to distinguish these two types of violent encounter. As previously argued, a high inclusive fitness or fitness correlation does not preclude conflicts among related individuals; we can, however, expect that it will move these conflicts toward the *e-contests* end of the spectrum. The reason is evident. *E-contests* are defined as conflicts where the cost for the winner is equal or closely similar to that of the loser. When the fitness of opponents in a conflict is strongly interdependent, the harm that one inflicts on the other also reduces the first individual's own inclusive fitness. The higher the correlation in the fitness of two individuals, the more likely it is that the cost to one will simultaneously constitute a cost to the other. This will tend to equalize the damage sustained by the contestants whether they win or lose. A high degree of correlation between the fitness of two individuals, when caused by close genetic relation, cannot actually equalize the losses two organisms may experience in a conflict pitting them against each other, but it will nonetheless reduce the differential of their respective losses. This should draw our attention to the fact that the "equality" of organisms engaged in an *e-contest* cannot be reduced to their direct ability to inflict harm upon each other, since it refers to all the factors making for the fitness in the two organisms—so, for instance, allies who prevent a stronger opponent from "getting away with it," or any form of kinship bond making the fitness of one adversary dependent on that of another.

Interestingly enough, in both chimps and humans we find these two types of conflicts, as well as an apparent shift toward *e-contests* in conflicts that take place between closely related individuals. Many primatologists have defended what they call the "chimpanzee model" of intergroup aggression. One of the central characteristics of this model according to Wrangham and Glowacki (2012) is that chimpanzees only engage in the killing of members of other groups when that killing can be carried out safely. "Lethal attacks have been reported only where there is a strong asymmetry of power between subgroups, typically when several males encounter either a lone male from a neighboring community or a lone mother with her dependent offspring."

Killing of conspecifics also takes place within communities of chimpanzees, and not only during encounters between different groups. Most of these murders are infanticides carried out by parties of females who are unrelated to the victim and who attack the mother to take and kill her infant. Again we are not dealing here with *e-contests,* but with a situation where there is an important power imbalance between the victim and aggressor (see Pusey et al., 2008). Furthermore, in the cases of the few adult victims that we know of, the killing took the form of a *u-encounter;* many members of the community gang up against one of them and treat him as if he were a stranger (Watts 2004). Yet *e-contests* between chimpanzees living in the same group are quite frequent. According to Wrangham, Wilson, and Muller (2006) nonlethal physical aggression among humans (recently settled hunter-gatherers) is probably two to three hundred times *less frequent* than among chimpanzees. These conflicts that never lead to the death of an animal are always terminated before it is too late either by fleeing the aggressor or by signs of submission that lead to or reinforce patterns of dominance that, on average, render the issue of future conflicts between the two individuals predictable—and combat therefore less necessary.

Is there a relationship between these two forms of conflict among chimpanzees? Wrangham and Wilson (2004) compare collective violence between youth bands and chimpanzee groups. They argue that in both cases collective violence between groups is a consequence of status competition between males within groups. This suggests that external violence, *u-encounters,* could be related, in two important ways, to internal conflicts, which mostly take the form of *e-contests.* First, and this is Wrangham and Wilson's main hypothesis, violence between gangs of youths (and of chimpanzees) is a means for individuals to assert their status inside the group. Among the group there is fierce status competition between males, but at the same time, relationships are "regulated by codes that suppress overt competition and therefore create a norm of respectful treatment from other gang members" (2004, 238). According to this hypothesis, violence *between* groups occurs because it cannot take place *within* groups. Because norms restrict violent competition between group members, violence against outsiders becomes a means whereby rivals decide their rivalries. Second, violence against outsiders is a way for individuals to discharge the frustration that comes from conflicts between insiders and from restraint on violence within the group. According to this hypothesis, violence against outsiders occurs in order that it should *not* take place *inside* the group. The two hypotheses of course are not exclusive, but the first one fails to explain why violence toward outsiders so often takes the form of *u-encounters.* Such encounters, which carry little or no risk for the perpetrators, would have but a small demonstrative effect upon internal rivals vying for status. Because *u-encounters* involve a large number of attackers ganging up on a lone victim, they do not seem appropriate for assailants wishing to demonstrate their superiority. However, if violence against outsiders takes place in order for violence within the group to remain limited, it is not surprising that this violence should take the form of *u-encounters,* which allow many individuals to simultaneously relieve their frustration.

Human Violence and the Chimpanzee Model

R. Wrangham and collaborators argue that the "chimpanzee model" constitutes an appropriate starting point for understanding the biological and cultural evolution of human warfare. According to them, "chimpanzees and humans are equally risk-averse when fighting. When self-sacrificial war practices are found in humans, therefore, they result from cultural systems of reward, punishment and coercion rather than evolved adaptation for greater risk taking" (Wrangham and Glowacki 2012).[12] This interesting claim needs to be qualified.[13]

One difficulty with this claim made by Wrangham et al. (2006), as formulated, is that it overlooks the importance of nonlethal intracommunity conflicts among chimpanzees, and the interrelation between this internal violence and external violence among groups, which Wrangham and Wilson (2004) postulated. Such conflicts are extremely frequent and usually settled without any one of the combatants being seriously harmed. This rampant nonlethal intracommunity violence is also part of the "chimpanzee model." To some extent we know why such conflicts rarely lead to fatalities. Relations of dominance allow weaker animals to submit and thereby to avoid major damage. Positions in the dominance hierarchy are often challenged, but whether such challenges fail or are successful and lead to dominance reversal, the correlated strategies of dominant and dominated animals continue to play their role of limiting conflict. Further, Wrangham and Wilson (2004) have argued that the two types of violent behavior are related; that violence between communities has something to do with regulation of conflicts within each one.

Not only are *e-contests* and *u-encounters* found in both humans and chimpanzees, but the distribution of each type of violent encounter is somewhat similar in both species. As many anthropologists have shown, hostile relations within segmentary societies can be represented by three concentric circles in the center of which stands the individual.[14] In the first circle, resorting to open violence to resolve conflicts is strictly forbidden. This is the domain of the family and the household, where one gives without demanding anything in return, and where failings and refusal that elsewhere would give offense are accepted with little or no protest. Beyond this circle—outside the family or the lineage, but still within the tribe or the village—is the domain of limited conflicts and ritualized warfare. Here the use of violence as a way of resolving disputes is allowed, but efforts are made to limit violence and to ensure equilibrium between the adversaries. Finally there is a third circle, often referred to as the domain of extreme hostility, where utterly destroying more distant enemies is not only permissible, but encouraged, and where unequal conflicts, surprise attacks, or early morning raids against defenseless villages constitute the rule. Among humans, as among chimpanzees, meetings with distantly related others often turn into *u-encounters,* while conflicts among close associates tend to be *e-contests.*

However, between the two species, differences in the distribution of conflicts are certainly as important as similarities. Essentially, while among humans the space of hostility is divided into three concentric circles, among chimpanzees it is partitioned in two, the *inside* and the *outside* of the community. Recent studies have indicated that kinship relations have a limited influence on cooperation among chimpanzees. Males form coalitions and preferentially associate with particular other males, but these associations— for grooming, for status promotion, and for defense against others—are not made on the basis of kinship relations (see, e.g., Mitani 2006; Langergraber et al. 2007). This is another way of saying that among chimpanzees there are no families or households. Within the community all relationships take place in a public space where rules of dominance apply. This circle where dominance constitutes the rule is also the space where violent encounters take the form of *e-contests.* Here challenges to the hierarchy are made, and frequent disputes, for food or access to a female (etc.), are resolved either by the submission of one of the parties or by avoiding the animal who is displaying aggressively. Outside of the community, inversely, dominance rules play no role; alpha males neither lead, nor initiate, nor even necessarily participate in border patrols or in murderous incursions into the territory of other groups (Watts and Mitani 2001). As violent conflicts with strangers are *u-encounters* in which a lone victim is massively outnumbered, whatever status the victim may have had in his or her community is clearly irrelevant.

In segmentary societies, the first circle, where violence is excluded as a means of resolving conflicts and where unlimited solidarity is the rule, corresponds to the domain where dominance rules. It is false to believe that this space is free of all violence: husbands beat their wives, older siblings beat younger siblings, mothers-in-law beat their daughters-in-law, and the head of the household punishes and may even kill his dependents. This author-ity (dominance) is rarely challenged, and when it is, the challenge can be met by extreme violence, a definitive retaliation, a final punishment that is considered legitimate by everyone. Legitimacy aside, this is not the domain of *e-contests*. The absence of violence to which anthropologists refer is nev-ertheless not an illusion: no one can resort to violence to resolve his or her conflicts, and everyone must bow to the authority of those who are higher in the dominance hierarchy. A fundamental difference is that among humans, in this space where dominance reigns, *e-contests* have no place.

When we move outside that first circle, we enter into a domain where *e-contests* predominate. Here force is allowed in the settlement of disputes, but the use of violence is codified and limited. The use of weapons is regulated as a function of the distance from the heart of the community; but mostly, as Evans-Pritchard noticed, the regulatory systems seem to be set up so as to ensure that at all times there is an equality between adver-saries (Evans-Pritchard 1940). This balancing act is also true of vendettas, systems of vengeance and counter-vengeance that ensure that the cost for the winner will ultimately be equal to the cost to the original loser. This is also the domain from which dominance is by definition excluded. The key concepts to describe such systems of violence are *reciprocity* and *equality*. No one should win, no one should lose, and conflicts are over when adversaries accept that this point of equilibrium has been reached.

Wrangham is probably right in claiming that such phenomena are cul-tural. The efforts that are made to ensure that none of the combatants uses a more dangerous weapon than the other, to supply the weaker side with allies, to make sure that tomorrow it will be the turn of the loser to win and of the winner to lose are *cultural constructs*. They rest on conventional rules that vary from culture to culture. Does it follow that they are "unnatural"; that they are deviant variations added on to a basic model of violent behavior? These rules seem designed on purpose to ensure a parity of damage inflicted as between combatants; and they appear to reflect and underline the essen-tial structure of *e-contests*. Among chimpanzees, dominance functions to reinforce the effect of fitness correlation in reducing violence in intraspecific conflict within groups. Among humans, dominance and *e-contests* have become separated, while dominance itself appears endowed with a greater authority, which the entire group is at times ready to enforce.

Meetings with individuals from outside of the community, in both humans and chimpanzees, often take the form of *u-encounters*. However, here also there seems to be a fundamental difference. To my knowledge there is no instance of an attacker being killed or seriously wounded during conflict between a boundary patrol and a lone foreign chimpanzee. Chimpanzees not only prefer safe killing, they are also very good at it; in other words, they are very prudent. Humans may also prefer safe killing, but when they engage in early morning raids against enemy villages or other violent action marked by a sharp power imbalance, some attackers are often killed or seriously wounded. Humans are not quite as good as chimpanzees at safe killing; but they nonetheless continue to engage in it. Chimpanzees would avoid such situations. Humans are clearly less risk-averse than chimpanzees when fighting. But *why* is this so? Here we touch a strategic enigma, to which Girard has a "breakthrough" answer, centered on the concept that gives mimetic theory its name.

Mimesis

Imitation has also been an important focus of research during the last forty years. One of the important things we have learned is that chimpanzees and great apes in general *do not imitate*—or if they do, *only a little*. In spite of the common claim "monkey see, monkey do," chimpanzees are not very good at imitating. Today, more than ever, it seems that Aristotle was *right* when he claimed that *humans are the most imitative of all animals:* imitation is far more highly developed among us than in any other species. However, one of the major areas of dispute in the study of imitation has been to define and to distinguish "true imitation" from other related behaviors, like emulation, stimulus enhancement, response priming, or "mere mimicry." The distinction between these different types of "imitative" behavior essentially refers to the *cognitive investment that is assumed to be necessary* in order for an organism to reproduce the actions of another.

It is clear that humans can imitate—in the true sense of the word—more, and more accurately, than most other animals. It is also clear that they not only copy the *actions* of others but also *reproduce or reenact their intentions*. Even young children who are exposed to a failed attempt at separating two pieces of equipment will *imitate the attempt* and rejoice at their success in mirroring *this,* rather than simply registering and copying its more visible outcome of failure (Meltzoff 2011). Furthermore: consistent with Girard's claim, we know that in order to achieve this degree of mimesis they do not need to be able to form a representation of the behavior that they imitate (Revel and Nadel 2007; cf. Gallese 2011).

Mimesis, however, *is not imitation:* it does not correspond to, and cannot be reduced to, imitation as it is currently construed and debated in ethology or cognitive science. Rather, it resembles more "imitation" in the sense in which it is understood in social psychology or in robotics, as a form of "social glue" or as the basis of social communication.[15] Yet, what is missing from these disciplines is the conflictual aspect of mimesis. Mimetic rivalry, mimetic desire, imitation, our ability to learn from each other, our willingness to help one another, the intensity and stubbornness of our conflicts all stem from the fact that we *take an interest in each other's interest.* This statement should be understood both in the sense that we are interested in *what* interests others, and that not only what concerns others concerns us, in the sense of fitness correlation, but also that we have concern for it (and them). *At the heart of mimesis lies the interest that we have in each other's interest—the flip side of which is the desire of each of us for others to take an interest in what interests us.*

Therefore, *emulation,* for example, which is described as "[observing] another achieving a goal in a certain way, finding that goal attractive, and attempting to achieve that goal yourself by whatever means" (Hurley and Chater 2005, 14–15), which is contrasted with "true imitation" because of the "by whatever means" clause, clearly falls within the ambit of mimesis. The same applies to what are usually described as *stimulus enhancement* and *response priming.* In all these cases, what we are dealing with are mechanisms through which the actions of one animal bring another to perform either the same action or an action related to the same goal. In *stimulus enhancement* the action of the first draws the attention of the second to a stimulus that triggers an innate response—so it is not imitation, because the second organism does not learn anything—and in *response priming,* for example the way in which yawning is contagious, body movements are copied—but not learned—as a means to a goal; so again, it is considered that this also is not "true imitation." Both phenomena, however, rest on the fact that organisms are attuned or attentive to each other.

According to Girard, the interest that members of our species take in each other's interest and desire is much stronger than is found in other species, and this is what underlies our greater ability for imitation and emulation. It also colors our reaction to stimulus enhancement and response priming. However, here is Girard's central point: if you find attractive the goal previously attained by another organism and "attempt to achieve that goal yourself *by whatever means*," there are no *a priori* reasons to exclude from those means the taking away, by force, from the other, of the prize that has suddenly become attractive to you. If the interest we take in each other's interest augments cooperation by making us attentive to each other's needs and desires, thereby providing more reasons to collaborate toward shared goals, it *simultaneously increases occasions of conflict.* As argued earlier, the simultaneous augmentation of conflict and of cooperation is neither surprising nor paradoxical. *Cooperation and conflict are not polar opposites; they are interdependent, reciprocal functions.* Conflict limits and often puts an end to all possibilities of cooperation; yet cooperation also inevitably occasions conflicts. It seems, therefore, that there should be an upper limit to the extent to which cooperation is possible within a group, a limit beyond which cooperation cannot be carried, because conflicts threaten to dissolve or destroy the group.[16]

Human Violence and the Birth of Culture

Wrangham, Wilson, and Muller (2006) claim, as we have seen, that the rate of nonlethal aggression among chimpanzees is two to three hundred times higher than among recently settled hunter-gatherers. This figure may be somewhat exaggerated because they base their evaluation of nonlethal human violence on a study by Burbank (1992) that, in evaluating aggression among humans, did not take into account, as they note, juvenile delinquency, punishment of children, sorcery, vandalism, or sexual coercion (Burbank 1992; see also Wrangham, Wilson, and Muller 2006, 16). Even if, in view of this uncertainty, we halve either the highest or the lowest figure, the rate of nonlethal physical aggression among chimpanzees still remains two orders of magnitude (i.e., one hundred times) bigger than what it is among recently settled hunter-gatherers. This is a huge difference! It means that in a community, instead of having, for example, one case of nonlethal physical aggression per day, you would have, at the least, 100 cases (and, at most, 900); and in one month, instead of 30 such aggressions, you would have at least 3,000 (and at most 27,000)!

What would happen in a human community where there was such a high rate of nonlethal physical aggression? Two consequences seem likely. First, *the high levels of cooperation*—in hunting together, cultivating fields, performing rituals, sharing food, caring for the weak and the sick, etc.—that we find in every human community *would be impossible*. Even the relatively simple division of labor that exists in some hunter-gatherer societies would collapse. Second, *the rate of lethal physical aggression within the community would rise dramatically*. Why so? Because humans bear grudges—they are *resentful* animals. The most significant result of Wrangham, Wilson, and Muller's comparison (2006) of the rates of intraspecific aggression in humans and chimpanzees is not that the rate of intraspecific murder is about the same (i.e. of the same order of magnitude) between the two species. It is that, given the much higher level of nonlethal aggression among chimpanzees, their level of *lethal aggression* is about the same as among humans. Some may want to interpret this as signifying that humans are much more or much less violent than chimpanzees; but the important point to grasp is that this discrepancy *requires an explanation*. It suggests that there is something *radically different* between human and chimpanzee violence.

Human violence is different because of its "runaway" character. *Conflict breeds conflict and violence only leads to more violence.* Human violence easily gets out of bounds and out of hand, unless it is checked by some external sanction. Allowed to let rip, it tends to intensify and to proliferate. This is especially true when the parties are about evenly matched; but even when they are not, as recent wars suggest, violence once begun is not easily stopped. This continuation of violence against apparently disproportionate odds indicates that once spurred to violence, humans do not easily give up.

According to Girard, it is the *greater power of mimesis* characteristic of our human species that explains this difference. Humans take offense and seek revenge. When aggressed, they may flee in the moment, but they usually, sooner or later, come back for more. They care not only about the *damage* they have suffered, but also about the *affront*. Of course dogs and chimpanzees sometimes bear grudges against particular individuals and may act upon them, but the resentment of humans seems different. It is more frequent, and it often appears disproportionate in relation to the damage sustained. Among the reasons why, according to Hobbes, unlike men, creatures without reason can live in society *without coercive power,* is that "irrational creatures cannot distinguish between *injury* and *damage* (1994, 18).

To say that humans distinguish between damage and injury or offense is another way of saying that they care more about the aggression itself than about its immediate physical consequences. The resentment and animosity we manifest to those who have aggressed us are an expression of the fact that we humans are more interested in each other than are other social animals. This *reciprocity of Other-interest* is both an expression of, and the means by which is realized the *greater interdependence* that exists between us.

Among humans, less violent aggressions easily tend to evoke more violent responses, and a higher level of nonlethal physical violence thus leads rapidly to a higher level of violence, resulting in murder. Societies as we know them—from bands of hunter-gatherers to the immense cities of the twenty-first century—*only exist because humans have succeeded in maintaining a sufficiently low level of intraspecific violence within their communities.*

How was that achieved? Girard's theory of culture and of the sacred provides an answer to that question, which shows how we did, in fact, at the threshold of hominization, survive our origins—but which has perpetually, ever since, reawakened the question of whether that *survival* is assured, and whether it amounts to *salvation.*

Notes

1. This remains true of mixed strategies: where an animal plays one strategy with probability p and the other with probability 1-p, the two strategies remain conceptually distinct and are intrinsically unrelated.

2. Of course this interpretation assumes that, empirically, such "particular circumstances" are relatively rare. If, as Roughgarden (2009) argues, they turn out to be extremely common, they are not "particular" anymore, and we should *review the predominance we generally give to selfishness as what drives evolution.*

3. Eusocial animals, like ants or termites, are animals that live together where there is (1) reproductive division of labor, (2) overlapping generations, and (3) cooperative care of the young.

4. Http://www.nationmaster.com/encyclopedia/Social-animal.

5. Http://encyclopedia2.thefreedictionary.com/Social+animals.

6. Http://www.britannica.com/EBchecked/topic/550897/social-behaviour-animal.

7. Of course this definition could be extended to include relations between individuals from different species.

8. See Muller and Mitani (2005) for an analysis of the relationship between cooperation and conflict among chimpanzees.

9. The value of the prize depends on its nature and therefore will vary from conflict to conflict; the expected cost, however, depends on the adversary. It is independent of the prize and can remain identical while the value of prize varies.

10. This assumes that there is a strong correlation between the parties' ability to inflict damage upon each other and their ability to win the conflict. This condition seems rational enough, but it is clear that it will not always be satisfied.

11. This will usually be true as far as the initial use of violence is concerned. However there is an asymmetry between costs and benefits, which our analysis should reflect. If in an *e-conflict* the gain is uncertain, the cost, on the other hand, is by definition certain. Energy is expended and damage is sustained before the game is decided, and this is particularly true of conflicts between well-matched adversaries. In an *e-conflict,* therefore, once violence has begun, we can expect agents to focus on the damage sustained and inflicted as the only reliable index of how they are doing. Once hurt, agents will either give up immediately or strive to equal or to outdo the damage that they have received. The continuation of the unresolved dispute will then progressively disjoin the cost of the conflict from its expected benefit. When that occurs, the conflict will appear completely irrational, as the *level of damage—the violence—will become disproportionate* relative to the expected gain. This, of course, will only be the case as long as the parties remain sufficiently equal in their ability to inflict harm on each other, and as long as no one succeeds in bringing about a rapid end to the conflict that would break the correlation between damage inflicted and cost incurred. It will then be optimal for each party in the conflict to aim for such a "quick kill," and this will lead to a continuous intensification of the level of violence.

12. Note that our two authors here adopt the same hypothesis as Lorenz (and Rousseau), which makes human violence somewhat "unnatural: a creation of culture."

13. Wrangham and collaborators recognize important resemblances between human and chimpanzee violence, but they also note significant differences—which, however, they *immediately attribute to "culture."* It is not clear why these differences should be attributed to culture rather than "nature," and more generally why we should assume that culturally developed traits do not also reflect "nature." In order to understand the relation of human violence to chimpanzee violence, Wrangham et al. focus on similarities between warfare among (some) nomadic hunter-gatherers and aggressions among chimpanzees from different communities. The underlying methodological assumption is that the conditions of present-day hunter-gatherers are the closest we can get to the original condition of humankind. Comparing their warring behavior to conflict between groups of chimpanzees should thus allow us to identify what is fundamentally "natural" in human warfare—and that is what is similar in both cases: differences are then attributed to culture. Apart from the dualism between nature and culture that it contains, such an assumption implies an unjustified historicist bias. As Lévi-Strauss argued long ago, present-day hunter-gatherer societies are quite different from each other and have a long history behind them. There is no particular reason to assume that any one of them corresponds to how our ancestors were, or illustrates the early stages of mankind. See Lévi-Strauss (1952).

14. See, for example, Evans-Pritchard (1940); Gellner (1981); Montagne (1930); Sahlins (1972); Simonse (1992); Verdier (1984).

15. See, for example, Dijksterhuis (2005) and the essays collected in Nehaniv and Dautenhahn (2007). (The first work mentioned above shows why mimesis is related to "group intelligence," something that is preconscious and highly developed in many species, and becomes (partly) conscious in man. It is the basis of the structures of "reciprocity," invoked by Girard in describing mimetic desire—Ed.).

16. This limit should not simply be pertaining to the size of the group, but also to the level of cooperation that can be attained between individuals.

Cited Texts and Further Reading

Burbank, V. K. 1992. "Sex, Gender and Differences: Dimensions of Aggression in an Australian Aboriginal Community." *Human Nature* 3: 251–77.

Dijksterhuis, Ap. 2005. "Why We Are Social Animals: The High Road to Imitation as Social Glue." In *Perspectives on Imitation,* vol. 2, *Imitation, Human Development, and Culture,* ed. S. Hurley and N. Chater, 207–20. Cambridge, MA: MIT Press.

Evans-Pritchard, E. E. 1940. *The Nuer.* Oxford: Oxford University Press.

Gallese, V. 2011. "The Two Sides of Mimesis: Mimetic Theory, Embodied Simulation, and Social Identification." In *Mimesis and Science: Empirical Research on Imitation and the Mimetic Theory of Culture and Religion,* ed. Scott R. Garrels, 87–108. East Lansing: Michigan State University Press.

Gellner, E. 1981. *Muslim Society.* Cambridge: Cambridge University Press.

Hobbes, T. 1994. *Leviathan.* Edited by E. Curley. Indianapolis: Hackett Publishing Co.

Hurley S., and N. Chater. 2005. "Introduction: The Importance of Imitation." In *Perspectives on Imitation,* vol. 1, *Mechanisms of Imitation and Imitation in Animals,* ed. S. Hurley and N. Chater, 1–52. Cambridge, MA: MIT Press.

Langergraber, K. E., J. C. Mitani, and L. Vigilant. 2007. "The Limited Impact of Kinship on Cooperation in Wild Chimpanzees." *Proceedings of the National Academy of Sciences* 104, no. 19: 7786–90.

Lévi-Strauss, C. 1952. *Race et histoire.* Paris: UNESCO.

Lorenz, Konrad. [1963] 1969. *L'agression: Une histoire naturelle du mal.* Paris: Flammarion.

Meltzoff, A. 2011. "Out of the Mouths of Babes: Imitation, Gaze and Intentions in Infant Research—the "Like Me" Framework." In *Mimesis and Science: Empirical Research on Imitation and the Mimetic Theory of Culture and Religion,* ed. Scott R. Garrels, 55–74. East Lansing: Michigan State University Press.

Mitani, J. C. 2006. "Demographic Influences on the Behavior of Chimpanzees." *Primates* 47: 6–13.

Montagne, R. 1930. *Les Berbères et le Makhzen dans le sud du Maroc.* Paris: Alcan.

Muller, M., and J. Mitani. 2005. "Conflict and Cooperation in Wild Chimpanzees." *Advances in the Study of Behavior* 35: 275–331.

Nehaniv, C. L. and K. Dautenham. 2007. *Imitation and Social Learning in Robots, Humans and Animals.* Cambridge: Cambridge University Press.

Pusey, A., et al. 2008. "Severe Aggression among Female *Pan troglodytes schweinfurtii* at Gombe National Park, Tanzania." *International Journal of Primatology* 29: 949–73.

Revel, A., and J. Nadel. 2007. "How to Build an Imitator." In *Imitation and Social Learning in Robots, Humans and Animals,* ed. C. L. Nehaniv and K. Dautenhahn, 279–300. Cambridge: Cambridge University Press.

Roughgarden, Joan. 2009. *The Genial Gene: Deconstructing Darwinian Selfishness.* Berkeley: University of California Press.

Sahlins, M. 1972. *Stone Age Economics.* Chicago: Aldine.

Simonse, S. 1992. *Kings of Disaster.* Leiden: E.J. Brill.

Verdier, R. 1984. *La vengeance: Études d'ethnologie, d'histoire et de philosophie.* 4 vols. Paris: Cujas.

Watts, D. P. 2004. "Intracommunity Coalitionary Killing of an Adult Male Chimpanzee at Ngogo, Kibale National Park, Uganda." *International Journal of Primatology* 25, no. 3: 507–21.

Watts, D. P., and J. C. Mitani. 2001. "Boundary Patrols and Intergroup Encounters in Wild Chimpanzees." *Behaviour* 138: 299–327.

Wrangham, R., and L. Glowacki. 2012. "Intergroup Aggression in Chimpanzees and War in Nomadic Hunter-Gatherers." *Human Nature: An Interdisciplinary Biosocial Perspective.* Http://www.springerlink.com/content/w240447t728304tp/fulltext.html.

Wrangham, R., and M. Wilson. 2004. "Collective Violence. Comparisons between Youths and Chimpanzees." *Annals of the New York Academy of Sciences* 1036: 233–56.

Wrangham, R., M. L. Wilson, and M. N. Muller. 2006. "Comparative Rates of Violence in Chimpanzees and Humans." *Primates* 47(1): 14–26.

Zahavi, Amotz, and Avishag Zahavi. 1997. *The Handicap Principle: A Missing Piece of Darwin's Puzzle.* Oxford: Oxford University Press.

Liminal Crises

The Origins of Cultural Order, the Default Mechanisms of Survival, and the Pedagogy of the Sacrificial Victim

Pierpaolo Antonello

I n *2001: A Space Odyssey* (1968), the American film director Stanley Kubrick resorts to a strange, fictional device to plot key turning points in the cultural evolution of humans: an ominous black monolith, seen to be something like a "black box" (which, in science and engineering, designates a device, system, or object that can be viewed solely in terms of its input, output, and transfer characteristics, without any knowledge of its internal workings).

This eerie object serves in particular to highlight and problematize the quantum leap implied in human emergence: the leap involved, in the first instance, in our passing from visibly animal-like groups resembling roving bands of chimpanzees, to the technologically endowed and properly humane humanity we all recognize today; and then, in a second phase, millions of years later, from our contemporary world of organized technological capabilities and powers, to a further developmental stage, seen to represent a sort of proto-divine level.

As typically happens in science fiction movies, that ominous and puzzling alien presence is a secular metaphor for an *unavowed* form of the divine. It is deployed, in this case, in a peculiarly "iconoclastic" manner, since Kubrick is self-consciously guarded and coy about explicating this transcendental symbol. One could conceivably interpret Kubrick's film according to a creationist or ID (Intelligent Design) model, although this latter hypothesis sits uncomfortably with the notion and name of a "black box." The monolith could be interpreted more convincingly as a metaphor for our inability (precisely) to account fully for the emergence of human intelligence and of human culture: i.e., the "something more" for which Kubrick can offer no explanation within a strictly naturalistic, evolutionary framework of Darwinian antecedence, but which he represents as having operated de facto, albeit in an "opaque," i.e., intrinsically mysterious, *deus-ex-machina* sort of way.

We shall assume here that the black monolith stands for an inarticulable or, at least, non-articulated symbol of liminality, identifying the points of inflection or phase change, the "punctuated equilibria" (to pick up here the terminology of Niles Eldredge and Stephen Jay Gould) in the long and "bumpy" trajectory of human evolution. Highly significant transformations, we do know, have occurred quite abruptly in the course of primate and human evolution, but we do not have a clear explanation about how and why. We have only a "black box."

I will attempt to say here what is the content, and the meaning, of this "black box," as interpreted by Girard's fundamental anthropology; and to focus this attempt, I would propose to invoke the concept of the "liminal," as developed in social anthropology by Arnold van Gennep and Victor Turner in their studies of initiation rites considered as a category of cultural experience (van Gennep 1960, 21; Turner 1969). According to the two anthropologists, liminality refers to in-between situations and conditions that are characterized by the dislocation of established structures, the reversal of hierarchies, and uncertainty regarding the continuity of tradition and future outcomes. Ronald Grimes has described the liminal as "a moment of ritually generated limbo . . . an antistructural moment of reversal" (Grimes 1995, 151). The "essence of liminality," Turner states, is "its release from normal constraints, making possible the deconstruction of . . . the meaningfulness of ordinary life" (Turner 1985, 160). Liminality is "a time outside time in which it is often permitted to *play* with the factors of sociocultural experience, to disengage what is mundanely connected; what, outside liminality, people may even believe to be naturally and intrinsically connected, and to join the disarticulated parts in novel, even improbable ways" (Turner 1985, 238).

What is particularly interesting, from the standpoint of our discussion, is the definition of a *suddenly nonstandard regime of functioning* of a system, process, or social entity that is localizable, at least approximately, within the history of the system, and that is characterized by free play and the emergence of novelty. It is this free play that represents the *potential* of a system and that modifies the system's subsequent development. Thus explicated, "the liminal" is a concept, which, rather like Kubrick's "black box," highlights and problematizes an enigma: here, the enigma of "threshold emergence."

Defined in this way, the liminal is a cogent interpretive concept, addressing particularly well the needs of our own discussion: that of the origins of cultural order and its legacy to all of us. It will help us conceptualize a functional regime developing at some point within the process of hominization, in which the radical transformations that both established the foundations of culture and enabled us to survive the birth pangs and the perils of becoming human could and did occur.

We are asked to imagine, at the threshold of this major evolutionary phase change, a zone of free play involving an event-scenario that is transformative and game-changing; even if "changing the game" may be viewed as a distinctly mixed blessing for *Homo sapiens,* its agent and beneficiary, since it implied, as we shall see, not simply new and transformed, specifically human potentials and energies, but also acquired *default mechanisms* that still mortgage our future. The elucidation of this spatially and temporally situated zone of free play, and the pharmacology stirring within it, will help us to achieve a decipherment of origins that is *naturalistic* (as all theories of culture-origins are bound to be), while avoiding any philosophically *reductionist* implications of this term.

We may note that the way modern scientific discourse tackles the problem of origins normally leaves little scope for concepts like the "liminal." The liminal is characterized by ambiguity, openness, indeterminacy, undifferentiation, disorder, unstable borders—i.e., all the elements that the scientific mind is primed to reduce and to eliminate, and that are hard to embrace in any general account of the origins of human culture, although it is otherwise congruent with accounts of the *self-organizing systems* often invoked by evolutionary theory as a whole.

One might argue that there is no account of liminal space in the current conceptualization of cultural origins, because there is *no origin* as such, but *only* the progressive accumulation of genetic and physical traits judged likely to bring about at some point the emergence of culture. (But we note: the word "emergence" is very frequently used to "explain" *without explaining* how novelty *as such* arises.) There are, in this scheme of things at least, no "punctuated equilibria." The evolution of culture is seen rather as linear and progressive; as something embedded in a form of "phyletic gradualism." Culture, morality, religion, the symbolic order, are explained simply as a result of encephalization and the growing of the neocortex, or referred, as in Jared Diamond (1997), to the transformation of the larynx and the vocal apparatus, the sudden appearance of language as genetically preprogrammed and neurologically wired in our brain, while rituals and taboos are very often "accounted for" via the platitudes of cultural materialism (Harris 1979).

Culture, in other words, seems to steal up on the theorist as an unobserved deus ex machina precisely because it is often mis-taken for a sufficiently explained "given." To echo Derrida, the origins of culture imply a "supplementary" nature (Derrida 1976, 144). More broadly speaking: according to the evolutionary psychologists John Tooby and Leda Cosmides, "most social scientists believe they are invoking a powerful explanatory principle when they claim that a behaviour is 'learned' or 'cultural.'" However, "as hypotheses to account for mental or behavioural phenomena, these terms are remarkably devoid of meaning. At this point in the study of human behaviour, learning and culture are phenomena to be explained, and not explanations in themselves" (Tooby and Cosmides 1989, 46).

What seems to be missing in the general theory of the origins of culture is mainly a *theory of symbolization* and how symbols emerged in humans or proto-humans; and, we may add, a theory linking human emergence to the other greatly neglected "given" of our evolutionary origins, the problem of the special intensity and significance of human violence. Girard claims our attention to the extent that he addresses both "blackspots" of understanding—linking their common elucidation, indeed, in a single movement of theorization.

In fact: "some of the most strenuous objections to human sociobiology come from anthropologists who [rightly] believe that symbols are the essential feature of human culture, often defining culture as a set of symbols whose meanings are shared by members of a human society" (Allott 1999, 67). As empirical evidence gathered by primatologists suggests, primates in fact already have culture, and they have tool-making, as well as forms of cooperation and proto-morality—but they do not have symbols. It is the symbolic order that makes possible the free-floating of signifiers, enabling their *recombination;* hence also the constitution of metaphorical and analogical thinking, the possibility of language, religion, myth, and rituals.

Girard's Mimetic Theory and the Quest for Origins

How does René Girard's theory of hominization, as set out in *Things Hidden since the Foundation of the World* (1987) and further discussed in *Evolution and Conversion* (2008), come to play a decisive role in opening up the conceptualization of origins, and showing the role of the liminal in the agency of change and transformation?

Rather than an accountancy of the genetic accumulation of physical traits, Girard's theory is relational and systemic—although this dimension, it is true, is firmly predicated on the increasing mimetic capacity of proto-humans. It is not a sociobiological theory *stricto sensu,* i.e., it does not posit that religion and the sacred can be explained solely and sufficiently via genetic determinism, or merely as an accumulation of artifacts or mentifacts; religion is rather, if we follow the Girardian account, an outcome—the principal and pivotal outcome—of the selective pressures that shape collective behavior in determining *the coevolution of the physical and the cultural.*

Social order and structures, argues Girard, emerge out of a primordial, mimetically driven chaos: they arise through an exasperation of the violence and conflict that, for natural or systemic reasons, periodically emerged within primitive societies, above all when the number of individuals composing human groupings increased above a certain critical level. This aggravation is magnified by the strength of human mimetism, or imitative capacity, which is a spontaneous reflex and not a conscious act.[1] Imitation in humans, in fact, does not account solely for the positive aspects of cultural transmission but also for the negative ones: acquisitive or competitive imitation for any given resources is far stronger in humans than in primates, triggering conflicts that can easily overcome any instinctual control of intraspecific violence.

Mimetism is so powerful that it overrules the instinctual constraints that both structure social ranking and control intraspecific killing. Also, when social crises erupt, the mimetic contagion of reciprocal violence is bound to get more rapidly out of control and to plague the whole group, if not restrained by means of cultural, i.e., socio-symbolic mechanisms. In those circumstances, our band of hominid primates will either disappear through mutual extermination, or else, if it is to survive, some self-regulating mechanism must be found *within the violence* that threatens them (Dumouchel 1992, 79–80). As Dumouchel writes: "[Girard's] theory postulates a self-regulating mechanism of violence, in which the social order emerges from the self-regulation of violence" (78).

A "pharmacological" action or transaction is involved, which represents a limiting and "homeopathic" use of violence itself. That self-regulatory mechanism, which is a systemic event and not a deliberate and conscious act (there is no scope for any form of contractualism in primordial times), takes the form of a sudden *externalization of endemic violence,* in the shape of spontaneous scapegoating. Much as in any episode of panic, the collective system in disarray finds (or rather produces) an endogenous fixed point on which to converge (Dupuy 2003): one randomly identified element of the social group, who is expelled and/or killed. The collective rage of the mob abates and disappears when that fixed point is found and the entire horde discharges its fury in a "lightning strike" directed at that point. This point of fixation is normally a member (or members) of the group that may present elements of "externality" (he/she looks slightly different, or displays nonstandard features differentiating her from the majority of the group). Of course the scapegoaters do not see this strike-point individual for what she actually is—a random victim; and they fail to do so because, by this killing, peace is suddenly restored.

Causal agency, making the victim responsible for the violence thus terminated, is projected onto her retroactively. If, by killing this victim, social peace is restored, it is sufficiently evident that the scapegoat victim "caused" it in the first place (cf. Girard's interpretation of the Oedipus myth, which operates on this same basis; Girard 2004). Here we have a collective *misrecognition* of a specific group behavior taken, cognitively speaking, to be the "cause" of the social disease. A dog or cat will similarly "misinterpret" its sense of being attacked by physical disease, and actually *hide* from its "attacker." The mythical misrepresentation in humans needs to be much more potent, however, since it has to overlay and "cover up" all the evidence pointing to the killing or "murder" of one's own kind.

The picture, for Girard, is even more complex than this: for the very act of victimization produces a sudden collective experience of positive relief and communal bonding; there is an intense and deep focalization on the victim, perceived as thaumaturgic, and the whole process is seen as possessing some sort of healing power. It is then taken up and used as a "fail-safe" or "default" mechanism, i.e., it is interiorized culturally by the self-programming social pyche as a process that has the capacity to *ward off* the ever-threatening recurrence of conflict and crisis. This trial-and-error mode of cultural invention, protecting humankind from its own violent shadow, is the beginning of the sacred and of the socio-symbolic ritual system of bonding-and-binding we call "religion." The victim is sacralized both because of her terrible potency in bringing disruption, violence, panic, crisis, and because her expulsion or sacrifice has brought a resolution to the crisis and a reestablishment of viable social order. For this reason, in polytheistic religions, the gods often come to represent both positive and negative forces. The victim must be a god; for who else could effect the saving reversal of transcending life-energies from a negative to a positive valency?

Prohibitions and Rituals

Girard is suggesting that in this primordial scenario, what emerges are two interconnected phases that contribute to structuring the symbolic order. The first one is related to the *emergence of prohibitions:* "If people are threatened, they withdraw from specific acts; otherwise chaotic appropriation will dominate and violence will always increase. Prohibition is the first condition for social ties, hence one of the first elements of cultural programming as well. Fear is essentially fear of mimetic violence; prohibition is *protection* from mimetic escalation" (Girard, Antonello, and de Castro Rocha 2008, 109–10). Religion developed out of the most basic feelings and passions of proto-humans: fear, and in particular fear of violence—violence that may be produced by both external and internal causes: predators, natural events, and endemic recycling (as in feud and vendetta); and we cannot be sure that the primitive mind was able to make a clear-cut distinction between the self-generated and the externally generated causes.

The second phase is related to the *structuring of rituals.* As an antidote to these moments of dreadful crisis, proto-societies felt compelled to repeat that *ur*-event that saved them from self-destruction: scapegoating—ritually *reprised* as "sacrifice." This is how Girard explains the origin of sacrificial rituals and of the symbolic order in general.

Sacrificial rituals stem from the repetition of this systemic proto-event, which is seen to be required once more in particular moments when a new cycle of regression into social disorder and mimetic crisis threatens. Their intention is to call down the same curative and salutary pharmacology by immolating ritually another scapegoat victim.

It may be useful to remark that ritualization still lies at the threshold between cultural phenomena and their biological preconditioning. We are in the "liminal zone" between nature and nurture. Forms of ritualized behavior are in fact instinctively activated in animals during moments of crisis, and the same phenomenon is also visible in humans. One could also refer here to the connection that has been observed, by anthropologists like Alan Fiske or Pascal Boyer, between OCD (obsessive-compulsive disorder) and religious rituals (Boyer 2001, 273).

According to Girard, rituals (and then eventually myths) stage and represent this primordial *ur*-scenario of collective scapegoating, in which a two-phase dialectic is distinctly observable: (1) an initial moment of undifferentiation, of disorder, mimicking the archetypical mimetic crisis; and (2) the subsequent sacrificial expulsion of a "surrogate victim" who brings back social order, producing what we define as *the sacred,* always held by the earliest humans to be the origin of the entire panoply of the myths, rites, institutions, traditions, practices, and laws that, developing over time—and very variously in different spaces and places—came to make up what we call "culture." Thus Girard explains the long-recognized dual function of all cultures: they regulate-and-enable communal life, and they bond-and-bind the members of the social community.

Rites of Passage

This *ur*-scenario helps to clarify the intrinsic constitutive dynamic of the so-called "rites of passage," as studied by van Gennep, which denote rituals marking transitional phases (like the passage between childhood and full inclusion into a tribe or social group).[2] Van Gennep points out how for pretechnological societies, the crossing of any threshold, limit, or border had to be governed, controlled, authorized, by ritual, in particular by ritual sacrifice: the trespassing or trans-gression of which is marked by a sacrificial offering to the divine, to the gods.

Mindful of Girard's theory of the origins of culture, one can easily understand the intrinsic structural "grammar" operating in rites of passage, since these simply particularize the grammar of any rite managing the relationship between transgression and sacrifice. In *Evolution and Conversion,* Girard explains:

> Ritual always intervenes at points of crisis, it will always be there at the same point of the mimetic crisis. Therefore, ritual will turn into the institution that regulates the crisis: like the crisis of adolescence and the rites of passage; like the crisis of death, which generates funeral rituals; like the crisis of disease, which generates ritual medicine. Whether the crisis is real or imaginary makes very little difference, because an imaginary crisis may cause a real catastrophe. (Girard, Antonello, and de Castro Rocha, 2008, 71–72)

The etymology of *crisis* is the Greek *krinein,* meaning to "decide," which refers at an earlier stage to "slitting the goat's throat"—a clear ritualistic and sacrificial gesture. In a similar fashion, the latin word *de-cidere* (to decide) meant, originally and etymologically, to "cut off" or "kill."

However, Girard inverts the etiological and classificatory order proposed by van Gennep, who claimed that foundational sacrifices are a subcategory of the rites of passage (van Gennep 1960, 23). According to Girard, it is the rite of passage that reproduces and repeats in different fashion the foundational sacrifice. This is also true for myths, which display, according to Girard, an inverted causal and temporal logic. In the mythical account of the foundation of Rome, for instance, Remus leaps across the ditch that Romulus was digging to act as defensive perimeter of the soon-to-be-founded city (transgressing the *limes*), and for this reason he is killed with the same tool that Romulus has used to make the ditch, and he is then buried in that ditch. In Girard's understanding, Remus is the foundational sacrificial victim, his transgression of the *limes* being the—arbitrary—accusation that led the

community to sacrifice him. Because of the sacred character normally attaching to the victim (and to any sacrificial practice as such), the tools with which
the ritual was performed are then used to mark out the sacred space of the
city (Girard 1986; Serres, 1991).

Van Gennep also contends that it is a mistake to see in the rites of
passage surviving variations or distortions of archaic human sacrifice (van
Gennep 1960, 24). On the contrary, for Girard, they are precisely ritualistic
byproducts of sacrificial rituals: crises are resolved and composed through
sacrifice, and the proto-sacrificial ritual very often involved a human victim.

As an instance of liminality, Victor Turner, in his book *The Ritual
Process,* describes the ritual enthroning of the Ndembu chief, who has first
been exiled from the village in a hut that is named *kafu* or *kafwi,* a Ndembu
term derived from *ku-fwa,* "to die"—i.e., he is *symbolically* killed (in Ndembu
liminality, as Turner notes, "imagery of death abounds") (Turner 1969, 100).
The ritual subject is dressed like a beggar and he is insulted by everybody,
each expressing *resentment* against him (101). Only Girard's mimetic theory
can make sense of this staged, symbolic inversion of power structure in such a
ritual. As we can read in *Things Hidden,* the emergence of sacred kinship was
produced by a peculiar development of sacrificial rituals:

> In all human institutions it is necessary to reproduce a reconciliatory
> murder by means of new victims. The orginal victim is endowed with a ter-
> rifying, super-human, prestige because it is seen as the source of all disorder
> and order. Subsequent victims inherit some of this prestige. One must look
> to this prestige for the source of all political and religious sovereignity. . . .
> It is necessary and sufficient for the victim to take advantage of the lapse
> of time before the sacrifice and to transform veneration into real power.
> One might therefore expect that the interval between the selection of the
> victim and the sacrifice will be gradually prolonged. This extension, in
> turn, will permit the future victim to consolidate progressively ever-greater
> power over the community. At some point, this power and the resulting
> submission of the community would become sufficiently effective and
> extensive as to make an actual sacrifice of the monarch impossible if not
> unthinkable. (Girard 1987, 53)

The Liminal Dialectic: Self-Protection Is Inventive

What van Gennep or Turner describe as "the liminal" is for Girard in particular the ritualistic reenactment of the crisis of undifferentiation, which stages the primordial mimetic violent disorder, out of which the sacred order came about. If it is to be effective, the sacrificial ritual needs to repeat the original event in all its phases: "the singular genesis of rituals and prohibitions from the mimetic crisis would . . . explain the strange contradiction between them which anthropologists have often noticed: *the rituals often prescribe exactly that which prohibitions prohibit*" (Dumouchel 1992 81).

Because they *represent and stage* the primordial disorder and undifferentiation of the mimetic crisis, rituals deliberately enter that "liminal state" that would require the transgression of the whole set of taboos and prohibitions, the erasure of all possible *differences* (i.e., lines of differentiation drawn between human and animal, between genders, between different social positions and functions, etc.). Dionysiac and carnivalistic rituals attest to this process of *de*-differentiation. They effect a "pharmacological" or "homeopathic" *innoculation* by a chaotic moment of radical transgression: a *contagion* operating, however, within ritualistic parameters that help the community to find a form of structural stability among the deregulatory and disaggregating forces that constantly threaten to rip it apart. Just like the sacred itself, this liminal zone has an ambivalent charge, for it would also allow for a partial or temporary redefinition of the internal structure of differentiation within the social and cultural sphere; and this in turn may produce new patterns that at first are kept within the ritualistic space but then progressively "overspill" into the "secular" sphere as technical, practical, social, or symbolic "spinoffs" (the above-cited example of sacred kinship is a case in point).

We tend to think that technical discoveries are inventions of the utilitarian and practical mind; but in so doing, we project our modern cognitive and pragmatic "freedom" retroactively onto primitive cultures, which were, on the contrary, enmeshed in all sorts of prohibitions and taboos; they could not and dared not act in certain ways, venture into certain zones, handle certain objects (etc.).

It is only within the space of ritual that the reorganization of the symbolic, social, and material elements of a given culture is allowed, and that the options possible within the strongest parameters stand open to the invention of novelty. In order to reproduce the beneficial effects of sacrifice, communities had to enter the liminal and dreadful zone of social crisis and of potentially contagious violence, as performed by rituals. For this reason, there are strict procedures for regulating and containing this experience; they are codified as stringent ritualistic and liturgical protocols to be observed. Transgression and transformation are ritualistically managed. However, this dangerous zone is also highly productive. The ritualistically staged reproduction of the primordial "genetic chaos" would create a space for experimental potentiality, just as it would allow the mixing up of elements that are normally kept separated by taboos and laws.

Because rituals regulated any form of uncertainty, as well as the transition through anomic zones, they would also favor the emergence of divinatory practices, based on the arbitrary interpretation of random events and facts. Moreover, as Girard argues, because of the intrinsic arbitrariness of the selection of the sacrificial victim, rituals would also codify mechanisms of random choice based on *agôn* (competition) or *alea* (chance), to use Roger Caillois's anthropological classification of games (Caillois 1961, 36; Girard 1987, 101–2).[3] This insertion of elements of chance into ritual practice would add a further layer of creativity, in terms of its symbolic and technical outcomes, to the ritualistic space.

Cultural, symbolic, and technical creativity is perhaps nothing but what we could call the "grammaticalization of ritual practices," through the manipulation of sacred elements, objects, symbols, people, animals (etc.) that perform a specific function within the ritual space. There is an *interplay* between the need to *manipulate* the sacred for healing purposes and the *necessity of keeping it at some distance* because of its intrinsic danger; in this peculiar space, we may hypothesize, were progressively constructed the cultural and symbolic elements that will eventually *find a use also* outside the sacrifical and ritual framework.

To offer a few examples: ritual sacrifice involves the body-manipulation of the victim, which then produces elaborate dressing, body painting, tattooing, mummification, but also healing practices and actual anatomical knowledge. Mimicking and staging the primordial disorder stimulated the development of dance, theater, rhythm (i.e., music and prosody); primordial chaos and undifferentiation, as achieved through ecstatic techniques,

through drugs and intoxication, triggered the development of winemak-
ing and pharmacology. Equally, the sacrifice of human and animal victims
would often entail the consumption of their bodies, which would trigger
the invention of ritualistic cuisine. All these procedures need to be handed
down through generations, and therefore mnemotechnique and mythmak-
ing ensue. In the *Rg-Veda,* for instance—which is one of the oldest texts in
any Indo-European language, composed in the northwestern region of the
Indian subcontinent, roughly between 1,700 and 1,100 BCE—we can read
how the world, the social structure, domesticated animals, poetry emerged
from the dismembered body of the sacrificial victim:

> FROM THAT SACRIFICE in which everything was offered, the verses and
> chants were born, the meters were born from it, and from it the formulas
> were born. Horses were born from it, and those other animals that have
> two rows of teeth; cows were born from it, and from it goats and sheep
> were born. When they divided the Man, into how many parts did they
> apportion him? What do they call his mouth, his two arms and thighs
> and feet? His mouth became the Brahmin; his arms were made into the
> Warrior; his thighs the People, and from his feet the servants were born.
> The moon was born from his mind; from his eye the sun was born. Idra
> and Agni came from his mouth, and from his vital breath Wind was born.
> (*Rg-Veda,* 10.90: 9–13)

Victimary Pedagogy: Human Peril Converted into Invention and Possibility

As is clear from this passage, and as Girard explains carefully, any serendipitous technical discovery would become irrelevant if not referred to the center of signification provided by the sacrificial victim (Girard 1987, 99–104).
When speaking about liminality, creative disorder has always been stressed
by anthropologists, but we must note also that cultural *order* is *originally
established and developmentally structured* by the sacrificial obliteration of
a surrogate victim who acts as a metonymy or a synecdoche for the social
whole. The creative dynamic of rituals, including the rites of passage, operates then at two levels. At one level, the disorderly permutation of factual and

symbolic elements of the rite produces new combinations and serendipitous discovery—and only within the ritualistic context would this be allowed because of the normal enforcement of prohibitions and taboos; at the second level, there is the *fixed point* of the victim, as the primordial token through which the whole social system constructs its meanings. As Girard argues, the victim, and in particular the surrogate victim, is the *ur*-symbol for any and all differential thinking:

> In the "superstitious" repetition of the event, a form of "staging" in the shape of a killing of a surrogate victim had to be set in place. This victim is no longer presumed responsible for the crisis, but it is both a *real* new victim that has to be killed, and a *symbol* of the proto-event; it is *the first symbolic sign* ever invented by these hominids. It is the first moment in which something *stands* for *something else*. It is the *ur*-symbol. (Girard, Antonello, and de Castro Rocha 2008, 106–7)

The liminal should, then, always be considered in relation to the role and the position of the sacrificial victim, and in all liminal states (i.e., in all ritualistic events) one should be looking for this fixed point, for this converging principle of order and recomposition. The victim is in fact the liminal figure *par excellence:* she belongs to the community, but not entirely so (since there are signs of victimary aptitude that distinguish her). The victim is integrated, but then she is also strange or a stranger, liable to be outcast; she is an insider/outsider. That is, for instance, the way in which Girard interprets the Tupinamba's ritual cannibalism:

> The individual who was captured was also kept alive inside the group for a considerable period of time. He was very well treated and was even given a wife. He had to be "domesticated" (i.e. acculturated), to become enough of an insider. Only then would he be a good sacrificial victim. In other words, the outsider is first turned into an insider and then the ritual enactment of the scapegoat mechanism occurs when this outsider/insider is ritually killed and actually eaten. (Girard, Antonello, and de Castro Rocha 2008, 116)[4]

This dynamics becomes especially clear and cogent when we view the so-called "rites of initiation" as proto-forms of *pedagogy*. If, in the historical

development of ritual *techniques,* there has been the progressive loss of the
center of signification, i.e., the sacrifice of a member of the community, while
retaining the liturgical apparatus and the technical invention stemming from
the ritualistic practices, in the case of the rites of initiation, we are still in the
presence of an evident victimary mechanism, albeit "purified" of its most cruel
and climactic moment. The neophyte stands in the position of the designated
sacrificial victim. The initiation process is in fact often likened to a simultaneous symbolic "death" and "rebirth," because as well as being a beginning it
also implies an ending, as existence on one level drops away in an ascension
to the next (van Gennep 1960, 75). The neophyte is also presented in a state
of undifferentiation: "sexlessness and anonymity are highly characteristic
of liminality" (Turner 1969, 102). These rites may involve ablation of body
parts, as in the case of circumcision, infibulation, the cutting off of the little
finger above the last joint, the perforating of the earlobe or the septum, etc.
(van Gennep 1960, 71–72). In a Girardian perspective, personal humiliation,
physical mutilation, and the exposure of the neophyte to life-threatening
circumstances constitute the symbolic reproduction of the sacrificial victim
position. By making the neophyte transit through the position of the victim,
the ritual makes him/her acquire a new "subjectivity," with a symbolic "resurrection" (which reproduces the circular productive pattern of any rite by
which from sacrificial death stems new life). The characteristics attached to
this process of transformation, as listed by Turner, also keep pointing to the
role of the victim: "homogeneity, equality, anonymity, humility, unselfishness,
obedience"; "suspension of kinship rights and obligation . . . , simplicity of
speech and manner, sacred folly, acceptance of pain and suffering (even to the
point of undergoing martyrdom)" (Turner 1969, 111–12).

We can also see the productive side of the sacrificial framework in the
moment in which the expulsion of the victim is at some point symbolically
elaborated as a ritualistic process of exclusion and integration, and not simply as a brutal, unreflecting force generated by scapegoating and sacrificial
unanimity, which eventually helps in constructing a sense of "identity"—a
proto-form of "selfhood," still enmeshed in the collective and the social, but
also clearly demarcating a space that we could call, in a modern terminology, "personal"—and a moral structure and set of rules of behavior that are
imposed upon the individual; all these things are directed to fostering community cooperation and harmonious cohabitation.

The theoretical implications of this perspective are quite far-reaching. They can be glimpsed, providing one allows the temporal leap or time compression involved, in Kubrick's film, which represents the first tool used as a weapon morphed into a futuristic spaceship. This insight resonates revealingly with Julia Kristeva's discussion on the notion of the "abject" in subject formation (Kristeva 1982). The issue of abjection has been addressed and discussed mostly in its psychoanalytical constitution,[5] but it is in fact rooted principally in an anthropological understanding of the economy of sacrifice, stemming from Kristeva's reading of the structuralist tradition, as well as of the works of Mary Douglas, Georges Bataille, and Girard himself.

We see here that for Kristeva the sacred is the special and original locus of the abject: "abjection accompanies all religious structurings"; "abjection appears as a rite of defilement and pollution"; "the various means of purifying the abject—the various *catharses*—make up the history of religions" (Kristeva 1982, 14). The abject, according to Kristeva, is always situated in a liminal space, neither subject nor object; however, it remains the location for subject formation and renegotiation, particularly in emancipatory terms (Reineke 1997). It could be easily mapped out so as to include the ritualistic space of the rites of passage: a sacrificial crisis, marked by the exercise of violence (suffered or perpetrated), is reenacted so that the chaotic elements of a child's personality are transformed and "jell" together, forming a "subject."

The overall implication of this perspective is that our modern categories of "identity," "self," "consciousness," "subjectivity" are rooted first of all in the mechanisms of persecution, exclusion, victimization. As Michel Serres has put it:

> What is meant by the subject we call *you* or *me? Sub-jectus,* someone who, thrown down, thrust under, cast beneath the stones which kill, dies under the excluding shields, the scapegoating votes, the crowd clamoring for the death penalty. And what abominable glue is it that sticks these collective entities together into this plural we call *us?* This awful cement is the sum of our hatreds, our rivalries, our resentments. (Serres 2008, 14; my translation)

The individual subject is dialectically created vis-à-vis the mythical unanimity: she is a *sub-jectum* not in terms of being submissive or dependent on some specified military power or national law (such is the *modern* reading of this etymology), but as *victim,* inasmuch as she is (ritualistically) *singled out and persecuted.*

In the dialectical process of scapegoating, we observe, on the one hand: sameness, undifferentiation, false differences perceived as objective boundaries of the subject, sudden metamorphoses, the singular always enmeshed in the faceless collective. On the other hand, we find the isolation of the victim, singled out, abjected, suffering; then, gradually, questioning that violence; and then gradually awakening to the logic of scapegoating: a process that resonates with the cry of the Psalmist, the laments of the Hebrew people and its prophets, the prayers of the suffering Servant and of the Crucified—and, displaced, also with the hearing of divine victimhood that "converts" St. Paul: "Why do you persecute me?" (Acts 9:4).

If religion is the "mother of all culture," as Girard states (following Durkheim), the process of sacrificial scapegoating carries intrinsically, or else has *developed* in historic/evolutionary time, a "redemptive" element that made it possible, at some point and to some extent, to overcome or transcend the logic of violence. We might then conclude that it is by progressively enlarging the borders of this ritualistic space, by the amplitude given to the liminal space of the ritual, that human culture is able to make further steps in its development and emancipation—providing always that we recall that invention is predicated on peril, and that violence contained is never *eliminated* by its inventive containment.

Can we, then, outrun the shadow that impels or compels our movement?

Conclusion: Evolutionary Freedom and Its Shadow

We enter at this point the vast territory of the ultimate questions about the liminal spaces of human evolution. How far do they account for, authorize, and predict the reach of our self-fashioning freedom? How far, on the contrary, do they record and explicate the "default" programming that conditions us and weighs down any attempt to escape the gravitational pull of our evolutionary antecedents and origins?

Turner states that liminal experiences find a rare and diminished echo in modern industrial societies, where they have been largely replaced by "liminoid" experiences, i.e., experiences presenting the characteristics of liminal experiences, but only in optional mode, since they do not involve the resolution of any crisis, personal or collective (Turner 1982). Play, sports, and the arts are typical examples. This alleged disappearance of liminal experiences might be held to chime with the progressive cultural influence of the Judeo-Christian revelation, which, so Girard contends, has acted as a deconstructive force in relation to the archaic-sacral symbolic-and-religious order, by revealing the arbitrariness and injustice of the scapegoat mechanism, and all the laws and rites irradiating from this "sacrificial" center.

Our modernity corresponds, in other words, to history's progressive entry into a phase in which symbolic and actual scapegoating are becoming less and less effective in conferring authority on the social structures and practices that formerly contained violence; whereas, at the same time, they project humankind into an everlasting "liminal state" of frantic experimentation and reconfiguration. We might argue that what accelerates with modernity is, on the one hand, the creative dimension of humankind, and its propensity to seek to overcome limits, taboos, and restrictions, relying for this purpose on merely technical capabilities; and on the other, the demystification and loss of the symbolic structures of containment, accentuating modern humanity's propensity to become caught up as never before in its own self-generated tendency to extremes. Hence the ambivalence attributed by Girard to modernity: it represents for him an everlasting "liminal space," in which the potential for *both* human creativity *and* cataclysmic and terminal violence is increasing.

This perception of a hidden ambivalence sets him at odds with Steven Pinker's thesis of a simple de facto correlation between the spread of education, increased reasoning abilities, the enlargement of moral horizons, the opening up of circles of cooperation, etc.—and the statistical lessening of the sum of human acts of violence over historical time (Pinker 2011, 260). For Girard, the dynamics of Progress and Abyss are subtler and starker, given our *capacity to regress* to archaic patterns of violence; our *vulnerability* to the perils of our own demons, to which the loss of archaic socio-symbolic protections exposes us; and the godlike technical powers we wield without a correspondingly godlike wisdom or purity of heart. Certainly, Girard allows us to glimpse the *negative* face of human liminal space, something largely concealed in the social anthropologists' understanding of creative reconfigurations.

Is any reconcilation of these positions possible; or can we at least glimpse some form of mediation between them? We might conceptualize such "creative reconfigurations" under the umbrella of the so-called *katechon* (Kirwan 2009, 96–99), a biblical concept, borrowed by Carl Schmitt, that defines the powers or the social mechanisms that restrain history "in its accelerating drift toward world revolution (sacrificial crisis)" (Hamerton-Kelly 2007, 21). From the point of view of the mimetic theory, the *katechon,* as much as the sacred, contains its own violence, in the two senses of the term: it keeps violence at bay, but it is enmeshed with sacrificial practices and mechanisms. The *katechon* neither knows its own violent shadow, nor confronts it as it is, but runs before it, taming it partially and perpetually by the ad hoc devices of ritual *exclusion* and *exorcism.* Its therapeutic pharmacology diffuses its violence throughout the very structures and institutions of its culture-invention. *Homo sapiens sacrificator* thus wins a space of "peace" and "civilization" at the price of perpetual repression, exercised to conjure an ever-deferred—but ever-haunting—peril of self-destruction. The very "fail-safe" or "default" mechanisms programmed into us, in that liminal space at the threshold of hominization, may be more deep-seated and potent in recycling violence than in combating it. That is why, to *survive* our origins truly, Girard looks to a transcendent and trans-historic hope. In *his* black box, programmed "from the foundation of the world," is Christian salvation.

If we adopt a historical standpoint, we can and may take into account, as Girard already does (Girard, Antonello, and de Castro Rocha 2008, 234–63), both the regression to sacrificial practices in the Christian era, and the expansion of sociocultural features that made humanity more and more complex, creative, and diverse in terms of geographical and cultural outreach, as attested by Pinker's accountancy—and by humanity's de facto survival hitherto. In point of fact, the Christian revelation has been inserted, and has built its irradiating power of salvation, not in a vacuum, but within a history of increasing awareness of the injustice of the mechanism of persecution, as first attested by the "figural" elements present in the Hebrew scriptures. Moreover, as Giuseppe Fornari has observed, Christian redemption necessarily inscribes within itself the history of humankind *as such* "since the foundation of the world." On this score, it is important to point to all those elements in pre-Christian cultures and religions that prepare the advent of Christianity with all its redeeming power (Fornari 2006, 333–50). At which point, the space of the victim becomes indeed the pedagogical pivot upon which modern rites of passage and the modern liminoid space of invention hinge; it is the focal point by which the mechanisms of exclusion and victimization acquire a proto-revelatory value. On the one hand, one must emphasize how much elements of awareness of the dangers of mimetic mechanisms are present and dealt with institutionally and culturally in non-Christian culture;[6] on the other, we could map and analyze all those liminoids in which a "figural" dimension is present outside and beyond any explicit reference to Christian belief or moral understanding.[7]

One simple example of such conciliatory syncretism might be found in the history of the modern novel, as understood by Girard in his first book, *Deceit, Desire, and the Novel:* the novelistic hero experiences a symbolic "resurrection from the underground"; that is, his *Bildung* is constituted by his initial position of outcast, by the isolation and exclusion from a given community, before finding a redemptive space of meaning outside that circle (Girard 1965). Scapegoating and the sacrificial structure are not seen, as Girard sometimes allows a rapid reader to think, simply as a blind mechanism, perpetually tied to a form of radical misrecognition; rather, they build up, if only by sheer repetition, a progressive awareness of their own constitutional injustice. Otherwise, we could not really understand either the presence of prophetic elements in Judaism in respect of Christian revelation, or those anti-sacrifical and antiviolent ethical, moral, social, and cultural elements that have been developed by all sorts of world religions. We would also fail to grasp the historical meaning of the so-called "souci pour les victimes" (concern for victims), which, according to Girard, has become a universal value in contemporary political and ideological discourse (Girard 2001, 161–69).

In and through the violent and sacrificial element ever-present in modern history and culture, the voice of the victims can still be heard. That voice can and will contribute to our chances of outrunning our shadow and transcending our origins.

Notes

1. On this score the recent discovery of the so-called "mirror neurons" has helped a great deal in understanding how imitation is a key basic tool for the development of the human mind. See Gallese (2011); Garrels (2005–2006).

2. Rites of passage, according to van Gennep, have three phases: separation, transition, and reincorporation: "I propose to call the rites of separation from a previous world, preliminal rites,

those executed during the transitional stage liminal (or threshold) rites, and the ceremonies of incorporation into the new world postliminal rites" (van Gennep 1960, 21).

3. The categories of games are comprised of physical prowess and strategy (*agon*), chance (*alea*), imitation (mimicry), and exhilaration (*ilinx* or vertigo). According to Caillois they are residues of ritualistic and sacrificial activities: "Hopscotch indeed symbolized the labyrinth through which the initiate must first wander. In the game of tag, beneath the childish innocence and activity, is recognized the terrifying choice of a propitiatory victim. Chosen by decree of destiny, before being selected by the sonorous and hollow syllables of counting-out rhymes, the victim could (at least in theory) rid himself of his defilement by passing it through touch to [someone whom he had overtaken in the race]. In Egypt of the Pharaohs, a checkboard is frequently represented in the tombs. . . . Above the player are inscriptions referring to the sentences in judgment of the dead, over which Osiris rules. The deceased plays for his destiny in the other world and wins or loses eternal salvation. In Vedic India, the sacrificer sways on a swing in order to help the sun rise. . . . The games played periodically in Greece were accompanied by sacrifices and processions" (Caillois 1961, 59–60).

4. For Girard this is also the origins of animal domestication (Girard 1987, 68–73; Girard, Antonello, and de Castro Rocha 2008, 116–18).

5. In psychoanalytic terms, "the abject is that which marks as untenable the identity of the subject in its objective worth" (Reineke 1997, 44).

6. Analyzing the Ndembu rituals, Turner underscores, for instance, what we could call the "mimetic" qualities of "the pedagogics of liminality," which condemn the basic separations from the generic bond of *communitas,* particularly those that involve expressions of selfishness. The ritualistic expression of "white laughter," in particular, represents "fellowship and good company. It is the reverse of pride (*winyi*), and the secret envies, lusts, and grudges that result behaviourally in witchcraft (*wuloji*), theft (*wukombi*), adultery (*kushimbana*), meanness (*chifwa*), and homicide (*wubanji*)" (Turner 1969, 104–5): all elements also structuring the biblical Decalogue, which, according to Girard, is mainly concerned with the prohibition of mimetic desire (Girard, Antonello, and de Castro Rocha 2008, 62–63).

7. An interesting remark in reference to this issue was made by Philip Tove, who notices that "in Christianity rites of passage and sacrifice have been divided. Thus catechumens do not receive communion at baptism . . . or at confirmation. . . . Perhaps the division of sacrifice and passage is another factor in making Christian rites liminoid" (Tove 2004, 53).

Cited Texts

Allott, Robin. 1999. "Evolution and Culture: The Missing Link." In *The Darwinian Heritage and Sociobiology,* ed. J.M.G. var der Dennen, D. Smillie, and D.R. Wilson, 67–81. Westport, CT: Praeger.

Boyer, Pascal. 2001. *Religion Explained: The Human Instincts That Fashion Gods, Spirits and Ancestors.* London: William Heinemann.

Caillois, Roger. 1961. *Man, Play, and Games.* Translated by Meyer Barash. New York: Free Press of Glencoe.

Derrida, Jacques. 1976. *Of Grammatology.* Baltimore: Johns Hopkins University Press.

Diamond, Jared M. 1997. *Guns, Germs, and Steel: The Fates of Human Societies.* New York: W. W. Norton & Co.

Dumouchel, Paul. 1992 "A Morphogenetic Hypothesis on the Closure of Post-Structuralism." In *Understanding Origins: Contemporary Views on the Origin of Life, Mind and Society,* ed. F. Varela and J.-P. Dupuy, 14–27. Dordrecht-Boston-London: Kluwer.

Dupuy, Jean-Pierre. 2003. *La panique.* Paris: Le Seuil.

Fiske, A. P., and N. Haslam. 1985. "Is Obsessive-Compulsive Disorder a Pathology of the Human Disposition to Perform Socially Meaningful Rituals? Evidence of Similar Content." *Journal of Nervous and Mental Diseases* 4: 211–22.

Fornari, Giuseppe. 2006. *Da Dioniso a Cristo: Conoscenza e sacrificio nel mondo greco e nella civiltà occidentale.* Genoa: Marietti.

Gallese, Vittorio. 2011. "The Two Sides of Mimesis: Mimetic Theory, Embodied Simulation, and Social Identification." In *Mimesis and Science: Empirical Research on Imitation and the Mimetic Theory of Culture and Religion,* ed. Scott R. Garrels, 87–108. East Lansing: Michigan State University Press.

Garrels, Scott R. 2005–2006. "Imitation, Mirror Neurons, and Mimetic Desire: Convergence between the Mimetic Theory of René Girard and Empirical Research on Imitation." *Contagion: Journal of Violence, Mimesis, and Culture* 12–13: 47–86.

Girard, René. 1965. *Deceit, Desire, and the Novel: Self and Other in Literary Structure.* Baltimore: Johns Hopkins University Press.

———. 1986. *The Scapegoat.* Baltimore: Johns Hopkins University Press.

———. 1987. *Things Hidden since the Foundation of the World: Research undertaken in collaboration with Jean-Michel Oughourlian and G. Lefort.* Stanford, CA: Stanford University Press.

———. 2001. *I See Satan Fall Like Lightning.* New York: Orbis Book.

———. 2004. *Oedipus Unbound: Selected Writings on Rivalry and Desire.* Edited and with an Introduction by Mark R. Anspach. Stanford, CA: Stanford University Press.

Girard, René, Pierpaolo Antonello, and João Cezar de Castro Rocha. 2008. *Evolution and Conversion: Dialogues on the Origins of Culture.* London: Continuum.

Grimes, Ronald. 1995. *Beginnings in Ritual Studies.* Columbia: University of South Carolina Press.

Harris, Marvin. 1979. *Cultural Materialism: The Struggle for a Science of Culture.* Walnut Creek, CA: AltaMira Press.

Harris, Marvin, and Eric B. Ross, eds. 2001. *Food and Evolution: Toward a Theory of Human Food Habits.* Philadelphia: Temple University Press.

Kirwan, Michael. 2009. *Girard and Theology.* New York: Bloomsbury.

Kristeva, Julia. 1982. *Power of Horror: An Essay on Abjection.* Translated by Leon S. Roudiez. New York: Columbia University Press.

Pinker, Steven. 2011. *The Better Angels of Our Nature: Why Violence Has Declined.* New York: Viking.

Reineke, Martha J. 1997. *Sacrificed Lives: Kristeva on Women and Violence.* Bloomington: Indiana University Press.

Rg-Veda. 1981. Edited by W. D. O'Flaherty. London: Penguin.

Serres, Michel. 1991. *Rome: The Book of Foundations.* Stanford, CA: Stanford University Press.

———. 2008. "Réception à l'Académie française de René Girard, Réponse de M. Michel Serres au discours de M. René Girard." In *René Girard: Cahiers de L'Herne,* ed. M. R. Anspach, 13–24. Paris: L'Herne.

Tooby, John, and L. Cosmides. 1989. "Evolutionary Psychology and the Generation of Culture, Part I. Theoretical Considerations." *Ethology and Sociobiology* 10: 29–49.

Tove, Philip. 2004. *Inculturation of Christian Worship: Exploring the Eucharist.* London: Ashgate.

Turner, Victor. 1969. *The Ritual Process: Structure and Anti-Structure.* London: Routledge & Kegan Paul.

———. 1982. *From Ritual to Theater: The Human Seriousness of Play.* New York: Performing Arts Journal Publications.

———. 1985. "Images of Anti-Temporality: An Essay in the Anthropology of Experience." In *On the Edge of the Bush: Anthropology as Experience,* ed. E. Turner, 227–46. Tucson: University of Arizona Press.

van Gennep, Arnold. 1960. *The Rites of Passage.* Translated by M. B. Vizedom and G. L. Caffee. Chicago: University of Chicago Press.

Victims, Sacred Violence, and Reconciliation

A Darwinian-Girardian Reading of Human Peril and Human Possibility

Harald Wydra

an René Girard's "fundamental anthropology" help make sense of humanity's immense "progress" during the short time of its existence—and contrariwise, of its prospects of transcending the seeming fatality of its own violence? The centrality of Girard's thought for these questions derives from the fact that Girard, relaying Darwin, gives us the most precise and complete understanding of what role the control of violence plays in permitting civilizational progress—and at what cost.

Like Darwin, Girard presupposes that the highly differentiated, elaborately constructed forms of life can be brought back to very basic, simple principles. In both cases, there is "one long argument from beginning to end" (Girard 2007, 96). Unlike Darwin, however, Girard conceives the struggle for existence as more than a biological or physiological fact. Mimetic theory, he says, demands an "existential understanding" (172); human beings are conceived of in unitary terms, thus joining up the biological-instinctive and meaning-giving (symbolic) spheres of human life.

Girardian mimetic theory sees the distinctive threshold between animal societies and human communities in the appearance of prohibitions that are accepted as symbolic centers. The victim is the *ur-symbol,* the first symbolic sign ever to emerge. While the sacrifice of a single victim occurs through an instinctive-emotional act, this irrational act of collective violence needs to be transferred into ritual forms that become lasting structures of meaning. Ritual forms symbolize the original sacrifice and thus keep violence outside the community.

A double "transference" occurs between victim and victimizers. The victim is first identified as a source of all the evil that afflicts the community. But then, given the cathartic effects of his scapegoat murder, the victim comes to be venerated as the source of all the good (i.e., restored social cohesion and peace) resulting from his death. By a process of symbolic and sacral transformation, obscure to those who practice it, the community's crisis of violence becomes the organizing center around which structures of meaning arise that, supposedly and mythically, keep violence away from the community. More exactly and in fact: their effect is to "contain" violence, at least provisionally, within it.

My proposal here is to explore the *cultural and ontological potential* of Girard's fundamental anthropology, in particular the conditions under which reconciliation may be achieved today, in an age of negative reciprocities spiraling out of control (as Girard suggests most fully in *Achever Clausewitz*). My argument is that surviving our origins ultimately depends on the ontological capacities of mimetic beings. Mimetic theory sees human beings not as naturally violent in a biologically deterministic sense, but simply as social beings of evolutionary inheritance. Mimetic desire, we recall, is a positive and creative emotion underlying learning, education, language, communication, trust, love, or cooperation. The reciprocity, however, can be negative, and mimetic relations can make us competitive, vying with each other, and so ultimately conflictual and violent. In an age where victimhood has become one of the primary objects of desire in terms of securing recognition, admiration, compassion, status—and even (in the political domain) independent statehood—the competition between victims may resonate in conflict and new forms of war (Wydra 2013). But if mimetic reciprocity of social interaction is the recurrent feature of human relations, and if it works two ways, humans not only have the capacity for absolute violence; they have also, in principle, the freedom to achieve reconciliation.

Sacrifice and Reconciliation

How does my Girardian "existential reading" qualify some important dimensions of Darwin's theory of natural selection? According to Darwin, the struggle for existence drives evolution because each living being is on the threshold of death. Only because an organism and its ancestors have the disposition to *want to live* but *have to die* could they come to be alive in the first place. Darwin holds that if many offspring die and if individuals in all species vary among themselves, then on average, survivors will tend to be those individuals with variations that are fortuitously best suited to changing local environments. The accumulation of these favorable variants through time will produce natural selection. In *The Descent of Man,* Darwin extended his interest in biological evolution to explanations of human behavior, including morality, art, and religion.

Darwin did stress the importance of imitation (in conjunction with intelligence and experience) in the progress of intellectual capacities, once the ancestors of humans became social (Darwin 1871, 161). Apes learn through experience to imitate the prudence of their fellow animals. If now some human being who is smarter than others invents a new trick, weapon, or any other means of attack or defense, then other members of the tribe will imitate him and acquire all benefits (Darwin 2006, 269).

Mimetic behavior patterns become crucial, he says, when heredity cannot assure the transmission of genetic traits because of voluntarily assumed death. People who sacrifice their life for others or excel by heroic deeds in warfare are likely to perish earlier and have smaller numbers of offspring (Darwin 1871, 163–64). The habit of performing benevolent actions, due to the love of praise and dread of blame, strengthens the feeling of sympathy—which gives the first impulse toward benevolent action.

For Darwin's process of natural selection, the "soul" or the "spirit" has no relevance. Imitation, however, is also an act that involves forms of sociability, communal action, and symbolism. As the ultimate frontier of life and an irresolvable enigma, death requires us to make sense of it. Antigone's revolt of conscience against the royal order to refuse the burial to her brother is only one testimony among many of the much older public control of death by authorities who perform ceremonial and symbolic acts for the sake of meaning-making. The death of family or members of a community, be it religious, ethnic, or national, may incite hatred, revenge, and vindictive violence. Conversely, death is also about mourning, compassion, consolation, and the future of one's soul. For Girard's fundamental anthropology, the creation of the symbolic center (an activity, a meeting, a form of ritualized worship, perhaps following mythical narratives) is not only a biological and physiological process, but also a spiritual act that is lived through subjectively within the contagion of passions and subject to processes of imitation.

As anthropologists have long since recognized, the central principle in ritual is imitation (Hocart 1970). The master of ceremony in a ritual—not elected but designated by descent—imitates the original act, and is imitated by the community in the worship of a surrogate victim that wards off uncontrolled mimetic violence. Mimetic responses can quickly contaminate other persons, especially in sexual behavior, but also in drinking or the exercise of power. Etymologically, contagion and contamination have common roots in the Latin word *con-tangere,* which means to touch somebody (we might imagine two circles that touch each other). In the case of a viral infection, the transmission of a disease occurs through the contact between two bodies. In the mimetic case, there is a contact between two spiritual bodies, two persons whose personal essences or "souls" touch each other.

The "sacrificial act" (at least in its concerted ritual elaboration) responds to a profound disequilibrium in the social fabric that precedes it: a deep internal crisis where conventional forms of social boundaries, hierarchies, and rule-bound norms break down. The killing that affects the transfer of moral blame onto the scapegoat victim transforms him or her into a symbol of intra-group reconciliation, and this killing becomes refracted in a series of cultural markers of reconciliation, peace, and stability. The emotional discharge is perceived as salvation, making this act representative of the divine, the ancestors, or God.

Such an act cannot be immoral or illegal, as no legal boundaries apply. Hubert and Mauss (1929) recognized the paradox that it would be criminal to kill the victim because it is sacred. Yet, the victim would not be sacred had it not been killed. Equally, "perpetrators" assign meaning to their action, but they are not really morally conscious of what has occurred. Although the "original" and "founding" character of sacrifice cannot be definitively "proved," mythological accounts and archaeological excavations of cemeteries confirm very widespread sacrificial practices, showing that ritual violence can be studied in exact analogy to paleontological fossil records.

Religious sacrifice is any sacrifice where one or more of the central parties involved is believed to be, or to represent, an agent of the superhuman realm. Understood as supernatural, spiritual, divine, or sacred, this agent is most commonly the recipient during the sacrifice (i.e., the God/ancestor receiving an offering). The Sanskrit word for Vedic sacrifice (*yajna*) is derived from *yaj,* meaning "to offer," and the German "*Opfer*"—combining victim and sacrifice in one term—is most likely derived from the Latin "*offere*" (to offer, to present), referring to gift-giving and the sense of grateful obligation. In popular use, sacrifice often refers to renouncing or "giving up" something, thus emphasizing the deprivation resulting from sacrifice. Often, this renunciation carries an expectation of a more valuable return; so that giving up, e.g., money, food, or pleasure will achieve some higher goal. The three dimensions—"making sacred," "gift-giving," and exchange (*do ut des*)—thus point to the three distinct participating entities of sacrifice, and determine their status and relationships. Between two of them, gifting or exchange takes place, while a third is the "object" that is given or exchanged.

This triangular configuration makes differentiation between the parties involved in sacrifice difficult. The Latin word *sacrificium* is derived from "*sacer*" (holy) and "*facere*" (to make). It describes a process of sanctification, a consecration (Carter 2003, 1–9). The divine and the thing sacrificed may be one and the same. As Hubert and Mauss show, in Mexico, at the feast for God Totec, where captives were killed and their skin was pulled off, a priest put their skin on himself, thus becoming the image of the God; he carried his ornaments and his costume, sat down on a throne, and obtained in lieu of the God the images of early fruit. The sacrifice to the God is here just a derived form of the sacrifice of God. Originally, it is always the God who suffers sacrifice, being the victim. Hubert and Mauss say: one offered God to himself (see Dupuy 2005, 96–97). In Christianity, the single divine being can be both sacrificing and sacrificed in the same event. In reality, the confusion between the one who sacrifices, the victim, and the divinity is the very essence of sacrifice.

How did this symbolic substitution of violence become an adaptive advantage? In Girard's view, control of affects, differentiated systems of communication, legal and institutional order, stable beliefs, conventions, etc., are rooted in a complex system of prohibitions that ritual commemorations of such sacrifice establish, develop, and deepen. The "natural" instinctive process of killing is commemorated by the substitution of the sacrificial victim by a totem, a dance, a mask, or a meal. Such practices of the sacred depend on interpretive acts that cannot be rationally arrived at. Symbols are collective representations of something that goes beyond human understanding and reason. The scapegoat mechanism is effective as long as it remains hidden and the perpetrators are convinced that a victim was not innocent but guilty. Eyewitness accounts by participants in a collective mob lynching are not to be trusted! Their cognitive failure is to assume that one never belongs to the persecuting party, and that one's group antagonism toward others is only ever legitimate.

According to Girard, if people emancipate themselves from their mimetic instincts, this is not by an achievement of intellect and the cognitive mind on their part. It is the fruit of the slow cultural osmosis and spread of Christian revelation, which fundamentally differs from archaic religion and mythology in that, for the first time, the founding Christian narrative and its symbols *lay bare the scapegoat mechanism,* and *offer to repair* human moral obliquity and escapism. The death of Jesus and its subsequent representation by his disciples are said by Girard to have induced a positive mimetic process by which a number of Jews became dissenters from the majority view and recognized the innocence of Jesus—although Girard did initially hesitate to accept the inherited notion of "sacrifice" as applying also, in any way at all, to Jesus's death on the Cross.[1]

While victims within archaic culture were presented as truly "guilty" by their persecutors, Jesus's *self-sacrifice,* at all events, as a redemptive act of salvation, has been highly significant in eradicating practices of ritual sacrifice we now call "archaic," including of human sacrifice—a fact that Darwin himself acknowledged. In his journal of the *Beagle* voyage he praises the introduction of Christianity, which abolished human sacrifices, idolatrous priesthood, infanticide, and wars, making the morality and religion of the inhabitants highly creditable (Darwin 1845, 414).

The Symbolization of Sacrifice and Its Problems

Stephen Jay Gould urges us to complete Darwin's revolution by accepting that natural selection should integrate the concept of the progress of humanity (Gould 1996). Progress is not about entities on the move to a "higher degree" of organization. It refers to the increase or contraction of variation in an entire system: a "full house," rather than a "thing" moving somewhere.

In a thoughtful consideration of the philosophical potential of evolutionary theory, Christian Illies pointed to the limits of evolutionary approaches to human culture (Illies 2010, 31–33). Fundamentally, human beings are free to transcend their instincts and drives and therefore are free to choose which idea or theory to accept and to integrate into a given culture. Eventually, the crucial limitation of evolutionary theories is in *their incapacity to formulate an ethical imperative*. Natural sciences can describe *what is* and *how it came about*, but they cannot explain *what ought to be*. They cannot by their own methods create their own justifications; but they also require categories by which to interpret their results. Functional theories of adaptation cannot, for instance, unmask morality as there is no obvious reason why they should have any privileged access to reality of the type required to make their criteria true.

Indeed, ideas about perfection and natural selection would not have been formulated without important precursors (Kant, Laplace, Lamarck, Spencer). Nietzsche even linked Hegel's transcendental philosophy to the concept of evolution: "without Hegel, no Darwin" (Nietzsche 1997, 2:226–27). While some symbols appear to be "eternal" and span different periods of human civilization, others go through major transformations. Hero myths, myths of rebirth, golden age, or the friend-enemy distinction appear to be anthropological constants.

Yet, the equivalence of symbols is not in the meaning but in experiences of the people who produce symbols. As Bernhard Giesen has recently argued, the foundation on which cultural order is based is approximate and ambivalent, unclear and equivocal (*uneindeutig*) (Giesen 2010). Cultural order becomes possible only once a common perspective on the world is adopted by participants, which is not based on constraint, purpose, or decision, but somehow arises without foundation, intentionality, or justification. We orient our lives by means of *vanishing points, which are symbolically mediated*—in the past or future, in mythical narratives, ritual performances, iconic representations, or in figurations of the sacred. These vanishing points, however, categorical and compelling as they may be, remain fundamentally unattainable. They enable the construction of meaningful actions precisely because they ultimately cannot be justified rationally themselves. Eventually, cultural frames obtain their strength because they transcend logical, rational, or empirical enquiry.

The semantic evolution of the modern conception of progress, for instance, has been an ever-changing vantage point (Koselleck 2006, 159–81). It forms, from antiquity to Rousseau, a fascinating study, not to be undertaken here. It was Condorcet who completed the transition from "perfection" toward *"perfectionnement,"* which turned the destination into a processual category of movement. *Perfectionnement* is at the same time the objective of humanity (*terme*) and it is indefinite (*indéfini*). The destination is integrated into the process of continuous perfection (improvement). According to Darwin's self-acknowledgment, the reading of Malthus's *Essay on Population* in 1838—which, on his own admission, was crucial for understanding the principle of selection, and a milestone in the elaboration of evolutionary theory—was mediated through Condorcet's ideas on progress. While Malthus approved of Condorcet, he argues that the latter clearly underestimated the disastrous consequences of indefinite progress and thus belittled the pressing urgency of remediating overpopulation (Malthus 1999, 12).

Political authorities use representations of life symbolism, including constructs of origins and of ends in order to legitimize regimes. The "beginning" of states, nations, or empires is by definition a "lost object." Political theory, that is, needs to refer scenes of violence and death to myths of origin—be it a social contract or by glorifying some founding historical events. Original violence becomes "the death that made it all possible," thus acquiring an "active" role, in the sense of *structuring* social relations. People imagine and commemorate the foundations of their political communities by heroic stories of unremitting struggle against the profane, violent, destructive, and evil forces. The complete destruction *de facto* of a people, however, will erase the possibility of successor generations, oral tradition, or iconic representation in cultural memory. Until archaeological evidence in the late nineteenth century, we knew about Troy or Carthage exclusively through the winners (the perpetrators of destructive violence: the Greeks and the Romans).

The official adoption of the Christian religion by the Roman Empire in 325 AD enforced a policy repressing pagan sacrifice, whose slaughtering of animals was repulsive to many Christians (Veyne 2007). This fusion of empire and Christianity required that the secular power incorporate the cults and rituals of the God and accept its own role as servant of the divine majesty. Consequently, the marriage between temporal power and Christian religion would constitute some form of *regression* to the archaic sacred within Christendom. The papacy would launch Crusades and support the Inquisition. The colonial expansion of European empires would see massacres committed in the name of civilized Christians against barbarians who did practice actual human sacrifice. Even the most fervent defender of the cause of the Indians, Bartolomé de las Casas, promoted the import of black slaves in order to relieve Indians from forced labor. The revolts against oppressive power structures in the French and Russian revolutions initially included the fight against the death penalty, taken as the symbol of the *ancien régime*—until the new regime put up its own altars and celebrated in blood masses of the new faith (Camus 1994, 96).

Yet, the triumphant self-representation of the nation and the victorious principle of popular sovereignty largely overlooked the victims it left behind. The building of democracies in Australia or the United States was preceded by the ethnic cleansing of native populations. Following the *levée en masse,* the revolutionary armies of Napoleon not only carried the revolutionary spirit, but also triggered forms of collective redemption that included nominally secular, but bloody and violent, nationalist fanaticism. The growing democratization of communication, the overt desacralization of traditional authority, and certain notable public scandals continued the unmasking of the truth about scapegoating. Since the Dreyfus Affair in France, after the horrors of technological warfare in the trenches, the eyewitness accounts of genocide in the gas chambers, and the massacres running through all the many conflicts in the twentieth century, there are memories and counter-memories that witnessed and transmitted the horrors of violence to posterity.

The idea of progress offered to emancipate mankind from metaphysics (and, in one sense, did so, to the benefit of ideology); but it also increased a readiness to engage in sacrificial violence in the name of purifying the community from heretics and enemies. As Eric Voegelin has argued, sectarian and heretical currents of Christianity transformed Christian symbolism by transferring transcendental symbols, such as the end of time and the Second Coming, *toward world-immanent questions of power* (Voegelin 1987, 112–14). One of the essential symbols of Gnostic spirituality that have guided the self-interpretation of modern political society up to the twentieth century is the conception of history as a sequence of three ages, of which the third age is seen as the final Realm. This characteristic mental structure associated with Gnostic spirituality has found its equivalent in so-called "scientific" periodizations of history as claimed by Hegel, Comte, Marx, or Spencer. Marxism, for instance, elevated the cogs in the wheel—the weak and the suffering proletarian class—into the masters of history and the redeemers of humanity. The social struggle pursued by revolutionary leaders and millenarian movements of early modernity lacked concrete political objectives, but rather was sectarian, radical, aiming at boundless and cataclysmic attempts to totally transform and redeem the world (Cohn 2004, 281).

Modern thought of the liberal-utilitarian school has rejected public sacrifices as incompatible with reason. While in "normal" conditions, people cannot be literally sacrificed today, more covert forms of archaic sacrifice flourish exuberantly. In situations of war, allegiance to papal or imperial authority or to nation-states could match the religions in meaning-giving power and sacral potency. To die in Crusades for the Holy Land was equivalent to achieving salvation for one's soul. But the sacrifice of citizens on the battlefield *too* would have a religious meaning, attaching salvation to the collective sacred of the nation: "No freedom without sacrifice" has been one of the rallying cries from Pericles through Abraham Lincoln up to Winston Churchill, Great War patriotism, or indeed the rhetoric of today's wars. We cannot live if others don't die for us. Yet, the conquest of territory, the exercise of power by force, also made the Free perpetrators of violence, producing victims. The totalitarian age made "sacrificial" politics not only an ideology, but a political model of social engineering as well.

Totalitarian regimes used victimhood and sacrifice in two fundamental ways. The Bolsheviks grew to political maturity by identifying themselves as suffering victims of persecution by internal and external enemies. The very logic of communism was based on the dehumanization of the enemy (as bourgeois, capitalist, Jew, heretic, or terrorist) and the systematic sacrifice of innocents. This cultural model of self-victimization and inflicted suffering became a model and tool of political and social engineering under Stalin's dictatorship (Wydra 2007). According to Vasily Grossmann, the violence of a totalitarian state is so great as to be no longer a means to an end. It becomes an object of mystical adoration and worship (quoted in Wydra 2007, 125). At the same time, however, it claimed to be the avant-garde of modernity and progress, capable of creating a "red paradise." This liberating promise of redemption was pursued by the systematic destruction of the past, the built environment, and traditional social relations. Redemption by destruction had systematic social consequences, a concrete social and political "function." The identification of the enemy became the representational principle of the Bolshevik party-state (Wydra 2007).

The imaginary Other was crucial in two respects: on the one hand, the definition of the enemy was constitutive of the identity of the People-as-One; on the other hand, this enemy permanently threatened the people's unity and had to be removed. The Third Reich enacted sacred cults, fixed rites that re-represented mythical events such as the torchlight procession of the seizure of power by the Nazis on January 30, 1933, or April 20, the Führer's birthday. The most potent cultic force was the blood baptism of 1923, the failed putsch of November 8. Hitler's rhetoric presenting Germany as the victim of a stab-in-the-back and a conspiracy from within by Jews was rooted in Germany's long-term inferiority complex before Western imperial powers. In reality, both ideologies claimed to purify the race or prepare the advent of a stateless and classless society by securing the extinction of enemies. "Enemies of the people" connoted a kind of social prophylaxis ensuring an insider group's identity by expelling its waste matter. The archaic models of founding murder and ritual sacrifice are close at hand here.

The magnitude of mass extinction in the world wars and genocide of the twentieth century, as well as the absurdity of heroism in an age of technological mass killing entailed fundamental reversals of meaning of sacrifice and victimhood. The perhaps most powerful symbols are Hiroshima and Auschwitz, the nuclear bomb and the genocide of Jews. In both cases the military strategic value was very low. The atomic bombs had the performative impact of terrorizing the Japanese population and impressing the Soviet Union. They shocked the world much more in the sense of the potential of an atomic overkill than in terms of empathy for the several hundreds of thousands of concrete victims. This also accounts for Auschwitz, the paradigmatic symbol of genocide. Victim and perpetrator exchange roles; in the camps there is only *fraternité* in abjection (Agamben 1999, 18). As a consequence, using the term Holocaust as the "supreme sacrifice" is deeply problematic. Not only does it carry a strong anti-Semitic legacy, as this concept had been used by a certain woolly-minded post-Christian rhetoric in order to describe—e.g., patriotic or humanitarian—sacrificial practices. When applied to the destruction pursued by Nazis in gas chambers and in crematoriums, any notion of this systematic mass killing as self-renouncing dedication to higher purposes and sacred principles degrades and mocks the memory of the victims (Agamben 1999, 34–38). The actual sense is, again, *archaic:* ritual slaughter and bloody immolation.

Conversely, in specific contexts victimhood has fundamentally changed self-representations and identities. The relationship between sacrifice and victimhood (*Opfer*) in the German context is illustrative here (Koselleck 2006, 232–33). The central memorial of the Federal Republic of Germany at the Neue Wache in Berlin now carries the inscription to the "victims of war and tyranny" ("Den Opfern von Krieg und Gewaltherrschaft").[2] This formula refers to the passive *Opfer* (the victims), i.e., the soldiers that were seduced and corrupted, and who died for a wrong cause. Eventually, their sacrifice (active *Opfer*) is finally reinterpreted. It is even more difficult in the case of the Jews: while they objectively were passive victims (being destroyed practically without resistance, without the possibility of active self-sacrifice themselves), the victim status actually supports the Nazi ideology, which actively wanted the Jews to be victims in order to cleanse the world of them. The ambiguity of the term *Opfer* indicates the limit of patriotism. Victims cannot fulfill the symbolic "function" of pacification, partly because the roles of the perpetrators and victims of violence have become blurred.

Paradoxically, the protection of victims has become a practice in international politics as a result of the major catastrophe of mass genocide during the Second World War. The idea of international justice was born in the wake of the Nuremberg tribunal, which was followed by the Declaration of Universal Human Rights. Within nation-states, the decline of ideology and the Cold War has brought with it a "duty to remember." At the level of nation-states, especially in those with prior colonial settings, policies of apology or regret for the extermination of native indigenous populations, such as those in Canada and Australia, answer the pleas of ethnic minorities who were victims of ethnic cleansing. Following the moralization of politics in the wake of the disasters of genocide and crimes against humanity, self-representations of political communities and the commitments of leaders have increasingly adopted the discourse of a politics of regret (Olick 2007).

Reciprocity and Reconciliation

Sacred victimhood is not a thing of the past, but a permanent anthropological constant. Liminal crises continue, causing imitative processes of contagion within which the exchange of intensified emotions constitutes new models. Redemption through disaster, destruction, and catastrophe has made a powerful return in the twenty-first century. In religiously motivated terrorism, for instance, suicide bomb attacks are not *simply acts of self-sacrifice* by terrorists. In reality, they *immolate* innocent victims and thus commit a bloody sacrifice, harking back once more to archaic practices. They thus de-symbolize the victim as a substituted Innocent and re-symbolize him—following archaic models—as representative mythic Guilt-Bearer (Juergensmeyer 2000).

From a mimetic perspective, this return to archaic forms of sacrifice has different implications. On the one hand, it suggests that the ritual capacity of religion—as a communal practice to avert disaster by keeping internal peace—is ever less able to contain the destructive elements of violence. Girard argues that we have not yet realized that emissary victimization, as an instrument of the containment of violence, has lost its efficiency. Religious ethics, possibly the only stabilizing force, have been overwhelmed by events, by self-conscious mimetic individuals who think they are free and insist on their authenticity and their false differences (Girard 2007, 62). The dilemma in a global world with intense communication and the possibility of continuously reinterpreting former acts of war and violence is this: *we are all potential or real victims now.* At the same time, our enmities are always "legitimate," so we cannot admit to "scapegoating." Nevertheless, the world is . . . full of scapegoats.

On the other hand, this *globalized empathy for victims* has also increased the self-attribution of the label "victim" in the modern world. Often, killing others is justified by externalizing guilt and *revisiting on others,* in *scapegoating transfers of pain,* the wrongs inflicted on one's own community. Thus, self-victimization has a creative role in bolstering political identities—and not only in crisis-ridden communities such as in Northern Ireland, ex-Yugoslavia, Kashmir, or Israel. The many and various victims of the Holocaust themselves became embattled in a fight about the singularity and the uniqueness of the memory of the Holocaust, relative to other victims of Nazism and other genocides (Chaumont 1997). According to Edward Said, the Israeli-Palestinian conflict is one that pits "victims" against each other. Military interventions by the North Atlantic Treaty Organization (NATO) such as in Kosovo in 1999 or in Libya in 2011 were justified on humanitarian grounds. Yet, they were carried out through air strikes that caused significant numbers of victims in the name of concern for victims. Humanitarian aid for civilians has become the single most important resource for opposing sides involved in low intensity wars to support logistically their "low-intensity" warfare (Münkler 2007, 131–74). Revenge and retaliation are also part of everyday life. The justice system often only masks our deep desires for revenge (Todorov 2003, 170–73). As the HIV scandal in France suggested, parents of victims wanted the errant officials to be found guilty of murder, so that their sentences would be as close as possible to their children's fate.

Rather than being deterministic about "good" and "evil" in human nature, mimetic anthropology recognizes that humans change. It proposes an original solution for what Kant called the a-social sociability of man. For Kant the development of human capacities relies on the competition between individuals for honor, power, or property. Unlike the Kantian perspective, reconciliation is not primarily a question of doctrine or cognitive processes. Rather, it acknowledges the exchange of intensified emotions as reciprocal and repetitive. According to Georg Simmel, struggle is not the end of sociability but actually its transformation into new forms (Simmel 1992, 284–382). Once a fight has started, its aim is to achieve some form of unity, even at the price of destroying the other party. In other words, the temporary integration of the collective whole depends on contingent configurations of these individual parts. The basic unit of analysis is not the individual, but relationships between individuals—which can be expressed in terms of "interdividuality" (Girard 1987, 35).

Since World War II, our enhanced moral awareness has been ever-ready to see humanity itself as transcendent victim. Yet, this moralization of politics has a reverse side: collective victimhood has also become an aspirational model of identity formation. Aggressions between rivals are increasingly justified by claims of pursuing one's own defense, often in seeking revenge for one's own self-attributed victimhood (Wydra 2013). Revenge, we recall, can appear to us a powerful and justifying moral motivation. So the impulse of revenge seeks to remain faithful to one's own dead, to honor their memory by taking up their cause. It is about faith between generations, making violence a ritual form of respect. Kant's sixth preliminary article in his pamphlet on eternal peace grasps this point when he insists on the fundamental need for reciprocal trust in our way of thinking of the enemy. According to Kant, a war of extinction (*Ausrottungskrieg*) would not only destroy the parties to war; it would continue the "hellish" arts of war, making peace possible only as a peace of the cemetery.

After Hiroshima and Nagasaki, the possibility of total annihilation became rationalized in the sense that nuclear deterrence would contain the "rise to extremes" (i.e., for Girard: the structural tendency of mimetic crises to develop in a crescendo-toward-paroxysm). Yet Osama bin Laden repeatedly insisted on the reciprocity of his movement's actions, claiming that al-Qaeda's attacks were a response to humiliations suffered by Muslims at the hand of the infidels at the end of the fifteenth century, at the time of the expulsion of the Arabs from Spain, of Israel's invasion of Lebanon in 1982, but also of the atomic bombs launched by the United States in 1945.

True: the strong *moral* value that nations have attached to warfare stimulated the extraordinary creativity of science and technological innovation. Despite the ban on interstate warfare and despite moral universalism, the goal of completely eliminating violence in international relations is therefore illusory (Wydra 2008a). Still, the collapse of totalitarian and colonial regimes affords us some cautious optimism. Despite their capacity to kill, either individually or collectively, human beings *do not have to be violent.*

If violence is a deeply transformative process affecting mind, body, emotions, and memory, why may such experiences of violence not, moreover, generate new forms of *resistance* capable of breaking the spirals of vengeance and retaliation? Given that it is the mimetic reciprocity of social interaction that is the recurrent feature of human relations, humans do not only have the *capacity* for absolute violence; they have also the freedom to achieve reconciliation.

The very idea of self-preservation as the primary goal of each individual has been vigorously called into question by biologists, social theorists, psychologists, philosophers, and political activists. Questioning this motif as the driving force of evolution, Roughgarden argues that the evolutionary biology of kinship selection is inadequate to determine what an "individual" is (Roughgarden 2009, 8). What does "survival of the fittest" really mean when we cannot say exactly who or what it refers to?

Alessandro Pizzorno's work, for instance, has also shown how untenable is the idea of individualistic self-preservation. The identity of the self cannot be taken for granted, but it is based on recognition (Pizzorno 1991). Such recognition may require an act of communication beyond the established images. This means that self-preservation must be more than a biological or physical category. Even under conditions of hunger, scarcity, disease, threat of annihilation, people may act in ways that do not do away with these conditions, but actually seek out *something else*. This something else relates to *the preservation of identity through recognition by others*. Even enemies are caught up in the illusion of being authentic *in difference* from the other; whereas it requires a symbolic act to break the logic of revenge. Such a symbolic act can never, properly speaking, be an "individual act"; it is embedded in the solidarity of self-and-other.

People often do things that cannot be comprehended by an individualistic logic of self-preservation. Sacrificing one's life for somebody else, for instance, can be rational if it is accepted by a certain "circle of recognition" and the community supportive of, or based upon, such a circle. Feeling empathy with the victim is a relational process. It is not so much about being close to the thought patterns of the others; it requires, rather, a spiritual conversion inside oneself.

As Roberto Farneti argued, attempts at peace-making must include reflective practices that psychologize the causes of discord. It requires inward-looking moves by individuals in order to accept the humanity of others by "reflective justice" (Farneti 2008, 554–55). In other words, the purely cognitive and/or egocentric view of "being aggressed" needs to be relocated: from the external space of facts-about-the-world to a critical historical examination of the space internal to one's own community. Elucidating the collective unconscious of one's own group, party, or community thus requires an "alterocentric" approach; our animosities, impulses, and hatred of the other are ontological commitments that are created in-and-through mimetic processes.

In a fundamental critique of Freud's atomistic constitution of personality as a conglomerate of ego-drives, Viktor Frankl's logotherapy suggests that the instinctive and the spiritual fundamentally differ (Frankl 2000, 32). Freud saw human beings as prey to their passions, drives, and instincts and thus deliberately excluded the human capacity for spirituality. Yet, human beings can transcend their drives and instincts, often by articulating quests for meaning and choices that are informed by spiritual realities. Self-transcendence is a matter of choice, along the lines of Karl Jaspers's *"entscheidendes Sein."* For Frankl, conscience is essentially intuitive, the unique possibility given to particular persons of actualizing their given potential in a specific situation. Drawing the analogy between the "irrationality" of conscience and of love, it is possible to postulate that "what love anticipates . . . is not an ethical necessity but, rather, a personal possibility" (Frankl 2000, 40). Frankl's testimony from his three years as inmate in Auschwitz suggests that even in the hell of a concentration camp, existential choices can make a difference (Frankl 2004). An act of a dissidence, asserted in complete despair, and without any immediate effect, may affirm humanity where it has been lost.

Detachment from glory and blame, from the instinctive urge to join the crowd, is both a biological feature and a historically contingent element of human freedom. Max Scheler's philosophical anthropology argued that our biological nature also allows us detachment and reflexive interrogation about our aims, desires, and needs. Due to our spirit, the human being can relate to life in ascetic ways, by suppressing instincts. Whereas animals always say "yes" to reality, man is capable of saying "no" (Scheler 1928, 55).

Similarly, Mohandas Gandhi's views about breaking the spiral of retaliation relied upon a deep sense of moral obligation toward fellow human beings, expressed in his idea of truth-force (*satyagraha*) (Gandhi 2009, xviii–xix). If the modern state claims that the beneficial outcomes of security and stability cannot be guaranteed other than by violent means, the risk is that violence as a means becomes an end in itself, thus perpetuating violence endlessly.

Gandhi's radical solution consists of extending the horizon of politics beyond the immediate. In his conception, power is not just an outcome, but something malleable and ongoing, always in the making. A tyrant is limited by the physical threat of an assassin or the moral resistance of a martyr.

Similarly, the most formidable empire is limited by the potential decay of its power in the long run. Postulating that means and ends are interchangeable, Gandhi arrives at a conclusion radically different from modern political theory. Peace and justice are not to be achieved by means of violence; rather, the means have to be treated as if they were coterminous with the ends.

Is a pessimistic anthropology, as expressed in Hobbes's famous metaphor of man's wolf-like nature (*Homo homini lupus*) therefore *warranted?* It may be worth giving Gandhi's reformulation of this problem a second thought: "The true problem does not seem to be whether a few saints can impose an ideal law on the world, but whether a few wolf-natured people are enough to impose the law of the wolf on everybody" (quoted in Wydra 2008a, 192).

Conclusion

In his polemical *Anti-Darwin,* Nietzsche argued that the struggle for survival is the exception; the general aspect of life is not the emergency, the situation of hunger, but rather richness, abundance, even absurd waste. If struggle happens, according to Nietzsche, it usually has the opposite outcome to that one might wish for in following the Darwinian school of thought. The weak impose themselves on the strong, being more numerous and smarter. The reason for this is that Darwin forgot the "*Geist*" (spirit). "By *Geist,* I understand ... prudence, patience, cunning, camouflage, great self-control and all which is mimicry (to this latter belongs a great part of so-called virtue)" (Nietzsche 1997, 998–99). The weak—so Nietzsche considers—have more *Geist* because the powerful deprive themselves of spirit, as they do not really need it.

For Nietzsche, as we know, the Christian faith is *Opferung* from the start: synonymous with self-mutilation, servitude, weakness, and subordination of the spirit (Nietzsche 1997, 610). On the contrary, as has been argued here, even when victims proliferate, one has to not succumb to the pathologies of psychological-instinctual irrationality and the processes of mimetic contagion. Human freedom can seek potential salvation not in the destruction, but in the affirmation of life.

Mimetic theory suggests that "conversion" can only occur once it is realized that enemies are often like brothers (demanding solidarity), rather than like twins, who attempt, in Girard's hermeneutic of myth, to combat *identity* and assert *difference* conflictually.

Acts of conversion are acts of dissidence, breaking the obvious biological-psychological impulse of rallying with the crowd against the stranger, the outsider, the potential scapegoat victim. They require detachment—either with reference to an open-time horizon or to the transcendence of the religious—and critical engagement that acknowledges the other's humanity in difference. Mimetic beings still have the freedom to turn negative reciprocity, vengeance, and retaliation into empathy, solidarity, and recognition.

Notes

1. Editor's note. This was a key point of difficulty in the early reception of Girard's theory. For a fuller account of Girard's current position, see notes 8 and 13 of the chapter by Paul Gifford in Part 2 of this volume; and, in Part 4, Kirwan.

2. It features the sculpture "Mother and Her Dead Son" by Käte Kollwitz and was inaugurated in 1993.

Cited Texts and Further Reading

Agamben, G. 1999. *Ce qui reste d'Auschwitz*. Paris: Bibliothèque Rivages.

Camus, A. 1994. *Der Mensch in der Revolte*. Reinbek: Rowohlt.

Carter, J. 2003. *Understanding Religious Sacrifice: A Reader*. London: Continuum.

Chaumont, J.-M. 1997. *La concurrence des victimes: Génocide, identité, reconnaissance*. Paris: La Découverte.

Cohn, N. 2004. *The Pursuit of the Millennium: Revolutionary Millenarians and Mystical Anarchists of the Middle Ages*. London: Pimlico.

Darwin, C. 1845. *Journal of Researches into the Natural History and Geology of the Countries Visited during the Voyage of* H.M.S. Beagle *Round the World, under the Command of Capt. FitzRoy, R.N.* 2nd ed. London: John Murray.

———. 1859. *The Origin of Species by Means of Natural Selection, or the Preservation of Favoured Races in the Struggle for Life*. London: John Murray.

———. 1871. *The Descent of Man, and Selection in Relation to Sex*. London: John Murray.

———. 2006. *Darwin lesen*, ed. by Mark Ridley. München: dtv.

Dupuy, J.-P. 2005. *Petite métaphysique des tsunamis*. Paris: Seuil.

Farneti, R. 2008. "A mimetic perspective on conflict resolution." *Polity* 41:4, 536–58.

Frankl, V. 2000. *Man's Search for Ultimate Meaning*. New York: Basic Books.

———. 2004. *Man's Search for Meaning*. London and Sydney: Rider.

Gandhi, M. K. 2009. *Hind Swaraj and Other Writings*. Edited by Anthony Parel. Cambridge: Cambridge University Press.

Giesen, B. 2010. *Zwischenlagen*. Göttingen: Velbrück.

Girard, R. 1987. *Things Hidden since the Foundation of the World*. Baltimore: Johns Hopkins University Press.

———. 2001. *Celui par qui le scandale arrive*. Paris: Desclée de Brouwer.

———. 2007. *Achever Clausewitz*. Entretiens avec Benoît Chantre. Paris: Carnets Nord.

———. 2008. *Evolution and Conversion*. With Pierpaolo Antonello and João Cezar de Castro Rocha. London: Continuum.

Gould, S. J. 1996. *Life's Grandeur: The Spread of Excellence from Plato to Darwin*. London: Jonathan Cape.

Hocart, A. 1970. *Kings and Councillors: An Essay in the Comparative Anatomy of Human Society*. Edited and with an introduction by Rodney Needham. Chicago: University of Chicago Press.

Hubert, H. and M. Mauss. 1929. *Essais sur la nature et la fonction du sacrifice*. 2nd ed. Paris: Librairie Félix Alcan.

Illies, C. 2010. "Biologie statt Philosophie?: Evolutionäre Erklärungen und ihre Grenzen." In *Evolution in Natur und Kultur*, ed. V. Gerhardt and J. Nida-Rümelin, 15–38. Berlin: de Gruyter.

Juergensmeyer, M. 2000. *Terror in the Mind of God*. Berkeley and London: University of California Press.

Jung, C. G. 1990. *Man and His Symbols*. London: Penguin.

Koselleck, R. 2006. *Begriffsgeschichten*. Frankfurt/Main: Suhrkamp.

Kropotkin, P. 1902. *Mutual Aid: A Factor in Evolution*. London: Heinemann.

Malthus, T. 1999. *An Essay on the Principle of Population*. Edited by Geoffrey Gilbert. Oxford: Oxford University Press.

Münkler, H. 2007. *Die neuen Kriege*. 3rd ed. Reinbek: Rowohlt.

Nietzsche, F. 1997. *Werke in drei Bänden*. Darmstadt: Wissenschaftliche Buchgesellschaft.

Olick, J. 2007. *The Politics of Regret*. London and New York: Routledge.

Pizzorno, A. 1991. "On the Individualistic Theory of Social Order." In *Social Theory for a Changing Society,* ed. P. Bourdieu and J. Coleman. Boulder, CO: Westview Press.

Roughgarden, J. 2009. *The Genial Gene: Deconstructing Darwinian Selfishness*. Berkeley: University of California Press.

Scheler, M. [1928] 1975. *Die Stellung des Menschen im Kosmos*. Bern: Francke.

Simmel, G. 1992. *Soziologie*. Frankfurt/Main: Suhrkamp.

Todorov, T. 2003. *Hope and Memory: Lessons from the Twentieth Century*. Princeton, NJ: Princeton University Press.

Veyne, P. 2007. *Quand notre monde est devenu chrétien*. Paris: Albin Michel.

Voegelin, E. 1987. *The New Science of Politics: An Introduction*. Chicago: Chicago University Press.

Wydra, H. 2007. *Communism and the Emergence of Democracy.* Cambridge: Cambridge University Press.

———. 2008a. "The Recurrence of Violence." *Sociology Compass* 1, no. 2: 183–94.

———. 2008b. "Towards a New Anthropological Paradigm: The Challenge of Mimetic Theory." *International Political Anthropology* 1, no. 1: 161–74.

———. 2013. "Victims and New Wars." *Cambridge Review of International Affairs* 26, no. 1: 161–80.

Empire of Sacrifice

Violence and the Sacred in American Culture

Jon Pahl and James Wellman

Innocent Domination USA
Jon Pahl

American self-understanding has been brutally efficient in producing "innocent domination" (Pahl 2012b). Throughout American history, death-dealing, pursued as a matter of public policy, has been cloaked repeatedly in a sacralizing aura of rhetorical innocence. According to this "exceptionalist" narrative, usually asserted in direct contrast to the evidence, killing is an unfortunate accident, "collateral damage" in the otherwise noble history of American progress. American domination, even and especially where violently pursued, is *innocent*.

Usually, this killing is dressed up as "sacrifice," i.e., as heroic and costly self-dedication to an ideal or value (Denton-Borhaug 2011). The trope is remarkably mobile—and exceptionally slippery in the semantic ambiguities it generates. The "sacrifice" of others (and of American "boys")—implying their bloody immolation (i.e., sacrifice in its archaic and original sense)—has been invoked as necessary across the centuries (Ebel 2010). The removal of Native Americans, the enslavement of Africans, the conquest of the Spanish in the South of North America, the revolution against the English across the

71

Atlantic seacoast, and the pushback of the French to what became Canada were all justified, already in the seventeenth and eighteenth centuries, by rhetorics of "sacrifice" (Jewett 2008). In the nineteenth century, the Civil War was described by both sides as a sacrificial struggle "upon the altar of the nation," as Yale's Harry Stout has aptly put it (Stout 2006). Most recently, the dawn of U.S. empire in the Philippines, the (belated) entry into World War I, the "good war" against the Axis Powers in World War II, the "Cold War" against the Soviet Union and Communist China (via proxies in Korea and Vietnam), and the military adventures in Iraq (twice) and in Afghanistan were all shrouded in sacralizing discourses of "sacrifice" (Stout 2006).

American interventions have thus always been presented as exceptional necessities justifying exceptional measures. Such violence, no matter how sadistic, "preemptive," and domination-driven, has been cloaked as "defensive" action, hence as innocent. Domination, so the exceptionalist narrative goes, is invariably "good" for the peoples Americans have invaded and fought. Religion itself has been pressed into service as a key component in an ongoing rationalization of violence-in-the-name-of-evolutionary-"progress" (progress being understood in racial, economic, nationalist, and gendered terms and marked by potent binaries of "us" versus "them"). Indeed, the production of sacralizing narratives out of violence tends to institute a *civil religion* parallel and rival to Christianity, operating essentially with transposed structures of thought and language (mis)appropriated from it.

The thought of René Girard insightfully illuminates this trend in American history, since for Girard, such phenomena are to be understood most fundamentally as "regressions" characteristic of Christendom and its aftermath, to primitive archaic patterns programmed by our evolutionary history. In his most recent (and probably final) writings, especially *I See Satan Fall Like Lightning; Christianity, Truth, and Weakening Faith; Evolution and Conversion;* and especially *Battling to the End,* René Girard has emphasized insistently what he calls his "realist" approach to anthropology, while also taking a decidedly theological turn (Girard 2001, 2008, 2010; Girard and Vattimo 2010).

For our purposes, Girard's emphasis, in particular, on the historical actuality of a "founding murder" at the beginning of human civilization can point us toward a fully "realist" refusal to blink in the face of violence, or be deceived by its sacralizing disguises. Girard's theological turn too can help us to recognize in American history the dynamics of a paradoxical oscillation, of "apocalyptic" tenor, between a "crescendo towards extremes" of violence (producing domination) and what Pierpaolo Antonello has identified as the "containments" of violence (presented as innocence)—a paradox operating via what Girard calls forms of "false transcendence" (Girard 2001, 46, 98–100, 119, 185).

This "realist theology," if we may so call it, embodies Girard's most mature reflections not only on human nature and Christianity, but also on an American culture that he called "home" for most of his adult life. It is true that the American empire (as Hardt and Negri observed [2008]) now operates as a global regime of transnational corporate power (one is tempted to say *banking* power). Yet the exchanges and flows (of weapons as well as cash) within this system are no less, for being global, part of a "sacrificial" economy than they were when tied to the nation-state and its policies (as is, in fact, still largely the case). Even more, the capacity of these sacrificial processes to produce victims has escalated, as Girard observes throughout *Battling to the End*—while also being at least temporarily contained in modern judicial rituals and systems of economic exchange. We have to understand here, however, that when violence is "contained," for Girard, it is also *redistributed* and *recycled* around the body politic.

What Girard helps us to realize, then, is that the system of false transcendence that marks American exceptionalism takes two primary forms. First, the ideological construct of innocent domination operates through overt, physical warfare rationalized and sanctified as (noble) "sacrifice"—at which construction Americans have proven themselves to be exceptionally skilled, not least in recent decades. Secondly, the "false transcendence" of superordaining necessity and sacralized innocence is deployed in various forms of "cultural warfare." Here, the battle is over symbols or "truth" more than actual physical territory. In these battles, what is "sacrificed" is not as evident (perhaps) as an actual human victim, but these ossifications of human reasoning that produce both the ideology of American exceptionalism and the false transcendence it secretes are, in the long run, no less destructive—are, indeed, perhaps more dangerous—than actual warfare.

For ideological rigor mortis is the exact opposite of devotion to a living God (not to mention devotion to living human beings and commitment to alleviating their suffering, insofar as possible). Such ideological certainty (which can have the function of masking a deeper want of assurance) marks a deep-lying strain in American history from its origins to the present.

Of course, American history is not to be reduced to any single deconstructionist narrative of anti- or para-Christian American exceptionalism cloaking domination with innocence through the workings of a false transcendence. There is also a deep stratum of trust (what Robert Putnam has identified as "social capital") manifest in spiritually grounded, pragmatically realistic, nonviolent movements for social change that give some empirical and cultural "heft" to what Kant long since identified as the conditions for perpetual peace, and that might collectively point (ironically enough) to the prospects for a *Pax Americana.*[1]

For the moment, however, we must explore and expand the fruitfulness of the present exercise in the application of Girardian theory. To which end, my colleague and I here present a series of four selected culture-readings, designed to illustrate the logic of sacred and "sacrificial" violence.

In Guns We Trust: The Origins of American Exceptionalism
Jon Pahl

"American" identity, according to this reading of the culture-story, originated in murder. From the very beginning of European settlement, shifting alliances between indigenous tribal groupings and English settlers produced competing, and largely unresolved, charges of murder and injustice. For instance, in 1636 an English trader named John Oldham was murdered in Massachusetts Bay Colony. The English accused various Native Americans of the crimes. These accusations were apparently driven less by the facts of the case than by the benefits that accrued to the English from playing on tribal rivalries that pitted the Mohegans and Narragansetts against the Pequots. English-speaking clergy preached repeated sermons demanding that the Pequots punish the murderers of Oldham, and when the Pequots refused and began carrying out raids on English villages, the English escalated the conflict with an attack on the Pequot village in what is now Mystic, Connecticut, on May 26, 1637. Captain John Mason led a band of ninety English soldiers, accompanied by several hundred friendly

Narragansetts, and torched the entire village, killing hundreds of Pequots, most of whom were women, children, and the elderly.

Commander of the attack John Mason explained the religious rationale for the mass murder afterwards, claiming that God "laughed his Enemies and the Enemies of his People to scorn making them as a fiery Oven. . . . Thus did the Lord judge among the Heathen, filling the Place with dead Bodies!" (Mason 1763, 10). A few decades later, Nathaniel Morton imagined the scene in vivid terms for readers, and explicitly justified it as a "sacrifice": it "was a fearful sight to see [the Pequots] thus frying in the Fire, and the streams of Blood quenching the Same; and horrible was the stink and scent thereof; but the Victory seemed a sweet Sacrifice, and they gave praise thereof to God, who had wrought so wonderfully for them, thus to enclose their Enemies" (Morton 1669, 101).

In the coming years, New England's Puritan settlers actually secured their dominance by promising free trade with various indigenous peoples in exchange for the severed heads and hands of murdered Pequots as tributes—thus establishing early connections between religion, violence, and commercial exchange in the "New World." And lest the theological point be lost—namely, that encouraging the murder and dismembering of an enemy could be an act of love on the part of Christians committed to Enlightened moral values like not killing—William Bradford of Plymouth Plantation opined that "cutting off [Pequot] heads and hands, which the [Indians] sent to the English, [was] a testimony of their love and service" (Lipman 2008).

In the decades to come, the English came to specialize in this method of dividing and conquering the first peoples of North America. They did so by using a murder as a pretext for more killing, although of course the killing was also legitimized by inquests, trials, and other legal procedures. The case of Sassamon—a "praying Indian" found dead near Plymouth in January of 1675—is the best-studied example. As a Christian, Sassamon was an ally of the English, although he also advised Wampanoag sachem Metacom (King Philip). Three Wampanoags were charged with Sassamon's murder, tried in English courts, and found guilty and sentenced to death. Metacom protested, and eventually began organizing raids against English settlements. The conflict escalated into total war—something Girard comments on with great insight in *Battling to the End*. Historian Francis Jennings has estimated that six of seven Native Americans and six of thirteen English in New England died during the war (Jennings 1976).

King Philip's War, as it came to be called, ended with the death of Metacom in 1677. After being captured by the English, he was first tortured, then beheaded. His head was then displayed on a pole in Plymouth for decades. According to Jill Lepore, the war—triggered by the murder of Sassamon, and ending with the murder of Metacom—rigidified cultural distinctions between "Indians" and "Americans," and established a dualistic pattern for cultural conflict that defined "American" identity (Lepore 1999). Murder, war, torture, destruction—the "sacrifice" of some to preserve others— these are the themes with which American history ought rightly to begin. Throughout the centuries, of course, Native Americans continued to bear much of the violence that flowed from this *us-them* dualism and its sacrificial operations—from the Sand Creek Massacre of 1864 (led by Colonel [and Methodist Reverend] J. M. Chivington), to the Wounded Knee Massacre of 1890, to the repression of the AIM uprising in 1973, to untold murders and crushing poverty down to the present.[2] All of this was done, of course, in the name of "progress"; in the name of the "modern" (if not putatively "Christian") renunciation of "primitive" religion and ritual.

It would not be difficult to trace the way this initial incident spiraled into ideological trajectories that take us quite directly to Iraq and Abu Ghraib.[3] Instead, however, let us, with Girard's help, draw out the historical and evolutionary significance of this "founding murder." He writes:

> The modern shedding of ritual brings to light the psychosocial substratum
> of ritual phenomena. We cry "scapegoat" to stigmatize all the phenomena
> of discrimination—political, ethnic, religious, social, racial, etc.—that we
> observe about us. We are right. We easily see now that scapegoats multiply
> wherever human groups seek to lock themselves into a given identity—
> communal, local, national, ideological, racial, religious, and so on. (Girard
> 2001, 160)

It is the *mobility* and *pluriform diversity* of the religious phenomenon—the construction, within the *gap* created by the "secularization" of inherited traditions, of hybrid civil religions and of self-sacralizing "cultural religions" or "identities"—that has marked the modern world. Girard again draws the conclusion: "All discourses on exclusion, discrimination, racism, etc. will remain superficial as long as they don't address the religious foundations of the problems that besiege our society" (Girard 2001, 210).

I have said something of the religious foundations of American violence in this brief excursion on the founding murder(s) in American history. For other case studies in the history of innocent domination, readers are invited to explore my book *Empire of Sacrifice* (2010a), which discusses in turn: the execution of the Quaker Mary Dyer on Boston Common in 1660; the sacrifices associated with slavery in North America, as outlined by Frederick Douglass; the ruthlessly mimetic "war on drugs" that is, in effect, a war on youth and adolescents in American policy; and (finally) the exclusion of women, gays, and lesbians from full participation in American society, in what I call the "sacrifice of sex." Each of these trajectories offers an enduring thread, open to a Girardian reading, throughout American history; and each demonstrates quite real "sacrifices" *of ritual immolation* illustrating America's ideology of innocent domination, albeit in forms that are not immediately and evidently identifiable as *religious.*

Other "sacrificial" trajectories of reading in American history are explored in my previous book, *Shopping Malls and Other Sacred Spaces: Putting God in Place* (2003), which tracks the ways shopping malls, Walt Disney World, or the suburban home—and especially domestic sanitation and lawn care—originate in a "desire to acquire" in America, and produce "sacred places" that reinforce what I call the "violence of banality."

But too many examples are wearisome. The point is the same in any event. Mimetic rivalries operate contagiously in America, through market and social systems that bear religious significance without appearing to be religious. In other words, innocent domination stems from a false transcendence, the falsity of which is evidenced by the existence underneath a religious rhetoric of innocence of a brutal, and escalating, system of interrogations, surveillance, torture, prisons, military expansion, and weaponry, the ballistic capacity of which is matched only by its destructive intent (Bacevich 2010).

Unfortunately, the most troubling and insidious of the forms of innocent domination is the way in which truth itself suffers under the fixed ideology of American exceptionalism. This is the case in the "warfare" between science and religion in America, which has been concentrated, with special heat, on the topic of evolution, and which deserves special attention.

Creationism as "Culture Warfare" in the Defense of American Exceptionalism

Jon Pahl

Girard himself tends to dismiss creationism as uninteresting, but there may be more to explore than he allows. He writes, in *Evolution and Conversion*, that "the compatibility between theism and evolution is not an issue for me, and the whole debate between Darwinists and creationists (or advocates of intelligent design) is simply *passé* and not very interesting from my point of view" (Girard 2010, 97).

In many circles around America, however, this debate is hardly passé—and even more, it may be important to read creationism and intelligent design as themselves variants of the modern tendency to create hybrid new sacrificial systems to bolster the decline of Christendom and its long-standing dependence on Constantinian sacrificial models. I hope to offer, in what follows, a brief Girardian reading of the creationism debate in America. Seen in this light, creationism is a rear-guard attempt to sacrifice science to the inerrant Word of God. Or, more accurately, opposition to evolution in America is constructed in such a way as to defend a sacrificial model of "Christianity" that obscures human (and natural) violence in favor of a sentimental (but profoundly destructive, if not actually vindictive) false transcendence grounded in American exceptionalism. Creationism in America is thus the *deviant transformation of Christianity into American myth*. It is dangerous precisely to the degree that it is false, and precisely to the degree that it claims transcendent warrant for its falsehood.

At root, creationism (including "intelligent design") posits an absolute beginning—but *not* a "Big Bang" (much less a "founding murder"). What is odd about creationism is how profoundly it mirrors "primitive" anthropocentricism or anthropomorphism. The human "word" is the center of everything, and the absolute beginning is an idealist project: "Let there be . . ." This seems nice, even nonviolent. But in fact the entire edifice of Creationism is built on a reaction—a mirroring of scientific epistemology declared as the "double" of mimetic crises. Creationism arose, of course, out of public debates over Darwin, leading to the publication of *The Fundamentals* in 1910 and the Scopes Trial in 1925.[4] It endures, largely unchanged, in the form of "intelligent design" down to this day.[5]

What creationists did then, and do now, is to graft a scientific episte-mology (Baconian common-sense realism) onto the biblical texts (Marsden 2006). Creationists read the Bible in a way that sacrifices all of the layers of its meaning and truth, including (curiously enough) *both* its literal *and* allegorical truth, in favor of defending its "scientific" veracity (which is the meaning, generally, of "inerrancy"). They call this a "literal" reading, but of course it is anything but literal—since it is usually dependent upon the King James Version, and since it rips all texts from their contexts (original and contemporary) and imposes on them a "scientific" context consistent with fundamentalist ideology.[6] In short, by "defending" the scientific truth of sacred scripture, science itself is *sacrificed* (if not *scapegoated*), and so too is the truth of the biblical text.

What takes the place of biblical truth, then, is in fact a sanctified sci-ence—the false transcendence of a trust invested in technology, "literalism" understood as a facile empiricism, and power understood as (American) military and technological force conducive to domination. It is as if mili-tant scientific atheists Richard Dawkins and Sam Harris had converted and turned Christianity into a "religion of science" (just as a cleverly grotesque 2006 *South Park* cartoon episode "Go, God, Go" implies!).[7] But "conver-sion" as creationists imagine (and practice) it then entails *not* the recognition of one's own participation in persecution (confessing one's "sin" is held to be old-fashioned), but rather one's choice to overcome (through "sacrifice" of them) some desires or enemies (usually sexual) that constitute the sins to be negated in order to complete one's righteousness.

This essentially Pelagian theology is, again, only one of many manifesta-tions of the American "empire of sacrifice." Here, science is sacrificed (i.e., cut away, surrendered, offered up), as indeed is the Christ, on the altar of Ameri-can exceptionalism and its "innocent domination," albeit masquerading as an imperative of Christian inspiration. Creationism is largely a U.S. phenom-enon. In it, fixed ideas (what else is "inerrancy"?) always involve a sacrifice of truth. Biblical exceptionalism, in other words, here reinforces American exceptionalism. What we then have is a total system of sacrifice that ranges from epistemology (what we know to be true in daily life, e.g., about meteo-rology, must be sacrificed to defend biblical inerrancy), from a scientifically verifiable Noah's Flood, to domestic policy (scapegoating people along the lines of age, race, gender), or foreign policy (scapegoating the socialists or communists or Muslim Others), or global economics (effectively: "to hell with the poor"). Girard, again in *Evolution and Conversion,* rightly describes such a scenario as a form of totalitarianism. He rightly envisions that

> this kind of totalitarianism is not only alive but it also has a great future. There will probably be some thinkers in the future who will reformulate this principle in a politically correct fashion, in more virulent forms, which will be more anti-Christian, albeit in an ultra-Christian caricature. When I say more Christian and more anti-Christian, I imply the figure of the Anti-Christ. The Anti-Christ is nothing but that: it is the ideology that attempts to outchristianize Christianity, that imitates Christianity in a spirit of rivalry. (Girard 2008, 236)

In America, in short, this ideology is not only future, but very much past and present, in creationism and its corollaries.

Seen from a Girardian viewpoint, creationism represents precisely an anti-Christian ideology that imitates evolutionary, progressive, catholic Christianity in a spirit of rivalry, trying to outchristianize Christianity: it is an ultra-Christianity, with an *über*-Christ, as if the Crucified One wasn't enough. If this reading requires verification, then a visit to the Creation Museum in Petersburg, Kentucky, just outside Cincinnati, will be in order. There you can "Walk through the Garden of Eden. See the scaffolding, smell the freshly-cut timbers in the busy work site of Noah's Ark. Dig up dinosaur bones—or come face to face with *T. Rex.*" And if you survive that experience, you will have taken a

> walk through biblical history. This walk through history is the centerpiece of the Creation Museum and features amazing scientific and biblical answers for the world we live in today. Witness the true time line of the universe unfold through the 7 C's of History (Creation, Corruption, Catastrophe, Confusion, Christ, Cross, Consummation)—illuminating God's redemptive plan.[8]

Here is the fixed ideology of American exceptionalism—"God's redemptive plan" *imposed on* or *forced into* the "scientific" history of the cosmos—domination rendered innocent in Kentucky.

Needless to say, this "plan" at the Creation Museum does not include much in the way of repentance for American or any other violence; you come out feeling convinced of your creationist Christian righteousness. It does, however, cost you $24.95. Over a million people had visited it within the first three years of the museum's founding.

What makes this variant of innocent domination particularly troubling is the way it constructs a romantic (death-defying and death-denying) system of sacrifice in which truth is the victim. Sacrifice is most powerful when it operates psychologically; when it operates unconsciously to give people hope in the face of mortality.[9] In America, as Harvard's president Drew Gilpin Faust has suggested in *This Republic of Suffering: Death and the American Civil War,* the American version of civil religion has often dealt with the trauma of death by trusting in various sanitizing discourses and practices, none of them more prevalent than "sacrifice."

"Death created the American nation," Faust writes (2008, 6). This cultural system originated in the murder of a single English trader in 1636, but has now developed through memorializing the "sacrifices" that united the nation in many and various adventures. Girard's deconstructionist realism, on the other hand, can help us to uncover, critique, and transform this civil religion and its false transcendence that substitutes force (physical or ideological) for the actual power of the ability of people to act in solidarity—a contrast made famous by Hannah Arendt (1969).

Hence, the "coming religious peace" to which I look forward.

Religious Sadism and American "Preemption"
James Wellman

Continuing to explore and diversify Jon Pahl's theme, I will argue that the seed of American preemption (i.e., the myth of American preeminence, insofar as it rests on violence—"containing" it, but also *recycling* it in the guise of preemptive aggression at home or abroad) lies in a form of religious sadism.

Girard, by virtue of the definition of desire given in *Deceit, Desire, and the Novel,* argues that the driving force of culture is, at its heart, "metaphysical desire." He suggests that "mimetic desire," whereby humans imitate the desire of the other and then use this mediator-model as a motivating source, are seeking to borrow from him godlike qualities and the power to exist in a godlike mode. Of course, for Girard, this ferocious need always "ends in enslavement, failure, and shame" (1961, 176). Since these desires are always just beyond reach, so that desire is thwarted and rivalries form, which in the end produce conflict and violence, and eventuate in scapegoating. Blood is shed, and through these conflicts, the archaic process of sacralizing the victim produces a new—if fragile and provisional—glow of unity and potential prosperity.

The cycle of violence contained by sacrifice continues as a natural flow of cultural construction. We might protest against this bloody dynamic of history, but as Walter Benjamin remarked, "There is no document of civilization which is not at the same time a document of barbarism" (Benjamin 1968, 256). Indeed, Girard argues that the sacralizing process is precisely the way in which this barbarism is transmogrified into myth, so that the community's "founding murder" becomes the community's project of salvation. In America, the ongoing violence (against Native peoples, slaves, women, and minorities of every kind) has been authorized by a specific type of Christianity—an American Calvinism, which is enrolled and mobilized in the process of sacralizing and rationalizing forms of preemptive war, thus producing a myth that vindicates American forms of exceptionalist nationalism, and justifies steps taken in pursuit of world domination. This particular species of American Calvinism, I will argue, acts as a seedbed for this desire for dominance, arising out of a metaphysical craving to mimic the mediator and become the divine sadist, whose dominance American leaders both seek and suffer from.

Girard writes in *Deceit, Desire, and the Novel:*

> We know that all victims of metaphysical desire seek to appropriate their mediator's being by imitating him. The sadist wants to persuade himself that he has already attained his goal; he tries to take the place of the mediator and see the world through his eyes, in the hope that the play will gradually turn into reality. The sadist's violence is yet another effort to attain divinity. (1961, 185)

The empirical evidence for this peculiar American DNA is everywhere in plain sight. The Calvinist creed of the obligation of rebelling against unjust tyranny is well documented in David Hackett Fischer's *Albion's Seed: Four British Folkways in America* (1989). Fischer paints a picture of the four primary folk cultures making up American culture. Fischer never describes them as *religious* cultures per se, but simply as "cultures"; and yet in each case, the heart of this civilization is the sacralization of revenge, and a desire to overcome past grievances—using the ferocity of the Calvinist God as a motive force for moving forward and dominating one's rivals.

Thus each culture in its own way uses theories of Reformed Calvinism to fight against forms of real or felt tyranny: the Puritans resisting the British; the Anglicans holding down the Catholics; the Quakers struggling against almost everyone; and the Scots-Irish against anyone not Scots-Irish. This latter group put it best: "The best enemy is a dead enemy." Each group carries a strain of Calvinist theology that promoted the fight against tyranny and yearned, in one form or another, to dominate in the name of this God. And this Calvinist God (the one orthodox Calvinists worship and believe in) is indeed a ferocious and even sadistic god. Conservative evangelical theologians themselves—i.e., those defending strict Puritan-evangelical theologies—admit the vengeful nature of this god. In fact, if they argue against it, they do so precisely because this theology "impugns the good character of God" (Olson 2011, 179). Roger Olson, speaking directly to the recent rise of an American-based younger generation of New Calvinists, describes their view of God as a picture in which God "ordains, designs, controls, and renders certain the most egregious evil acts such as the kidnapping, rape, and murder of a small child and genocidal slaughter of hundreds of thousands in Rwanda" (178). Olson warns against this image of God, but to no avail. For these "young, restless and Reformed Calvinists glory in a God who takes no prisoners—quite literally—proudly proclaiming a God that . . . only saves some when he could save all" (179). Many would blanch at these images, but the core texts of Calvinism, at least in the most extreme and unrevised versions, depict a sadistic—and impenitently Old Testament—God who arbitrarily commits acts of global genocide, whether in time or beyond time.

As Girard argues: "Divine punishment is demystified by the gospels; its only place nowadays is in mythic imagination, to which modern scepticism remains strangely attached" (1987 [2003]: 195). We are curiously faithful in part because our primary metaphysical desire, mimetically enhanced, is to sacralize our violence as a way of maintaining our dominance and as a way of rationalizing the motive force of American exceptionalism. But more than that, the god desired is a god who is arbitrarily violent and who needs no justification for his violence. This god makes commands, chooses whom he wants, destroys whom he wants, using whatever means are necessary to get what he wants. Seen through this lens, a domestic or foreign policy that imitates these kinds of arbitrary divine rigor makes absolute sense. Thus, forms of violence and torture are normal and to be expected from such culture-generated forms of mimesis: this is the way of the god.

Early American figures in this form of Calvinism give us quintessential and spectacular exemplars of the movement. The eighteenth-century Reformed thinker and Calvinist Jonathan Edwards, the revivalist minister who spearheaded the First Great Awakening, who is often lauded as the greatest American theologian, and who is a hero to many of the New Calvinists, often chastised his fellow ministers that it was their duty to scare the hell out of their people—literally.[10] Edwards famously did this by preaching "Sinners in the Hands of an Angry God," which literally imagined a god who would dangle the sinner over the fires of hell, waiting for repentance from the sinner. In Edwards's classic *Religious Affections,* he argued that even the devil can mimic the affections of conversion, further putting his congregation in a state of terror about that state of their salvation (Edwards 2009). How does one know if one is saved? In fact, Edwards, as well as his fellow ministers, terrified their congregations to such an extent that suicides were reported across the Northeast region—a man in Edwards's own congregation took his life. Not long afterwards, the revival plateaued, at least in part because congregations had had enough of the manipulation. Edwards was shortly thereafter dismissed from his pulpit. We see in this example a form of terror, a religious sadism, a way of coercing consent by dangling the possibility of arbitrary violence from which one has only one outlet—to give in to the same god who is simultaneously the source of the threat.

In his chapter "Masochism and Sadism," Girard, quite intentionally, puts masochism as the first term of the two. He argues that the sadist "persecutes because he feels he is being persecuted." The masochist becomes a sadist because he realizes "the key to the enchanted garden appears to be in the hands of the tormentor" (1961, 185). The tormentor in this case is "Yahweh, the God of revenge," who condemns whom he wishes and saves whomever he wants. This god legitimates an arbitrary form of terror, which the sadist seeks to mirror and model, in part to overcome his own fear and in part to express his sense of revenge. Thus, Girard makes clear that these characters are neither essentially good nor evil, but damaged persons, victims of their own metaphysical desire. He quotes Dostoevsky: "Do not hate the atheists, the professors of evil, the materialists, or even the wicked among them, for many are good, especially in our time" (190). Moral illumination means understanding the terror that haunts sadists, even in the midst of their persecution.

We are, then, identifying Calvinism as the bulwark religion of America: a sadistic and sacrificial religion where one's success is a marker of blessing and a providential promise of sacred acceptance. American exceptionalism is legitimated through sacral and sacrificial forms, and its arbitrary nature is hidden behind paeans raised to the glory of its promise, and to all who bow to its power. Disciplined moral action demands that one *have victory;* one must not *be a victim,* because this is the mark of defeat, both morally and in respect of one's salvation. Grace is limited in this system and thus it must be sought, even though one can't earn it, and yet one's *success* is a sign of it, as are the sobriety and iron will of those who follow the creed. The warp and woof of masochism and sadism keeps many in its grip—another kind of Weberian "iron cage."

Preemptive aggression is thus a natural extension of this creed—when in doubt, act first, ask for forgiveness later. Scots-Irish culture simply takes the victor's right to an extreme, in an ethic of radical freedom whereby contests over scarce resources create an ecstasy of battle—as illustrated by the violence in American football and in military academies, and by the anger of Second Amendment rights groups. Scott Appleby's "ecstatic asceticism" in which one's joy is founded in solidarity with the power of the state, triumphant over all enemies, is a further extension of this sacrificial ethic (Appleby 1999). To sacrifice one's life for this power sacralizes not only one's own life but the life of the nation. Violence becomes a *sacrament* by which one wins glory for oneself, one's family, and the state.[11]

This ecstatic asceticism reigns supreme in the ethic of the American military—deeply entrenched in the South and Midwest—which carries on the legacy of their Scots-Irish heritage. The Navy Seal 6 team that was able to find and "take out" Osama bin Laden code-named their target "Geronimo"—thus rehearsing an early episode of American Indian scapegoating involved in America's "winning" of the West. Following this murder (in its own way, a founding murder), scenes were shown of various American military academies; cameras panned the literal dance of ecstasy, in which soldiers chanted together, "U.S.A., U.S.A., U.S.A." The fervency of this sacramental ritual was as powerful as any I have ever witnessed.

One might, once again, say: this is a kind of inverted gospel—in which the one who comes in peace and in the name of the Lord only *arrives* in and through the act of murder. And, of course, the model is not the Jesus of the Sermon on the Mount or of the Cross, but rather the apocalyptic Christ from the Book of Revelation, who comes on a white horse and tramples his enemies underfoot. This god is then interpreted as a Sovereign War God, a sadistic Master—and, of course, one who can and should be imitated in the pulpit, whether in church or in the White House. And, to be sure, there are many masochists who love this god, who love this kind of leadership, and who take pleasure in the demanding nature of this gospel. Again, we see an inverted gospel of peace—a powerful culture-construct (and culture-constructing) god who motivates a righteous and unrelenting violence, as efficient as it is arbitrary.

The American Megachurch
James Wellman

My final example is one that is less obvious though fascinating in its own right: the American megachurch. Empirically, these churches are defined as those that have 2,000 or more attendees each week; they are now the dominant form of church structure in the United States. The surge of this phenomenon is recent, only since 1970 (Chaves 2011). These large churches tend to be non-denominational and generically Christian even when they represent specific denominations. Americans don't, today, want to be affiliated with denominations; nor do they want much in terms of theological specificity. They do want spiritual growth, which they feel they receive from megachurches; and they do like the way their needs are met at these mall-like religious operations.[12] As institutions, however, megachurches are at once one of the most sophisticated sites of modern-day technology and communication, and yet harbor, in their theological framework itself, an interesting species of religious archaism (or, as Girard would say, "regression").

Our studies cover a dozen of these megachurches, and I have visited most of them.[13] One in particular stood out as exemplary of the general trends. I visited Rock Church in San Diego; there were five worship services on the Sunday I visited, all exactly the same. I estimated that 12,000 people came through these services—people of every ethnic background, mostly younger—the diversity was stunning. As with many megachurches it took place in an old naval warehouse, remodeled as a theater. The show—and it was a show—was well done, with high-definition screens across the front, so one could see every pirouette of the singers and every movement of the band. One of the soloists stood out; he was a Hispanic young man whose voice was stunning, and who stood in front of us like a kind of southern god. I kept thinking about his ethnic history: by what Catholic tributary could he have been nurtured or forced into this quite remarkable future, and into this rushing river? Needless to say, all my dreaming was taking place as a prelude to what was coming—Miles McPherson, an ex–San Diego Chargers football player, an African American man who came bounding onto the stage, decked out in stone-washed jeans and a casual but stylish dress shirt; his broad smile and energy hit me. Miles's charismatic personality was evident, as was his intelligence and articulate manner.

His sermon was engaging; he was going over well-trodden ground: arguing for a design theory of God's existence—if we see order around us, there must be a designer. (Intuitively, this makes sense, though as Kant has shown, there is no necessary inference that can be drawn about a first cause; but of course, I wasn't expecting Miles to be quoting German philosophy.)

At the end of the "talk" each time, Miles would start the altar call, making the claim that our sinful blood is damning, and that only the innocent blood of our savior Jesus Christ can "cover" for us. This is hardly original or unusual in the evangelical Protestant mainstream; and the blood atonement theory seems nearly universal in these megachurches. But here was the sacralizing of the founding murder right at the heart of a dazzlingly modern and sophisticated performance—the *sacrifice* (meaning here specifically: the *bloody immolation as scapegoat victim*) of Jesus. Jesus must die for our sin, to purge us of the punishment we deserve from God. There is no other way for any human being to be saved—past, present, or future. Here we have a quintessential piece of archaic religion: God is the one who scapegoats his Son—whose innocent blood, however, "atones" for human sin, i.e., makes the reparation required by the god's own sadistic and rigorous Purity. [14]

Analysis of more than four hundred interviews convinced my team of researchers that *desire* is at the heart of what megachurch members want—they seek salvation, acceptance, a leader, and a sense of purpose larger than themselves. Desire is in the body, and so emotion rules this territory. Charismatic leadership is critical precisely because it evokes these emotions. The mimetic nature of desire hovers hotly around every expression that we heard from the megachurched, just as predicted by the Girardian claim that its etiology makes human desire a primarily social construct—we see what the Other desires and we replicate their desire for the same object. The whole power of these institutions to evoke and nurture—but also to bring cathartic satisfaction to these desires—was impressive on so many levels. I noticed, even in my own body, this rising desire of mimetism.

Rock Church, the day before I got there, had sent out 600 volunteers to completely refurbish an entire city park, something city officials said would take them five years to complete. On that same Sunday, Miles announced that Rock Church would be giving out free vouchers to their thrift shop to all 2,000 police officers and firefighters in the city of San Diego. This was impressive, by nearly any standard, in terms of direct social service. It was easy to imagine desiring what Miles desired—imagining how so many wanted to be close to him, as Randall Collins talks about: be close to the energy star, to the source of power (Collins 2004).

And true to this process, as I read in the megachurch interviews, they wanted to catch the desire of the energy stars in their churches, wanting what those charismatic figures wanted. Particularly in churches that were at the height of their growth—peaking, as it were, in popularity and power—the talk about these charismatic figures constructed them as sacred objects. Yes, the Bible was talked about and music was mentioned, but the sacralization of leadership was something I noticed consistently. Thus, my latest—at least partial—definition of "religion": *Religion is the socially enacted desire for the ultimate.*

My sense is that humans want and desire forms of emotional energy that can last—ultimate sources that appear and are claimed to be unlimited. And religion in this sense provides the ultimate promise of a source that can never run down. What has struck me about megachurches is that when mega-church members talk about them and why they attend, it is almost never because of a specific theology or dogma, it simply is not about any cognitive content. It is strictly because they can say: "I came home." "He speaks to my heart." "I feel like he knows me." "He has a pastor's heart." "It's never dull." "I never fall asleep." "It doesn't feel like church." "It's applicable to me."

At which point, Randall Collins's Interactive Ritual Chain theory may serve to specify the source as well as the means whereby religious experience is ritualized. It all begins with a desire, a willingness to focus on something that is of interest. But this focus is always relationally situated; there is a co-presence, whether real (as with other human participants) or perceived—that is, an observation that others are interested in the same object. Humans want to be with other "desiring" people, and this "co-presence" enables one to "see," to feel inspired, and to be moved with, in, and toward other people. Co-presence is often accompanied by a charismatic leader: this emotional charging agent is now the source of desire, and now its focus; and, of course, sometimes this leader facilitates a focus on other objects of interest—symbolic or otherwise. This, in essence, constructs the core stimulation: an *emotional charge* occurs, a "shared mood threshold," and sometimes there is a peak, a collective threshold of effervescence where the air is filled and "something more" takes over—with some sensing deliverance, others enlightenment; some satiated in the moment, and some moved to act, or sometimes to think more deeply; often to feel and almost always to somehow make it happen again and again. Here we have a promising—if still very general and indeterminate—poetics of natural religion as a psychosocial phenomenon.

Megachurches have conquered the American church marketplace in empirical fashion, by creating a bonanza of desire; stimulating every aesthetic body part; uplifting the middle class of America to seek success, not just for its own sake, but to serve others: they send out battalions of servants and missionaries across the globe. But at their theological heart is a binary choice, the blood of Christ—signifying Heaven—and being without Christ, signifying Hell. The archaic religious here is right at the heart of a multimillion-dollar display of American ingenuity, creativity, and entrepreneurialism.

◆   ◆   ◆

We may conclude with this bold display of continuity-in-time, rendering perceptible the perennial legacy of archaic religion: in molding desire, in motivating social groups, in producing solidarity, in engendering loyalty to a leader, in creating social movements that valorize a specific way of life, in rationalizing righteous causes, and, at times, as we have shown, in creating a sense of righteousness and of belief in the nation.

Even as Miles McPherson called sinners to repent, he consistently lifted up the work of the police and the military as "sacrificial" and noble occupations, servants to all. The church was truly a chaplain to a righteous state, and this state—the United States of America—figured, here again, as a nation called to righteous domination. As we have seen, archaic religion feeds on violence; and when it is righteously ordained violence, it becomes a truly sovereign Power.

Religious sadism is a seductive god; but in lifting its disguises, we observe that in the end it *also* preempts perhaps the one and only thing that can genuinely save us from its ill effects—namely, a God who forgives not only those who love, but also those who hate.

Notes

1. See Putnam and Campbell (2012) and Pinker (2011). I develop the latter theme in what my article "Clashing Minorities, Converging Majorities: Toward a Coming Religious Peace" calls "a coming religious peace."

2. I explore these and other incidents in more detail in Pahl 2010a and Pahl 2010b.

3. See, for example, David P. Gushee, J. D. Zimmer, and J. H. Zimmer, eds., *Religious Faith, Torture, and Our National Soul* (2010); and Lincoln (2007).

4. The entire twelve-volume set of the *The Fundamentals* is available online, in a four-volume 1917 Baker Book edition, at http://www.ntslibrary.com/New_Online_Book_Additions.htm.

5. The classic history, recently updated, is Numbers (2006).

6. On this theme, see "America's King of Kings: The King James Version of the Bible and American Civil Religion" (Pahl 2013).

7. The episode comes from Season 10 (2006) of the cartoon, and is a satire of militant atheism in the context of the debate over evolution. Dawkins comes in for particular scorn. See the entire episode online at the South Park Studios website, at http://www.southparkstudios.com/full-episodes/s10e12-go-god-go.

8. Creation Museum website, "What's Here," online at http://creationmuseum.org/whats-here/exhibits/.

9. See along these lines "Sacrifice as Renunciation" by Gavin Flood (2013).

10. See George Marsden's biographical magnum opus (2003). However, I am sure that Marsden doesn't agree with my interpretation of Edwards.

11. Pat Tillman, the ex–Arizona Cardinals football player, who quit his million-dollar football contract to fight in the Afghanistan War, is a quintessential exemplar of both ecstatic asceticism and the sacralizing of human sacrifice. Tillman, in the midst of his duty, realized that the war was counterfeit. Nonetheless, his accidental death in battle was sacralized precisely against his own will. See Krakauer (2009).

12. The research that shows these findings is documented in an article written with Katie Corcoran and Kate Stockly-Meyerdirk, "'God is like a Drug': Explaining Interactive Rituals in American Megachurches," *Sociological Forum,* 2014.

13. See Kelley (2012).

14. It's important to note that this sadist god is not the only one desired in Christian history. After two decades of meditating on visceral showings of Christ's Passion, Julian of Norwich reflected that the "sin" for which Jesus dies—a common trope also in Calvinist penal substitution—is not the individual commission of sin, but a general failure of all humankind, the "generalle man." It is thus that the redemption by which Julian finds that "all shall be well" is applicable to everyone, for "alle man whych is synfulle and shall be in to the last day, of whych man I am a membre, as I hope, by the mercy of God" will find the "blessyd comfort that I sawe" as "it is large inough for us alle" (Julian of Norwich, XVI.79).

Cited Texts and Further Reading

Appleby, Scott. 1999. *The Ambivalence of the Sacred: Religion, Violence, and Reconciliation.* Lanham, MD: Rowman and Littlefield Publishers.

Arendt, Hannah. 1969. *On Violence.* New York: Harvest Books.

Bacevich, Andrew. 2010. *Washington Rules: America's Path to Permanent War.* New York: Metropolitan Books.

Bellah, Robert N. 1967. "Civil Religion in America." *Daedalus* 96 (Winter 1967): 1–21.

Benjamin, Walter. 1968. *Illuminations.* Translated by Harry Zohn. New York: Schocken Books.

Chaves, Mark. 2001. *American Religion: Contemporary Trends.* Princeton, NJ: Princeton University Press.

Collins, Randall. 2004. *Interaction Ritual Chains.* Princeton, NJ: Princeton University Press.

Denton-Borhaug, Kelly. 2011. *U.S. War-Culture, Sacrifice and Salvation.* London: Equinox Publishing.

Ebel, Jonathan H. 2010. *Faith in the Fight: Religion and the American Soldier in the Great War.* Princeton, NJ: Princeton University Press.

Edwards, Jonathan. 2009. *The Religious Affections.* Vancouver: Eremetical Press.

Faust, Drew Gilpin. 2008. *This Republic of Suffering: Death and the American Civil War.* New York: Knopf.

Fischer, David Hackett. 1989. *Albion's Seed: Four British Folkways in America.* New York: Oxford University Press.

Flood, Gavin. 2013. "Sacrifice as Renunciation." In *Sacrifice in Modern Thought,* ed. Johannes Zachhuber and Julia Mezaros. London and New York: Oxford University Press.

Girard, René. 1961. *Deceit, Desire, and the Novel: Self and Other in Literary Structure.* Translated by Yvonne Freccero. Baltimore and London: Johns Hopkins University Press.

———. 2001. *I See Satan Fall Like Lightning.* Translated by James G. Williams. New York: Orbis.

———. 2003. *Things Hidden since the Foundation of the World.* Translated by S Bann and M Metteer. New York: Continuum. Original edition (London: Athlone Press, 1987).

———. 2008. *Evolution and Conversion: Dialogues on the Origins of Culture.* With Pierpaolo Antonello and João Cezar de Castro Rocha. New York: Continuum.

———. 2010. *Battling to the End: Conversations with Benoît Chantre.* Translated by Mary Baker. East Lansing: Michigan State University Press.

Girard, René, and Gianni Vattimo. 2010. *Christianity, Truth, and Weakening Faith: A Dialogue.* Edited by Pierpaolo Antonello. Translated by William McCuaig. Cambridge: Cambridge University Press.

Gushee, David P., Jillian Hickman Zimmer, and J. Drew Zimmer, eds. 2010. *Religious Faith, Torture, and Our National Soul.* Macon, GA: Mercer University Press.

Hardt, Michael, and Antonio Negri. 2008. *Empire.* Cambridge, MA: Harvard University Press.

Jennings, Francis. 1976. *The Invasion of America: Indians, Colonialism, and the Cant of Conquest.* New York: Norton.

Jewett, Robert. 2008. *Mission and Menace: Four Centuries of American Religious Zeal.* Minneapolis: Fortress Press.

Julian of Norwich. 2005. *The Showings of Julian of Norwich.* Edited by Denise N. Baker. New York: Norton.

Kelley, Peter. 2012. "God as a Drug: The Rise of American Megachurches." *UW Today.* Http://www.washington.edu/news/2012/08/20/god-as-a-drug-the-rise-of-american-megachurches.

Krakauer, Jon. 2009. *Where Men Win Glory: The Odyssey of Pat Tillman.* New York: Random House.

Lepore, Jill. 1999. *The Name of War: King Philip's War and the Origins of American Identity.* New York: Vintage.

Lincoln, Bruce. 2007. *Religion, Empire, and Torture: The Case of Achaemenian Persia, with a Postscript on Abu Ghraib.* Chicago: University of Chicago Press.

Lipman, Andrew. 2008. "'A means to knit them together': The Exchange of Body Parts in the Pequot War." *William and Mary Quarterly* 65 (January 2008): 1–18.

Marsden, George. 2003. *Jonathan Edwards: A Life.* New Haven: Yale University Press.

———. 2006. *Fundamentalism and American Culture: 1875–1925.* New ed. London: Oxford University Press.

Mason, John. 1736. *A Brief History of the Pequot War.* Boston: S. Kneeland and T. Green.

Morton, Nathaniel. 1669. *New-Englands Memoriall.* Cambridge: S.G. and M.J for John Usher of Boston.

Numbers, Ronald L. 2006. *The Creationists: From Scientific Creationism to Intelligent Design.* Expanded ed. Cambridge, MA: Harvard University Press.

Olson, Roger. 2011. *Against Calvinism.* Grand Rapids, MI: Zondervan.

Pahl, Jon. 2003. *Shopping Malls and Other Sacred Spaces: Putting God in Place.* Grand Rapids, MI: Brazos.

———. 2010a. "Homicide and American Religion." In *Religion, Death, and Dying,* vol. 2, *Special Issues,* ed. Lucy Bregman, 135–58. New York: Praeger.

———. 2010b. "Shifting Sacrifices: Christians, War, and Peace in America." In *American Christianities: A History of Dominance and Diversity,* ed. Catherine A. Brekus and W. Clark Gilpin, 445–65. Chapel Hill: University of North Carolina Press.

———. 2012a. "Clashing Minorities, Converging Majorities: Toward a Coming Religious Peace." *Gülen Movement.* Http://www.gulenmovement.us/clashing-minorities-converging-majorities-toward-a-coming-religious-peace.html.

———. 2012b. *Empire of Sacrifice: The Religious Origins of American Violence.* New York: New York University Press.

———. 2013. "America's King of Kings: The King James Version of the Bible and American Civil Religion." In *The King James Version of the Bible at 400: Essays,* ed. David G. Burke. Saarbrücken, Germany: Scholars Press.

Pinker, Steven. 2011. *The Better Angels of Our Nature: Why Violence Has Declined.* New York: Viking.

Putnam, Robert D., and David E. Campbell. 2012. *American Grace: How Religion Divides and Unites Us.* New York: Simon and Schuster.

Stout, Harry S. 2006. *Upon the Altar of the Nation: A Moral History of the Civil War.* New York: Viking.

Wellman, James K. Jr., Katie E. Corcoran, and Kate Stockly-Meyerdirk. 2014. "'God is like a Drug': Explaining Interaction Rituals in American Megachurches." *Sociological Forum.*

PART TWO

Rebooting Evolutionary Survival: Is Christianity Crucial?

From Closed Societies to the Open Society

Parochial Altruism and Christian Universalism

Wolfgang Palaver

Recent research on human altruism has shown that altruism often relies on a common enmity vis-à-vis other groups, which strengthens internal cohesion. Today this typical pattern of human solidarity is called "parochial altruism," and it is seen as referring back to the origin of human civilization. The French philosopher Henri Bergson mentions such a pattern in his description of closed societies, representing the first stage of human evolution. According to Bergson, closed societies were characterized by a static religion fostering a parochial altruism.

With the help of René Girard's mimetic theory it is not too difficult to interpret these societies as derived from, and as offspring of, the "founding murder." For Girard, while following closely Bergson's distinction between "closed" and "open" forms of social organization, emphasizes the fact that it was the Judeo-Christian revelation that has overcome archaic religion by exposing its origin in collective violence against a single victim.

In the following analysis, I will compare parochial altruism as an offspring of archaic religion with Christian universalism. This contrastive comparison will lead us to a deeper understanding of our current world, which is characterized by an ongoing weakening of parochial altruism without, however, being, as yet, able to follow the way of Jesus. René Girard, on this basis, interprets our age of globalization as an "apocalyptic age." Without traditional forms of parochial altruism, we run the risk of destroying our world—a world no longer able to contain the rivalrous and destructive effects of enhanced competition. This, however, does not mean that we have to wait fatalistically for the end of the world. The "apocalyptic" stage of today's fast-globalizing world community may instead force us towards a deeper understanding of the gospels; and this, hopefully, will enable us also to overcome Constantinian versions of Christianity, which remain, despite their global outreach, parochial—but *also* imperialistic!—exemplars of the closed society, rather than illustrations of the open society.

Parochial Altruism: How Enmity between Groups Fosters Solidarity within Groups

Recent anthropological research has shown how consistently throughout history human solidarity has relied on enmity directed outwards, towards "Other" groups; while altruism within human groups seems almost always to go along with a parochial preference for insiders over outsiders. Enmity against outside groups, in other words, is one of humanity's most powerful means of fostering in-group solidarity. Samuel Bowles, an economist heading the Behavioral Sciences Program at the Santa Fe Institute, concluded recently in an article in *Nature* that "generosity and solidarity towards one's own may have emerged only in combination with hostility towards outsiders" (Bowles 2008, 326). The title of this article—"Conflict: Altruism's Midwife"—clearly articulates a strong relationship between solidarity within groups and enmity between groups. Bowles and his collaborators studied the synergy between "parochialism," meaning "favoring ethnic, racial or other insiders over outsiders," and "altruism," that is: "conferring benefits on others at a cost to oneself." With the help of computer simulations creating artificial histories of early human development, Bowles and his team found out that parochialism and altruism tend to join hands:

> In millions of simulated evolutionary histories, the populations emerging after thousands of generations of selection tend to be either tolerant and selfish, with little warfare, or parochial and altruistic with frequent and

lethal encounters with other groups. Occasional transitions occur between the selfish peaceful states and the warring altruistic states. But neither altruism nor parochialism ever proliferate singly; they share a common fate with war, the elixir of their success. (Bowles 2008, 326)

Bowles also refers, of course, to examples from the early period of human history to illustrate his thesis, not forgetting, however, that parochial altruism is not just something that explains the past of humanity—it is a pattern that is still with us:

> Thus, in ancestral humans, evolutionary pressures favored cooperative institutions among group members as well as conflict with other groups. These were complemented by individual dispositions of solidarity and generosity towards one's own, and suspicion and hostility towards others. This potent combination of group and individual attributes is as characteristic of the contemporary welfare state in a system of heavily armed and competing nations—in short, modern nationalism—as it was among our ancestors. (Bowles 2008, 327)

Bowles's research shows strong parallels to anthropological insights acquired with the help of René Girard's mimetic theory. According to this theory, a first form of human solidarity inside a group holding down internal rivalries and competition emerged from the scapegoat mechanism that resolved a mimetic crisis inside this group by killing or expelling one of its members, who subsequently became sacralized as the god of that community. Émile Durkheim's "mechanical solidarity" comes very close to Girard's understanding of the violent sacred stemming from the scapegoat mechanism (Durkheim 1984, 31–67). This type of solidarity is religious by nature and consists in a repressive law punishing every transgression of social order. Durkheim refers to Hesiod's description of divine vengeance as an example of mechanical solidarity (29, 66). Hesiod's poem *Works and Days* describes Zeus's justice by retelling the myth of Oedipus, who was punished for his hubris: "Often even a whole city suffers because of an evil man who sins and devises wicked deeds. Upon them, Cronus' son brings forth woe from the sky, famine together with pestilence, and the people die away; the women do not give birth, and the households are diminished by the plans of Olympian Zeus" (Hesiod 2006, vv. 240–45). Hesiod's indirect reference to Oedipus mentions Girard's archetypal case of a mythic scapegoat (Girard 1977, 68–88; 2001, 107–15).

Mechanical solidarity, however, is not the typical political form of solidarity that we find throughout human history and that is still with us today. This type can be called "antagonistic solidarity" connected to political friend-enemy patterns, fostering internal solidarity (Höffe 2002, 91). Antagonistic solidarity is at least as old as Aeschylus's tragedy *The Eumenides*. In this tragedy, Aeschylus describes the overcoming of civil war by the establishment of a political order. The vengeful and violent Erinyes are transformed into the gentle and fruitful Eumenides. It seems that violence has fully disappeared from the city. This, however, is only superficially true. Open violence, in the sense of revenge, has been transformed into a form of structural violence that helps to create peace inside the city, but can be used against foreign enemies and internal troublemakers at any time. The pacified Eumenides promise that common love *and* unanimous hatred will overcome civil war:

> I pray that discord, greedy for evil, may never clamor in this city, and may the dust not drink the black blood of its people and through passion cause ruinous murder for vengeance to the destruction of the state. But may they return joy for joy in a spirit of common love, and may they hate with one mind; for this is the cure of many an evil in the world. (Aeschylus 1983, vv. 977–87)

Civil war is here prevented by enmity towards the outside world. Wars against foreign enemies have helped to create peace inside the city. Athena recommends political friend-enemy relations as an antidote to internal bloodshed. According to Girard, Aeschylus's tragedy *The Eumenides* represents the political dimension itself of the social group as a product of the scapegoat mechanism (Girard 1987b, 146–53; Palaver 1998, 38–45). What was originally laid upon the scapegoat is now channeled outside the city. In rituals we can find the necessary link between the political and the scapegoat mechanism. The political builds upon the ritual channeling of internal violence toward the external world, whereas in the scapegoat mechanism a member of the group itself is killed. Ritual sacrifice already tended to sacrifice foreigners. The political prolongs the ritual focus on the foreigner and takes a friend-enemy relationship between two different groups as an always-already given starting point. Using the example of the Canadian Tsimshian tribe, Girard reflects on the original function of religious-ritual wars and, by extension, friend-enemy relations:

> Ritual violence is always less internal than the original violence. In assuming a mythico-ritual character, violence tends toward the exterior, and this tendency in turn assumes certain sacrificial characteristics; it conceals the site of the original violence, thereby shielding it from this violence, and from the very knowledge of this violence, the elementary group whose very survival depends on the absolute triumph of peace. . . . In sum, the groups agree never to be completely at peace among themselves. We see here the principle behind all "foreign" wars: aggressive tendencies that are potentially fatal to the cohesion of the group are redirected from within the community to outside it. (Girard 1977, 249)

Antagonistic solidarity—the friend-enemy pattern uniting the group or social community against an outside third party—as we have discovered it in the *Eumenides* has been one of the most important political containments of competition right up to the present day. It characterizes Rousseau's patriotism—"a common emulation in all to live and die for their country" (Rousseau 1990, 150; Palaver 1999, 96–97), always directed towards a common national enemy—at the beginning of the modern nation, as well as Carl Schmitt's *Concept of the Political,* with its emphasis on the distinction between friend and enemy, Huntington's *Clash of Civilizations,* or recent European emergences of right-wing populist parties to strengthen a national "we" against an outside "they" (Schmitt 2007; Huntington 1996).

Antagonistic solidarity is a type of parochial altruism that has been powerfully described in Henri Bergson's book *The Two Sources of Morality and Religion.* In this book, Bergson wrote about closed societies at the beginning of human civilization that were characterized by a closed morality and a static religion. These early forms of social life are characterized by either an antagonistic solidarity or a parochial altruism:

> Who can help seeing that social cohesion is largely due to the necessity for a community to protect itself against others, and that it is primarily

as against all other men that we love the men with whom we live? Such is the primitive instinct. It is still there, though fortunately hidden under the accretions of civilization; but even to-day we still love naturally and directly our parents and our fellow countrymen, whereas love of mankind is indirect and acquired. (Bergson 1935, 22)

According to Bergson, the natural pattern of early human communities "required that the group be closely united, but that between group and group there should be virtual hostility" (Bergson 1935, 44). Closed societies are characterized by an internal solidarity that is strengthened by enmity towards the outside. These closed societies are fostered by a static religion emerging as a form of "natural religion" at the beginning of human civilization:

> What binds together the members of a given society is tradition, the need and the determination to defend the group against other groups and to set it above everything. To preserve, to tighten this bond is incontestably one aim of the religion we have found to be natural; it is common to the members of a group, it associates them intimately with each other in rites and ceremonies, it distinguishes the group from other groups, it guarantees the success of the common enterprise and is an assurance against the common danger. (Bergson 1935, 175–76)

Seen from the perspective of mimetic theory, it seems to be clear that static religion as an essential dimension of these early forms of parochial altruism stems from the scapegoat mechanism. Static religion is identical with the violent sacred enveloping closed societies in the beginning of humanity. The closure of tribal communities "is achieved through constant recourse to the expulsion of the Other" (Girard 2004, 89), be it an internal scapegoat or an outside enemy.

Christian Universalism: Towards the Open Society

Parochial altruism, however—if it is indeed an evolutionary "default" pattern—is not something to which humanity is bound forever. It is not rooted in an ontology of violence governing the entire cosmos; rather, it is simply a pattern that developed as the most likely and evolutionarily successful way in which human beings have lived socially from the earliest beginnings. And even today, we ourselves are still struggling with remnants of this pattern. From a *theological* point of view, parochial altruism is an offspring of original sin or evolutionary process, or both, but *not* in the unmovable "given" of divine creation. Also: Samuel Bowles ends his article with a clear rejection of a fatalistic attitude that does not recognize possibilities of overcoming parochialisms: "Even if I am right that a parochial form of altruism is part of the human legacy, it need not be our fate" (Bowles 2008, 327).

Human beings are able to transcend the natural pattern of parochial altruism because they are essentially characterized by their freedom and by their spiritual stature. Especially in the Christian tradition to which I will confine myself in this paper—not excluding therefore similar potentials in Judaism, Islam, or the traditions of the East—it is humanity's openness towards a transcendent God that allows it to transgress patterns of closed societies towards an open society. Again it is helpful to draw on Henri Bergson's work on the two types of religion. According to Bergson, "there seems to be no doubt that . . . the passage from the closed to the open, is due to Christianity" (Bergson 1935, 61). He clearly distinguishes in this regard Christianity from mere philosophy, which was not able to go that far.[1] In the eyes of Bergson, it is a "dynamic religion" such as can be discovered in *mysticism* that overcomes parochialism:

> In our eyes, the ultimate end of mysticism is the establishment of a contact, consequently of a partial coincidence, with the creative effort of which life is the manifestation. This effort is of God, if not God himself. The great mystic is to be conceived as an individual being, capable of transcending the limitations imposed on the species by its material nature, thus continuing and extending the divine action. (Bergson 1935, 188)

Bergson recognized the prophets of Israel as an important although limited source of Christian mysticism that reached its completion in those great Christian mystics that imitated the Christ of the Gospels (Bergson 1935, 61, 205–6).

Much more could be said, of course, on the Jewish roots of Christian universalism. The Protestant theologian Reinhold Niebuhr, as well as the

British historian Herbert Butterfield, have gone much further in this regard than Bergson. They both understood clearly how the prophetic inspiration within the ancient Hebrew tradition overcame the collective pride typical of closed societies, and how it undermined the identification of the nation with God (Butterfield 1954, 75–88; Niebuhr 1986, 3–6; 1996, 1:208–19).

Being unable to explore here the prophetic roots of Christianity more deeply and carefully, I will turn directly to the Gospels as a key example of a dynamic religion that has overcome parochial patriotism profoundly.

In the New Testament, we can find in the demand to love our enemies the clearest expression of this type of religion that turns closed societies towards the open society:

> You have heard that it was said, "You shall love your neighbor and hate your enemy." But I say to you, Love your enemies and pray for those who persecute you, so that you may be children of your Father in heaven. (Matt. 5:43–45)

Not infrequently in times past, this passage was read in order to prove that Christianity breaks completely with its Jewish past: a parochialism that had to give way to universalism. Such an anti-Jewish (sometimes anti-Semitic) reading, however, does not do justice to the biblical text. Universalism—as I have already noted—did not begin with Christianity but with the Jewish prophets. The saying against which Jesus puts the exhortation to love our enemies can only partly be found in the Hebrew Bible. In a letter to Ernst Michel from April 1933, the Jewish philosopher Martin Buber maintains vehemently that there is no commandment to hate one's enemies in the Hebrew Bible (Buber 2010, 733–34). Indeed, in Lev 19:18 we can find the commandment to love thy neighbor, but there is no explicit command to hate your enemy. Buber even refers to passages recommending the love of enemies.[2] What Jesus quotes has to be understood, however, in a much broader way. It is a saying that refers to humanity's affinity with parochial altruism, and to general folk wisdom going along with it. This antithesis established by Jesus poses a "new standard for obedience to God, not in opposition to the Torah but over against conventional attitudes and interpretations of the Torah" (Hays 1997, 327). Martin Buber understood it as a reference to an attitude that was influenced by a pagan type of vulgar morality (Buber 2010, 734). From the perspective of Girard's mimetic theory, the exhortation to love our enemies means a decisive break with the closed societies emerging from the scapegoat mechanism. Whereas the scapegoat mechanism leads to a "closed kingdom," Jesus's command to love one's enemy belongs to a "Kingdom of love," explaining "all that people must do in order to break with the circularity of closed societies, whether they be tribal, national, philosophical or religious" (Girard 1987b, 197–98). According to Girard, it is ultimately the very special image of God in the Gospels that enables us to break with the sacred violence of the past, and its parochialism. He again and again refers to a God "who is alien to all violence" because—in the words of Jesus—-He "makes his sun rise on the evil and on the good, and sends rain on the righteous and on the unrighteous" (Matt. 5:45), (Girard, 1987b, 183; cf. 206, 269; 1987a, 156; 2001, 14).

The parable of the Good Samaritan in the Gospel of Luke (Lk. 10:25–37) is also a clear example of how Jesus challenged traditional friend-enemy patterns when he referred to a political enemy of his people as a positive example to show what it means to love one's neighbor. The essential passage is Jesus's answer to the question "Who is my neighbor?":

> A man was going down from Jerusalem to Jericho, and fell into the hands of robbers, who stripped him, beat him, and went away, leaving him half dead. Now by chance a priest was going down that road; and when he saw him, he passed by on the other side. So likewise a Levite, when he came to the place and saw him, passed by on the other side. But a Samaritan while traveling came near him; and when he saw him, he was moved with pity. He went to him and bandaged his wounds, having poured oil and wine on them. Then he put him on his own animal, brought him to an inn, and took care of him. (Lk. 10:30–34)

Today we do not immediately understand this parable properly because we quickly equate a "Samaritan" with "a charitable or helpful person" (Waldron 2003, 336). But in Jesus's days, a Samaritan was to ordinary Jews an enemy, belonging to the group of a despised Other: "For centuries Judeans had treated the Samaritans as a despised outgroup and subjected them to the processes of negative stereotypification" (Esler 2000, 329). Jesus challenged severely this traditional pattern of identifying with one's own group against an outside other by telling this parable:

> In the body of the parable Jesus has refused to engage in the processes of
> group differentiation and stereotypification, indeed he has positively sub-
> verted them. Rather than accept an invitation to add to the way in which
> the Israelite ingroup maintains and develops its social identity in the face
> of negatively regarded outgroups by formulating more tightly a critical
> indicator of membership, Jesus exposes this discussion as completely inad-
> equate and morally inferior in the face of the particular human need he has
> set out. (Esler 2000, 344)

Instead of maintaining traditional friend-enemy patterns, Jesus's parable represents a universal moral attitude that includes all human beings as possible
neighbors in need of our help. The French philosopher and mystic Simone
Weil clearly emphasized the universal attitude of Jesus's illustration of his
commandment to love our neighbor: "The neighbor is a being of whom
nothing is known, lying naked, bleeding, and unconscious on the road. It is a
question of completely anonymous, and for that reason, completely universal
love" (Weil 2001, 50). But this universalism has nothing to do with those
abstract types of universalism that are completely occupied with claiming to
love all of humanity while easily overlooking the needy nearby. Again, Weil
justly claimed that "love is not real unless it is directed toward a particular
object; it becomes universal without ceasing to be real only as a result of analogy and transference" (Weil 2001, 119). Jesus's universal attitude cares for the
neighbor close by, while undermining, at the same time, all those traditional
cultural or religious patterns that often prevent people from caring for those
who are in need. According to Amartya Sen, Jesus's parable is a "reasoned
rejection of the idea of a fixed neighborhood" (Sen 2009, 171; cf. Waldron
2003). It does not depend on an ethnic or a communal solidarity, but "transcends all such boundaries" (Waldron 2003, 350).

From an age-old political perspective, the parable of the Samaritan is
dangerously subversive. It was "utterly destructive of ordinary decency, of
what had, until then, been understood as ethical behavior" (Illich and Cayley
2005, 51). Elijah Benamozegh (1823–1900), the Orthodox rabbi of Leghorn
(Livorno) for over half a century, and a Cabbalist philosopher, is a perfect
example to illustrate the challenge to traditional political thinking signified
by this parable. Benamozegh, who had—quite similarly to Carl Schmitt—
some affinities to pagan thinking and a high estimation of political enmity,

accused Jesus of destroying patriotism with this parable. According to Benamozegh, Judaism surpasses Christianity regarding its attitude towards one's
country. "Without a political enemy, there can be no country" (Benamozegh
1873, 73). In his eyes Jesus chose the example of the Samaritan in order to
destroy political life, because asking the Jew to love the Samaritan would
have been, in Benamozegh's nineteenth century, to ask "the Pole to love the
Cossack, or the Italian, the Austrian soldier" (Benamozegh 1873, 84).

   According to Ivan Illich, a Catholic priest and social critic, the only way
to understand this parable today is "to imagine the Samaritan as a Palestinian ministering to a wounded Jew" (Illich and Cayley 2005, 50) or, to even
sharpen this point, a Hamas fighter helping an Israeli soldier. This story
marks a significant break with all forms of ethics that are based on a special
care of one's own family, group, or race. "This deeply threatens the traditional
basis for ethics, which was always an *ethnos,* a historically given 'we' which
precedes any pronunciation of the word 'I'" (Illich and Cayley 2005, 47).
Jesus brings a new form of love into the world that undermines and exceeds
all traditional understandings of it. Illich comes in such insights close to
mimetic theory and its insight into the biblical overcoming of the scapegoat
mechanism. The ethnically closed ethos of a group gives way to individual-
ity and universalism as soon as the scapegoat mechanism is uncovered. One
can refer, for instance, to Girard's reading of Sophocles's *Antigone,* where
he criticizes Creon's traditional attempt to distinguish between friends and
enemies from a Christian perspective by likening Antigone's protest against
Creon's political attitude to Jesus's repudiation of enmity. Echoing Simone
Weil's understanding of Antigone, he states: "The City of Man is founded on
hating together, and whatever mutual love it enjoys rests on that foundation,
which Antigone, like Christ, brings to light in order to repudiate it" (Girard
1987b, 244).

Globalization and Its Apocalyptic Threats

Ivan Illich's book in which we find his reflection on the parable of the
Samaritan is a deeply *apocalyptic* book in which topics like the Antichrist
or the "mystery of lawlessness" (2 Thess. 2:7) play a central role (Palaver
2007b). According to Illich, we are not living in a "post-Christian" but in

an "apocalyptic world" (Illich and Cayley 2005, 177, 179). What Illich says about our modern world in general is particularly true in regard to the ongoing weakening of those traditional patterns that helped to contain internal rivalries and competition by parochial altruism, invoking a common enemy. Biblical revelation is slowly undermining parochial politics, leading to a planetary mimetic crisis in which competition runs hot. Global terrorism and the global war against terror are very visible signs of this dangerous crisis. Several conservative political thinkers were partly aware of how the biblical revelation contributed to this crisis and tried to slow it down by strengthening political forms of parochial altruism as far as possible. Carl Schmitt, a German law scholar who was closer to Christendom than to the message of the Bible, struggled hard to reconcile his political emphasis on the friend-enemy distinction with the perspective of the Gospel (Schmitt 2007, 29). According to him, the demand in the Sermon on the Mount to love our enemies is not related to the political enemy at all, but only to our private enemies. Leo Strauss and Eric Voegelin, too, understood that the biblical message threatens closed societies and leads step by step to the modern crisis we today call globalization (Ranieri 2009). Both these thinkers identified themselves at least partly with Celsus, a pagan philosopher criticizing Christianity in the second century, on the grounds that it tries to bring the entire world under one law, particularly at the risk of provoking a global civil war (Palaver 2007a, 80, 82, 92–93). According to Leo Strauss, natural law without the assistance of divine revelation views closed societies and not a universal society as according with nature (Strauss 1971, 130–64). He clearly favors this unassisted type of natural law: "Classical political philosophy opposes to the universal and homogeneous state a substantive principle. It asserts that the society natural to man is the city, that is, a closed society" (Strauss 1995, x). Girard's mimetic theory is capable of explaining why the biblical revelation contributed to the development of our globalized world, with its positive potentials as well as its new threats. According to Girard, the biblical revelation slowly transformed all closed societies derived from the scapegoat mechanism into our globalizing world of today:

> The gradual loosening of various centers of cultural isolation began in the Middle Ages and has now led into what we call "globalization," ... The true engine of progress is the slow decomposition of the closed worlds rooted

in victim mechanisms. This is the force that destroyed archaic societies and henceforth dismantles the ones replacing them, the nations we call "modern." (Girard 2001, 165–66)

According to Girard, the truth of Christianity is "destroying everything by depriving us of our enemies" (Girard 2010, 199). By "everything," he means the entire set of accommodations by which we evade the challenge and the reproach of the Kingdom, and its "absolute peace."

Post-Constantinian Christianity

Before I focus on the answer that is needed in this critical situation of our contemporary world, I must first come back to Christianity's role in the ongoing process tending towards globalization. It is important to note that Christianity has contributed to this process not only positively, but also negatively. Historically speaking, Christianity is not a completely dynamic religion transcending any and all remnants of static religion; rather, it is a "mixed religion" in which pagan patterns still play a role, although they have been slowly transformed by mysticism (Bergson 1935, 183).

We can first realize this fact in the term "parochialism" itself, which stems from the Latin term for "parish," and which is therefore not alien to historical Christianity at all. Simone Weil, who identified deeply with the universal attitude of the parable of the Samaritan, and who pleaded for a "new saintliness" in our world of today that has to be universal in a very broad understanding of being "Catholic," was very critical of a church to which many of its members attached themselves "as to an earthly country" (Weil 2001, 49–51):

> Less vast things than the universe, among them the Church, impose obligations which can be extremely far-reaching. They do not, however, include the obligation to love.... Our love should stretch as widely across all space, and should be as equally distributed in every portion of it, as is the very light of the sun. Christ has bidden us to attain to the perfection of our heavenly Father by imitating his indiscriminate bestowal of light. (Weil 2001, 49–50)

Historical Christianity often failed to emulate its divine model.

Regarding historical Christianity, we must be aware, consequently, of its mixed character, the product of an intermingling of static and dynamic religion; but we have also to take the measure of an even more complex problem. The Constantinian shift resulted in a Christian universalism that only seemingly resembles dynamic religion and its outreach towards an open society. This type of universalism is a form of imperialism that looks like a form of universalist mysticism but remains bound to static religion and to closed societies (Bergson 1935, 268–69). Bergson was very well aware that a merely gradual enlargement of a social entity does not lead to an open society. The expansion of closed societies does not change their nature: "It is not by widening the bounds of the city that you reach humanity; between a social morality and a human morality the difference is not one of degree but of kind" (Bergson 1935, 25; cf. 22–23; Niebuhr 1960, 168). Similarly, Girard also makes clear that the notion and practice of empire remains close to the scapegoat mechanism because it wants "peace" by "domination" and is "based on exclusion" (Girard 2010, 200; cf. Girard 1991, 200–209).

Imperialistic universalism only seemingly leads towards an open society. In reality it remains a closed society, even where it aspires to take in the whole world to be governed by a world state. If Christianity wants to contribute to an open society and a unified globalized solidarity without the need of outside enemies, it has to overcome its own temptation towards collective pride. It has to detach itself from Constantinianism and its inherent imperial temptation. Girard clearly criticizes the Constantinian distortion of the message of the Gospels:

> Beginning with Constantine, Christianity triumphed at the level of the state and soon began to cloak with its authority persecutions similar to those in which the early Christians were victims. Like so many subsequent religions, ideological, and political enterprises, Christianity suffered persecution while it was weak and became the persecutor as soon as it gained strength. (Girard 1986, 204 [corrected translation])

John Howard Yoder, a Mennonite theologian who taught until his death in 1997 at Notre Dame University, was very much aware of the Constantinian danger (Yoder 1984, 135–47). He recommended Catholic and Christian repentance from Constantinianism in a lecture on interfaith dialogue he gave in Jerusalem in 1976 (Yoder 1994, 242–61: "The Disavowal of Constantine: An Alternative Perspective on Interfaith Dialogue"; cf. Hauerwas 2007, 66–72). This kind of repentance means a new concern for the Jewish heritage and the meekness, humility, and nonviolence of Jesus Christ. Instead of imperial pride, Yoder refers us to the particular Jewish tradition of the Suffering Servant in Second Isaiah and the particularity of the example of Jesus. In Yoder's eyes, particularity and universalism are not alternatives in the Bible. Christians are first of all asked to love their local neighbors and live with them in solidarity by following the particularity of the way of Jesus. As we have seen above in discussing the parable of the Good Samaritan, Jesus did not recommend an abstract and cosmopolitan universalism neglecting the needy nearby, but instead showed a universal concern for all the different people in his proximity. Such an approach will contribute much more to peace in our pluralistic world than all attempts to find a common denominator rejecting all particular traditions at a global level. We are in need of the spirit of humility flowing from different religious traditions to overcome collective pride governing closed societies, as well as all forms of universal imperialism (cf. Niebuhr 1960, 135, 151).

According to the mystic philosopher Simone Weil, it is the *supernatural,* i.e., a world-transcending reality, that enables us to love our neighbors in a universal manner—something exemplified by Jesus. Only by reaching out to a "reality outside the world" are we really enabled to love and to act justly in this world (Weil 1998, 132). This emphasis on the supernatural has, of course, to be understood broadly because it includes Buddhism as well as other traditions that do not explicitly believe in a personal God. It even includes certain humanistic traditions. But all these traditions are only true as far as they allow us to overcome our pride and our natural inclinations towards worldly power by leading us on a path of renunciation enabling creative love. According to Weil, only an act of renunciation enabled the Good Samaritan to help his neighbor. "In denying oneself, one becomes capable under God of establishing someone else by a creative affirmation" (Weil 2001, 91). Similarly, the Christian philosopher Nicholas Wolterstorff also understands the Good Samaritan's compassion as an act of renunciation: "Compassion is *kenotic,* to use a term common in contemporary theology; compassion is self-emptying" (Wolterstorff 2008, 217). Weil understood very well that all true religions emulate God's restraint and renunciation by which he creates, thereby contradicting many all-too-human imaginings of divine power:

The religions which have a conception of this renunciation, this voluntary distance, this voluntary effacement of God, his apparent absence and his secret presence here below, these religions are true religion, the translation into different languages of the great Revelation. The religions which represent divinity as commanding wherever it has the power to do so seem false. Even though they are monotheistic they are idolatrous. (Weil 2001, 89)

I think that Girard's mimetic theory is deeply rooted in a mystic experience that opened his eyes to precisely this God who brings together renunciation and creative love. Working on his very first book, Girard discovered the God of the Gospels. He took over Simone Weil's expression "creative renunciation"—albeit without citing the French mystic at all—to summarize the pivotal last chapter of his first book, *Deceit, Desire, and the Novel* (Girard 1966, 307; Weil 2001, 99). It is this insight that enabled Girard to understand the deep difference between the parochial altruism as it emerges from the archaic past and Christian universalism.

Notes

1. Also Reinhold Niebuhr maintains a clear distinction between the prophetic religion in the Old Testament and Greek philosophy, which did not reach the same level of universalism (Niebuhr 1996, 1:215). See also Girard's distinction between the logos of Greek philosophy, or of Heidegger, and the Logos of the New Testament (see Girard 1978, pt. 2, chap. 4: "Le logos d'Héraclite et le Logos de Jean").

2. "When you come upon your enemy's ox or donkey going astray, you shall bring it back. When you see the donkey of one who hates you lying under its burden and you would hold back from setting it free, you must help to set it free" (Ex. 23:4–5). "When an alien resides with you in your land, you shall not oppress the alien. The alien who resides with you shall be to you as the citizen among you; you shall love the alien as yourself, for you were aliens in the land of Egypt: I am the LORD your God" (Lev. 19:33–34). On potentials to overcome enmity in the Hebrew Bible, see also the work of Marc Gopin (Gopin 2002, 41–42, 78–79).

Cited Texts and Further Reading

Aeschylus. 1983. *Aeschylus in Two Volumes.* Vol. 2, *Agamemnon, Libation-Bearers, Eumenides, Fragments.* Loeb Classical Library. Cambridge, MA: Harvard University Press. Original edition, 1926.

Benamozegh, Elijah. 1873. *Jewish and Christian Ethics with a Criticism on Mahomedism.* San Francisco: Emanuel Blochman. Original edition, 1867.

Bergson, Henri. 1935. *The Two Sources of Morality and Religion.* Translated by R. A. Audra, C. Brereton, and W. H. Carter. London: Macmillan & Co. Original edition, 1932.

Bowles, Samuel. 2008. "Conflict: Altruism's Midwife." *Nature* 456, no. 7220: 326–27.

Buber, Martin. 2010. *Politische Schriften, Zweitausendeins Klassiker-Bibliothek.* Frankfurt am Main: Zweitausendeins.

Butterfield, Herbert. 1954. *Christianity and History.* London: Bell. Original edition, 1949.

Durkheim, Émile 1984. *The Division of Labor in Society.* Translated by W. D. Halls. New York: Free Press. Original edition, 1893.

Esler, Philip F. 2000. "Jesus and the Reduction of Intergroup Conflict: The Parable of the Good Samaritan in the Light of Social Identity Theory." *Biblical Interpretation: A Journal of Contemporary Approaches* 8, no. 4: 325–57.

Girard, René. 1966. *Deceit, Desire, and the Novel: Self and Other in Literary Structure.* Translated by Y. Freccero. Baltimore: Johns Hopkins University Press. Original edition, 1961.

———. 1977. *Violence and the Sacred.* Translated by P. Gregory. Baltimore: Johns Hopkins University Press. Original edition, 1972.

———. 1986. *The Scapegoat.* Translated by Y. Freccero. Baltimore: Johns Hopkins University Press. Original edition, 1982.

———. 1987a. *Job: The Victim of His People.* Translated by Y. Freccero. Stanford, CA: Stanford University Press.

———. 1987b. *Things Hidden since the Foundation of the World: Research undertaken in collaboration with J.-M. Oughourlian and G. Lefort.* Translated by S. Bann and M. Metteer. Stanford, CA: Stanford University Press. Original edition, 1978.

———. 1991. *A Theater of Envy: William Shakespeare.* Oxford: Oxford University Press.

———. 2001. *I See Satan Fall Like Lightning.* Translated by J. G. Williams. Maryknoll, NY: Orbis Books. Original edition, 1999.

———. 2004. *Oedipus Unbound: Selected Writings on Rivalry and Desire.* Edited and with an introduction by Mark R. Anspach. Stanford, CA: Stanford University Press.

———. 2010. *Battling to the End: Conversations with Benoît Chantre.* Translated by M. Baker. Studies in Violence, Mimesis, and Culture. East Lansing: Michigan State University Press. Original edition, 2007.

Gopin, Marc. 2002. *Between Eden and Armageddon: The Future of World Religions, Violence, and Peacemaking.* Oxford: Oxford University Press. Original edition, 2000.

Hauerwas, Stanley. 2007. *The State of the University: Academic Knowledges and the Knowledge of God.* Oxford: Blackwell.

Hays, Richard B. 1997. *The Moral Vision of the New Testament: Community, Cross, New Creation, a Contemporary Introduction to New Testament Ethics.* Edinburgh: T&T Clark. Original edition, 1996.

Hesiod. 2006. *Theogony. Works and Days. Testimonia.* Translated by G. W. Most. Loeb Classical Library. Cambridge, MA: Harvard University Press.

Höffe, Otfried. 2002. *Demokratie im Zeitalter der Globalisierung.* München: Verlag C.H. Beck. Original edition, 1999.

Huntington, Samuel P. 1996. *The Clash of Civilizations and the Remaking of World Order.* New York: Simon & Schuster.

Illich, Ivan, and David Cayley. 2005. *The Rivers North of the Future: The Testament of Ivan Illich as told by David Cayley.* Foreword by Charles Taylor. Toronto: Anansi.

Niebuhr, Reinhold. 1960. *The Children of Light and the Children of Darkness: A Vindication of Democracy and a Critique of Its Traditional Defense.* New York: Charles Scribner's Sons. Original edition, 1944.

———. 1986. *The Essential Reinhold Niebuhr: Selected Essays and Addresses.* New Haven: Yale University Press.

———. 1996. *The Nature and Destiny of Man: A Christian Interpretation.* 2 vols. Library of Theological Ethics. Louisville, KY: Westminster John Knox Press.

Palaver, Wolfgang. 1998. *Die mythischen Quellen des Politischen: Carl Schmitts Freund-Feind-Theorie, Beiträge zur Friedensethik.* Stuttgart: Verlag W. Kohlhammer.

———. 1999. "Mimesis and Nemesis: The Economy as a Theological Problem." *Telos* 117: 79–112.

———. 2007a. "Carl Schmitt's 'Apocalyptic' Resistance against Global Civil War." In *Politics and Apocalypse,* ed. R. G. Hamerton-Kelly, 69–94. East Lansing: Michigan State University Press.

———. 2007b. "Review of *The Rivers North of the Future: The Testament of Ivan Illich as told by David Cayley,* by Ivan Illich and David Cayley." *Bulletin of the Colloquium on Violence & Religion* 30: 13–15.

Ranieri, John J. 2009. *Disturbing Revelation: Leo Strauss, Eric Voegelin, and the Bible.* Columbia: University of Missouri Press.

Rousseau, Jean-Jacques. 1990. *The Social Contract and Discourses.* Translated by G.D.H. Cole, J. H. Brumfitt, and J. C. Hall. London: Dent. Original edition, 1986.

Schmitt, Carl. 2007. *The Concept of the Political.* Translated by G. Schwab. Chicago: University of Chicago Press. Original edition, 1932.

Sen, Amartya. 2009. *The Idea of Justice.* Cambridge, MA: Belknap Press of Harvard University Press.

Strauss, Leo. 1971. *Natural Right and History.* Chicago: University of Chicago Press. Original edition, 1953.

———. 1995. *Liberalism Ancient and Modern.* Foreword by A. Bloom. Chicago: University of Chicago Press. Original edition, 1968.

Waldron, Jeremy. 2003. "Who Is My Neighbor? Humanity and Proximity." *The Monist* 86, no. 3: 333.

Weil, Simone. 1998. *Writings Selected with an Introduction by Eric O. Springsted.* Edited by R. Ellsberg. Modern Spiritual Masters. Maryknoll, NY: Orbis Books.

———. 2001. *Waiting for God.* Translated by E. Craufurd. New York: Perennial Classics. Original edition, 1951.

Wolterstorff, Nicholas. 2008. *Justice: Rights and Wrongs.* Princeton, NJ: Princeton University Press.

Yoder, John Howard. 1984. *The Priestly Kingdom: Social Ethics as Gospel.* Notre Dame, IN: University of Notre Dame Press.

———. 1994. *The Royal Priesthood: Essays Ecclesiological and Ecumenical.* Grand Rapids, MI: William B. Eerdmans Publishing Co.

Girard, the Gospels, and the Symmetrical Inversion of the Founding Murder

Paul Gifford

The figure of sense I propose to examine is neatly summarized by René Girard himself in a recent text, "On War and Apocalypse" (2009):

> What I call (after Freud) the "founding murder"—the immolation of a scapegoat victim who is both guilty of disorder and able to restore order— is constantly reenacted in the rituals at the origin of our institutions. Since the dawn of humanity, millions of innocent victims have been killed in this way to enable their fellow humans to live together or at least not destroy one another.
>
> This is the implacable logic of the archaic sacred, which myths dissimulate; [but dissimulate] less and less as humans become increasingly self-aware. The decisive point in this evolution is Christian revelation. . . . *Christianity is a founding murder in reverse* [my italics].

In *Achever Clausewitz,* where he first coins this same thought, Girard adds: "Christ came to take the place of the victim. He placed himself at the heart of the system to reveal the hidden springs of the system. The 'second Adam'—to pick up St Paul's expression—reveals to us how the 'first' came about. The

Passion teaches us that humankind comes out of sacrifice, that it was born with the religious" (Girard 2007, 19 [2010, xix]).

That figure of *antithetical reprise,* linking those two figures of *scapegoat murder,* is of extreme interest to us because it opens up to understanding the space of peril and of possibility sketched out, ambiguously, *in between*—the space of evolutionary "survival" (first figure) and of Christian "salvation" (second figure).

My ground plan for exploring it is simple. Take a standard isosceles triangle. Flip it out sideways at one corner, producing two triangles standing side by side along the same baseline; then swivel the *second* of these around its center of rotation in the same plane.[1] You obtain, between figure A and figure Z, a relation of *symmetrical inversion.* The *identical* second figure is now presented *inversely, antithetically—"in reverse."*

How we do interpret that formal relationship? What significance does it have for our larger theme: can humankind escape, override, or transcend the default mechanisms programmed by our evolutionary history? Can we, in a word, "survive our origins"?

Figure A: The "Founding Murder"

Our volume introduction has sketched out elementarily what Girard means by this; but some elucidation is in order.

A number of otherwise intelligent readers simply "do not get it"; or perhaps, rather, they are scandalized and dissuaded from further thought by what they do get. The shorthand label, with its "mythic" resonance, is troublesome—as is also, these days, the reference to fallen idol Freud. Social anthropologists have been known to respond badly to Girard's text-based theoretical model. ("What is this vast, evidence-light hypothesis purporting to describe the origins of culture, and the way all human cultures generate and manage violence? Where's the *fieldwork?*") And is this theory not, anyway, just a "video nasty"? Darwin told us we were all descended from apes; and we were just getting over that shock to human self-esteem when along came Girard and added that our evolutionary emergence implies also that we are the children of Aztec-style blood sacrifice.

It seems important here to specify how Girard comes by his notion of a "founding murder" and what sort of theory this is. If the theory seems strange, as it can at first sight, we might try thinking of the Girardian hypothesis as some sort of equivalent, in the domain of the *human social psyche,* of what, in the field of theoretical physics, is understood by "Big Bang" theory—this analogy or model providing a suggestive *first approach* to its heuristic form, its epistemological standing, and its potential fruitfulness.

Girard too starts from a quite observable (yet very ill-observed) universal, not unlike microwave radiation noise—a phenomenon that, as physicists belatedly realized, is present everywhere, all unnoticed and undeciphered, in the background of all their observations.[2] For his part, Girard notices that all human desiring is "mimetic": it is *desire-upon-imitation,* mediated and modeled by *other people* within a *social* field of overlapping and mutually interactive desires. He then sees what immense virtualities exist, within the social desire-field so conceived, for generating rivalry and conflict. Already, in his first work on the novel, the negative energy crackles, making that Girardian "triangle of mimetic desire" spin on its axis and morph into a virtual black hole, capable of decisively warping social space (Girard 1961).

To that basic *structure of negative reciprocity,* Girard then adds an account of its *dynamic quality.* The conflictual charge of mimetic rivalry in humans will increase exponentially, and become contagious externally, precisely because it is a mimetic phenomenon. We are asked to grasp that a *runaway dynamic* is at work here—which means that the "black holes" represented by feud, vendetta, or crusade will tend, fatefully, to deepen, proliferate, and fuse, thus engaging all relationalities within a given community. Here is a radical new light on what anthropologists are accustomed to call "group intelligence" in humans: it represents the obverse face of human superiority, as gifted by evolution—the peril that answers human potential.

What it suggests is that any human grouping is subject, visibly or invisibly, to an extreme peril of violent implosion—from which it follows (eventually, but in all deductive rigor) that *containing* and *managing* self-generated violence must be (visibly or less visibly) the *prime possibility condition* and the *number one imperative* of human social life at all times and in all places.

Our theoretical physicists, following the inferential trail of their background radiation noise, knew they had to run backwards, in evolutionary space and time, the scenario of the implosion of stars and planetary systems that confirmed their theory. In so doing, they arrived at a scenario of explosion: hence a theory of the generating origin in time-and-space of an expanding physical cosmos. Is there, analogously, evidence of an *anthropological* big bang in the human (i.e., cultural and social) space-time of life on earth?

The suggestive basic datum, long known to anthropologists, is that the process of hominization is itself an accelerating emergence of novelty, and that it introduces into evolving physical and biological nature a formidable new principle of accelerated change. From the appearance some 8.5 to 10 million years ago of hominid primates, via the advent of the genus *Homo* some 2 million years ago, through the emergence of *Homo sapiens* half a million years ago, it reached a stable threshold (*Homo sapiens sapiens*) some 100,000 to 32,000 years ago. Over a few tens of thousands of years, *Homo sapiens sapiens* conquered every climate region of the earth. Starting some ten thousand years ago, agriculture and domestication of animals began; cities and writing soon followed; and history records an accelerating rhythm of transformation ever since.

At the heart of this quickening novelty, Girard sees, in effect, something akin to a contained explosion—the first evidence for which is to be found in the earliest oral and written traces that have come down to us in the form of religious mythologies the world over, and, nearer to home in respect of Indo-European cultures and civilizations, in ancient Greek tragedy (Girard 1972). These earliest forms of collective self-representation, if we know how to decode the signals they emit, form a kind of relay or listening ear reaching back in time to human evolutionary origins, which are, to all seeming, irretrievably lost and unknowable. Both genres resonate still with consistent and convergent patterns referring us insistently back, as if to some obscurely discerned proto-Event that they half-remember.

The figure of sense suggested by these convergent echolocations of origin is that there is indeed, at the root and origin of human social groupings, a *mimetic crisis*—a threatening black hole of collective self-destruction. Not, of course, one single proto-event (as Freud imagined in his *ur*-scenario of the "slaying of the Father" by the Primitive Horde); but a prototypical event-series. The prototypical crisis—attested with extraordinary consistency in these "culture-fossils"—is resolved by a mechanism of group survival discovered, through the play of autoregulatory variation, by hominid and early human groups under threat of extinction. It is then rehearsed as a secret of group survival, and interiorized culturally in the long process of hominization as a *default response against recurring crises.*

The mechanism known in Girardian theory as *emissary victimization,* or more problematically as "scapegoating," is described in our volume introduction. This overview will have explained sufficiently why, despite its attendant disguises and occultations, this is "murder." We might perhaps object that, if we accept the—relatively early—attestation of the Hebrew Bible, which refers to a period spanning nearly a thousand years BCE, the Book of Leviticus (Lev. 16:8, 10, 21–22, 26) indeed acknowledges scapegoats (in fact, *two* of them); save that, in this text, they are *animals*—and they are *not* "murdered." One is, indeed, slaughtered for sacrifice, but the eponymous other ("Azazel") is driven off into the wilderness on the Day of Atonement (Yom Kippur), charged with the sins of the people. On reflection, however, it will be seen that this apparent divergence from type shows, on the contrary, the prescient accuracy of the theory—provided it is applied with an imaginative suppleness due in respect of all evolving phenomena.

Girard thinks of *animal sacrifice,* in this context, as representing a *modulation,* intervening over time, of *ritual human sacrifice* (Girard 1978). Read in this perspective, the two animals and their differential fates attest very precisely the psychodrama of a *dawning—that is: partial and still hesitant—demystification,* separating out (in fact, by a process of drawing lots) two perceptions that properly archaic sacrifice fused and confused: "our sin" is *both* something requiring an expiatory sacrifice to God *and* a diabolical burden that "we" wish to see lifted from us and carried away by a condemned and rejected sin-bearer . . . or "scapegoat."[3]

But in what sense is it "founding" murder; and is this a *real* or a *mythical* foundation? On the second point, the answer is *both:* each as properly understood. "Founding murder" is a myth-like concept in the sense that it models imaginatively something that is not susceptible to direct scientific observation: the process of human threshold emergence, by which the *extreme threat* of social implosion is *contained and managed,* thus driving outwards and forward, in the place of the threatened implosion, the *expanding universe of human culture and culturally driven change.*

In the constituted mythologies-and-religions so attentively scrutinized by Girard, the "founding murder" at the origin of one's own tribe, tradition, or ethnicity appears in self-justifying misrepresentation (Girard 1972,

1978). The mythology of the tribe, the city, or the people *always* points, albeit obliquely, to a foundational victim—sometimes buried under the actual *foundation stone*—of "our" institutions and achievements (Romulus kills Remus, etc.); except that he is never *shown as* victim, i.e., as a murdered scapegoat whose blood is on "our" hands. The mythic model (despite its pertinence as poetic truth) is thus *also a travesty,* mystifying and untrue insofar as it *camouflages* the blame-transfer, the scapegoat murder, and the guilty moral agency of the collective subject of the mythic tale of identity and origin (Girard 1978, 146–67).

From *Things Hidden* (1978 in the original French text), Girard's modeling hypothesis is set to work in accounting for the actual process by which the hominid line negotiated the threshold of "hominization." Redeveloped by an adequate hermeneutic, which reclaims it from its embeddedness in myth, the model becomes a fully respectable scientific hypothesis, of real explanatory power, subject to verification and falsification.[4] Deductively, the very fact of established group self-identity supposes the excluded Victim (originally: the murdered or ritually sacrificed Victim) as surely as the enactment of algebraic equations, and all the combinatorial operations deriving from them, supposes an equation-forming equivalence ($= 0$).

Can we be as sure as Girard that our earliest ancestors, even in a testing evolutionary environment, stood in dire and crucial need of such a protective default mechanism? Readers skeptical on that point might perhaps be encouraged to listen to recordings of chimpanzee screams of rage, and then be asked to imagine those fearsome animal warriors, or their *habilis* second cousins, transmuted into erect, plain-roaming hominid groups armed with artifact weapons—but also with superior group intelligence and tactical skill, *and* the capacity to remember hurt and take revenge . . . *and* to use artifact weapons to devastating effect . . . *and* to fight to the death intraspecifically (Girard 1978).

If we then factor in adequately the great human specificity highlighted by Girard—the runaway dynamic of negative mimetic reciprocity—we gain a realistic *aperçu* of why humankind nearly failed to make it across the threshold (Girard 1978, 133–45). Formidable as they were, environmental challenges may yet turn out to have been less menacing overall to the emergent hominid line than were the perils of social implosion and mutual destruction between groups. What we already know is that the challenges of environment often compounded and exacerbated the perils of intraspecific violence.

• • •

Scapegoat murder is thus seen as genuinely foundational for human societies in a primary, if limited, first sense: it enables them to survive the successive crises generated from within the group, and to bond together socio-symbolically, thus realizing the differential advantage of human group intelligence and cooperation. But the selfsame default mechanism is seen by Girard as foundational also in a much stronger, more irradiating sense.

For we have to factor in the set of implications and consequences that this mechanism serves to enfold deep into the practices of human socio-symbolicity and cultural invention, as these things develop in evolutionary/historical time. In this respect, too, "the" founding murder is, ultimately, to be understood as a generic event series: i.e., repeatable, as well as various and developing in its concrete historical expressions. The term serves here to model the way in which the default mechanism itself evolves; how it is interiorized and programmed over time, and elaborated culturally (no doubt retracing genetically transmitted propensities) by the newly complex and mimetically enabled collective psyche; and how this evolutionary development opens to *Homo sapiens* (as we must now call him) the era of mind-generated sociocultural and civilizational advance. It can thus stand for Girard's entire threshold-process scenario.

The process of cultural invention is driven by the formidable need of proto-humans to manipulate symbolically, if also magically, the transcending life forces they experienced within their own communities as so deeply threatening—the attempt to convert these transcending collective energies and forces from a negative to a positive valency, by means of an all-important sacralizing belief in supernatural agency. We have seen how the process of sacralization might have worked in terms of group understanding. The dead victim comes to be seen as the potent bearer of a power of life and death, and then as *the* Power capable of reversing the current of life-energies from negative to positive: such terrible wrath, such amazing beneficence! And the immanent god of the crowd then becomes the center and focus—indeed, the attributed origin—of all social and moral codes developed (always vainly) against a recurrence of internal crisis and the specter of social catastrophe.

What is involved, we perceive, is a *transactional manipulation in the socio-symbolic order*—this movement of the collective psyche being at first, no doubt, totally self-unaware, yet still manipulating, as if in a dream, the brutal resolution by which conflict, disorder, and violence had issued in the collective murder of the scapegoat victim. We have seen that Girard, from this single scenario, derives a generative logic of laws, legal systems, moral codes, and institutions. He explains likewise the ritual forms and practices known to anthropologists, most especially ritual "sacrifice," which is seen as re-enacting ceremonially the founding murder. It does this—here is a further signature leap of Girardian insight—through the bloody immolation of new scapegoat victims.

Ritual sacrifice thus reenacts, ceremonially, the movement of expiation-and-appeasement, which is obscurely remembered to be the community's own saving life-principle. The sacred action that represents these foundational things is staged and replayed ritually (i.e., repeatably), to newly bonding, and newly salutary, effect. We can perhaps already say: to "salvific" effect, since *survival* is here believed to be due to divine agency—survival, peace, and human flourishing being readily construed and received as a form of *deliverance from on high.* Such things are intimated immediately by powerful surges of awed affectivity as registered by the emergent archaic psyche. Primitive man is, indeed, definable as the *sacralizing animal.*

The modern mind, with its greater disembeddedness in immediate experience and its culturally transmitted capital of analytical expertise, might see only a form of psychosocial pharmacology, in which is writ large a pattern already extant in biological nature: the pattern whereby the inoculation of limited and specialized forms of an infected tissue can immunize an organism against a more deadly and general contagion. Here, a ritually prepared and limited dose of violence holds in check, and protects against, the worst effects of generalized mimetic violence. In the archaic mind, a form of crude, pragmatic psycho-theology, rendering account of the *transaction* practiced, is assuredly at work, albeit obscurely, mythically, without explicit self-consciousness. If we spell it out—*as archaic-sacral minds never could or did*—it might look troublingly like a first draft of the particular atonement theory still extant today among the twelve or thirteen such theories known to Christian theologians, and still used by some "fundamentalist" believers to account for the effects of the crucifixion of Jesus: the theory known as *penal substitution.* ("Troublemakers? Offered up to the gods, they are: representing us, substituted for us, punished in our place. Anyway, that's us off the butcher's hook. And I don't mind saying: thanks be to the gods!")

This genetic account of "sacrifice" (in its first, primitive or "archaic-sacral" acceptance) retraces the "enfolded" meaning of the "founding murder." Society's scapegoat victim, at first sacralized, then hypostasized, becomes the god (or gods); and the god magically disculpates the bloody human hands and the acquisitive, rivalrous, and warring human hearts at the real origin of the mimetic crisis—meanwhile blessing and consecrating all the laws and moral codes that *Homo sapiens* is busy inventing so as to inhibit a return of the mimetic crisis, and thereby guarantee (at least until the *next* descent into turbulence and crisis) the necessary goods of social coherence, stabilizing confidence, authority, and order. In this sense, the default mechanism defined *founds the very possibility of all human cultural and social development.*

◆   ◆   ◆

"Founding murder" thus represents an empirical survivalist outcome in the image of many other ingenious "solutions'" thrown up and programmed by self-organizing evolutionary process. But, of course, the "deal" (or transaction) involved, if neat and advantageous, is too good to be *true*—just as, conversely, it is also *too bad* to be an entire or exclusive truth about the origins of religion and human moral nature.[5] The divinity invoked is actually a self-mystifying fiction of the violence-ridden human community; and that fiction obscures from view the truly explanatory phenomenon of moral imperfection in humankind—something *enfolded* deep into all practices, behaviors, institutions, and values of our psychosocial being, just as it has come in turn to *enfold* collective self-perception, like a *mystifying dreamsphere.*

That dreamsphere is precisely what Girard calls "myth": and it represents the third culture-founding practice generated by emissary victimization. Religions-and-mythologies tell the identity story of the community, *while disguising its "founding murder."* They project a *dreamsphere remembrance* of origins, since they speak always from the point of view of the victimizers. They thus constitute, implicitly, *persecutory narratives* or *sacrificers' tales.*

For which there is a real price to be paid: the self-justifying mythic dreamsphere imprisons *Homo sapiens* in an unsightedness of self-mystification. It opens him to all the delusions of religious transactionalism. And a cruel and tragic prison this is. Human civilizational progress, human spiritual development, remain thereby *mortgaged* to a defective symbolico-sacral defense mechanism, ignorant of itself and which is only partially and very provisionally effective in managing human violence. This condemns humankind to an eternal and, potentially, *infernal* "return of the same"—a condition Girard shows to be represented as "accursedness" and as "fate" in Greek tragedy.

If we attempt to summarize this ambiguous evolutionary inheritance, therefore, the most exact account of "founding murder," with its ritualized prolongations in the form of archaic-sacral "sacrifice," is that it *contains violence*. It "contains" it in the double sense that it *holds it in check*, while also *recycling, reproducing,* and *refracting* it indefinitely, *not knowing what it does.* The evolutionary emergence and "survival" of the species depends on it, since without it, our species could not have cleared the threshold of hominization. And yet, as we must shortly proceed to observe, *survival,* for humankind, is *not yet salvation.*

Already, however, we are able to establish a clear discernment of difference as between (1) archaic-sacral (or so-called "natural" religion), and (2) the *phylum* of more evolved or higher religions, notably the Abrahamic faiths. It is here that we begin to see the *ground plan* of the Girardian "chateau," and the entire point and purpose of its second wing.

This distinguishing or differential reading commands Girard's entire approach to the Hebrew scriptures. They always "remember" archaic practice (Abraham believes he is called to *immolate* his son, and prepares to do so—only to find God truly *Other,* and consequently the object and practice of "sacrifice" likewise). Yet, in the Genesis story of temptation and exile, for instance, or the immediately following account of "founding murder" (in the story of Cain and Abel), and in so many more episodes, Girard detects at work a ferment of subversive novelty, challenging, reworking, and replacing elements of the archaic sacred. He is fascinated by and deeply admiring of these "figures" foreshadowing the insights of the gospels—observing, as he believes, the *opening up* of inherited archaic religion to light and grace "from above."

If space allowed us to follow his reading, we should, however, see that not even at the point of its fullest emergence from the logic of archaic sacrality—a point he identifies in the conception of the Suffering Servant of Deutero-Isaiah—can the process of "demythification" be said to have been carried through to its logical term. The sacrificial Temple survives—and with it, the legal prohibitions, and the mythical stories, and the theocratic

state. Above all, a "monstrous Double" survives: the God of the archaic sacrificial system—the wrathful, retributive, and often bloodthirsty Jehovah of
Hebrew tribal imagining. Save that now, if we are reading from the script
of that singular Girardian grammar of violence and the sacred, we must
remember to add: which is *also our own "default-imagining," as programmed
by evolutionary process.*

With the same Girardian primer of archaic sacrality in mind, we can
see how the originality of the Hebrew Bible is expressed and attested—not
in some exceptional and suspect obsession with violence, but in the way it
addresses, grapples with, and profoundly modifies the *deep-laid and obscure
foundational link between actual human violence and the archaic sacred.*

Equipped with these insights, we should not be taken aback to recognize
the figure of founding and sacrificial scapegoat murder as *summoned up, represented,* and *reworked* in the Christian gospels.

Figure Z: The Crucifixion of Jesus

The classic formulation of the victimary mechanism is given very precisely by
Caiaphas, promoter of the plot to kill Jesus: "It is better for you to have one
man die for the people than to have the whole nation destroyed" (Jn. 11:50).
The formulation is "classic" in that the mechanism of emissary victimization
itself has become a well-rehearsed, self-aware gambit: a cynical calculation
of the *raison d'état,* deployed with the intent of *economizing* violence and
destruction self-protectively, even as it *recycles* these things.

For that very reason, the default mechanism will, in this presentation,
appear worn down in its sacral potency—not as good as it once was at ward-
ing off violent catastrophe. True: it will suffice, immediately, to stave off
the riot Caiaphas fears (Lk. 22:2; Jn. 11:48); and it will reconcile those rival
power-brokers Pilate and Herod (Lk. 23:12). But apocalypse still looms; and
the human sacrifice made to Roman power will not prevent the destruction
of the Second Temple in 70 AD.

We have no trouble, either, in recognizing in the Passion of Jesus a concerted ritual sacrifice; or of discerning, embedded within the complex ritual
elaboration surrounding it, a *collective lynching,* reminiscent of the most
primitive forms of founding murder. The cosmopolitan Passover crowd is

worked by rage-modeling leaders. Responding to Pilate, it vociferates: "Crucify him!" (Matt. 27:23; Mk. 15:14; Lk. 23:21; Jn. 19:15). Pilate is seeking from the crowd both political sanction for killing and exemption from blame: *vox populi, vox dei* (this very Roman theme is well illustrated in the film *Gladiator*). The gross, crowd-pleasing practice of condemnation-by-acclamation of the victim goes back to the need for mimetic unanimity in the *carnival* or *festival* practices associated with archaic religious sacrifice (see Girard 1972, ch. 5). Specifically, the process of choosing the victim—Jesus or Barrabas?—recalls, ironically, the lot-drawing of Leviticus. The essential action accomplished, at all events, is the most primitive one possible: a collective rejection or expulsion of the Victim, henceforth marked out for death by a mimetically realized unanimity-in-violence.

The voice of the collective god is terrifying, paralyzing. "For they were afraid," says gospel writer Mark (Mk. 16:8), noting cryptically how he himself (or some avatar of his) had run away, shameful and naked; and how that same denuding archaic-sacral fear had gripped the disciples still, even at the empty tomb, before the dumbfounding fact of the Resurrection.

Luke, for his part, gives us the collective curse mimetically transmitted, even on the Cross, by the unrepentant "thief" (i.e., brigand) (Lk. 23:41–42). All four gospel writers stress the way in which the disciples themselves, with Peter emphatically foregrounded, are also caught up in this same tide of mimetic persuasion or contagion, as they unanimously flee or deny Jesus. Then there is the derision and cursing of the bystanding crowds (Lk. 23:35–36), familiar to us from accounts of the public executions practiced still in the seventeenth and eighteenth centuries in Europe—another attestingly "primitive" feature.

Nor must we forget, in the sheer diabolical perfection of its institutionally concentrated and transmitted violence, the modality of this scapegoat murder. Crucifixion is a form of execution-by-torture, reserved for slaves, criminals, and foreign enemies of the state; it is practiced at the margins of the city from which the victim is expelled; and it is visibly derived from the most primitive sacrificial ritual (Girard 1982, 260). It enacts, in agonizingly slow motion, a *sentence of collective reprobation* writ pedagogically large. It is *par excellence a scapegoat death,* albeit enacted here *judicially,* and pointed up, for public edification, by an inscribed textual commentary (Lk. 23:38; Jn. 19:19–23). In this sense, it is part of a concerted cultural elaboration, transmitting spontaneous crowd violence institutionally, to maximum socio-political effect.

There are other, prior, ritual aspects familiar from archaic-sacrificial traditions: the derisive ritual of robing, crowning, and "royal" acclamation; the scourging of the victim; the casting of lots for the seamless garment. Yet still, despite this ritual character, resonant with an entire inheritance of sociocultural practices, and freighted with reminders of all archaic-sacral ritual immolations, this particular instance of crucifixion re-effects, in principle, a primitive form of scapegoat murder. "It is because it reproduces the founding event of all rites that the Passion is related to all the rites of the planet" (Girard 1978, 249ff.; cf. 1977, 119–26).

At one level, therefore, Jesus is a scapegoat victim of human violence *like any other*. Girard declares explicitly that there is *nothing unique, or even unusual, in the malefic or malignant dimension of this crucifixion*—only, he insists, in its work of redemptive revelation (1982, 166), which concerns its dimension of goodness and love: "There is only one transcendence in the gospels, that of the love divine which triumphs over all manifestations of violence and the sacred by revealing their nothingness" (284).

This typological conformity—we might almost say: this representative banality—is *integral to its pertinence and meaning,* as is its recapitulative character, displaying so clearly the logic of this key piece of human psychosocial functioning. Both features are integral to the immense resonance and effect in human history of this event. The Cross, says Girard, *must be recognizable,* if it is to be *operative.* "The event represented has to be the same; otherwise, the gospels could not refute and discredit point by point all the illusions characteristic of mythologies, which correspond to illusions gripping the actors of the Passion" (153).

◆   ◆   ◆

So what, then, is actually *different* about *this* "scapegoat murder," *this* "sacrifice"? Where does Girard think the "inverting" and the "converting" come from? Two points may (all too briefly) be made here.

For Girard, the *innocence of this Victim* is such as to cause the default mechanism of unanimous condemnation, hence also the entire machine of sacral mystification and cover-up to *malfunction.*

No, if we look again, there is *not,* in this scapegoat murder—save fleetingly, at the apex point of the mimetic crisis—a flawless *unanimity*. Pilate, in his rational and equitable moment, has already seen through the charges laid against his victim (Matt. 27:24; Mk. 15:14; Lk. 23:4; Jn. 19:38. See Girard 1982, 159). His wife intervenes urgently, if vainly, to protect this Innocent from capital execution (Matt. 27:19; see Girard 1982, 160). The penitent thief answers the cursing thief in Luke: "this man has done nothing wrong" (Lk. 23:40–42); and in Mark, even the executing centurion's verdict is that this was a just man, in the image of God (Mk. 15:39; cf. Matt. 27:54).

To which conviction, the Resurrection experiences of encounter add a swelling tide of new and freshly motivated counter-conviction.[6] True: if we judge abstractly and quickly, the resurrection retraces the archaic-sacral "second moment," divinizing the victim. But no, this is *no mere replay; it too is a symmetrical inversion:*

> It is no longer men fabricating gods, it is God who has come to take the place of the victim. . . . This victim is divine before any sacralisation. The divine precedes its sacralisation [i.e., it does not *proceed from* it]. This re-establishes the rights of God. (Girard 2007, 109)
>
> In some way, it is because Christ enters into the matrix of false resurrections that he is truly risen. (20)

Phenomenologically, the Resurrection is that which surprises all the actors; which throws into reverse gear and eventually overthrows the mimetic process of sacralization, hence also of self-mystification. So that not only has the scapegoat sentence not "stuck"; not only is the scapegoaters' hatred exposed for what it is ("They hated me without a cause"; Ps 35:19); but the entire enfolded-enfolding system of emissary victimization and scapegoat violence is, for the first time, pierced through and fully exposed by it:

> We have to understand what is played for and lost in the passion; the hold of persecutory representation over humanity as a whole. . . . What the gospels portray for the first time is: the refusal of the stereotyped accusations that persecuting crowds forever accept, eyes closed. (Girard 1982, 154–55)

For the first time, humankind is delivered from its imprisonment in the archaic dreamsphere of self-deceiving mythic falsehood. So much so that the words of Jesus: "They know not what they do" must, *pace* Freud, "be accounted as the first and most decisive declaration *of the unconscious* in human history" (165).

That unveiling, he says, has been, is now, and will be in historical culture-time, world-changing: "It is out of this knowledge that humankind will learn, slowly, very slowly . . . to slip underneath the persecutory representation of violence" (Girard 1982, 162). Where the world's religious mythologies were universally complicit in the mystifying cover-up of humankind's enfoldment within violence, the gospels represent *the archaic-sacral mystification machine working at full tilt and failing;* and they enable us, in its *represented failure,* to deconstruct the very mechanisms of religious authority, political power, mystified sacred rage, social advantage, and double-think that allow "the system" as such to function "below the line," subterraneously.

Girard thus speaks of "this extraordinary work of the gospels: persecutory representation abrogated, broken, revoked" (Girard 1982, 156). In other words, the gospels declare the very thing that, historically, has made and still makes "archaic religion" *archaic.*

This is *not* the work of just any scapegoat victim. A slight shift in the title with which this victim has come to be recognized is significant. This is *not* any banal and malodorous sacrificial *goat.* Looking steadily at the foregrounded Victim, the gospels speak rather of the *"Lamb* of God" (Girard 1982, 173–74). That sense-shift within a functional sameness *preludes* the larger figure of inversion being developed.

I recall at this point the dissenting view expressed by the Norris-Hulse Professor of Divinity (Cambridge), speaking in 2009, at our first Darwin-Girard conference. Girard's reading of the Cross stuck her as partial and suspect, a kind of reductive Gnostic theology, predicated on the idea of saving illumination.

I do not myself think a comprehensive reading of Girardian gospel analysis (as distinct from an impression derived from the one-sidedly "anti-sacrificial reading" initially sketched out in *Things Hidden*) will support the view that Girard is engaged in reducing Christian salvation to illuminated knowledge; still less of cutting theology down to anthropology (nor even of reducing moral evil to its paradigmatic manifestation of violence).[7] He is, rather, as it seems to me, engaged in making the *fullest theological affirmation* of the gospels *comprehensible,* by first *specifying their anthropological content cogently.* As Simone Weil, quoted by Girard, points out, the gospels first reveal humankind, the better to effect the revelation of God.[8]

Girard certainly points us to the key question broached by the gospel texts, a question situated at the frontier between anthropology and theology: "But who do you say that I am?" (Matt. 16:15; Mk. 8:29; Lk. 9:20; cf. Jn. 6:69). And from the direction of anthropology, he does, it seems to me, cast genuine new light on the central actor of the Passion—a light entirely consistent, in the final reckoning, with the attestation of the main New Testament theologians Paul and John.

Showing this adequately would require a book in itself. In default of which, I offer, baldly stated, what I take to be the main thrust of the Girardian reading. The gospel texts, Girard shows, alert us to something new and quite startling: for the first time, the "founding murder," with its process of emissary victimization, its constitutive logic of concealed untruth, and its irradiating consequences of renewed murder and cyclical crisis, is already in *the teaching and healing ministry of Jesus* entirely grasped, explicitly named—and challenged as incompatible with the "Kingdom."

The most immediate evidence of this understanding lies just where we were too embarrassed to seek it: in the so-called "cursing of the Scribes and Pharisees." (To "politically correct" modern ears, and no doubt to many post-Holocaust Jewish ones, this reads spontaneously like early Christian sectarian polemic, even inflamed anti-Semitism—i.e., it reads like a precursor form of religious violence!)

Not so, says Girard. He shows Jesus, addressing the representatives of the Law, challenging them with the consistent record of murder by which the religious leaders of Israel have dealt with the accusing prophets of their common Hebrew tradition, in a continuous series reaching back, via the most recent murder of John the Baptist, to the slaughter of Abel. He challenges them with the recognition of things hidden "from the foundation of the world" (Lk. 11:47–51; cf. Matt. 13:35).

They are addressed, that is (here is an audacious novelty, acutely picked up by Girard), as *spokesmen for the archaic sacred* within the Jewish religious tradition. In one (structural) sense, of course, it could in principle be *any other* religious tradition—since the common substratum of archaic religion is precisely what "survives," genetically speaking, in *all religions.*[9] Abel is not, as Jesus must have known, a canonical prophet of Hebrew tradition. But is he not a "prophet and apostle" in the more universal or fundamental sense that he reveals the truth of the innocent victim and the founding murder?

The true adversary of Jesus is not "the Jews," therefore. It is (in Mark) "the satan" (i.e., God's licensed public prosecutor) or (in John) the "Prince of this world," simply and etymologically known as "the Accuser" or "Satan." These names are exactly translated in the conceptual language of Girardian anthropology as the "principle" or "subject" of the system of the archaic sacred. When John's gospel describes Satan as a "murderer from the beginning," as well as a "liar" (Jn. 8:44), we see stirring, under the appearances of heavy-hitting but obscure religious polemic, the suddenly transparent and luminously apposite sense: what indeed attracts those qualifiers is the *symbolic matrix* of all violent significations realized in all "religions"—i.e., the "founding murder," camouflaged and consecrated as something divinely ordained, protecting its own lie, mendaciously, by means of ongoing, serial murder. "Things hidden from the beginning of the world": exactly so! The expression is precision-engineered and expresses a clear intelligence of "founding murder."

The exposing of the lie at the root of the archaic sacred, this challenge in principle to sacred violence, causes Satan's house to become divided against itself (Mk. 3:23–27; Lk. 11:14–23).[10] Many episodes of the gospel texts analyzed by Girard develop this understanding; they feature so many encounters between Jesus and archaic-sacral human violence. Thus: the aborted stoning of the woman taken in adultery (Jn. 8:1–11; see Girard 1982, 97–99); the decapitation of John the Baptist, presaging the crucifixion of Jesus (Matt. 14:1–12; Mk. 6:14–29; Lk. 9:9; see Girard 1982, 187–220); the healing of the Gerasene demoniac (Mk. 5:1–20, Lk. 8:26–39). This latter essay is a brilliant reading of the psychodrama of violent mimetic reciprocity between scapegoat victim and expelling crowd—a story that *expels* not just actual "demons" but ancient demonology itself (Girard 1982, 243–69). All such readings bear witness to the fact that the default mechanism, *the archaic-sacral expulsion of violence by violence,* is now itself being "expelled," i.e., *lifted.* "But if, by the Spirit *of God,* I expel demons, then for you, the Kingdom of God has arrived" (Matt. 12:28; my italics). For what expels violence and disables the reciprocity of negative mimesis is the perfect imitation of the God-who-is-Love (see Girard 1978, 313–19).

Who, then, *is* Jesus? Girard answers *anthropologically, in the logic of his theory.* Jesus is the One who says: "I see Satan fall like lightning" (Lk. 10:18).

This perspective opens up to real understanding the "apocalyptic" theme of the gospels. Girard insists: the apocalyptic warnings in the gospels refer not to divine, but to manmade, this-worldly violence; more precisely, to a version of the mimetic crisis discernible in the storm clouds once more gathering within and around Israel, a crisis no longer containable by its worn-out and increasingly exposed mechanisms of symbolico-sacral ritual control. Beware, he sees Jesus saying, the paroxysm of Satan challenged. Deprived of its founding control mechanism, the principle of enfolded-enfolding violence that dominates humanity "will know a formidable recrudescence when it enters its death throes" (Girard 1978, 287).

The "powers of heaven" that are said in apocalyptic discourse to be "shaken" (Lk. 21:26) are not Jesus's own, therefore; nor are they those of his heavenly Father. They are those of the sacralized authorities and institutions, values, energies, and cosmic forces *of this world*—insofar as they have been induced, imprudently from their own perspective, to commit an act that exposes once-for-always—and thereby also breaks in principle—their hold over the mimetically suggestible desires of men.

In the end, the reflective judgment of the gospel writers is that the subject of the action, the true *author of the Passion,* is not the Crowd, or the Jewish leaders, or their Roman masters; nor is it even the Fear-and-Violence at the center of established sacral-sacrificial religion. The Passion is shown to involve all of these agencies (which is already remarkable). But what is so much more remarkable is that the gospels display these things traversed and transfigured by the true subject of the action, who is . . . the *Victim himself.*[11]

◆ ◆ ◆

We saw triangle A flip open, declaring its own "double," as the mystifying mechanism jammed. But, in Girard's submission, the gospels give us to observe the movement of *inversion* (and conversion) causing the entire figure to pivot around its *real axis.*

The Victim of the founding murder, in this *reprise,* is entirely lucid about the nature and meaning of the confrontation undertaken; entirely heroic in facing its direst implications; and so utterly assured of its meaning, action, and effect in the world beyond his own death that he consecrates that new figure of sense ritually, in advance, in the form of the transformed symbolic meal.

The Last Supper, in turn, harmonically converts the sense it recalls. It of course retraces the Jewish Passover (complete with its own potent memory of violence and divine counterviolence, even if what it essentially commemorates is "salvation"—i.e., deliverance out of slavery in Egypt). But way beyond and before that reminiscence, back upstream (in evolutionary terms), it recalls the most archaically primitive cannibal *diasparagmos* (Girard 1982, 132). This primitive referent is, however, here transformed into its antithesis: a *sign* of the act of self-offering enacted by the Love divine; and a *sacrament* of participation in the banquet of the Kingdom that comes ("Thou on earth both Priest and Victim / In the Eucharistic feast," as hymn writer Chatterton Dix very succinctly puts it).

The reversal effected could hardly be more complete. "Sacrifice" once meant: "bloody immolation of scapegoat victim"; it *signified,* that is, in the image and logic of the founding murder. Here, it signifies in the image of this ultimate *self-offering of Jesus,* undertaken for the sake of the world—out of love, in response to the Love divine, in the perfect image and likeness of that first Love.[12] The second, reworked figure of sense is no mere replay; it is "abyssally different" from the first (Girard 1978, 316).[13]

In the last analysis, Girard's novel and transforming figure of sense is this: Jesus, knowing *intimately* the "founding murder," consents to enter into it and assume it *self-sacrificially*—as *Victim.* The Love divine must, in the end, itself suffer in full the most extreme worldly consequences of human violence, in order that the lie at the heart of the archaic sacred be ultimately . . . "nailed." Only so can the very spring and principle of violence in the human heart, the principle enfolded deep into all its works and systems and, even before that, afforded by the Creator a permitted place within a free, self-organizing creation, be *reworked* into a triumph of Love. Only so does the mimetic creature have an adequate model of mimesis.[14]

We can hardly fail to see that a veritable semantic *somersault* is here accomplished in respect of that one small word "sacrifice." Moreover, the somersault accomplished retraces a *vast semantic arc* that leaps from pole to antithetical pole, recapitulating evolutionary time and transfiguring human psychosocial space with the new and real hope of salvation. Whoever grasps or is grasped by that new figure of overarching sense would seem likely to be changed in outlook and in being—and likely, in turn, to change things. "For you the kingdom of God has arrived."

Survival and Salvation: Interpreting "Inverse Symmetry"

The implications for our problem of the relation between *survival* and *salvation* are considerable, too, at the level of theory; but here the dossier is so vast that we can do no more than open it, laying down a few basic pointers and some questions.

Demonstrating the "'anthropological pertinence" of the Christian Cross, showing how it addresses so precisely humankind's hidden nerve-point of evolutionary genesis, Girard offers to bring Christians and non-Christians closer to understanding each other than at any time since Darwin. (There is, no doubt, a considerable chicken-and-egg question to be negotiated first: does Girard illegitimately invent the Origin that suits his faith; or does his faith, as he believes, legitimately illuminate his tracing of evolutionary Origins—the Second Adam declaring "how the first came about"?)

If we can transcend the mere hermeneutics of Suspicion, evolutionary and Christian frames of reference may become newly complementary and even the key to understanding each other.

> Christ will have sought to bring humanity to an adult stage, but humanity will have refused that possibility. I employ the future perfect tense deliberately, for there is here an intrinsic failure. . . . That is why the eschatological framework, if one assumes a Darwinian perspective, is simply the obverse of a scientific reality. It is because humankind was unfinished, because it had recourse to the lie of [archaic] "sacrifice," that Christ came to complete our "hominization." (Girard 2007, 212)

One might remove the quotation marks and write, with respect to the theological obverse of evolutionary process, our humanization. Girard continues:

> This finishing is an advent [i.e., a world-changing arrival, the coming of a New Thing]. We must then take seriously the word of Christ when he says that he comes to *bring war;* [for] it is the old world that he comes to destroy. . . . Of course, two thousand years, compared to several millions, is not much: it is the time before the Return i.e. the "perdition" that will fall upon humankind, like the labor-pains of a woman giving birth. (212)

This might well alarm the new atheist "four horsemen"! They would undoubtedly jump to interpret the martial metaphor (at least) in *archaic-sacral* fashion: that is, as an involuntary avowal of the complicity-in-violence of Christian sacralizations.

Yet Girard is pointing here to *both* a continuity *and* a painful tearing loose—the *breakup* of a previous totality, and the divisive *breakaway* involved when an art of *survival* (in horizontal time) is recast "vertically," into a potential and a call in the order of divine relationality (i.e., is declared as *salvation*).[15]

We jib at the thought of the cosmic process of creation involving a prodigious "squandering" of atoms, stars, animal and human lives; although, following Darwin, we are beginning to see that prodigality at this level is balanced and complemented by an inbuilt or intrinsic principle of organizational sifting, certain later stages of which are recognized by Darwin under the name of "natural selection." Yet if we were more imaginative and more consequent in our scanning of natural process, might we not conclude that "founding murder" is the *cultural expression of the same sacrificial principle*, bringing human moral liberty into being, riskily, out of the play of chance and necessity? We might then be able to recognize in turn that the *Christian Cross is the pivotal reworking of this sacrificial principle itself*, since it "converts" sacrifice itself, allowing it to recognize, to imitate, and to return towards its good and loving Author.

As viewed through this prism, an apparently self-organizing play of chance and necessity, more easily than hitherto, may be seen as disclosing and bringing to birth—"in the fullness of time"—an authentic, and authentically divine, "authorial" initiative of "saving" encounter, and invitation to co-creation. Specifically, the figure of symmetrical inversion and reversal, as we have explored it, would seem to make evolutionary process newly thinkable as the expression of *ongoing* divine "creation"—compatible with, and complementary to, the model of the open and emergent universe developed by twenty-first-century cosmology.

We have seen in passing that Girard's theory explains what is, in effect, the emergence of one evolutionary *phylum* among ancient "religions," that of the Abrahamic faiths. Within that phylum, with its further branching, we could follow the progress of a transforming illumination of "grace from above" (i.e., "revelation"), registered in the changes in the practice of sacrifice;

or in the adventure of Hebrew prophecy; or the treatment in the Old Testament of "divine wrath and punishment" (we think here of the Book of Job); or the difficulties of the Israelites in disentangling their *survival* as a nation from their *salvation* as a covenant people. We are enabled to follow the logic of sacred rage and its "revelatory" Christian transformation in the conversion and subsequent theology of St. Paul. Girardian theory thus opens up, freshly, the received truths of faith to modern understanding.

Girard aids believers and skeptics alike to see Christianity as "the religion of the exit from religion" (to quote one of France's best contemporary theologians of the time of "interfaith" and of the inflamed interface between faith and contemporary secularism); but then *also* to refind, beyond the deconstruction of Western metaphysics, the point of distinctiveness that enables us to rediscover and retranslate the logic of theological tradition. For Girard, conspicuously, Christianity is "the religion of the Gospel" (Geffré 2012).

What is perhaps most significant in this perspective is that our figure of the reversal of founding murder attests a self-similar signature in both "first" creation and "redemptive" or "new" creation—the recognition of which requires only that we take due account of evolutionary time, on the one hand, and its divine "fullness," on the other. The God who respects the self-organizing liberty of his created universe is the *same* who appears as Victim within the scenario he invents; and, again, the *same* who refuses to call down legions of angels to evade the crucifying consequences of so doing.[16]

The entire dialogue between faith and science would seem to be potentially renewed and relaunched within the parameters of such recognitions. In which respect the Girardian perspective offers to render otiose, or at least to bracket, the nineteenth-century debate between Darwin and a natural theology or theodicy in the image of William Paley.

In respect of Christian soteriology itself, Girard's *figure of inverse symmetry and reversal* offers to help bridge the historic divide between the two extant poles of classic "atonement theory." Cross-and-Resurrection are traditionally seen by theologians as forming a *re-founding Event* of cosmic significance. But ambiguously so—and not without difficulties of unitary understanding. Does this Event imply a divine *course correction* rescuing humanity from "fall" and "original sin"; or is it not rather the *completion* of a divine purpose *always-already* operating in creation?

When viewed through a Girardian lens, these historically posited alternatives cohere into a single figure of intelligible sense. With and without "perversity of will," *Homo sapiens* is, according to the Girardian account, quite tangibly subject to distorting forces before and beyond himself. This inheritance constitutes the "unfinishedness" *that also alienates humankind* from its own *divinely purposed potential.* "Fall" is henceforth established, to all hearing, as an echo of *Call.*[17] The advent within evolutionary time of nature's Original liberates and heals in respect of this alienation, in the self-same movement by which it inaugurates, models, and enables the Completion originally purposed in creation.

More fundamentally still, we learn here to distinguish two figures of sense: a "horizontal" logic of *survival* in evolutionary time, and a "vertical" time of God's *salvation,* traversing and interacting with it.

Is it not in this sense that the coming itself of "the Kingdom" represents in well-considered Christian theology the true principle of all genuinely "apocalyptic" discourse? As embodied and proclaimed by Jesus, the Kingdom inaugurates within evolutionary and human time God's own eschatological end time, thus constituting the Event on which universal history pivots.

Conclusion

Deprived of archaic sacrificial protection against our own self-generated violence, we stand, in Girard's view, as never before, at unlimited risk of self-destruction as a species—of actual *non-survival.* We can, for the first time in history, destroy our world (Girard 2007, 47); and we are more exposed *culturally* than ever before to extinction, even as we are invited—but not yet *converted* in authentic and operative spiritual persuasion—to the universal promise of *salvation.*

Yet, with the help of Girard's "apocalypse thinking" (64), we may perceive invitation, as well as threat, in the new dispensation that makes war unthinkable as a "prolongation of diplomacy by other means":

> The Passion reveals both mimetism and the only way out of it. . . . We are not headed towards reconciliation in any *necessary* way, but the idea that men have no other saving recourse than to be reconciled is indeed the

complementary face of the escalation to extremes. This truth points to the
founding murder—and draws its sting. (Girard 2007, 185 [2010, 101])

In short: the more firmly we grasp the *difference* between (evolutionary) survival and (Christian) salvation, and the essential complementarity
between them, the closer we may be to acceding to both.

Notes

1. Girard, as anthropologist, must be regarded as operating in this first (horizontal) plane. Yet
   theologians may wish to notice that the selfsame effect can be obtained by swiveling the figure
   around its center of rotation in another (vertical) plane.

2. So unnoticed was it that when Arno Penzias and Robert Wilson were working on an experimental
   microwave antenna at the Bell laboratories in New Jersey in 1965, they at first put down the
   insistent hissing they were capturing to pigeons roosting on the antenna. That it was in fact the
   "afterglow" of a primal cosmic explosion had been first proposed in 1948 by Ralph Alpher and
   Robert Herman. The big bang was essentially what Abbé Georges Lemaître had envisaged in 1927
   under the name of the "primordial atom"—which may have owed something to the cosmological
   scenario of the expanding universe, imagined under the name of the exploding "primordial
   particle" by the American romantic poet Edgar Allan Poe in *Eureka* (1848). The term "big bang"
   was coined, as a derogatory term of dismissal, by Fred Hoyle, author of the rival "steady state"
   theory.

3. It will be observed, however, that the scapegoat acknowledged in Leviticus is not yet "scapegoated"
   in the fully modern sense of being made the innocent victim of an illicit and reprehensible transfer
   of blame. On the "double semantic loading" of the word scapegoat, see Girard (1978, 199–210).
   Girard suggests that the modern sense did not formally enter the French or English languages
   before the seventeenth century (see the "Interview with René Girard" (2009), on the Imitatio
   website).

4. The present state of empirical confirmation is explored in the introductory chapter of our
   companion volume *How We Became Human*.

5. Girard gives new pertinence to Bergson's thesis of the "two sources" of religion and morality. See
   my chapter "Homo religiosus" in *How We Became Human*.

6. The Resurrection theme as such is beyond the compass of this essay. Girard's view of it as an
   "objective fact," in counterdistinction to Bultmann, is expressed in "The Anthropology of the
   Cross" (Girard 1996, 280–83). His chapter on Hölderlin in *Achever Clausewitz* suggests that, for
   Girard, the Resurrection completes the pattern of inversion by speaking of the withdrawal of God:
   see "Un dieu tout proche et difficile à saisir" (2007, 215–30 [2010, 120–35]).

7. Prof. Coakley may not have known of the important revision, occasioned by his dialogues with
   Raymund Schwager, of Girard's critique in *Things Hidden* of the "sacrificial" theology of the
   Letter to the Hebrews: "I revised my critique of the Letter to the Hebrews . . . which was all that
   remained in me of anti-christian modernism. The critique of a timeless-essential Christianity,
   which I had thought to pick up in Hegelian fashion was absurd. Christianity has, on the contrary,
   to be thought out as something essentially historical; which Clausewitz helps us to do. The
   judgment of Solomon says it all, really: there is the sacrifice of the other, and there is self-sacrifice;

archaic and Christian sacrifice. But, yes, we are still talking 'sacrifice'" (Girard 2007, 80 [2010, 35]).

8. Quoted on the jacket cover of *Je vois Satan tomber comme l'éclair* (Girard 1999). See also the conclusion of Girard's interview with James Williams: "Mine is a search for the anthropology of the Cross, which turns out to rehabilitate orthodox theology" (Girard 1996, 288).

9. See "The Question of Anti-Semitism in the Gospels" (Girard 1996, 211–21).

10. On this theme, see chap. 14 of *The Scapegoat,* "Satan Divided against Himself" (Girard 1982).

11. An awareness of the "true agency" of the Passion figures prominently in Girard's explanation of his shift of position on "sacrifice": "I agree with Raymund Schwager that Jesus is scapegoat for all—except now in reverse fashion, for, theologically considered, the initiative comes from God rather than simply from human beings with their scapegoat mechanism . . . Paul speaks of . . . God making Christ to be sin, but also our wisdom and righteousness" (Girard 1996, 280). For a fuller account of Girard's "exodus" from sacrifice, see Michael Kirwan, in this volume.

12. James Williams points out that Girard himself was led by this instance-in-principle to affirm, in relation to his historically derived and anthropological notion of "sacrifice," a new and positive sense: "a willingness to give oneself to others and to commit oneself to God . . . out of love and faithfulness to the other" (Girard 1996, 70). This considerable inflection of his theory intervened after his conversations with Fr. Raymund Schwager, as acknowledged in his contribution to the latter's *Festschrift* (see Girard 1995, 15–29).

13. Culturally speaking, the powerful persuasion of this new Model, reversing the polarity of mimesis, at its originating point of sacrifice, explains why the word itself has, in our culture, passed, albeit still ambiguously, from a negative to a positive valency. We speak today of "the heroic *sacrifice* of Captain Oates"—without, however, eliminating the antipodally different, prior sense attaching to it (we *also* still say: "he was simply *sacrificed,*" i.e., cut off, victimized, butchered, immolated). In present-day usage, confusion between these senses is common—if not, indeed, constitutional; in which respect, language usage provides a highly suggestive pointer to the cultural "in-between" time we inhabit; and no doubt also to the ambiguity of human moral nature.

14. Hence Girard's statement of his contribution to theology: "If the Passion is regarded not as revelation but only as a violent event brought about by God, it is misunderstood and turned into an idol. . . . So what theology needs is a corroborating anthropology. This anthropology will open up the gospels again to their own generating center" (Girard 1996, 282).

15. His last work is, in this respect, markedly non-exclusivist and unsectarian: Christ justifies what was and remains true in *all religions* (2007, 20 [2010, xvi]).

16. Cf. the thought-provoking displacement of viewpoint practised by Girard: "The decisive moment of . . . evolution is constituted by the Christian revelation, a sort of divine expiation in which God, in his Son, asks forgiveness of men for having revealed to them so late the mechanisms of their violence" (Girard 2007, 10 [2010, x]).

17. As in the theology of Paul: "All have sinned and *fall short* of the *glory of God*" (Rom 3:23) (my italics).

Cited Texts and Further Reading

Alexander, Denis. 2008. *Creation or Evolution: Do We Have to Choose?* Oxford and Grand Rapids, MI: Monarch.

Barbour, G. 1998. *Religion and Science: Historical and Contemporary Issues.* London: SCM Press.

Barrow, John D., and Frank J. Tipler. 1996. *The Anthropic Cosmological Principle.* Oxford: Oxford University Press.

Bartholomew, David J. 2008. *God, Chance and Purpose.* Cambridge: Cambridge University Press.

Diamond, Jared. 1997. *Guns, Germs and Steel: A Short History of Everybody for the Last 13,000 Years.* London: Chatto and Windus.

Dumouchel, Paul. 1985. *Violence et vérité: Autour de René Girard.* Paris: Grasset et Fasquelle.

Geffré, Claude. 2012. *Le christianisme comme religion de l'Évangile.* Paris: Éditions du Cerf.

Girard, René. 1972. *La violence et le sacré.* Paris: Grasset.

———. 1977. *Violence and the Sacred.* Translated by P. Gregory. Baltimore: Johns Hopkins University Press.

———. 1978. *Des choses cachées depuis la fondation du monde.* Paris: Éditions Grasset et Fasquelle; quoted edition Le Livre de Poche, 1989.

———. 1982. *Le bouc émissaire.* Paris: Grasset et Fasquelle; quoted edition Le Livre de Poche, 12th ed., 2009.

———. 1987. *Violent Origins: Walter Buckhart, René Girard, and Jonathan Z. Smith on Ritual Killing and Cultural Formation.* Stanford, CA: Stanford University Press.

———. 1995. "Mimetische Theorie und Theologie." In *Von Fluch und Segen des Sündenböcke: Raymund Schwager zum 60. Geburtstag,* ed. J. Niewiadomski and W. Palaver. Thaur: Kultur Verlag.

———. 1996. *The Girard Reader.* Edited by James Williams. New York: Crossroads.

———. 1999. *Je vois Satan tomber comme l'éclair.* Paris: Grasset et Fasquelle.

———. 2003. "The Mimetic Theory of Religion: An Outline." In *2000 Years and Beyond: Faith, Identity and the Common Era,* ed. P. Gifford et al., 88–105. London: Routledge.

———. 2007. *Achever Clausewitz.* Paris: Éditions Carnets Nord.

———. 2009. "On War and Apocalypse." *First Things* (August/September).

———. 2010. *Battling to the End: Conversations with Benoît Chantre.* Translated by Mary Baker. East Lansing: Michigan State University Press.

Hamerton-Kelly, Robert G. 1992. *Sacred Violence: Paul's Hermeneutic of the Cross.* Minneapolis: Fortress Press.

Mahoney, Jack. 2011. *Christianity in Evolution: An Exploration.* Washington, DC: Georgetown University Press.

McGilchrist, Iain. 2009. *The Master and His Emissary: The Divided Brain and the Making of the Western World.* New Haven: Yale University Press.

Palaver, Wolfgang. 2013. *René Girard's Mimetic Theory.* Translated by Gabriel Borrud. East Lansing: Michigan State University Press.

Pinker, Steven. 2011. *The Better Angels of Our Nature: The Decline of Violence in History and Its Causes.* London: Allen Lane, Penguin.

Schwager, Raymund. [1986] 1994. *Brauchen wir einen Sündenbock? Gewalt und Erlösung in den biblischen Schriften.* 3rd ed. Thaur: Kultur Verlag.

Southgate, Christopher. 1953. *The Groaning of Creation: God, Evolution, and the Problem of Evil.* Louisville, KY: Westminster John Knox Press.

Ward, Keith. 2007a. *The Big Questions in Science and Religion.* London: Templeton.

———. 2007b. *Divine Action.* London: Templeton.

Survival and Salvation

A Girardian Reading of Christian Hope in Evolutionary Perspective

Robert G. Hamerton-Kelly[†]

Thinking about the "End of all things" is a prevalent and enduringly popular urge. It is also a terrain rich in confusions; these are reproduced throughout popular speech and writing on this theme, commonly invoking the terms "apocalypse" and "apocalyptic."

We are prone to ask: Will this world survive indefinitely or will it perish unless a "higher" power intervenes to save it? Will we survive indefinitely by our own determined ingenuity in protean adaptations, or do we need a saving intervention from "beyond"? Thus structured and formulated, the question of survival and salvation recalls the cosmological alternative of "big bang" or "steady state." Modern cosmology itself would seem to have decided in favor of the former scenario, which I understand to mean that there will eventually be an end to the world independently of any preference of ours. To quote Maynard Keynes, "In the long run we shall all be dead."

Are there, however, really only two horses in the race: survival by our own efforts on the one hand, or rescue from above on the other? The line of enquiry I wish to explore here acknowledges that "survival" is an immanent (or "first") imperative, imprinted in humankind, as in all creatures, by the process of natural and biological evolution. "Salvation" might then be viewed no longer simply as an *antithesis* to this immanent imperative, a proposal designed to cancel out or reverse the threat of collective extinction, but as a complementary realization of this first, evolutionary purpose, lifting it up into its "second"—"vertical," "transcending," and "ultimate"—dimension.

This way of articulating these two concepts within an evolutionary frame invokes, as will become progressively apparent, the potential for the emergence or coming-to-be of a "renewed" Creation, grounded in and capable of responding freely, in "the fullness of time," to divine purpose. "Salvation," if we are to maintain contact with the broad tradition of Christian theology, is to be seen as a self-communicating "grace" from above, respecting natural process, yet interacting freshly with it, such as to both amend and complete the first-creational programming ordered to "survival."

This *complementarity* between *survival* and *salvation* may thus be thought of as a *restoration* that enhances and completes its *original dynamic*—something occasioned by the fact that the program of survival in its original form, *being incomplete* (as we see more clearly since Darwin), had begun to go seriously wrong in the human spearhead of this process. For our culture, the Book of Genesis registers this view of cosmic-and-human history paradigmatically—even if the figure of sense it traces has, in the course of subsequent culture-history, under "apocalyptic" persuasions, been retraced in darker colors than the original warrants (Mahoney 2011, 49–70).

If we follow this view, the "apocalyptic" impulse arises not from the conviction that creation is metaphysically and morally aberrational and should be replaced by an eternal perfection of spirit; it arises, rather, from the perception that the conduct of humans in history can be, and frequently is, self- and world-destroying. The negative view of the material world is the view of the Orphics and their great popularizer Plato, and later it was known as Gnosticism. The affirmation of the original goodness of all things, and the hope that this excellence might be restored in a renewed creation, is specifically Christian. The Apostle Paul grasps the meaning of this hope for a new creation so well and so early in Christian thought that I choose to take him as a guide in this reflection.

My other mentor-in-overview is Teilhard de Chardin, who, in his day, was controversial both in theology and biology. Theology thought him "soft" on sin and the need for redemption, while biology regarded him as a poet and visionary rather than the scientist he claimed to be. In current discussion he would probably be regarded as a representative of an "intelligent design" form of evolutionary creationism; and, two generations back, of the "process theology" of Whitehead and Hartshorne.

He was, at all events, a *pan-en-theist,* i.e., he held the metaphysical view that the divine is "in, with, and under" the natural, and indeed comes to be *in* and, to some extent, *as* the process of natural evolution and change is accomplished—but which nevertheless views the divine as something distinct from the process. The pan-en-theist option stands between theism, where the divine is separate from and essentially unaffected by natural processes, and pantheism, where nature is divine without any separation of the divine from the natural.

Like the "spiritual materialism" of Heraclitus, Teilhard's vision is one of a continuity of matter, which starts crude and unfolds its latent potential towards spirit. He sees the coming into being of life on earth as a process of transformation from one type of matter to another: from inorganic to organic, and developing thereafter its potential to become conscious, self-conscious, and God-conscious, driven by the progressive increase of its inner complexity. The point at which self-consciousness emerged marks the beginning of culture.

This is, particularly, the point where the process of evolution became *co-evolution:* i.e., where the *synergy* of nature and culture began, nature forming culture and culture shaping nature. In Girard's thought, this is the critical point at the threshold of "hominization" where ritual sacrifice emerged from indiscriminate hominid violence, to give the order necessary for the exfoliation of the distinctions on which culture is based. Reactively, this culturally ordering sacrificial practice impacted, in turn, on the evolving structure of the human brain, making it a sacrificially enabled and programmed instrument (cf. Girard's etymological account of the verb *decidere*—to "cut away," i.e., "to decide" *and* "to kill").

This practice also enabled the symbolic function of the social psyche (the one victim *representing* the many of the community, and the social ordering of this practice providing the challenge that "kick-started" *complex symbolic communication,* hence also *language,* in a way more basic, need-driven "animal" functions did not) (Girard 1987a, 99ff.).

Girard thus explains cogently how emergent *Homo sapiens* came to create and develop both the culturally distinctive institutions that order our societies and the syntactical distinctions and recombinations that structure our intragroup communication and language. In the beginning, *anthropo-logically speaking,* was the deed, not the word—ritual, not myth; ritual kill-ing making possible the emergence of the word, shaping the evolution of the brain so as to make it competent for differentiation. Ritual sacrifice formed the sacrificially competent brain and together they constituted the sacrificial mind, whose subtleties Girard has so cogently illuminated.

We humans are the products of both nature and culture: we bring with us, as we emerge on the historical scene, the separation between culture as history and nature as prehistory, but preserving a seamless continuity between these realities.

"Survival" and the Shadow of Apocalypse

The "either/or" structure of survival/salvation is, as we must first verify, an existential datum of great antiquity, and a form of natural "gravity" that we escape or transcend in our thought processes with great difficulty.

Historically, this alternative is the characteristic matrix of all forms of "apocalyptic discourse," and will be so for as long as we view the genre simply as the naturally generated product of the collective mind of a culture. In positing this existential origin, we imply that this "either/or" is likely to be the basic framing and horizon of all human discussions about the fate of the world.

Before attending to mythic origins of the apocalyptic mind-form in the West, I would like to draw attention to the *contemporary resonance and pathos* of the apocalyptic theme still today. This year, 2012, is the fiftieth anniversary of the publication of the Port Huron Statement issued by the Students for a Democratic Society (SDS) at its national convention held from June 11 to 15, 1962, in suburban Detroit.[1] The manifesto ends with what one commentator calls "an apocalyptic downer": "If we appear to seek the unattainable, as it has been said, then let it be known that we do so to avoid the unimaginable." Our framing alternative here puts in a recognizable appearance.

And there is more . . . What is the *unattainable* they seek? "We would replace power rooted in possession, privilege or circumstance by power and uniqueness rooted in love, reflectiveness, reason and creativity." Compare this with the following excerpt from the founding principles of the Occupy movement (which often mimics SDS), and which envisages the ideal of "constituting ourselves as autonomous political beings engaged in non-violent civil disobedience and building solidarity based on mutual respect, acceptance, and love." The *hope for human authenticity,* so it would appear, never quite dies—even if innocence is *corrupted,* the young (of all ages) are traduced; and even though love falls silent. Alas Cordelia! This is a tragic dichotomy and a flaw inherent in all human moral idealism; we are well short of any idea of "salvation."

A second contemporary reference will also prove instructive. Public opinion in the United States has been much exercised of late by a debate around Steven Pinker's book *The Better Angels of Our Nature: Why Violence Has Declined.* The climate of pathos here is intensified by the political background of a clash between Israel and the United States on a preemptive strike at Iran, and the entry of this issue into U.S. domestic politics, through reckless politicians who will say and do anything at all to be elected. Their slash-and-burn politics revels in nuclear brinkmanship, while quietly—and not so quietly (if we refer to Pinker's website)—the *cognoscenti* try to convince themselves that "every day, in every way, we are getting better and better" at controlling violence.[2]

Pinker's position on this point represents, in my view, one more way station on the road pioneered by Émile Coué and then made an American highway by Dale Carnegie, Norman Vincent Peale, and Robert Schuller. It is paved with the fatuity of American optimism and leads to the city of self-deception. Pinker argues that, statistically, a human being is less likely than ever before to be raided, coerced, raped, or killed in his or her habitat. Robert Jay Lifton comments that this statistical approach invoked by Pinker leaves out of account some important items: the existential horror of technological killing; the satanic consciousness that, at the level of governments, our own included, there are plans to murder on a massive scale; and the reciprocal and answering malignancies of fundamentalist religion—not to mention the fiendish inventions of raging ideological cranks. Both governments *and* their fundamentalist opponents are willing, and some are actually planning, to poison or burn large numbers of the human race using the infamous "weapons of mass destruction." Pinker's statistics, furthermore, are open to question; and the naiveté with which he not infrequently draws conclusions from the data would be risible were it not so grotesque.

This debate—whether violence is abating and the human world improv-
ing—is surely the most tiresome, sophomoric, and characteristically American time-waster imaginable. There are no reliable points of reference in this
whole sphere of discourse; attitudes are confused with evidence. Thought is
bypassed by mechanical recourse to symbols (so for instance: the image of
the glass half full or half empty); and the gnarled texture of history is treated
as assimilable to the smooth surface of statistics. Hope is something we need,
assuredly; but it should not be conjured up by sleight-of-word arguments
and one-line squibs from the *Reader's Digest,* nor even by slogans drawn
from politicians' campaign biographies.[3]

Hope and despair (or, less abruptly, "depression") are existential opposites that correspond to the phenomenological opposites of life and death.
We shall later observe the Apostle Paul himself treating hope as an existential
phenomenon arising from the historical state of human being in this world.
The most elementary point we should retain in all these cases is that, existentially speaking, the "either/or" structure constitutes a fundamental mode
of human consciousness. We all live every moment under the existential
threat of death and the greater or lesser imminence of extinction that negates
our hopes and is more or less ever-present to our minds. This is our fundamental condition: we are programmed to worry about the risks of violent
termination, to foresee and to fear Catastrophe, just as we are programmed
for evolutionary survival; this worry is the *flipside of the same evolutionary
programming.*

The ramifications of this fact are evident in many cultural forms, not
least in religion itself. In this field, we can trace them back to the very earliest
layers of Stone Age temple sites known to the latest archeology. A recent
instance is the Göbekli Tepe site being excavated by K. Schmidt, as interpreted by Karl W. Luckert of the University of Northern Arizona and later
the University of Missouri (emeritus). Luckert thinks, plausibly, that the site
was a weapons factory, turning out flint spearheads and arrowheads, and
formalizing in ritual structures the collaboration made necessary by the need
for weapons—perhaps also by the need for an atonement to salve the collective conscience of a community in conflict about its death-dealing industry.
It might be conjectured that the rituals were those controlling conflict, to
avoid war and death, or else representing the unity-in-violence of contending
parties. However this may be, the weapons manufacture is clear evidence of

violence at the origins of society and culture, exactly as Girard invites us to expect.[4]

In Western historical thought, we find this primary, existentially generated dualism expressed most reliably and most revealingly in the literary deposits of the ancient Mesopotamian civilizations, whose myths of creation, seen as the ordering of chaos, we can rediscover in Sumerian, Akkadian, and Ugaritic texts from as early as the fourth millennium BCE (Pritchard 1955).

The social matrix of these myths was probably the invention of the irrigation systems that eventually controlled the flooding waters of the rivers on whose banks their builders lived, and made possible the defense of dry-land space and orderly agriculture. Periodically the waters would overwhelm the irrigation canals and surge chaotically over living space and fields of food. That is: periodically there would be an apocalypse-event, i.e., an occurrence of phenomena out of which reemerged the symbol of the end of order, the threatening memory of bewildering chaos. Genesis (1:1–3) calls this the *tohu wa bohu* (later to become the Yiddish phrase for "all f——d up").

The imagery of these myths has one fundamental theme, the battle of the savior god against the chaos monster, Marduk against Tiamat, Baal against Yam[5]—that is, a theme of violent dualism. In the beginning was violence; and this is presented as the necessary and beneficial violence that brings chaos to order. In the Akkadian epic *Enuma Elish,* the hero Marduk defeats Tiamat, horizontally cuts her body in two, and sets up one part as the roof of the world and the other as its floor. In the space between, we humans dwell secure; while Marduk keeps an eye on dismembered Tiamat, who always remains a threat.

Once a year, in the ritual of the Babylonian New Year festival, the world returns to chaos: the king, who represents the power of order, is dethroned and humiliated, and the world is plunged back into chaos. Then the drama pivots around the central axis of violence, and Marduk resurgent crushes Tiamat once again. The regular re-enthronement of the king as lord of the defeated chaos monster rejuvenates order and re-founds good governance.

The account of the creation in the Bible (Genesis 1) is, in some sense and at one level, a bowdlerized version of this myth. It eschews gods and monsters and cosmic battles in favor of the serene omnipotence of the God of Israel, who stills the chaos by his word and builds an upper and nether expanse (in the KJV: the "firmament") that separates the water above from the water below to make space for human existence.[6] Within this space we dwell secure, until God loses his temper in the days of Noah and allows the waters above (rain) to join the waters below (springs, seas, rivers) and drown the human world in resurgent chaos. So cosmos (order, regulation) is the—albeit uncertain—control of chaotic violence by calming violence; in fact, by what, in Girardian terms, might be termed the "godly" violence of ritual sacrifice.

In pre-Socratic Heraclitan terminology, the first principle (*arche*) of the world is violence. According to Heraclitus, violence is the father and king of all (*polemos pater panton*, fr. 53; cf. fr. 80); and, like the king of Babylon, he is Marduk's representative on earth, keeping order by the dragon-conquering power of "good" violence.

The point is that the catastrophic outbreak of a previously contained chaos—the resurrection of Tiamat the dragon—may well be a figure of *cosmic* and *cosmological sense* derived ultimately from, and originally referable to, the chaos of a violence experienced closer to home, within the social community, as the natural violence of flooded irrigation conduits and the mimetic conflict of failed differentiation and malfunctioning rituals—the "thing seen" providing the means to model and decipher the "thing unseen." Such magnifying projections have been a continuing possibility and a real danger in Western political thought for at least five thousand years; and this provides an important clue to the background of apocalyptic expectation in general. We have always lived with the anxiety of the end of all things—something that is always more dynamic and more "cosmic" than any matter of merely individual extinction, and is especially potent when the "times are out of joint."

Universal apocalypse, in other words, might be seen as an existential extrapolation out of individual worries, recalling the worrier or worriers to his (or their) metaphysical frailty, and consequently, to their sense of threat and/or their paranoia. Generating apocalyptic scenarios is certainly a way of sharing out globally the burden of mortality, which we all, as individuals, encounter allusively and piecemeal in our everyday lives.

We see this most clearly and paradigmatically in art, insofar as art provides a remediation and a therapy for the pain of our metaphysical frailties. No one can sing or hear one of our great Western Requiems (Mozart, Brahms, Verdi, Fauré, Duruflé) without feeling the solace of dread expressed, shared, and thus mitigated. Equally, no one can read that first and perhaps greatest of Western novels, the—misnamed—*Epic of Gilgamesh,* without recognizing the common bane-and-blessing we can be to each other, and which we share with each other through the representations of our art. "Epic" is a misnomer: we might, rather, think of this narrative text as the first *novel,* given that its major characters are not gods, as in myths, or semi-divine heroes, as in the epics, but humans; and its subject is not the creation of the world or the conquest of an enemy, but rather the defeat of love. Death trumps human love, and Gilgamesh fails to bring back his beloved, Enkidu, from the land of shadows. (What say we to the fact that the first great love in our literature is a same-sex love?)

Furthermore, while on this futile journey of love, the main character develops from a violent and capricious thug into a wise ruler. So we have the theme of most novels, of operas (and of soap operas!) ever since: how characters change on the journey of life in the search for and in service of love, to the enduring banality of which we seem abidingly addicted. Along the way of Gilgamesh's journey, we also see traces of the mechanism of ritual killing that controls violence, and detect the strong scent of mimetic desire.

Here, very clearly, we are entering Girardian territory.

Modeling the "Alternative" of Survival and Salvation: Pagan Religious Mythology

Girard, as we know, discovered mimetic desire in nineteenth-century European novels and labeled it "novelistic truth" (or "vérite romanesque") as opposed to the "romantic lie" ("mensonge romantique"). The truth of mimetic desire, however, is not something invented for the first time in nineteenth-century Europe. It is something we have known explicitly, at least since the earliest written Western witnesses to consciousness.

The Gilgamesh epic itself would provide an argument for what Girard calls the comparative study of texts, showing how a single mechanism of mimetic desire and reciprocal violence governs and shapes the creation and presentation of the entire set of such texts. All of them are "religious" texts in the primary sense that they are shaped and informed by the social technology of archaic religion, which, by ritually controlling internally generated violence through sacrifice, enables the coming-to-be (i.e., both the existence and the development) of society and culture. What artistic representation of such social technologies does is bring archaic religion within range of self-cognizance, hence also, potentially, of liberation and change. We may ultimately wish to say: within range of salvation.

Clearly Gilgamesh and his story are a deposit of the *earliest* stage of culture, the stage just after the hieratic phase, which was dominated by myth and liturgy. Here is an early break in the mythic cloud of unknowing, a very first dawning of novelistic truth. "Gilgamesh," writes editor Mitchell, "is the story of a hero's journey. One might say it is the mother of all heroes' journeys, with its huge uninhibited mythic presences moving through a landscape of dream. It is also the story of how a man becomes civilized, how he learns to rule himself and therefore his people, and to act with temperance wisdom and piety. The poem begins with the city and ends with it" (Mitchell 2004, 7).

A poem that begins and ends with the city, and tells of how a man becomes civilized by emerging from the fog of myth into the "through a glass darkly" insights of history, recalls the Hebrew Bible's account of Cain's founding of the city named Enoch as a direct result of the death of Abel, the brother he has murdered (Genesis 4:17); and Romulus's founding of Rome under the impulse of his murder of his twin, Remus. Abel dies to found the city of Enoch, and Remus dies to found the city of Rome (Serres 1991); and Enkidu dies to re-found the city of Uruk and to civilize its king, as we see in Sin-leqi-unnini's climax to the Prologue. Only the Bible, we notice in passing, regards this chain of founding events as unfortunate, because of the bloodshed and the vengeance that must follow—against which disorders it invents the novel and ambiguous "mark of Cain" (Gen 4:15–16).

At the climax of the Prologue, the SV (standard version) commands us to:

> Find the cornerstone and under it the copper box that is marked with his name. Unlock it. Open the lid. Take out the tablet of lapis lazuli. Read how Gilgamesh suffered all and accomplished all. (Mitchell 2004, 70)

This is an allusion to the *founding sacrifice* of Uruk, i.e., the sacrifice that both marks the founding temporally—and guarantees the foundations them-selves—of this city (which, in the text, stands for the known world). As is frequently the case in ethnology and in historical writing, buildings, bridges, shrines, and cities are literally "founded on" sacrifice, in the sense that the body of a victim is buried under the cornerstone. Thus, Uruk is *founded on* Gilgamesh, but not only in the literal sense that it rests upon his sacrificed corpse. Additionally, since the written account of all his mighty deeds and abject sorrows is interred in a copper box under its chief cornerstone, upon the narrative of his life and actions.

It is not the fact of the sacrifice alone, therefore, that founds the city, Uruk, but also the story, the narration, of its founding. The event and its description together become the mechanisms of a certain *transforming and creative effect*. If the text is a reliable account of the violence being subdued, it reads as a "novelistic" *truth;* if it falsely obscures the violence by tall tales of miracle and cunning, it is still *myth.* Our text is somewhere between these two possibilities.

The most striking feature of the narrative is that it deliberately reveals the pain and suffering that violence causes and presents the "conversion" of the agents of violence (i.e., their turning away from violence) as the *alternative and only real* basis for the foundation of the city. Therefore the narrative opens with the novelistic *revelation* of the city's dependence on sacrifice for its stability. By virtue of the metaphoric *distance* created by the written representation of this unpalatable fact of foundation—and thanks to the *metaphor,* which the writing establishes, of "sacrifice under the cornerstone"—the first "novel" in Western culture does in fact disclose a novelistic *truth.* We do understand—at least if we allow Girardian theory to focus and clarify our reading—the foundational role in human societies of sacrifice and its supporting or derived forms: vengeance, the scapegoat victim, and the whipping boy.

However, if Gilgamesh himself glimpses a novelistic truth, it is clear from this earliest novel that he cannot *sustain* the state of "converted" insightfulness. Upon finding the immortal one who has survived the flood, he restores the ancient rites, the temples destroyed by the flood, and the statutes and sacraments that the flood had rendered void. That is, he *re-founds* the city on sacrifice. We might comment: this is not "salvation."

Taken together, therefore, the narratives of the pursuit of eternal life, of the natural catastrophe of the flood, and of the restoration of ancient rites and prohibitions form a coded account of real sacrificial practices extant at the time of writing (i.e., the ancient rites that were held to renew the life of the city). The flood signifies a catastrophe of disorder for both the natural and the human worlds, and shows the tight associative, metonymic, or symbolic linkage between these two things in the collective consciousness of the historical community. In the text, most of the organized world succumbs to it, but Utnapishtim survives it and so, beyond trauma, he has a hold on eternal life (we might say: the intuition of a genuine salvation). How is trauma reckoned to have turned into immortality? The text answers: through the ancient rites of sacrifice, in which someone dies "instead of us," enabling his death, for us, to bring forth life.

The figure of Humbaba is especially germane to this larger sense. He is the guardian of the great cedar grove sacred to Ishtar, a monster who keeps even heroes away by his frightful roaring and hateful mien. Gilgamesh and Enkidu attack him and Gilgamesh kills him. Humbaba pleads for his life as follows:

> If any mortal, Enkidu, knows the rules of my forest, it is you. You know
> that this is my place and that I am the forest's guardian. Enlil put me here
> to terrify men, and I guard the forest as Enlil ordains. (v. 125; Mitchell
> 2004, 125–26)

The existential threat symbolically personified by the forest monster pleads for his life as something necessary in the scheme of things, and he goes on to warn that if the heroes kill him, they invite the revenge of the gods. Without the deterrence of sacred terror, vengeance will become an unbounded plague. Gilgamesh ignores the pleas and the warning; and as a result, his beloved Enkidu must die. Enkidu takes to his bed and sighs away his life, leaving Gilgamesh inconsolable and prompting the latter's journey of enlightenment. The attempt to eradicate evil causes the death of the beloved (in the plague of vengeance). In this world, there can be no final solution to the problem of the dark threat from the forest.

How is Humbaba necessary to the order of the world? He is the guardian of the Sacred, the marker of the line between the gods and men that must not be crossed. In the economy of sacrificial religion, the line drawn around the sacred precinct, the place of sacrifice, warns humans off, not because the humans will pollute the divine, but because the divine *in its archaic form is a distilled precipitate and projection of human violence,* and because, like high-tension electricity, it will kill the trespasser. So Humbaba the frightful guardian of the Sacred is also, within this frame of primitive, sacrificial religion, the beneficent guardian of human life. In order to emerge from the cocoon of violent religion, humans must break the Sacred open, invade the sacred space, and take the consequences—which in this case means the death of the beloved and the conversion of the lover.

So once again, in this harbinger of the great Western novels, we see the revelation of novelistic truth as an emergence from romantic mendacity in its most primary form: that of early mythic *misrecognition.* This emergence pre-traces a form of conversion, and it represents the only alternative to apocalypse (understood in the—equally primitive, or rather "regressive"—sense that survives still today in popular discourse). The point for us here is this: the *very attempt to remove the monster that terrifies us*—whether this "monster" is identified as class oppression, race pollution, capitalist bandits, democratic clowns, death itself—can bring on the mini-apocalypses we recognize so well from our terrible twentieth century, and which we observe to be alive and thriving in the faith-based politics of cruelty of the twenty-first century, that we recognize in the United States as "KKKristianity," in Israel as the Jewish "Haredist" settler pathology, and in the Muslim world as "Salafist" religio-fascist chagrin.

Survival "Opened Up" to Salvation: The Hebrew Scriptures

Gilgamesh shows us how, virtually from the beginning of our Western written record, the novelistic truth has been struggling to emerge from the romantic lie, how survival by myth and sacred violence has been opening to salvation by secular (i.e., post-religious) truth and succoring (i.e., "humanitarian") love.

This emergence has come down several streams; here I mention only the two classic Western conduits, which flow from Athens and Jerusalem respectively. Greek medicine, mathematics, drama, and philosophy, and especially Greek tragedy, show clear traces of an emergence from the house of mythology, but do not often make the conscious connection between mythology and sacrificial religion that Girard shows us so insightfully (often using Greek texts). Jerusalem, on the other hand, sends out a stream of disclosure that exposes sacrifice, myth, and prohibition for what they are, *the building blocks of the house that violence built.*

Typically, Girard identifies in the Hebrew scriptures outbreaks of an especially intense mode of historical narrative that might be called epiphanies of Gospel truth. This phenomenon has long been recognized in traditional exegesis as "typology" or "figuration." For Girard, the striking types or figures are the Joseph story (Gen. 30:24–50:26), the judgment of Solomon (1 Kings 3:16–28), the Suffering Servant of 2 Isaiah (40–52), and the story of Job (Williams 1991).

This last text, which is a protest against the cruel moralizing of the Jehovah of Hebrew tribal imagining, comes from the Wisdom tradition and claims that God is not the moral tyrant presented in the Deuteronomic histories. It may provide us here with a useful *tuning fork* for apprehending the Girardian reading of the Hebrew scriptures as a whole.

God, as shown here, paradigmatically, and for the first time, is seen to prefer a man who *speaks the truth* to one who blames the sufferer for his sufferings in order to *safeguard the moral reputation of God.* The truth of Job is that the high and invisible God, unlike the tribal deity often mistaken for Him . . . is *not* vengeful.

The modern reader, particularly if programmed by Enlightenment thinkers, or by modern Absurdists, is likely to respond: "But the philosophic price paid for this insight is high. His God might not be vengeful, but does He then not appear as unreliable, unpredictable, obscurely cruel in his failure to intervene savingly? God has allowed Job, on a whim, to be "tested"—for which *metaphysical* enigma, this text, markedly, *does not even attempt* to offer any explanation. Perhaps the moralizing of the Deuteronomist is preferable?"

Girard, however, applies here the deconstructivist thrust of his own theory of the archaic sacred. The x-ray shape he discerns beneath the fabulating and still mythic data of the story is that of Job, "Victim *of his people.*" In other words, the God Job wrestles with is not just that of a peculiar Hebrew tradition of retributive justice; he is, in part still, the sacralized *projection* of the "God" of *the archaic sacred* (or "primitive religion") *as such,* i.e., a monstrous Double, required, engendered, and consecrated by man's ancient, devious, and universal game of exorcising violently his own violent shadow, which fearsome deity, born of the social psyche, constitutes, in evolutionary terms, the *inherited default setting* of man "the-religious-animal."

This text stages, in fact, the entire ambivalence of the archaic sacred, and its "containment" of violence; and it epitomizes the gradual—and some-times fitful—Hebraic "verticalization" of *Homo religiosus*. Ultimately, says Girard, Job "wrests the deity out of the process of persecution" to envision him instead as "the God *of the oppressed and the downtrodden*" (Girard 1999, 185). The Victim, for the first time, can say: "I know that my redeemer [Heb. *Goel,* vindicator] liveth" (Job 19:25).

Far from being embarrassed by the residual presence of the archaic sacred, and of mythological elements shared with world religions-and-mythologies, Girard *goes out of his way to underline these things.* Within Israel itself, we recognize the *archaic-sacral patterns of religious culture:* such as the alimentary prescriptions, and the actual use of a "scapegoat" animal, marking perhaps the point of passage from human to animal sacrifice. Human sacrifice is not so far back that it cannot be recalled as a *displaced and rejected* form of faithful piety: we think of the story of Abraham and Isaac in Genesis 22, in which Abraham in obedience to God attempts to sacrifice his son. At the last moment God stays the father's hand and gives an animal instead for sacrifice.

Israel's institutions too—priesthood, sacral monarchy, temple—all fit into that picture, as does the memory of recurrent catastrophe running through the early books of the Hebrew scriptures. And what of Israel's often bloodthirsty "Lord of hosts" (*Yahweh sebaoth*)? We might be forgiven for sometimes wondering if He is merely the binding-bonding tribal God, the cornerstone of the *cultural identity* of the people of Israel, and the Guarantor of its historic *survival.*

The archaic pattern, in short, is *always-already there:* foregrounded in the prehistorical and overtly mythical first books of the Bible, still pres-ent as a background to the whole. Yet so is something else, which grows: a new perspective in the shaping of the mythic material, a specific honesty in relation to the Victim. Yes, we are confronted with a horizon of primi-tive religious-cultural practice entirely recognizable from archaic-sacral religions-and-mythologies. We recognize the environing world of the archaic sacred: sorcery, soothsayers, fertility cults, child sacrifice—the entire gamut of "idolatrous" (and very violent) sacralities unfolds in the background of

Israel's story. Yet such shared beginnings are stressed because they serve, pre-cisely, to measure an original and far more remarkable pattern of textual and historical emergence.

The Edenic prologue of Temptation and Fall establishes the very for-mula of the mimetic triangle: but here it is the rivalry *with God* that is being staged, and presented as the fact and the fault of mimetically suggestible, blame-shifting humankind, obeying its older and deeper—we might want to say its "evolutionary"?—"other voice": the Serpent. Accursedness and exile are still presented as divine punishments; but these are also shown, clearly enough, to be self-inflicted human wounds, and they signify *de facto* a prohibition placed on the greatest Object of sacralizing and rivalrous desire. This narrative *steps outside* the world of the archaic sacred; it recognizes it; it represents and critiques it—in the name of the Lord God who made would-be *sapiens* and under whose judgment *wanna-be sapiens* henceforth stands.

True, Girard's reading engages little with the "high road" of revelation passing through the prophets (to whom Jesus himself is so very attentive). The reason is clear: Girard is following the "low road" of anthropology: the opening up "from below" of things human. As it is, however, this reading has tremendous resonance for the theologian and Pauline scholar that I am. For the Apostle Paul, the Christian Cross is the wisdom of God that surpasses the wisdom of the world (1 Cor. 1:18–25). In the light of this divine wisdom, as he has come to know it, Paul sees—and we in turn see—the linkage that connects the murder of Jesus with such as Gilgamesh and, further back, with the original victim, "slain and hidden as the foundation of the human world" (Rev. 13:8; cf. Matt. 13:35 quoting Ps. 78:2).

For Paul grounds the universal horizon of humanity and its salvation in the utterly specific history of two men, Abraham and Jesus. He uses the figure of Abraham to nudge Moses out of the center of attention (see Gal. 3:10–20), and to show that the blessing promised to the Patriarch was spe-cific to the Abrahamic line, conceived as defining human faithfulness (atten-tive, trusting, and forward-looking) as such, and not a promise to his ethnic descendants specifically. This perspective is founding for the notion of "the Abrahamic religions."[7]

Biblical religion in its authenticity (Jewish and Christian) stems from this trusting turn from looking back to looking forward, from dwelling in the permanence of the sacred to wandering in the transience of history. This trusting obedience to the invisible God on the basis of his word alone is the very definition of faith for St. Paul—the faith that justifies apart from obedience to Mosaic Law, or attachment to place, or ritual, or prohibition. This faith, looking to the future not the past, leaves behind the sedentary sacred, symbolized by the graves of the ancestors, and becomes nomadic on the earth. "Idols" abide in sacred space, whereas the true God dwells in holy time. Timeless myth and time-bound narrative diverge; and the Abrahamic faith rides out of myth and ritual on the back of historical narrative.

One effect of the Girardian "neo-figural" reading, therefore, is to justify, in terms of evolutionary "emergence," the special status attributed, in the history of religions, to the Judaic root of the great monotheisms. Another is to allow us to distinguish its thin red line of "novelistic truth": the testimony given to the possibility of post-sacrificial, nonviolent fellowship with the divine, as prefigured in the Hebrew scriptures, and as integrally expressed in the self-sacrificing death of Jesus.

Girard and Christian Hope

My ultimate text must be from St. Paul: "For the creation waits with eager longing for the revealing of the sons of God; for the creation was subjected to futility, not of its own will but by the will of him who subjected it in hope; for the creation itself will be set free from its bondage to decay and obtain the glorious liberty of the children of God" (Rom. 8:19–21).

For Girard the narrative history of Jesus in the gospels is the definitive account of the revelation of the surrogate victim mechanism, which manipulates the violence that is generated abundantly from the evolutionary system, both in the free play of pre-human nature, and, albeit temporarily stabilized, in the world of human culture and human freedom. In the latter dimension, the victimary mechanism is the method by which the world was "subjected to futility"—the futility of the sacrificial ruse that kept the system operating by the sleight-of-hand deflection of violence onto a substitute—a measure that has to be repeated like a pharmaceutical dosage[8] about twice a day (as was literally the case in the temple in Jerusalem prior to its destruction in 70 CE; a "therapy" that, like the misnamed "painkiller," dulls and muffles rather than removes the pain.

Furthermore Girard reads the Passion story as a decisive disarming-by-disclosure of that *sacralizing victimary mechanism,* which now, in our own times, through the slow osmosis of Christianity into human culture at large, has become dramatically weaker, is losing control, and being pushed aside—thus ushering in the dramatically sharpened alternative characteristic of our times. *Either* the slouching beast will blow up Nazareth and all of us with it, *or else,* impelled by the *hope that comes* with knowing that violence cannot be contained by sweeping it under the carpet of sacrificial blood and mythic thunder, realizing that it *no longer needs to be*—we shall turn to loving.

That hope is "not yet seen," says Paul (Rom. 8:24), so its fulfillment in love can, in the here and now, be no more than an act of anticipatory imagination that endures because of faith's confidence that the witness of the record, despite appearances, is positive, or rather, *promising.* The long process from the inorganic to the consciousness beyond self-consciousness attests that the Spirit "in, with, and under" all things will not only endure but also triumph. We know that this hope is not just wishful thinking, because the love that wells up from the heart of all existing things pours especially into our human hearts as the Gift of the Holy Spirit, the quintessence of grace (Rom. 5:1–5). That same Holy Spirit brooded on the primal chaos *in illo tempore,* and uttered the first creating word, "Let there be Light" (Gen. 1:2b–3). That very light, "the true light that enlightens everyone" as he and she come into this world (Jn. 1:9, cf. 4–5), that light "has shone in our hearts" (2 Cor. 4:6), to give us a foretaste of the fulfillment to come (2 Cor. 1:21).[9]

The Apostle looks for his hope to "things unseen," to the Resurrection of Jesus in Jerusalem, and the gift of the Spirit in the heart. In that way he rises above the existential dualism of life and death, although the "unseen" remains wrapped in the mist of hope, until that day. In the meantime we feel that our inner self is being renewed as the outer self and its world decay (2 Cor. 4:16–18). The inner renewal is the work of love in us and through us, founded in the confidence of faith as a reading of the work of divine grace in our world, and hoping for the glorious liberty of the children of God.

For the Apostle, the existential tenor of this new creation shapes itself around three fixed points; he calls them faith, hope, and love (Greek: *pistis, elpis, agape*), presented definitively in 1 Corinthians 13:13. Here they are the eternal qualities of existence, not subject to the decay of time, enduring even into the real-and-ultimate presence of God. "These three abide (*menei*): faith, hope and love, but the greatest of these is love." They cannot be surpassed, since what *here* we must believe (take on trust), *there* we shall know. Yet even when we "know," when we see God "face to face," we shall need faith; which is to say that faith cannot be a purely cognitive (i.e., "cognitivist") category; it can only mean "validated trust in God," like Abraham's faith. Hope too endures, in that one continues forever to look forward to life from God, and love endures because love is the Holy Spirit that binds and bonds us, within ourselves, between us communally, and in communion with God.

These qualities are like three points of an isosceles triangle, with *love* at the apex and *faith* on the bottom left and *hope* the bottom right. Like the Holy Trinity, they are utterly inseparable; indeed they are the existential imprints of that very divine presence, the image of God in the life of a person. In Romans 5:1–5 the Apostle writes that believers have peace with God now, because by faith they have laid hold of hope, and know this hope is not wishful thinking, because love has poured into their hearts. Love testifies to the authenticity of hope, and hope attests the confidence of faith, while trust (faith) is the heart of love, and eager expectation (hope) its confidence.

Hope is integral to existence in God, the "converted" existence of the novelistic truth beyond romantic myth: that of the older, wiser Gilgamesh (temporarily), the dying Knight of La Mancha, back in his own bed and his right mind; and also of the dying Stepan Trofimovich Verkovensky, away in a strange bed in an inn in Dostoevsky's *The Demons,* realizing that "J'ai menti toute ma vie" ("I have lied all my life"). All three are disillusioned, and blessed, because this is the way of "conversion" in the Girardian sense; it is "a divine *dis*illusionment," *an awakening from the impossible dream.*

The existential hope, as we find it in 1 Corinthians 13 and Romans 5:1–5, is also an eschatological reality ("eschatological" means that it belongs in the class of the things ultimate, i.e., "beyond," on the axis of either space or time). The important passage here is Rom 8, which is a skillful integration of the historical and the existential dimensions of human hope and the most intense point of contact with the larger concern of this volume, evolutionary theory and Girard's thought:

> We know that the whole creation has been groaning in travail together until now; and not only the creation but we ourselves, who have the first fruits of the Spirit, groan inwardly as we wait for adoption as sons, the

redemption of our bodies. For in this hope we were saved. Now hope that is seen is not hope. For who hopes for what he sees? But if we hope for what we do not see, we wait for it with patience. (Rom. 5:18–25)

The Apostle even specifies the ultimate existentially: "For we know that up to the present moment the whole creation groans and writhes in every part of its body *like a woman in childbirth*" (Rom. 8:22; my translation). The Greek prefix *sun* attached to the two verbs emphasizes the totality of this agony, and the whole passage from which this sentence comes shows that the Apostle knows that violence drives the world of nature and humanity. That a violent explosion, a "big bang," set it all in motion would not have surprised him. That "war is the father and ruler of all" would not have surprised him. He knew that the world of nature and history is "founded on" a slaughtered Lamb (which, so my colleague Paul Gifford suggests, is the symmetrical inverse of the anthropological "scapegoat," who is foundational for "survival").

The whole argument of which the text in question is a part is that we can endure the painful process of life in a world of violence because the Spirit has infused us with hope for a good outcome. We have heard the Apostle describing this good outcome as "the apocalypse of the children of God," or "the glorious liberty of the children of God." Thus he signifies the other side of the coin of Crucifixion, namely, the Resurrection, which in this world exists as hope (Rom. 8:18–25). Hope is the existential presence of the Resurrection of Jesus from the dead.

How did Paul know this? He did not infer it from a disinterested reading of the phenomena; rather he learned it in a flash of insight, of "revelation" (*apocalupsis*), into the significance of the slow death by torture of one young Jew named Jeshua. The insight that this event is the unveiling (*apocalupsis*) of the inmost, consisting-and-constituting truth of all things, from the big bang to the tiny whimper, and from alpha to omega, occurred in what Girard calls "the miracle of Peter," that is, in the apostolic witness that "this is it." Among the many young Jews being murdered that week, a small group of young fishermen and other drifters, led by Peter, saw that this Jeshua is unique. They "got it."

This "apostolic miracle" of grace is the crux of Christian theology; and being miraculous it does not fall under the purview of natural theology, where the debates about creation and evolutionary theory are conventionally lodged. Like the Resurrection, which appears in this world as hope, Peter's apostolic moment of recognition is among us . . . as "*faith*."

Yet here, too, is the crux of the Girardian difference from so many current thinkers: the apostolic moment is also, at another—*anthropological*—level of discourse, *a statement of fact*—at least in the sense that it provides a hermeneutical key that, *like none other,* puts the facts into their adequate pattern of interpretation. When we "get it," we understand that the Cross discloses the natural and historical fact that escaped the author of Job; namely, that violence is the *obverse face* of our precious freedom, and that it drives all the world in all its parts, human and natural, just as the paroxysms of a birth mother's body drives a tiny fragment of new creation into the horror and hope of the world. The Resurrection is the light in *that* darkness; it discloses the ground and the shape of our Hope.

Conclusion

Hitherto, Christian theology has been handicapped, in post-Darwinian times, in its attempts to expound and apply the meaning of the Cross, because it has lacked a theory of violence. *Faute de mieux,* it entered, pre-Darwin, into an alliance with middle and neo- Platonism; this set it up for a fall—and it has indeed suffered much contempt in post-Enlightenment times (not least from Darwinians) because of this alliance. Post-Darwin, Girardian theory has at last made possible a genuine "theology of the Cross" (Luther's phrase, and Luther's ambition at the threshold of the modern world)—a theology made accessible, and supported, by an *anthropology* of the Cross. This is something more complete and more profitable than a mere *philosophy* of the Cross (as attempted impressively, for example, by Vattimo [2002] and Žižek [2009]).

Here is a vital measure of the difference made by the Girardian mimetic theory—and of its significance. Both evolutionism and Christianity are, in their different ways, approaches to the central fact of violence in nature; but how these approaches are reconcilable and complementary appears only in the light of mimetic theory.

Notes

1. See *New York Times,* March 4, 2012.

2. See http://stevenpinker.com, and *New York Times,* January 4, 2012, and January 9, 2012.

3. See, e.g., B. Obama, *The Audacity of Hope* (2006); film biography of W. Clinton, *The Man from Hope* . . .

4. Pre-publication draft (December 2012) of Luckert's forthcoming book, *Stone Age Religion at Göbekli Tepe: Atonement Twelve Thousand Years Ago and around the Planet* (Foreword by Klaus Schmidt).

5. *Yam* is "sea" in the NW Semitic languages. In Ugarit *mot* (death) is often used for the same idea of chaotic nothingness.

6. "And God said: 'Let there be a firmament [Heb. *raqia,* expanse] in the midst of the waters, and let it separate the waters from the waters.'" "And God made the firmament and separated the waters, which were under the firmament from the waters, which were above the firmament. And it was so" (Gen. 1:6–7, RSV).

7. Wolfgang Palaver claims that the *Akedah* ("binding") or story of the "transcended sacrifice" of Isaac by Abraham in Genesis 22:1–19 signifies the historical rejection of human sacrifice and the acceptance of the absolute value of human beings as such. See Palaver (2009).

8. The Athenian "pharmakos" figure is a form of sacrificial victim, like the scapegoat, and the name aptly recalls the "medicinal" role of sacrifice as a specific therapy against disorder that must be taken regularly, that is, *ritually.*

9. See 2 Corinthians 4:16–18: "For it is the God who said, 'Let light shine out of darkness,' who has shone in our hearts to give the light of the knowledge of the glory of God in the face of Christ [v. 6] . . . So we do not lose heart. Though our outer nature is wasting away, our inner nature is being renewed every day. For this slight momentary affliction is preparing for us an eternal weight of glory beyond all comparison, because we look not to the things that are seen but to the things that are unseen; for the things that are seen are transient, but the things that are unseen are eternal" (v. 16–18).

Cited Texts and Further Reading

Girard, René. 1966. *Deceit, Desire, and the Novel.* Translated by Yvonne Freccero. Baltimore: Johns Hopkins University Press.

———. 1987a. *Job: The Victim of His People.* Translated by Yvonne Freccero. Stanford, CA: Stanford University Press.

———. 1987b. *Things Hidden since the Foundation of the World* (*research undertaken in collaboration with Jean-Michel Oughourlian and Guy Lefort*). Translated by Stephen Bann and Michael Metteer. Stanford, CA: Stanford University Press.

———. 1999. *Je vois Satan tomber comme l'éclair* (Paris: Grasset, 1999). Translated by J. G. Williams. *I See Satan Fall Like Lightning.* Maryknoll, NY: Orbis Books, 2001.

Hamerton-Kelly, Robert. 1992. *Sacred Violence: Paul's Hermeneutic of the Cross.* Minneapolis: Fortress Press.

Mahoney, Jack. 2011. *Christianity in Evolution: An Exploration.* Washington, DC: Georgetown University Press.

Mitchell, Stephen. 2004. *Gilgamesh: A New English Version.* New York: Free Press.

Palaver, Wolfgang. 2009. "Abrahamitische Revolution, politische Gewalt und positive Mimesis." In *Im Wettstreit um das Gute,* 29–65. Munster: LIT.

Pritchard, James B. 1955. *Ancient Near-Eastern Texts Relating to the Old Testament.* Princeton, NJ: Princeton University Press.

Serres, Michel. 1991. *Rome: The Book of Foundations.* Translated by Felicia McCarren. Stanford, CA: Stanford University Press.

Vattimo, Gianni. 2002. *After Christianity.* New York: Columbia University Press.

Williams, James. 1991. *The Bible, Violence, and the Sacred: Liberation from the Myth of Sanctioned Violence.* San Francisco: Harper.

Žižek, Slavoj, and John Milbank. 2009. *The Monstrosity of Christ: Paradox or Dialectic?* Edited by Creston Davis. Cambridge, MA: MIT.

PART THREE

Violent Reciprocities and Peace-Making in the Contemporary World

Northern Ireland

Breaking the Inheritance of Conflict and Violence

Duncan Morrow

Ring the bells that still can ring
Forget your perfect offering
There is a crack in everything
That's how the light gets in
          —Leonard Cohen, "Anthem," 1992.

A s part of the wider Western world, Northern Ireland is deeply tied to the presumptions, movements, and expectations of those around us. Indeed, it is arguable that we live as close to the geographical center of the North Atlantic democratic community as anyone. But unlike most of Western Europe and North America, it is our predicament to live together without a shared and acceptable transcendence provided by nation or state or religion. All of these modern sacralities have "cracked."

In the course of centuries of increasingly ethnocentric struggle, both religion and nation have become the tools of a struggle for power. Control of the instruments of violence—also of the political apparatus of the *state*, therefore—has become the object of deep and continuous political rivalry. The consequences have been a kind of endemic insecurity, and a public life that exhibits all of the characteristics of model-obstacle and model-rival relation-ships. The question of being and identity has haunted Northern Ireland since it was born out of turmoil and violence almost a century ago: "To be or not to be?" (i.e., should this state exist at all?). That has been our question. The result has been semi-continuous political violence, which by turns polarized and fascinated the immediate population, and over time a wider political public.

I propose here a short exploration of what it means to live together in the shadow of this ambiguity and insecurity. My essay is also a brief explanation of what has happened to us since the decisions to call a halt to political violence, begun in the mid-1990s. Most importantly, it asks what kinds of ways forward are possible that can take us beyond mimesis with the "double" of our own fears, which has been the dominant political experience for so long.

Let me say, by way of personal preface, that I was born and still am a Protestant. This places me on the side of the historically dominant, who have their place as a direct result of buried-but-lingering violence and who fear the counterviolence of revenge to this day. I am also well-educated and materi-ally comfortable, which means that I and my family can live free of the most brutal consequences of our history.

Four factors, at least, have set my life at an oblique angle to the dominant obsessions of my homeland. My wider family were Presbyterian farmers who lived in a part of Northern Ireland where there were historically very few Catholics. All of their rivalries were within the Protestant community and against their more powerful family and neighbors. Their politics tended to sympathize with Catholics, probably more out of solidarity with a common dislike of the Protestant leadership rather than anything else. Secondly, in the midst of the worst of polarizing violence, I was brought up in a self-consciously ecumenical Christian community, which acted as a temporary respite center and gathering point for spiritual refugees from every and each community right through the last violent decades. My experience was to meet and hear both parallel and irreconcilable stories of threat and fear. Over time, in the midst of our own rivalries and struggles, we were forced unwill-ingly to recognize that we were not better people—life in this community is far from utopian. But we were freed of some of the political fascination: an inheritance that has made possible the job I do now.[1]

Thirdly, I lived part of my life in both the wider UK and in the Repub-lic of Ireland. They were and are my friends. I cannot and do not share the obsessive fears of cultural or political annihilation that haunt so many of my neighbors.

Finally, I was introduced to the work of René Girard by a magnificent Dutchman, Roel Kaptein, who tried to teach us to be humble. He taught that we were not the good people we thought ourselves to be; that our freedom was a freedom to choose whom to follow, *not* to have or to get what we wished; to be faithful and to be grateful; and to understand our lives not as autonomous individuals, but as children of a mimetic relationship, people whose lives and personhood were the gifts of God and of others, rather than personal possessions. I remain certain that any creativity that we have found is the gift of such people, and of this community.

A Politics of "Selfhood" for Northern Ireland

Over many centuries, the politics of Britain and Ireland gave many opportunities for division and bitterness. The British state, in its own deep rivalries with, and fears of, the Catholic powers of continental Europe, harnessed religion as the pretext to oppress the Irish Catholics, their politics and culture. Protestant domination was the transcendent politico-economic principle, and this was defined as freedom from authoritarian Catholic enslavement. In generating a system in which religious identity and political experience became deeply intermingled, it created a profound cleft between people with different political and religious experiences of the same events. The underlying relationship of rivalry and violence was "remembered" within the limping structures of politics, the law of the land, the rituals of daily life, and the myths of the people. This all-conditioning fact left Ireland vulnerable to ethnocentric division in later centuries.

Sectarianism, antagonism to others articulated on the basis of religious differences, has deep roots in Ireland and was recognized early on as a politically potent force in all localities. While in much of the island of Ireland, the Protestants were a numerically small ruling class, in the North, the settlement created two large but distinct parallel communities who also interacted in commerce and daily living. A complex pattern of distance and intimacy emerged, mediated by many local variations.

Early relationships with roots in colonialism and religious sectarianism now gave way to antagonistic ethnocentric rivalry about ownership of the state. After the formal emancipation of Catholics in 1829, Catholic democratic confidence grew, gradually demanding more political distance from Britain. Protestants, on the other hand, became more and more antipathetic to Irish nationalism and sought closer allegiance to the globally dominant British Empire. As the rivalry deepened, so each national movement became increasingly caught in patterns of mimetic rivalry and fascination, which inevitably spilled out into violence experienced in diametrically opposite ways. Each "community" was convinced that their cause was a "just" response to the threat they faced. As Catholics organized, so the Catholic struggle under Protestant British rule became the leitmotif for Irish nationalism. Consciously or unconsciously, Protestants, unable to acknowledge the violent roots of their settlement, sought to shore themselves up against a feared domination, perhaps even the revenge, of a rising Catholic majority on the island.

Although shaped in increasingly segregated worlds, Nationalism and Unionism, Protestant and Catholic life in the north of Ireland were essentially constituted by and through one another. While it is always complex to talk of a single national self, each was indelibly generated by its experience of and reaction to the other. Instead of a single transcendent national identity, each sought control of the means of violence represented by the state.

Shelving the Irish crisis during World War I bought time, but no simple solutions. Protestants took the opportunity to remind a jingoistic Britain of their blood sacrifice at the Somme, while Catholics held up the blood sacrifice of the leaders of the abortive Easter Rising by republicans in Dublin during Easter of 1916. For both parties, the war offered opportunities to underline the sacred nature of the national bond.

The peace treaties following the war concerned themselves with the territories of the defeated German, Austrian, and Ottoman Empires. Seeking to generate a moral international order from Armageddon, Woodrow Wilson, an American president of Scots-Irish and Presbyterian origins, promoted democracy and U.S. freedom as the antidote to the failed tyranny of empires. In supporting "small nations struggling to be free," he raised the principle of national self-determination to a new prominence in international affairs. But, as in much of post-empire Europe, no single national "self" could be identified. The doctrine of self-determination under conditions of rivalry was not so much an invitation to freedom as an encouragement to conflict. Because all change was now legitimated by winning and keeping a majority, the politics of territorial control and the suppression or expulsion of the other became logical political developments.

Instead of small nations struggling to be free, small nations rivaled for territorial control and political power. In the context of escape from empire, the atmosphere of fear and revenge was hard to avoid. The atmosphere of violence rose everywhere—not least, of course, in the bitterness of the new German losers. It is in the nature of rivalry that the bitterness of the defeated serves to maintain the fears of the apparent winners. European history tells us clearly enough that the rivalries unresolved in Czechoslovakia, Yugoslavia, and even Poland in 1919 all exploded into tragedy before the twentieth century came to an end. After domination came occupation, expulsion, and murder. Wherever Europe had once found a cultural melting pot now became its theater of death.

Ireland fell outside the scope of the Paris Peace Conference in 1919. But Irish nationalism sought to ensure that the doctrine of self-determination applied to the Habsburgs' Europe should apply also to the British Empire. Elections in the UK in 1918 underlined divisions across the island. Where Catholics were in a majority, the demand for Irish national self-determination was unmistakable. But where Protestants predominated, there was almost universal support for the Union with Britain.

In an atmosphere of crisis and violence, Britain sought the line of least resistance: first by trying to impose order by force, then by trying to grant home rule to Northern Ireland and Southern Ireland separately, and then agreeing to the independence of the southern part, leaving Northern Ireland within the United Kingdom but insulated from the rest of the state and the rest of the island.

Rivalry over the very existence of Northern Ireland was built in from the beginning. Northern Ireland was designed to have a Protestant majority through a careful choice of territory. Catholics were only a minority if they could be successfully separated from the rest of the Catholic population on the island. Amidst considerable IRA violence, the Protestant Unionists set out to establish Northern Ireland as "a Protestant Parliament for a Protestant people," thereby deepening the despair of their own Catholic population and simultaneously defining their own project in terms of its relationships with the greater Catholic Other to the south. The result was a political world shaped by complex mimetic relationships with events of the past (temporal mimesis), and with the fears of our own community, and with the fears of the others (spatial mimesis). The result was a world of polarization and fascination, which, like an earthquake, was always predictable in general terms, but hard to pin down to dates and times.

When an accepted transcendence has disappeared, attempts to claim or enforce transcendence can only be done with enormous violence. The very act of seeking to impose an order as transcendent exposes the *roots of all structure* in violence and the sacred. Once *competing* claims to the transcendent order face each other, there is nothing to stop their descent into enormous, and potentially unlimited, violence. Religious wars are always *about everything*. So in the secular world (where sacralities are displaced to a horizontal timeline), equally, are wars of ideology and nation. At the frontiers of the European empires, both nationalism and liberal democracy found themselves exposed as murderers.

Instead of providing a secure identity, the nation delivered up to rivalry is exposed as a god that failed: failed to assert, failed to protect, failed to *be*. The result is not security, but ever more desperate attempts, by ritual means, to reassert the transcendence and security seemingly promised by the autonomous nation. In spite of the rising fascination, the issue itself of nationality becomes in fact the scene, and often the scenario, of maximum insecurity, where identity is demonstrably not taken for granted, but has to be repeatedly, neurotically, and violently asserted. Inevitably, it is also immediately emotional and profoundly associated with anger, fears, and mistrust; and ultimately, in their crescendo to paroxysm, the angers, fears, and anxieties seek their discharge in scapegoating. As violence rises, any remaining free relationships are liable to be invaded by this pervading atmosphere.

For fifty years, the rest of Britain and Ireland *turned their backs on Northern Ireland*. Northern Ireland became, in this sense, the scapegoat of Leviticus, dispatched into the wilderness, "carrying away" those aspects of their own historically hopeless entanglement that it was impossible to resolve. Northern Ireland became a place apart, locked up in continuous rivalry and polarization, confined in perilous isolation—the delegated scapegoat of more powerful forces. It was a role we played well. In many ways, Northern Ireland also enjoyed the limelight of being at the center of such attention—there was a considerable "illness bonus." At the same time, for as long as Northern Ireland is handled as the identified patient of psychotherapy, it probably makes it impossible for real change to happen.

The price of driving Northern Ireland away has been paid in finance and material resources that were applied to maintain spatial separations and reduce the most obvious aspects of rivalry. The results to date have been an ethnic conflict played out in slow motion, where the resources and ingenuity of Western states have been applied to manage enmity without ever undermining or repairing it. Nothing fundamental changed; but the symptoms were well-managed (this is the exact *split-sense* in which the sacred is said by Girard to "contain" violence).

The logic of mimetic rivalry did not, therefore, escalate to its logical conclusion in Northern Ireland. Instead, after thirty years, the dynamics of the underpinning relationship had begun to become visible. Thousands of lives were sacrificed to the gods of self-assertion. Violence merely deepened hopelessness. And as killing followed killing, in an ever more circular pattern, fewer and fewer could really believe that our political world was divided into the intrinsically evil and the intrinsically good. Slowly, but inevitably, the costs of violence were becoming visible.

Keeping the Peace: Rituals of Self and Other

The "normal" reaction to the uncertainty of rivalry is an ever more desperate attempt to maintain order. Girard has shown decisively that difficulties in culture are resolved by the rituals of religious and cultural life. Fundamentalism and chaos are not opposites, but two sides, the plus and the minus, of the same reality. We live in a time when rituals have faded from public view, but the legacy remains.

When it is functioning, ritual allows a people to experience again that they are unified and at peace, a single entity forged out of disparate units. Coming into mimesis with the known order, people are freed of anxiety, becoming part of a whole rather than isolated as individuals. Critically, the price of ritual is always borne outside the community. For a people to become undivided requires, of course, that those separating or dividing the community are driven out; and thus a clear moral order of the good and bad is established.

The imperative to return to ritual, and hence to finally place the anxiety of the community onto a scapegoat, becomes greater as insecurity and anxiety rise. In a context like Northern Ireland, political ritual therefore takes on an unusual public prominence and a peculiar hopelessness. National flags fly from every lamppost in places where violence is greatest; and aggressive territorial marking creates a sharply segregated sense of public space. The Protestant tradition of parading through the countryside each summer acts as a lightning conductor for community tension, and self-consciously Irish sports create community solidarity for the Catholic population.

But because the rituals never fully succeed in driving "them" out, the underlying violence in the ritual is disastrously visible. While ritual temporarily unites the community internally, it never quite succeeds, either, in its primary function: that of transforming violence into sacred obligation. Ritual continues, but it can only really continue in bad faith. The remnants of cultural ritual generate, but cannot finally expel, the fears—while deepening the rivalry and fascination between competing communities and people. But precisely because of the increased anxiety, failed rituals also increase the drive to greater ritual effort. For those who fear that they will lose in the rivalry, ritual takes on an ever more desperate character, deepening the hopelessness rather than generating release.

The tragedy of the Christian churches in Northern Ireland is to have become co-opted as ritualizers of segregation and antagonism. The very fact that whole political groups can still be described in terms of denominational labels, however unsatisfactorily, suggests a close association between ethnic, national, *and religious* identity. During settlement, the north of Ireland spectacularly failed to follow the principle of territorial segregation that underpinned Germany's attempt to regulate religious warfare after the Reformation, and the "you in your world, I in mine" *modus vivendi* of Western ex-Christendom in the modern age. Instead, antagonistic versions of Christianity coexisted on different sides of a colonial expansion, cheek by jowl. The churches were therefore structurally at risk of becoming mouthpieces for ethnic identity, identifying the god of the scapegoats, in all partisanship, with *their own tribal predicament.* This disastrous half-truth is a trap into which they fell spectacularly.

In the absence of political security, churches were often the first available places for people to gather in security. The enemy was shut out in a context where real mutual antagonism deepened the sense of ritual exclusion. The rival claims to authority that are the legacy of Reformation and Counter-Reformation became in Ireland the fuel for community solidarity and mutual exclusion. While Protestants preached vigilance against Catholic imperialism, and therefore diverted attention from the impact of British (Protestant) imperialism on their Catholic neighbors, Catholics preached righteous resistance without reference to the implications of Catholic power for Protestants. Worryingly for the churches, their action as ritual antidote to anxiety increased their popularity; and it is ironically true that Northern Ireland is one of the *most religiously observant* parts of Western Europe. While the communities were united and calmed and the enemy was ritually excluded, forgiveness, contrition, and reconciliation could be systematically "contained" also.

Through their involvement in schools, our churches also played a critical religious role in forming parallel communities in the modern age. In the absence of a transcendent state, the British agreed to devolve schooling in Ireland to the separated and rival denominations. Understood as separate and parallel systems, the schools emphasized internal solidarity and external difference between Christian denominations and also between Christians and others. Separate religious instruction cemented and integrated separate understandings of history, different games, and different socioeconomic experiences. Instead of vehicles for humility and truth, churches became purveyors of myth. In many ways the denominational schools were the midwives of the modern national selves. And the churches patrolled their own boundaries with the same vigilance as the hardening boundaries of state and nation.

In recent years, two events have illustrated the ongoing complicity of organized Christianity with ritual exclusion. As a result of worsening sectarian youth riots in a largely Protestant town, a young Catholic boy was brutally beaten to death by a Protestant gang. Amid the subsequent shame and anger, it became clear that religious objection precluded the Protestant MP for the area from attending the Catholic funeral, and another member of his party remarked that the murdered victim was not fit for heaven. In another incident, three Augustinian priests celebrated the Eucharist with an

Anglican at a mass to remember the 1916 rising against the British. The result was a national Catholic panic, and the forced apology of the Augustinians. Of course this is not the whole picture. But in general terms, Ireland has deepened the secular suspicion that Christianity is implicated in violent religious exclusion rather than freedom, forgiveness, and love.

In the modern age, even the rituals of democratic politics have failed to generate structure or order. Northern Ireland was regarded by Catholics as an outrageous gerrymander, an artificial "construction" imposed to defend imperial power. For Protestants, of course, this refusal by Catholics to recognize the transcendent authority of the ballot box reinforced the sense that Catholics could not be regarded as citizens but only as enemies. For as long as national rivalry remained the basis for political life, only demographic change could alter the result. Elections degenerated from ritual occasions to choose and grant authority to governments to organized headcounts to ensure supremacy in the rivalry over the state. Without an experience of ritual belonging, neither the winners nor the losers of elections found any security. Instead, elections deepened the rivalry between self and other by ritually setting whole communities into rivalry as competing and antagonistic twins, and emphasized the *inadequacy of democracy as a ritual for resolving conflict.*

In a context of escalating rivalry, the drive to create ritual solidarity is enormously heightened. Where the enemy is still present, such rituals present the greatest opportunity for violence. In a context like Northern Ireland where neither side can finally drive the other out, the violence merely provides a pretext that requires further rituals but never results in security.

There is no way back to safety through ritual. As the ordained order fades, so the temptation grows and the descent into undifferentiated violence accelerates. While the transcendent order of the West—democracy, human rights, and civic equality—and some of the inheritance of Judeo-Christianity, especially around killing, have been hugely important, even these are now coming under visible strain across the West. There is no way to security through repeating the old myths of our own innocence. Instead, each failed ritual re-creates a radical sense of self and other, simultaneously dividing and polarizing at one level while drawing everyone into deeper fascination with one another in the violence that is generated. And if we have one political contribution to the world, it is this: Northern Ireland has already been down the road of *compensating for rivalry* through *increased homeland security*—with disastrous long-term consequences for all of our stated transcendences, already predicated upon violence, even where invoking justice and rights.

"That's How the Light Gets In"?

Change has come to Northern Ireland in part because it had to. Profoundly, in situations of fear and fascination, the fascination of others adds to the flames and reduces the space for action. Change in Northern Ireland was dependent on the fact that other people elsewhere found their own ways to go. For freedom to flourish, the core thing is always to find our way back to our own freedom and responsibilities, thus making new things possible for others. We are not and never were autonomous and separate from change elsewhere.

The crisis of Northern Ireland—how we live together as our structures wane—is the crisis of the world. Clear new shoots came from the changing international atmosphere after the Cold War; from changes in South Africa and (at that time) the Middle East; and from the wish to stop using Northern Ireland as a scapegoat in Britain, now increasingly fascinated by its fear of self-organizing Europe, and in Ireland, now wishing mostly to become rich within the EEC. Whereas, in 1920, Northern Ireland had been the fulcrum of a violent British-Irish conflict, by 1994 it was regarded as an obstacle to the interests of both Dublin and London.

And, of course, we had our own responsibilities. Northern Ireland is not poor or ill-educated. We speak English and have access to the global market; we have an open capitalist private-ownership system and have relatively little public corruption. We know how to vote, and we see from our neighbors how government is meant to work. At its heart, our crisis is a crisis of relationships. By the 1990s, there was an increasing hopelessness in Northern Ireland about the ever more visible cycle of violence. In the light of changes elsewhere, violence looked like violence, rather than any of its high-minded rationalizations. The age of Protestant domination was clearly over. And while Irish nationalism had failed by violence to dislodge the British from Ireland, there was no doubt that Catholics in Ireland had a greater sense of gaining ground than before. What Girard calls the "wearing down" of the efficacy of sacred violence was our opportunity.

Ethnocentrism is the result of spatial and temporal mimesis with deep and complex root systems. In a context where ethnocentric and sectarian rivalry has dominated the landscape, nearly every institution is infected. The reality is that real change—change where we stop the separation of people into good people and bad people, and in which the secrets of ethnocentrism are unveiled—will challenge all of our rituals and all of our institutions. Real change, real freedom will only be possible if we are willing to face our victims and meet in contrition and forgiveness.

What is already clear is that Northern Ireland is deeply ambivalent about this experience. Forgiveness and contrition are very painful; and it is my deep experience that all of us *fight like tigers* to avoid the unveiling of our secrets, and to keep the consequences of the revelation of our complicity with violence as far away as possible. The price of freedom, of knowing that we are all brothers and sisters, and of stopping the game of dividing between the good guys and the bad guys, is paid in profound and disturbing dis-illusion about ourselves.

We have to drop all our romanticism about conflict resolution. As Girard points out, on the day Jesus was crucified, Pilate and Herod made up a profound rivalry of mistrust and became friends. Surface harmony can hide murderous secrets, and the wish to be left alone without the unveiling of our secrets is deeply tempting. The intuition to return to ritual expresses in part the desire to return to innocence.

On the other hand, there is also a deep longing for the fear and violence to be over. In spite of the inadequacy, Northern Ireland has undoubtedly and tentatively embarked since 1994 on a journey toward a different political settlement. By calling it a "peace process," people have been prepared for a long journey. At the same time, by calling it a process, we again run the risk of hiding from ourselves that this is not merely a series of ritual steps to a known destination, but a series of costly existential choices made under the gaze of our rivals and in the face of our victims.

And yet, the decision to stop, to look for peace has created huge cracks in the edifice of ethnocentrism in Northern Ireland. One of the benefits of being in a place with resources of Western scale is that *time* has been given for these patterns of relationship to become visible and to be addressed—a chance that has elsewhere disappeared, carried away in rapidly escalating violence.

Slowly but inexorably, the truth about our complicity with ethnocentric violence is emerging into the public domain, in spite of the resistance of just about every interest. Of course it is also true that by investing so many resources, more and more people have a vested interest in keeping things as they are (should I perhaps count myself among them?). By safely isolating "the problem" by paying for it to be taken away, by creating an *industry of fascination* around our failure to find each other, we have generated an inheritance of interests contradictory to each other, but equally hypocritical. The overwhelming result is ambivalence and ambiguity in which aspects of the old and the promise of novelty coexist in uneasy relationship.

In an open society, so much is already known. All the cases that have been before Northern Ireland's courts give huge detail of what terrorism did. We know, even if we do not wish to acknowledge it, that the state *too* broke all of its rules in support of its security strategy. Yet there is a deep fear that a public truth process would lead to renewed, and even more desperate, rivalry, as each of us desperately seeks to prevent the impact of the unveiling of our complicity upon our current political projects. Unlike in South Africa, the political future here looks like a form of sharing, and until now, the possibility of sharing has been based on an unspoken mutual agreement that neither side could really stand the revelation of their own violence. Unfortunately, both sides still insist on unveiling the truth about *the other's* violence, and so rivalry about the issue continues to surface. At a recent meeting, the priest responsible for mediating with the IRA to achieve decommissioning of weapons told a heckling ultra-Protestant in his audience that Protestants were responsible for acting like Nazis when in power; to which his heckler responded that Catholics were engaged in collusion with genocide. While more extreme than usual, the exchange revealed a deep truth about the distance of the journey still to be made toward peace.

On the one hand, we live in a kind of bad faith: paying money to our victims but never allowing their story to divert us, continually paying lip service to their suffering, but keeping it as far away from our responsibility as possible and certainly scapegoating them again. And yet, inexorably, the human stories of victims count as one of the real cracks in Northern Ireland. Slowly but surely it has become clear that the murders and conspiracies of the past will either be our door into a new future or else the reason why we go back to war. Paradoxically much of the best and most profound work has been done among the relatives of those who were closest to violence. In my own work, I know of many examples of victims of violence meeting and finding peace with others who suffered from the other side; of people who were involved in violent action meeting those who they destroyed and finding forgiveness and real change.

The harder nut to crack has been the political interests and the wishes of average people, those who watched violence *from a distance,* so as not to be *disturbed.* At stake for many of us is the deeply hypocritical ideology of liberal individualism, postulating that only those who committed the act are complicit in violence. And by focusing on the victims and perpetrators and making them *the only players* and the only people *responsible for making change,* we are of course scapegoating them again.

Perhaps the most challenged in this regard are the churches. At a *global* level, they remain committed to rivalry and separation. And in an Irish context, that rivalry has had enormously destructive consequences. No amount of assuring ourselves that we have prayed for peace can take away from the fact that the Protestant churches have never been places to speak about what it means to be a people who arrived at where they are through colonial politics; or that the failure to recognize the Christianity in Catholicism had the effect of sacralizing religious hatred and murder. And has the Catholic Church ever really spoken about how its use of the power of exclusion from communion and its insistence on secular priestly authority has fueled the same dynamic of superiority and sacred cause and made all non-Catholics feel unsafe with the Church in power? Likewise the churches have continued to insist on separate education, no matter what the ethnocentric consequences. On the one hand, the experience of Northern Ireland is the experience that the gospel is deeply challenged, even in the bosom of its own carriers. And there is no doubt that change in Ireland, if it were really to undermine the sins of our rivalry and segregation, would touch on deep historic injuries and would shake the ritual certainties of many Catholics and Protestants all across the world.

And so, in spite of twelve years of a surface peace process, it remains extremely important that there are small "cradles of freedom," places where people can meet in a real sense. To be real cradles where freedom can be nurtured, they have to be places where the rivalries of wider society are distant.

These nurturing spaces or places really only fulfill their task when they make it possible to learn existentially and repeatedly that romanticism, the division of people into good people and bad people, is a lie; and that instead, and more truly, people meet as brothers and sisters.

If there is such a thing as the process of peace-building, it is the slow interaction of our rivalries with the freedom that this knowledge brings. It is thus inevitably fragile, contingent, and difficult. It is also deeply discomforting. In this too, we belong once more to the rest of the world. And it has to be renewed and refound again and again. And when we experience something of it, something new is brought out of nothing—the very definition of *creation*.

Northern Ireland perfectly reflects our ambivalence about all of this. While Britain and Ireland, together with the international community, guided the process, there could indeed be plausible talk of new relationships. In a deep sense they were renegotiating their own relationship in revisiting the scene of the things they had previously found too hard to cope with—Northern Ireland. In doing so, they were able to point to a degree of success in avoiding deeper fascination for violence, enabling them to subordinate territorial rivalry to wider Western values. British colonialism was now over; and, since at least 1945 and the discovery of the Holocaust, all Western states have made it a matter of policy to avoid alignment with Hitler's ethnic madness.

At the same time, they were revisiting the scene of some uncomfortable secrets: both had bought freedom from home-based conflict by deflecting the worst ethnic madness onto a small unresolved territory lying between them. While there was a sincere wish for change, there was an even stronger interest in getting rid of what had become an irritating problem. In the peace deal of 1998, sharing and partnership was to be the order of the day; but, problematically, that sharing was to be done mainly by the rivaling parties in Northern Ireland. The danger of course, for Britain and Ireland, is that both are in practice scapegoating Northern Ireland for their own difficulties once more, without being willing or able to take their own responsibilities.

After September 11, 2001, global desire to be a terrorist has probably risen, although within the Western world, the identification of terrorism with murder and crime has also increased sharply. With all avenues to political action blocked, the result of these competing forces has been a profound stasis, with no possibility of returning in innocence to the past, and no willingness to move decisively forward. Local political leadership has not yet found any freedom to really take leave of ethnocentrism. "Our people" continues to be a concept with clear lines defined by traditional divisions, with the danger that they will be made simply irrelevant over time. The fundamental picture of good guys and bad guys remains intact. And none of us has been truly willing to face the people injured in the past by the violence from our own side.

That this peace-bearing evolution could happen in Northern Ireland without social crisis and paroxysm is certainly an achievement of sorts. While it is always possible that the ceasefire will go into reverse, the emergence of a pause in escalation and a political culture in which parties now talk openly with one another has had important consequences. Irish nationalism has begun to make its peace with the legacy of so many Irish people fighting and dying as British soldiers in the two world wars, not least by attending memorials and laying wreaths. Irish sporting organizations have dropped their objections to British soldiers playing, and politicians of all parties now sit to debate political matters regularly. Unionist politicians now travel to Dublin without comment from their constituents. And last year, the Queen, memorably and to great healing effect, made the first official visit to Dublin by a British monarch since Irish independence in 1921.

Important institutional changes have also begun to emerge. A second official enquiry has laid the blame for the "Bloody Sunday" massacre of 1972 where it belongs: on the shoulders of over-nervous or gung-ho British paratroops. A new police service has emerged that has much wider support than before. For the first time it is possible for many Catholics to join safely in policing, with the possibility that more than a third of all officers will be Catholic within five years. This is in itself a huge change in the relationship with the law for many people; and it is fragile. In some areas, people have begun to stand up against the violence of local paramilitaries, most famously in the case of the Catholic McCartney family against the IRA.

The government has now produced a policy framework—called "A Shared Future"—that puts making new and nonviolent relationships at the heart of social and economic policy for the future. For the first time, Ireland has started to attract new people to live among us, rather than exporting some of our brightest and best across the globe. This too has changed the underlying reality, creating new relationships and bringing new challenges.

The road from Egypt to the Promised Land passed through forty years in the desert. The Hebrew Bible records that it was only by miracle that this rivalrous and rebel troop arrived. And the candor of the story shows that when they got there, the inheritors of the land of milk and honey remained very violent and singularly imperfect. "Every heart to love will come, but like a refugee."[2]

There is light in Northern Ireland. There are cracks in the transcendence of nationalism that call us forward into more complex recognition of our relationship with one another. Christianity is called to recognize its real and avoidable, if structurally determined, complicity in violence. The rituals of segregation are revealed as empty. And as a society, in spite of the very slow pace of change, there are signs of people edging toward finding other realities.

What Northern Ireland reveals to the world is that the rituals of the past are gone as a way to peace. There is no way to get to security through more violence. And it reveals ever and again that the path of contrition, forgiveness, and conversion is simultaneously a path of freedom and penitence. Change means that we stop making the old distinctions between people who belong to us and people who don't, between friends and foes. What continues to be required is people, groups, leaders, and institutions who know this reality existentially. The only decisive *difference* is whether we need each other or not.

But we should end with a word of caution. As Jewish folk wisdom says: "Jewish people are just like everybody else, only more so." The same can be said of places in conflict. Working for peace in Northern Ireland is no different to anywhere else, except that pressures of fascination are more powerful. And just because of that, the essential choice—the choice to go on finding security through ritual and violence, or the choice to find another way—becomes sharper.

Hope in history is not just, or even mostly, chronological. It is the possibility that everything can be brought into relationship with the profound truth that we are all complicit in violence; but also that we are forgiven, and that we are invited to find our way back to each other as humble, imperfect, and unique sisters and brothers. We have a way to go.

Peace and Creativity: Our Debt to René Girard

A good part of the way has been illuminated by René Girard. At the heart of the mimetic hypothesis is the rediscovery of relatedness as the core of human existence. Not only does everything and everyone exist in relationships, but relationships are foundational to being, rather than the other way around. Behind, before, and around each person is the "given" of relationality. Or, put another way, there is no human being outside some given nexus of relationships. Our only questions can be: "with whom?," "in which mode?," and "with what fruits?"

Girard's radical, operative, and vital insight is that human relationality extends past instinct, past dominance patterns (pecking orders, social class, empire, etc.), and past the laws of genetics itself, into the *mimesis* of desire: a preconscious relatedness continuous with what evolutionary science calls "group intelligence," something that, in humans, both enables creative freedom and connects us, perilously, to one another in complex patterns—as models, rivals, and obstacles. His key insight is that human singularity in this order consists of being mimetic in respect of each other's *desires;* and here Girard reveals both our opportunity-rich opening to human, and even divine, potentials, *and* the risk of violent destruction, the threat to our very survival as a species that uncontrolled mimetic desire places over us.

The emergence of culture, while it may involve a rational functionality traceable by the theorist, is not itself, in the human subjects it motivates, a rationally driven process; it is, rather, an existential *condition of human survival* in the face of uncontrolled mimetic desire. And it rests ultimately, so Girard tells us, on an "all-against-one" unity forged in foundational violence, always at the expense of some victim or other—a foundation preserved and perpetuated in ritual sacrifice, without its beneficiaries becoming totally demystified in respect of their own role in that process . . . at least until some expelled and wandering slaves, reviewing their own beginnings and opening a new phylum of religion, began to see things differently. As he openly acknowledges, even an explorer like Girard is only the latest in a long line of pioneers.

That which we call "the self" can therefore only be a "self" in relationship. If individual autonomy is the romantic myth that still haunts our time, then change cannot come through "self-discovery" or "reconstruction"—if that implies some kind of conscious or planned change exercised on an independent subject. It depends critically on, and it is defined by, a change in the relationships through which each and every human reality is constituted. To speak of the self is to speak of our place in a wider reality. The self cannot so much be reconstructed as reoriented, or "reborn from above" as the gospel would have it. In mimesis with each other, the defining reality is "with what or with whom are we in mimesis?" and "mimesis of what sort?" Not so much *who are we?* as ... *whose* are we?

René Girard's work is necessarily scandalous to the modern academic mind. Uncomfortably, Girard takes us back to interdependency and to dependency. Autonomous self-fashioning gives way to choosing to follow the way that opens up unexpected possibilities of change and freedom. Not only does he dismiss the autonomy of desire and postulate a "grand narrative" theory in the age of postmodern relativism and nihilism, he identifies his insights closely with those of the gospel, with Jesus, and with the Judeo-Christian tradition as a whole. For Girard, Jesus's absolute anthropological importance is his revealing and redemption of the victim, underlying human cultural and religious existence, and his invitation into a new reality founded on that grace itself.

Freedom from mimetic desire, new and positive mimesis following this Christic pattern, is something that breaks in and, like its opposite, spreads contagiously; it is not any possession of ours. The possibility of relationship with the scapegoat victim—available to us through the Judeo-Christian tradition, and through the ongoing grace that theologians attribute to the Holy Spirit—rather than with the victimizers, however much our own kin or kind they may be, brings in a decisively new anthropological reality. In a radical sense, we are either locked up in the mimesis of rivalrous and conflicting desire, or we are, in some sense, in some degree, or for some part of the way, following the Christic pattern of peace-making. The only real creativity, engendering genuine novelty in the world, in other words, is that which reworks human lives into mimesis with this reality.

The potential consequences of a world mediated by a relationship with the victim are literally revolutionary. Now at last we can meet each other in weakness rather than as rivals—so winding up, once and for all, the archaic notion, lurking still in all our discreetly concealed modern romanticisms, that the world is divided into good people and bad people; and, conversely, that being given the chance to be recognized and serve one another as brothers and sisters is both blessing and creative act.

Among the many uncomfortable conclusions of Girard's insights is that, *pace* all dissenters, Jesus *matters*—albeit in a manner inverse to the triumphalist, militant proclamation of ex-Christendom. We might struggle with this, as might our critics, were it not for the fact that Jesus is for humanity before humanity is for Jesus. Whether it likes to recognize it or not, this generation and all future generations in a globalized world will be facing this choice in the acutest form, as a matter of our own continued *survival* as mimetic creatures. And Girard is surely right to put this point with the required note of urgency (at the price of generating ripples of well-bred disquiet at his "particularism," his "apocalypticism," etc.).

After Girard, the search for peace takes on a radically different shape. The old presumption that peace is the absence of visible violence is hardly sustainable in the face of our modern knowledge. The tools of elimination, repression, expulsion, revolution, and forced assimilation have been exposed for what they always were: forms of violence and surrogates for murder; which singularly reduces the tools available to us, while exposing the *impotence of power*. With overwhelming evidence that the mimesis of desire has increasingly deadly consequences for human life, we have been stripped of the possibility of *scapegoating with a good conscience*. We can no longer plead equality between the world of the ancient Egyptians and that of the Hebrew slaves in the desert, between crucifiers and the crucified, between the logos of Heraclitus (violence) and the Logos of John (love).

Whether we know it or not, the search is no longer for the ultimate structure, but for the relationship in which we all can have a place. The choice is to go on in denial, to seek to drive out our enemies in ever greater numbers, and to be revealed at that point as the liars and murderers we then are; or to stop the hypocrisy and scapegoating, and to find our way toward one another, as sisters and brothers in forgiveness and service.

There is indeed a crack in everything: change, creativity, and blessing are dependent on the shafts of light which that crack lets in, and on finding our way into a new world. The Christic bell is for me one that still rings loud and clear (a case at least envisaged by Cohen). If it is the Love divine (rather than the very imperfect, cracked, and regressive bell of ex-Christendom) that first makes the light-bearing crack and becomes the new model, then, in my view, we may and should remember the one *"perfect* sacrifice."

Notes

1. Between 2002 and 2012 Dr. Morrow was chief executive officer of the Northern Ireland Community Relations Council (CRC), the body with primary responsibility for the funding and development of intercommunity relations, practice, and policy in Northern Ireland (Editor's note).

2. Cohen, "Anthem."

Cited Texts and Further Reading

Baillie, Gil. 1995. *Violence Unveiled: Humanity at the Crossroads.* Danvers, MA: Crossroads Publishing.

Bell, Ian. 2012. "Truth Is Fine—but Hypocrisy Saves Lives." *Glasgow Herald,* July 1, 4.

Garrells, Scott R., ed. 2011. *Mimesis and Science.* East Lansing: Michigan State University Press.

Girard, René. 1976. *Deceit, Desire, and the Novel: Self and Other in Literary Structure.* Baltimore: Johns Hopkins University Press.

———. 1977. *Violence and the Sacred.* Baltimore: Johns Hopkins University Press.

Girard, René, et al. 1987. *Things Hidden since the Foundation of the World.* London: Athlone Press.

Girard, René. 2010. *Battling to the End.* East Lansing: Michigan University Press.

Judt, Tony. 2005. *Postwar.* London: Penguin Books.

Kaptein, Roel, and Duncan Morrow. 1995. *On the Way of Freedom.* Dublin: Columba Press.

Morrow, Duncan. 2007. "From Truce to Transformation?" Northern Ireland Community Relations Council. Available at http://www.community-relations.org.uk/about-us/news/item/137/from-truce-to-transformation.

———. 2008. *The Real Work Begins.* Northern Ireland Community Relations Council. Available at http://www.community-relations.org.uk/about-the-council/speeches.

Ruane, Joseph, and Jennifer Todd. 1976. *The Dynamics of Conflict in Northern Ireland: Power, Conflict and Emancipation.* Cambridge: Cambridge University Press.

———. 2010. *Ethnicity and Religion: Intersections and Comparisons.* London: Routledge.

Van Erp, Stefan, and André Lascaris. 2005. *Who Is Afraid of Postmodernism?* Munster: Lit Verlag.

Wright, Frank. 1987. *Northern Ireland: A Comparative Analysis.* London and Dublin: Gill and Macmillan.

———. 1993. *Two Lands on One Soil.* Dublin: Macmillan.

Communities of Contrast

Modeling Reconciliation in Northern Ireland

Derick Wilson

The internal "ethnic frontier" of Northern Ireland has been a space of intercommunity relations permanently subject to rivalrous and conflicting desires. At this interface, the daily lives of people and the energies of political parties, religious, cultural, and civic groups have been—and can in a flash, still become—consumed in a vortex of emotions and destructive actions.

This ever-imminent vortex has been forged by the force field of our history of asymmetrical relationships (Wright 1987),[1] straining conflictually toward rival forms of belonging, both internally, in relation to the political establishment of Northern Ireland, and externally with its aligned cosmopolitan neighbors: the Unionists historically looking always to Britain, the Nationalists to the formerly British but (since 1921) now independent Republic of Ireland. Moreover, the majority within each Irish political entity has its geographically or politically "trapped" internal minority. Historically, until the Good Friday Agreement of 1998, each had their diaspora, assumed or real, to appeal to and had been able to give this relationship primacy over the need to meet and deal with the Other in their midst.

All of which made Northern Ireland, in Girardian terms, a place of "bad mimesis" permanently subject to experiences of destructive rivalry

(Oughourlian 1991, 72)—these rivalries, turbocharged by the falsely sacral-izing devotion to political goals, projects, and institutions, rose recurrently to paroxysms of intercommunity conflict. It is as though each community were attempting to secure ethnic purity by driving out or killing off the Other (Kaptein 1992); and, even since the Good Friday settlement, violent acts of scapegoating have populated the space of relationships between people, with their respective traditions and their cultural institutions.

The challenge now, consequently, is to develop ways that contrast with the forms of "bad mimesis" that have gone before, and develop invitations to be mimetic with experiences and models of freedom that undo these internal dynamics. More precisely, it is to create a "good mimesis"—for Girard often insists, in countering partial readings of his work, that a *good* form of mimesis does exist; that his scenario of mimetic crisis is reversible; and, indeed, that the model for its reversal exists precisely in the faith professed in Northern Ireland by both "Catholics" and "Protestants." "Good mimesis" has the dual task of modeling concretely new models of freedom between different iden-tities, thus meeting the intellectual and theological challenges of promot-ing the ways of "communion" and cutting out the old ways of "crucifixion" (Kaptein and Morrow 1993, 119–24).

It will be understood that these community labels reflect *first of all* the fact which Girard's scenario of human origins illuminates fundamentally: namely, that the prime principle of bonding-and-binding in any community is, by definition, "religious" (in all the *ambiguity* attaching to that word). Some of us engaged in the effort of reconciliation appreciate vividly this basic fact about cultural identity, but would consider that it does not invalidate or exclude the potential for "good mimesis" of the Christic model (Kaptein 1992, 71–72). It is certainly an important and singular feature of our situa-tion in relation to other theaters of inter-ethnic conflict, such as the Balkans or Israel-Palestine, that the conflicted communities can both refer directly to it. In making this move, however, we always remind ourselves centrally that Girard envisages "Christendom" and its offshoots and residues (of which Northern Ireland is one) as entirely capable of *regressing* to unchristian pat-terns of *archaic* religion, precisely under the persuasion of falsely sacralizing mimetic rivalries (Girard 1987 [2003], 224–27; 249–253).

In Girardian terms, Northern Ireland is a place fossilized in the "regres-sions" of the former Christendom: a place where the gods of the (different) nations have failed to protect their "children," and the differing sacred national traditions were never able to conquer the ethnically and religiously different Other, or expel or purge or win out through assimilating that Other.

A Curious Place of Peace-Making

The Good Friday Agreement of 10 April 1998 (also called the Belfast Agreement)[2] has left us in a curiously ambiguous and difficult place of peacemaking.

While demanding imperatively to be addressed, the legacy of violence of the Troubles leaves us haunted. Between 1969 and 2001, 3,529 people were killed as a result of the conflict (Sutton 2002). These numbers, small by comparison with the casualties of other world hot spots, loom large in the "narrow ground" or "postage stamp" that is Northern Ireland.[3] The differential impact of the conflict and the direct experience of violence fell primarily on people from the border areas between Northern Ireland and the Republic of Ireland; from contested rural areas of mid Ulster; from the urban areas with high levels of poverty in Belfast and Derry; on business people; and on staff in the security forces, policing, and the criminal justice system.

The victims are both visible, in that they are in the midst of the society, and invisible, in that the move to create a new peaceful narrative of the driving political forces has given many victims the feeling that their story and place in common memory is erased (CVSNI 2010, 4–5), an experience common in other conflicted areas of the world (Rothfield 2008, 15–27).[4]

Because there have been no agreed winners, no expelled or dominated losers—and because we are still in the midst of one another—the victims are at one and the same time expelled from many memories, yet always, discomfortably, returning.

The distinction between "legitimate force" and "violence," and with it the ability of the law to criminalize effectively, were eroded, if they had ever existed in this place. Such ethnic frontier societies need external transcending powers, preferably international ones, as well as the establishing of agreed policing and criminal justice systems; addressing discrimination in employment; securing diverse cultural identity and/or language rights, religious identity, and religious freedoms (Wright 1987, 112–63); and equity in education with, preferably, the harnessing of education to the goal of building a more shared, reconstructed society based on equity, diversity, and interdependence (Eyben, Morrow, and Wilson 1997).

What we have had hitherto is a process of sacralizing *some* victims, or creating a *hierarchy* of victims (CGAPNI 2009, 16) in which those killed, whom we believe to be part of "us," are elevated and those Others are demonized. This dynamic needs to be broken or it becomes part of the sacrificial vortex that sucks us in. The only lasting peace is one founded on a new acknowledgment of perpetrators and victims together. We have to see, in others, the face of the Other-like-us.

There is still, even within the framework of the Agreement, an ambivalence about facing into reconciliation, since this is an invitation to living in a new manner altogether, which escapes us in the scale of its moral challenge and in its political consequences. Many, including former peace and reconciliation workers, remain resentful and in rivalry with those now in power; and even those in power, needing one another to have that power, settle also for resentment. "Resentment" is somewhere between revenge, which we know destroys all, and reconciliation, which we know demands a whole new freedom (Morrow 2009). Yet we know such freedom has to be modeled, interpersonally, structurally, and intellectually, with the Other and with one another.

Alongside such disabling dynamics, there are traces also of something new: something we call a "contrast-culture" (Kaptein with Morrow 1993, 116), which is relational and centered on trust—a culture of relationships where people experience a freedom and openness with different Others; where there are experiences of learning together in often very robust relationships; so many fragile embryos capable of growing into new relationships and structures, re-linking very divided people and the traditions they come from. Crossing "the barrier from the past to the future is a hazardous enterprise where the essence of peace has come to mean making a future with the very people 'we' tried, and failed, to defeat" (Morrow 2007, 1).

These relationships and spaces belong to a history of diverse actions, motivated by reconciliation and by a knowledge, shared across diverse political, religious, civic, and cultural groups, that secret and private discussions, progressing eventually into public space, are needed if violence and conflict are to ever be ended, antithetical positions negotiated, and beliefs examined together—the whole within relationships that promote healing on a variety of levels (Shriver 2007, 2–3).[5]

The way of "crucifixion," the way of people of goodwill mimetically denying their own part, by acts of omission and commission, in the violence of a violent culture, henceforth discomforts us (this is one legitimate effect of the Good Friday Agreement!). The latent but life-bearing myth of the victims is henceforth that they deeply belong both to the perpetrator and to those—*all* those—who survived unscathed. And if we are to find ways to acknowledge this reality together, our divided community needs spaces and relationships where people can acknowledge the victims and perpetrators, all together exploring and consolidating new ways beyond fear and conflict.

The fact that there was not one winner, but an uneasy and haunted peace, has meant that we are faced by the need to recognize that we cannot build a new shared society without *all* victims and survivors being acknowledged; we cannot build a new and shared society without the "previously hated Other" being *also* included.

To meet together, learn, and build a new, shared culture within existing and new public and civic institutions between people from different sides of the fear line is a still fragile and delicate enterprise. For the immediate future, it will still be easier for people to be mimetic in respect of the old cultural wisdom, that "the Other is not to be trusted," the "Other is your enemy." However, it is our contention that there is already at work, in respect of past and future time, and in all places of our divided community, a strand of practice that builds experiences together, contrasting with the old cultural ways, and where the other is understood "to be a gift." This is what we call "experiencing the Contrast" (Kaptein and Morrow 1993, 116).

The group Acknowledging the Past, established in the wake of the Good Friday Agreement, recently conducted a review of how victims and survivors, of all sorts, from all different traditions—former combatants, as well as local politicians and the British and Irish governments—might deal with the past. They arrived at this overarching restorative principle:

> The past should be dealt with in a manner which enables society to become more defined by its desire for true and lasting reconciliation rather than by division and mistrust, seeking to promote a shared and reconciled future for all. (CGAPNI 2009, 13)

Meeting Together for a Change

In 1979, a study group on Girard's work modeled this form of practice within the wider work for intercommunity reconciliation of the Corrymeela Community. The mimetic hypothesis became, from then on, central to the practice of residential education programs and to the theological, political, and educational understandings of violence, scapegoating, healing, and reconciliation that the community promoted, involving children, young people, and adults from all areas of political and civic life. "Mimetic" understandings were developed and applied to politics, faith, civil society groups, education, and community work practice. The educational work was both relational and structural; it was pursued in support of a critical practice of community relations in Northern Ireland and beyond.

Finding a basis in mimetic theory (MT), the group was influenced by the work of the Dutch–Northern Ireland Advisory Committee (DNIAC 1977),[6] who brought diverse gifts in theology, literature, politics, philosophy, and psychotherapy; also, as I have already indicated, by Frank Wright, who brought us his political perspectives on "ethnic frontier" societies. We developed a style of group work that enabled people from very diverse and conflicting backgrounds to meet together and reflect on their questions and difficulties around the business of living peacefully together in the one conflicted place. Some working hypotheses on which that work has been based evolved out of our experiences with groups.

These inspirations were codified into a series of general principles or working presuppositions guiding our common encounters. For example:

> We work with people in groups from all social backgrounds, assuming that people initially choose to come together because they wish to be together and meet with other people. We assume that people who come into groups with us wish to find some new ways to understand the situations they are in and to order their lives in a new manner.
>
> In order to have this possibility, we hope that the people come to meet others as completely as possible, with their own histories and experiences, their own difficulties and fulfillments, their wishes and their hopes. The published and accepted themes of the group meetings give the possibility for the members of the group to do this.

Meeting together in this manner is only possible when there is freedom between the members of the group. This means that there is trust in
the group, or at least, trust in the group worker. Our responsibility as group
workers is to be free and trusting, yet we recognise that this is not always
completely possible, as we too live in the same place as the group members.
Our task is not to make any difference between the members of the group
and not to play any power game in, or with, the group. By modelling freedom through being in the group in this manner we give the other members
of the group the possibility to experience freedom and trust too. (Wilson
and Morrow 1996, 16–25)

The meetings we have had, and still continue to facilitate, in the wake of the
political agreement of 1998, have often been between people who have traditionally maintained distance from one another. In many cases, mimetically,
these embryonic meetings have been repeated and patterned, eventually
becoming new adult structures pursuing their own life and arrangements in
organizations such as faith and interfaith groups, trade-union groups, community organizations, members of reconciliation groups, members of school
boards and staff in the "controlled" (state), the Catholic ("maintained"), and
the integrated, and Irish Language sectors of the educational system (see
Eyben, Morrow, and Wilson 2002, 103).

We begin a group by asking the members to speak about their interest
in the published theme and identify the questions they have. Listing these in
turn, acknowledging without any comment to whom the questions belong,
we then decide together what the work of the group will be. This flexible and
very initial modeling process establishes the possibility for members to learn
deeply and to speak about themes that are important to them. Within it,
silence is welcomed as people find their voice and their questions.

The only conditions we place on group members is that the themes they
wish to speak together about are relevant to the actual life experiences of the
group members, and that they speak in the first person. We ask each person
to remain responsible for his or her own question, and the members of the
group write the agenda of the work together, through sharing their questions, shaping the sequence of the subthemes and taking responsibility with
the group worker for the manner in which the group moves forward with
these themes.

One of the results of group work is that differences between people become clearer, and at the same time, often unexpectedly, are accepted. This acceptance goes two ways. Every member of the group comes to understand herself or himself as being different, even unique, and, simultaneously, accepts that all are, in their own way, themselves not excluded, different.

When people really accept the fact of difference, this acceptance is decisive. Particularly so in what has been a politically contested "ethnic frontier" society, where the negative mimetic pressures on each person to belong to their own tradition can rest very heavily on an individual's shoulders. This reverses the mimesis of group solidarity, where the sense of collective responsibility diminishes the expression of individual difference within a tradition and feeds separation and mistrust. It promotes a dynamic of individuals, and then groups, becoming "critical lovers" of their tradition (Shriver 2005, 1); hence also the possibility of people freely meeting those who belong to different traditions.[7]

Our task is to make it possible for everybody in the group to say and share everything he or she wishes. Working in this manner, every member of the group gets as much space as possible to consider, and gain clarity about, his or her situation in life and society. The goal of group work is not that group members make decisions about their lives during the group sessions; rather it is that people get the freedom to make decisions in their lives as they need or wish, in the very moments that such freedom is needed or wished. In that group space, the experience of freedom is something to be mimetic with and has the power to curtail and relativize earlier experiences, often repeated, that ensnare and diminish people.

Dissolving "Bad Mimesis," Promoting "Good Mimesis"

An important aspect of our work is to make the mimetic influences more conscious by tracing them out in the stories that are told in the group, and in the relationships group members have with one another. It has been our continual experience, since 1979, that once people are opened up to the mimetic understanding, when they see how relationships and structures can promote models of freedom, or, contrariwise, constitute occasions of rivalry or stumbling blocks to human growth and development, participants and

facilitators alike begin to see ways in which they can, in beneficent emulation, promote "good mimesis" and dissolve "bad mimesis."

In these groups, we are enabled to acknowledge what is happening, and
to think and talk about how we experience living in this place. Becoming
conscious of what we are doing with one another, representing consciously
the processes of bad mimesis, we gain possibilities of choosing to live more
justly together, mimetically modeling freedom and inviting others also to live
in a "contrasting" manner.

One example of exposing bad mimesis is the recognition of our classic
strategies for "managing violence." Traditionally and communally, people
have found ways to limit emotions flaring up. We have often settled for
separation, avoidance, or politeness rather than take the risk of meeting one
another.

Here is an example of Politeness:

> In our town Catholics and Protestants are not afraid of each other, but
> there is a certain "standing off" from each other. Protestants are very much
> the majority. There are Catholics in the town who are civil servants and a
> lot of police officers too. All the locals agree that, if there is any trouble,
> it is caused by outsiders coming into the town. Any feelings of ambiguity
> on this, or any people who support political violence, keep quiet. (Wilson
> 1994, 213)

Communal politeness drives out any ambivalence people have; local peace is
assured by scapegoating outsiders.

There are also the strategies of Avoidance:

> In our town everyone knows about everyone else, on all sides. It is too small
> to be otherwise. The population of the town and its immediate area is very
> evenly balanced between the traditions. There have been incidents in the
> town between the traditions but there is a silence about who did it, even
> though, within each group, people know who did the different actions on
> behalf of their group. (Wilson 1994, 213)

Here, there is a knowledge that violence is close to the surface, but people
agree not to talk about it, hoping to live together without any major

explosions of emotion. The silence and communal politeness ritualizes the tension and makes it manageable. However, the ritual is incomplete as "the others" cannot be got rid of. If the townspeople agree that any violence done locally is always by "outsiders," that is incomplete too, because "outsiders" can have links with "insiders." All remains in an uneasy, polite peace.

Separation then happens easily:

> In our completely Protestant estate there is no politeness between us and the Catholic estate over the road. If boys from there come here to look for girls, the response is anything but polite. The same if our boys go over there. If girls do the moving then it is slightly different. They seem to be more open to us coming over. (Wilson 1994, 213–14)

Men are culturally associated with violence (Girard 1977, 125–26; Chidester 1992) and so when boys from the other side come into "the Other's" territory, they are evicted because they are more threatening. As the places in question are exclusively of one tradition, there is no equilibrium. Because local boys can bring in local girls from the "other" estate, there is tension between the local boys and girls. There are no possibilities for politeness here; there is no ritual way to be in the midst of each other or one another. Strict separation, between the men anyway, is what operates:

> In our town centre, if you're young and male, you know not to walk on the side of the street that does not belong to your tradition. There are shops we identify as being "one side" or "the other" and you stick to them. A boy got his head split when he walked on the wrong side, a gang of boys smashed a hardware shop window, took out a large shaft from it, and proceeded to lay into him with it. Any outsiders on the wrong side get beaten up. (Wilson 1994, 214)

Here, members of each tradition even provoke some of the others by invading "their territory" in the town center. Communal rivalry extends into the center of the town. Here, there is strict separation and frantic attempts to drive the other away if one group's territory is invaded.

The strategy of "comparative autobiographies," on the other hand, illustrates the power of positive mimesis. This method of "meeting together"

involves both the hearing and the telling of stories in which people are introduced to others who are understood to be different. People are invited to
share their experiences of how they were made aware of "Others" in different contexts, and to what extent they were brought into ways of rivalry and
fear of "the Other," or into feeling at ease with them. An example of this, in
a group examining how they were introduced to prejudice, difference, and
diversity, went as follows:

A. When I was very young my parents ran a public house and there were
often sporting events and other festivals locally where people got quite
drunk. When some people from the nearby public housing estates got
drunk they used to go out to the back of the pub and were sick. My mother
often took me to the window and pointed down at these people, saying
"that's what drink does for those people from the estates." Here I was introduced to prejudice about people from the estates and I was also given the
sense that we were better than them.

B. Around our corner there was a hostel for families who had been made
homeless in some way, it was called a "Half-way Hostel." We were always
pointed toward this hostel, and were reminded that many of the children
there had no dads and had families who weren't able to cope. In this manner I learnt that we were better than other people, especially the children
with no dads.

C. I remember being at school next to one we all called "a smelly girl" and
I remember joining with others in victimising this girl. I also remember in
class one day how we all laughed when the teacher brought her up to the
front and told her, in front of us all, that she would have to wash.

D. I remember a girl in our town becoming pregnant when she went with
a foreign student and the whole town felt that she should be ashamed of
what she did. It was even worse for us all when she married this person.
The whole street used to come out whenever he walked up and down to
his home gawking at him and treating him as somehow strange. They were
fascinated at how this girl could get married to this man and live such "a
strange life."

E. I remember our school shared a campus with a school for people with special educational needs who were taught in the huts nearby. Looking back now we had many times where we could have done things together but we were separated. We had different lunch times from them, we had a different play space from them, all in all we were brought up to see them as daft people and we were told not to play near them. (Wilson 1994, 220)

This exchange amounts to a "comparative autobiography" approach. Its potential is to explore how each was introduced, in myth and reality, to difference, and thence to aspects of communal mistrust and rivalry. Without a doubt, this technique will have similarities in other conflicted cultures; it is not peculiar to our particular ethnic frontier.

Of course, it is an important condition of success that the group worker understands, securely and well, the nature of mimetic conduct, and its consequences; and that he or she is able to recognize them in what is happening in the group and in what it is told. He or she needs the ability to make what is happening clear to the members of the group through assisting them to visualize their experiences in diagrams and examples (Wilson and Morrow 1996). For example:

The Dynamics of Separation, Avoidance, and Politeness

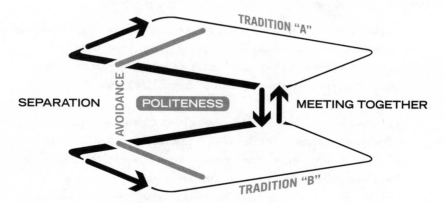

"Meeting Together" enables people to understand and visualize their situation more clearly.

At the same time, these explanations, which give everyone the possibility to locate their experience differently, must be given in a manner that the group members always understand—understanding also that they need not agree with the explanation, and that they are always free to question and reject it. In this form of group meeting, new insights come to group member and group worker alike. All the group worker is doing is offering a contribution in the hope that it is helpful to the members of the group who are seeking, and hopefully finding, for their own lives, their own ways beyond conflict.

A group worker, in fact, needs to model freedom within the group itself. This means that the group worker never rivals with the group as a whole or with particular group members for power within, or outside, the group. She never rivals with (a) member(s) of the group about knowledge or life experiences; and she accepts all the members of the group equally, not having regard, special sympathy, or antipathy for any member of the group. To be at ease with the task of facilitation, and with all those individual members of a group, means that each facilitator is free of the Girardian dynamic of excitement-and-fascination. In such ways facilitators are in "model-model" relationships and so able to work at their best.

To work with groups in a society where many people have traditionally remained apart is also to risk encountering feelings of isolation and loneliness oneself. The facilitators have experienced times, and places, where bringing people together across lines of enmity has not been welcome. There have also been times, especially before the more overt violence ended, where meetings continued to be held in the midst of much community violence and fear. Living, as group members and facilitators did, in the midst of these fears, the facilitator was not immune. If the facilitator allowed these fears to dominate him or her, then she brought no new possibilities into the meetings.

The sustaining purpose remains always to give people the possibility of finding their own questions, moving them away from relationships of rivalry and struggle, to share and exchange those experiences that are important for them.

Trust-Building within and beyond Civil Conflict

To work with groups of people of different backgrounds within a divided society means that the emotions associated with the conflict in that society are always near the surface. People from the different traditions, as equal citizens, will have times and situations where they are at ease, and times and places where they are not. These asymmetrical swings between people on different themes are fulcrums around which new understandings develop; and these may help build a contrast with the reality of meetings in more intransigent conflicts and more public arenas.

A person from the Protestant-Unionist (pro-British) tradition did not wish to share her experiences as she had a relative in the security forces: "I am fearful of having them marked out by people here from the other tradition, telling friends of theirs who may have associations with paramilitary groups" (Wilson 1994, 180).

A teacher from the Catholic tradition who lived in the middle of a solidly Republican (pro-Irish) area with a history of attacks on the police and army, during the conflict, said:

> A soldier was seriously injured in an ambush by a paramilitary group and was lying in our front garden. My mother rushed out to see what she could do for him, and it was clear there was very little she could do. As she cradled his head in her arms, a crowd of people gathered round her and jeered at them both. (Wilson 1994, 180)

In a contested society, explicit cross-community work has had an emotional charge associated with it, and often the emotions experienced include fear. Although the possibility of tapping these emotions is higher within groups explicitly dealing with the themes of community understanding, it is our experience that these realities also can dominate professional groups concerned with social welfare, education, or employment issues too. Often people choose silence, politeness, and avoidance within their daily work life. The spaces we offer enable people to "meet together" beyond these dynamics, often deeply.

To establish joint meetings with people who have traditionally looked after the needs of one tradition only, such as teachers in schools or clergy, and to invite them to explore what cross-community contact means, has often been to move in a very emotional atmosphere. Many, in moving out beyond their own traditional group and culture, believe that the experience will provoke more fear and confusion. People are often temporally mimetic with past experiences of having "cultural good reason" to fear or be suspicious of the other. In an open atmosphere where people experience freedom together, they can draw on, and be spatially mimetic with, trust and freedom.

We often need to cope with people who demand reassurance that the meeting will go well. In a contested society there can be few assurances that people in mixed groups will not meet experiences in which they are challenged, irritated, or caused to question basic ideas. On several occasions facilitators have been asked, "Can you reassure us that all will be well if we go on?" Understanding people's uncertainty about mixed meetings, being open to not giving blanket assurances, apart from offering the meeting their best efforts and understanding that this work is new and unfamiliar, is a reality the facilitators live with.

Seeking reassurance can often be a group's way of escaping the reality of meeting one another, denying that unexpected things can happen, which may be either pleasant or unpleasant. To collude with this request is to bring people into a false atmosphere of security. However to remain with them, whatever the experience, is to stay in relationship and meet whatever comes out. When people ask for reassurance, they are unsure what will happen if all ends in chaos. Deep within them, they know that chaos is not pleasant and that people are sometimes scapegoated.

Again, the strategic aim is to assist group members to move through any chaos into an experience of being in freedom with one another. It is to escape from, and transcend, the logic of the classic human blame game (i.e., "scapegoating," with its constitutional moral obliquity and unsighted partiality), and to come to know that such new ways are possible. To move in the vicinity of chaos, and experience coming out beyond it together, *without* scapegoating someone, is fundamental new knowledge and experience that builds new ways of being together.

Communal Rivalry and Differences in How
People Understand History

As trust builds, we attempt to tackle the all-conditioning weight of the past. In contested societies, each person's version of history is related to his/her ways of explaining his/her feelings, and especially fears in the experience of their families, friends, and everyday life. In such a place, history always lies close to the surface of daily life, and the normal rituals of more secure societies—which allow past events, even where hurtful, to be both acknowledged and placed at a distance—do not work.

Potentially, the past always has the ability to disturb the present, even as the society seeks to move on through new political agreements and mutually owned institutions. It takes time, and deep commitment, to build new institutions that propel people forward and build mutual ownership and cohesion. Meeting together in new ways is part of this moving forward. In contested societies, the past, temporally, often invades the present contagiously, especially at times of "annual remembrance" events. It is important, and painful, to recognize the circles in which people and traditions are caught.

In "ethnic frontier" conflicts, opposing sides often create "model-obstacles," establishing ethnocentric national identities. Many, on all sides, wish for a unilateral acknowledgment by the others of their violent actions, without acknowledging their own. The only way to break the endlessly circular pattern of competing reciprocal demands for one-sided Other-acknowledgment is that one's own demand for acknowledgment itself be free from the accusation that it is one-sided, and free also from the wish to rewrite history in a certain manner by predetermining the evidence to be used. Sometimes, in the midst of the most difficult discussions, such acknowledgment is given by all, and the circular double bind is then broken. Mutual acknowledgment becomes an instance and a model of freedom; and the process of dealing with the past moves forward.

New experiences can only come in where each person is secure. In group work, participants quickly begin to appreciate how relationships between people here are continually shaped by the different historical understandings of the same events—and how people see the same incident through very different spectacles. The histories within which people have been brought up have become so much a part of them that until trigger-events and/or mirroring confrontations occur, people do not realize the extent to which they have absorbed one version of history, and with it, a world view that prevents them from seeing the Other as a person. Yet finding their way back to their feelings about some notable event, and speaking about this in groups, can lead them to exorcise the baleful effects.

Openness to Surprises, Stories of Contrast

One way beyond scapegoating is for people not to expect the worst in situations, and be open to surprises.

> Emma: "I find my colleagues very supportive in the mixed projects we have developed. Initially I was so tight in myself and anxious at having this task. In my view, my colleagues, my parents and the staff of the other school would all be difficult to win over to the Mutual Understanding programme. I organised meetings down to the last detail, not wishing to be caught off guard or shown up. I was surprised by the quality and numbers of the responses. I now find it all very challenging." (Wilson 1994, 232)

Expectations were so great in Emma—she was expecting the worst of everyone—that she was nearly closed to good experiences emerging in group work. These are common themes: the burden of expectations and the place of surprises.

All meetings involve risk-taking and trust. Trusting is not an abstract attitude but a concrete experience with an Other:

> A member who worked with trade-unionists had found people in Northern Ireland quite prepared to discuss race and gender discrimination but not religious discrimination. They doubted whether the group could contain the tensions such a discussion might unleash. (Wilson 1994, 232)

This is the point where a Girardian lens assists facilitators to intervene to point out the deep-seated and fundamental ambiguities of the word "religion." It is a huge asset to have theorized for us this treacherous word embracing *both* the best and the worst in humankind (Girard 2011 x–xi).

The ability to discuss sensitive issues is, of course, a major requirement if people are to find ways forward together. If they always avoid the difficult issues with people from the opposite tradition, this means that they are perpetuating "the violent and humiliating traumas that make us who we are" (Wright 1988).

Meeting people, being at ease with them, and not forcing them to move in particular ways can create trust. As trust grows, the space where upheaval and chaos dominates is decreased. Creating relational spaces where rivalry is more or less absent is at the center of the community-relations task. One of the most important insights in meetings with peace groups has been that those who seek peace *can,* sometimes, move out of rivalry. In so doing, changes can occur; people can see one another as human beings just like themselves.

We are most heartened when people tell stories of situations in which they had experiences that provided a contrast to being prejudiced or sectarian:

> Although I went to a Catholic school and was very much caught up with political aspirations associated with that, I also got involved in a cross-community programme when I was younger in the local Protestant school. This gave me contacts there which changed me.
>
> When I grew older and worked in a mixed youth club, I got a chance to see things in a new way, this is what motivates me now in my work.
>
> The suffering that I have seen in my life has affected me and although I am very much within the Protestant tradition, I do want people to do things together. Meeting those who have suffered violence, yet who wished to promote reconciliation, motivated me some while ago to get further involved.
>
> When I moved away in order to do post-graduate study for a while I got a great sense of liberation and freedom. Now I have returned to work here, I really want to put the good experiences of life into this place and try to encourage others to turn their back on the old ways of living apart and in mistrust. (Wilson 1994, 234)

Without promoting the myth of women being the only people interested in peace-making, Northern Ireland's experience suggests that some women have often been freer and more central to seeking new ways forward. These women seem to be less deeply involved in the rivalries and less compelled to defend themselves. The responses of these women have often been a key to developing the experience of trust and openness. When they have risked speaking about difficult issues, often they have made it possible for others to follow. As an example, Michelle was a young woman from the Catholic tradition whose father was a police officer. She spoke of how

> I experienced people within my own tradition and from the other tradition. I felt I was always under scrutiny from both sides. As a member of the local youth council I had been involved in cross-community projects and in North-South [Northern Ireland–Republic of Ireland] programmes, with the support of my own family and the local youth tutor. I just got on with doing things and tried not to notice those who were against me. (Wilson 1994, 235)

Her friendship with Clare, a Protestant girl, was very important to her. Clare was a Protestant brought up within a very strong Protestant Unionist tradition and

> was supported in cross-community work by my family. When two buses, which had traditionally carried both children from Catholic and Protestant schools for years, became segregated through a sectarian incident, I refused to travel on the bus that was now identified as the Protestant bus. I preferred to stay beside my Catholic friend. My family supported me in this action too.
>
> I enjoyed doing cross-community projects, my father was happy as long as I wished it and so I went on my way. People who had taken sides over the bus segregation said privately to me how they wished they could have done what I did. (Wilson 1994, 235–36)

Clare spoke of the trust she had with Michelle. This prompted others in the group meeting to share experiences in which they were trusted by people from the other tradition. As Clare's father was a respected person within his tradition and did not prevent his daughter from doing community relations work, she had space in which to move that was greater than some others had.

The group explored the extent to which females were freer to take positions, such as these young women had done, although the threat was always there for the girls. People agreed that there were sets of cultural boundaries around male behavior within cohesive traditional groups that may be different for females.

Conclusion: Redeeming Relationships and Structures

In contested societies, people often seek security in the midst of fear, and yet the opposite of fear is not security, but trust. Real human security is experienced in relationships of trust and in structures where they have their place.

The task of peace-making for educationalists within in a contested society is the reestablishment of experiences of trust through the use of models of education whose main contribution to societal change or transforming experiences is to give people the opportunity of being with "the Other" in an inclusive, freeing way. The change sought is not carved out or fought for, but is an outcome of the relationship structures that give freedom and space to change.

Lederach (2005, 127–28, 182) argues that peace-building and reconciliation work is a "process-structure." The "meeting together" models developed out of the practice of the Corrymeela Community in Northern Ireland since 1965, and the particular forms of practice and understanding derived from the work of Girardian scholars since 1979, have underpinned such "process-structure" understandings. In the reconciliation practice of that ecumenical community and its residential learning programs, as well as the wider community and institutional practice in localities in Northern Ireland and beyond, it has also informed the wider advocacy and scholarship of what was the "Future Ways" program based in the University of Ulster (1989–2006), and it informs and infuses a number of practitioners and groups working in wider civil society.

The project of "Meeting Together," rooted in the Girardian mimetic hypothesis, underpins a wider engagement in promoting and sustaining the task of working for a more open and shared society. For as long as personal and group relationships are founded on fear and violence, trust in any sort of politics is very difficult. Inversely, when people meet together across traditional barriers and experience trust in which they can be secure and grow, then these experiences, at a pre-political level, model a reality in which new, hopefully inclusive political structures could, should—and perhaps will—come to be embodied.

Notes

1. The asymmetrical experiences of the state were initially dealt with through the responses to the demands of the Civil Rights Movement (1967). The full program of rights, agreed representation, law and public institutions, and safeguards were agreed in the peace-building agenda and the establishment of a devolved Assembly anchored in the Belfast Agreement (1998) and by an Ireland-wide plebiscite vote; the St Andrews Agreement (2006); and the Hillsborough Agreement (2010). The asymmetries in experiences of the law, while critically examined still by many human-rights activists, have been mainly attended to with the devolution of Criminal Justice to the NI Assembly in May 2010.

2. This new British-Irish Agreement replaced the Anglo-Irish Agreement of 15 November 1985. Multi-party talks, including both sponsoring governments, were brought to a successful conclusion by George Mitchell, the independent chairman. See http://cain.ulst.ac.uk/events/peace/pp9398.htm.

3. Of the total deaths, 3,271 occurred in Northern Ireland, 115 in the Irish Republic, 125 in Britain, and 18 elsewhere in Europe. Republican groups have been responsible for 2,061 of the deaths, Loyalist groups for 1,016, British Forces for 363, and the Irish Republic's Forces for 5. For the remaining 84 deaths, it has not been possible or appropriate to identify the killing group (Sutton: updated 2002). See http://cain.ulst.ac.uk/sutton/book/#append.

4. Philipa Rothfield writes: "This is the dilemma of reconciliation: to work with unspeakable suffering, and to cajole its utterance. To respect the victims and survivors of atrocity, yet broker their participation. National projects of reconciliation are about creating a viable social future out of the horrendous. If they enjoin victims and survivors to participate, and in a sense they must, they are also likely to pathologize resistance, to judge non-conformity and exert moral pressure to conform. Such is reconciliation's ambivalence" (2008, 26).

5. Reviewing diverse truth and reconciliation processes, Shriver (2007) identifies four aspects of a truth-that-heals rather than divides: (1) Forensic truth: what happened, when and where and with whom. (2) Personal or narrative truth: when victims speak, a truth that, though it does not bring back the dead, releases people from their silence. (3) Dialogical truth: when personal stories are heard as part of a process of sociopolitical change. (4) Truth that heals, being subtle, complex, and ambiguously comprehensive. Such an approach is a means of clearing the air; exposing the facts; digesting them in dialogue; clearing the public air; getting rid of the malignancy of evil.

6. Drs. J. Bakker, Aat Van Rhijn, and André Lascaris (Netherlands) were foundation members of the DNIC with William Arlow, Louis Boyle, and Colin Murphy (Ireland). They were later joined by Dr. Roel Kaptein.

7. Shriver in his (2005) text identifies three kinds of patriots, the best being the good patriot who carries on a lover's quarrel with his country. He invokes R. Niebuhr, who argues that "A democratic society requires some capacity of the individual to defy social authority on occasion when its standards violate his conscience and to relate himself to larger and larger communities than the primary family group" (*The Irony of American History* [Scribner's, 1952], 125–26).

Cited Texts and Further Reading

The Belfast Agreement ("Good Friday Agreement"). 1998. See http://news.bbc.co.uk/nol/shared/bsp/hi/pdfs/07_12_04_ni_agreement_01.pdf.

Chidester, D. 1992. *Shots in the Streets: Violence and Religion in South Africa*. Cape Town: Oxford University Press.

Commission for Victims and Survivors, Northern Ireland (CVSNI). 2014. "Report on the Dealing with the Past Conference." Http://blogs.qub.ac.uk/amnesties/files/2014/05/CVSNI-DWP-Conference-Report-March-2014.pdf.

Consultative Group on the Past (CGPNI). 2009. *Executive Summary*. Belfast: CGPNI. See http://cain.ulst.ac.uk/victims/docs/consultative_group/cgp_230109_report_sum.pdf.

Dutch–Northern Irish Advisory Committee (DNIAC). 1977. *Three Years of Conferences in Holland, A Report and Evaluation*. Netherlands: The Secretariat, Bergen, NH.

Eyben, K., D. Morrow, and D. Wilson. 1997. *A Worthwhile Venture? Practically Investigating in Equity, Diversity and Interdependence in Northern Ireland*. Coleraine: University of Ulster.

———. 2002. *The Equity, Diversity and Interdependence Framework: A Framework for Organisational Learning and Change*. Coleraine: University of Ulster. See also http://eprints.ulster.ac.uk/12598/.

Fitzduff, M. 1989. "From Ritual to Consciousness." D. Phil. thesis, University of Ulster.

Girard, R. 1977. *Violence and the Sacred*. Baltimore: Johns Hopkins University Press.

———. 1987. *Things Hidden since the Foundation of the World*. Translated by S. Bann and M. Metteer. London: Athlone Press. New edition, New York: Continuum, 2003. Page references are to the 2003 edition.

———. 2011. *Sacrifice*. East Lansing: Michigan State University Press.

Kaptein, R. 1992. "Northern Ireland and Ethnocentrism: Its Escalation into Violence and Terrorism." A Paper for the COVR Conference on Ethnocentrism and Violence, Stanford, CA.

Kaptein, R., with D. Morrow. 1993. *On the Way of Freedom*. Dublin: Columba Press.

Lederach, J. P. 2005. *The Moral Imagination: The Art and Soul of Building Peace*. Oxford and New York: Oxford University Press.

Morrow, D. 2007. "The Weight of the Past on the Way to the Future." NICRC. Http://www.community-relations.org.uk/about-us/speeches.

———. 2009. "Between Revenge and Reconciliation? Making Peace on the British/Irish Ethnic Frontier." Public lecture. INCORE Summer School, University of Ulster. Http://incore.incore.ulst.ac.uk/Seminars/DuncanMorrow_ref.html.

Oughourlian, J.-M. 1991. *The Puppet of Desire*. Stanford, CA: Stanford University Press.

Rothfield, P. 2008. "Evaluating Reconciliation." In *Pathways to Reconciliation: Between Theory and Practice*, ed. P. Rothfield, C. Fleming, and P. Komesaroff. Aldershot, UK: Ashgate Publishing.

Shriver, D. 2005. *Honest Patriots*. New York: Oxford University Press.

———. 2007. "Truths for Reconciliation: An American Perspective." Public lecture. Coleraine: University of Ulster & Northern Ireland Community Relations Council.

Sutton, M. 2002. *An Index of Deaths from the Conflict in Ireland*. INCORE. University of Ulster. The

CAIN Web Service—Conflict and Politics in Northern Ireland. Http://cain.ulster.ac.uk/sutton/index.html

Wilson, D. A. 1994. "Learning Together for a Change." D. Phil Thesis, Faculty of Education, University of Ulster.

Wilson, D., and D. Morrow. 1996. *Ways Out of Conflict.* Belfast: Corrymeela Press. See also http://eprints.ulster.ac.uk/12600/.

Wright, F. 1987. *Northern Ireland: A Comparative Analysis.* Dublin: Gill & Macmillan.

———. 1988. "Reconciling the Histories of Catholic and Protestant in Northern Ireland." In *Reconciling Memories,* ed. A. Falconer and J. Liechty. Dublin: Columba Press.

Responses to Morrow and Wilson

Girardian Reflections on Israel and Palestine

Mel Konner

I stand in awe of the accomplishments of people like Derick Wilson and Duncan Morrow in making the historic reconciliation in Northern Ireland possible on the ground, and also in explaining in such a personal and intimate way, but also so analytically and so penetratingly, what is at stake and what has happened there. At the conference where we all spoke, I was also asked to comment on the Wilson-Morrow session and to try to draw some parallels with the Middle East. (At the time I was in the middle of a six-week visit to Israel and Palestine. I had visited Israel many times, and had been to Palestine several times, as well as to Jordan and Egypt).

I am no expert; and I am not unbiased. I grew up as an American Orthodox Jew, and despite losing my faith I retain a certain tribal identity. I continue to believe that there should be, at least for the foreseeable future, a Jewish state. I also, however, believe that there must be, sooner rather than later, a Palestinian state next to it, preferably one that unites the West Bank with a peaceful Gaza. I have used the word "Palestine" for many years, long before the United Nations admitted that country to observer status as a non-voting nation. I believe in its present and (hopefully very different) future reality, just as I believe in Israel's right to exist and to defend itself, although I certainly cannot defend all that it has done in the name of those rights.

I grew up in a mixed neighborhood among Irish Americans; have always loved Irish music, literature, and culture; and have a dear friend, James Flannery, who has just retired as head of Irish Studies at my university and sometimes directs Yeats's plays at Dublin's Abbey Theatre. Reinforced by and educated in conversations with him, I have always seen parallels in the histories of the Irish and the Jews: long oppression, a literature and culture more than tinged by that oppression, attachment to a traditional—and, some claimed, moribund—language, outsider status, certain commonalities between the Irish Famine and the Holocaust, and a common resistance, over many generations, to British imperial power. To the limited extent that I see parallels between the conflict in Northern Ireland and the one between Israel and the Palestinians, I see them against this background of long, partly parallel histories.

I first visited Northern Ireland in 1998 at the invitation of Dr. Mari Fitzduff, then head of INCORE, the Institute for Conflict Resolution, who brought together people from all over the world to discuss various conflicts. It so happened that the same week the then-new Northern Ireland Assembly met for the first time, and we watched the seating of the delegates on live television—one step in a long process of reconciliation.

Derick Wilson has called our attention to the use of language, and I was struck that when Mari talked about the capital of Northern Ireland, she never said "Derry" or "Londonderry," but always "Derry/Londonderry," an awkward but necessary phrasing. Otherwise, you were immediately taking sides.

It later occurred to me that the equivalent might be if I were to say "Jerusalem/East Jerusalem" or "Yerushalayim/Al Quds." I would like to see that city become the capital of both countries. That is, I endorse a two-state solution there also, which is not feasible at least *within* Northern Ireland, although of course Northern Ireland and the Republic of Ireland have belonged to separate states for almost a century. Perhaps a better analogy would be to what the West Bank was before 1988, when it was still a part of Jordan.

Duncan Morrow's deft and subtle account of the history of the Irish Troubles reveals deep-seated and complex resentments and rivalries that may never be fully resolved; yet Northern Ireland furnishes at the moment a far better example of conflict resolution than anything at hand in the Israeli-Palestinian conflict. Morrow refers to "huge cracks in the edifice of ethno-centrism in Northern Ireland" despite ongoing tensions between the two sets of churches, and speaks of a "chance that has elsewhere disappeared, carried away in rapidly escalating violence."

Yet, as he indicates, reconciliation is not an event; it is a process only partway done. Although the Catholics in Northern Ireland have long been oppressed, they will likely become the majority religious group in Northern Ireland, after which, some Protestants fear, it may only be a matter of time before unification of the six Northern Ireland counties with the Republic; then the Protestants will be a small minority in a much larger country. How likely this really is, I am in no position to say. But I do hope that in that future the question will be moot; that is, the conflict will be such a distant memory that it will matter much less than it does today whether Northern Ireland is a part of the United Kingdom, the Republic of Ireland, or an entirely separate entity.

I am not a historian, but it seems to me that Europe as a whole—*sensu lato,* including the Irish and British islands—is moving in two directions simultaneously, where political power is concerned. I mean to say that (recent qualms notwithstanding) Europe matters more, and local cultural identities matter more as well. I see no contradiction here, as the nation-state was always something artificial and may be temporary. Thus Scotland, Catalonia, the Flemish and French halves of Belgium, and other intranational entities are taking power away from the nation-state from below, even while Europe, as well as entities like NATO, and even the relatively weak United Nations, take power away from it from above. My idea is that Ireland and/or Northern Ireland can have their independence, and that will matter less in a future day when Europe matters more. Perhaps this is far-fetched in current terms, but anthropologists take the long view.

How does this relate to the tragically fraught situation in the Middle East? There are many disanalogies. When Jews, who had never been absent completely from what is now Israel, began to settle there in larger numbers in the 1880s, the local Arabs, who did not see or refer to themselves as a Palestinian national entity, saw the Jews as European colonialists. The Jews did not have a national entity squarely behind them as the Northern Ireland

Protestants did, but they did bring economic and cultural capital that local Arabs had difficulty competing with. The Jews brought an ancient claim on the land—but the land was not, of course, empty, and the consciousness of Arabs as Palestinians formed gradually in a sort of self-defense. In Girardian terms one might say that mimetic rivalry and mimetic desire for the land created both Palestinian-Arab and Israeli-Jewish consciousness in parallel.

Part of the mimetic rivalry is that the two cultures have competing narratives of victimization and suffering. Each sees itself as the "David" in a battle against a "Goliath." Palestinians are obviously weak and have been victimized in relation to Israel, but Israel was always weak and victimized in relation to the vastly larger Arab and Muslim worlds. This is without even mentioning the Holocaust, which was the culmination of two millennia of Jewish suffering at the hands of non-Jewish Europeans—with, in the end, the full support of the Arab world. Thus, if anything, the mimetic hatred and fear in the Middle East is even worse today than it was in Northern Ireland at the peak of the "Troubles." And yet, in Northern Island, Catholics deeply fear British power, and Protestants would hardly embrace unification with the Republic.

My highly educated and intelligent Palestinian friends and acquaintances want to see a one-state solution now, with Arabs and Jews living side by side in the same democratic country, all rivalry diffused into ordinary politics. I can see that happening in Israel/Palestine perhaps in a distant future when the conflict—the mimetic rivalry and violent victimhood—matters even less than it does today in Northern Ireland. It will be hard enough to get to a *two*-state solution—Israel and Palestine side by side as separate entities; but perhaps a hundred years from now, we will view that as a transition to a single, unified state.

When I first visited Northern Ireland in 1998, psychologists had shown that very young children there could identify many differences between Protestants and Catholics, from clothing to haircuts to how they park their cars. While to my naive eye there were few obvious differences, they were already embedded in children's minds. Studies in the United States show that children are cognitively aware of the difference between black and white people by age three. As both Morrow and Wilson know only too well, these reciprocating fears and denigrations are deeply ingrained and generally breed more of the same.

But we know that a large difference between two groups of people is not needed for mimetic rivalry, even at its most aggressive and destructive. In Girard's model, the ultimate mimetic rivalry may be between twins. What is needed is a dichotomizing distinction to split what is really a continuum into two moieties that mirror each other's desires, goals, and behavior. What are the differences between the Montagues and the Capulets? Effectively none, except their mirrored pride, hatred, violence, grief, fear, and urge for revenge.

While I was at the Derry/Londonderry conference, my son was on a high school trip to Ireland, and had stayed with his group for several weeks in the town of Three-Mile-House, in the Republic near the Northern Ireland border. I traveled to meet him and sat for a few hours with the family he had been staying with. The father was a police officer, a detective in his mid-forties, who had spent his career chasing self-described IRA militants who crossed the border in both directions and were suspected of committing acts of violence in Northern Ireland and using the Republic as a refuge. He was a charming, handsome, humorous man, not at all forbidding, but his description of his job brought home to me the reality of the conflict, and the need for each side to control its own most violent partisans.

Derick Wilson points out that extreme positions dominate, and that is the tragedy of these situations. People who work toward reconciliation can find extremists on both sides an almost insurmountable obstacle. I know people on both sides of the Israeli-Palestinian conflict who support the reconcilers, and yet they can't control the situation as long as extremists are willing to take actions that generate great insecurity in the silent, peaceable majority.

Wilson also presents a very interesting psychosocial analysis, prominently including the Girardian viewpoint, of how to address those insecurities. Similar efforts are ongoing in the Middle East. For example, the Seeds of Peace program brings together teenagers from these two worlds and tries to give them the kind of contact with each other that might inoculate them against extremism. But by that age many of them on both sides have already had a good deal of the wrong kind of indoctrination.

To take another example, I spent a day with a group called Midwives of Peace, consisting of practicing Jewish and Palestinian midwives who consult on professional challenges and meet regularly in East Jerusalem in the interests of mutual understanding. These women literally have the next generation in their hands. One newcomer thinking of joining the group mistakenly called it "Midwives for Peace." "No," a veteran gently corrected her, "it's Midwives *of* Peace," thereby emphasizing with one simple preposition that they are hoping to help deliver peace into their corner of the world, in what they know can only be a difficult labor. Perhaps Seeds of Peace and Midwives of Peace are akin to an emerging Middle East version of what Morrow calls "cradles of freedom" in Northern Ireland, small protected communities where new relationships can be built.

Perhaps Derick Wilson's effort to use Girardian theory directly to increase awareness of the forces at play could also play a role in the Middle East?

Three years after that first trip to Derry/Londonderry, my eldest daughter spent a semester there working with Mari Fitzduff. When I visited her it happened to be St. Patrick's Day, which is much less celebrated in Ireland than it is in the United States. There are many more Irish Americans than there are people in Ireland, and they have not always played a constructive role. There are parallels here too with the role of some Jews in the United States vis-à-vis Israel. In both conflicts, people on the other side of the ocean are sometimes doing too much to influence a situation in which they have intense ethnic passions but much less at stake than those who are really in the conflict.

On that trip we had the chance to meet in Belfast a very elderly former IRA militant who had in his youth in the 1940s almost been hanged, but was pardoned at the last minute. Six decades later he remained as a living repository of the (often justifiable) resentment of British rule. We also took a Black Taxi tour of Belfast, to see the Republican Irish symbols, gravesites, murals, and other commemorations that people cling to. Derick Wilson talked about the need to throw out parts of your tradition, to break the cycle of mimetic rivalry.

This is a trope that you find in the Middle East on both sides: competing narratives of suffering. When the Israelis (mainly Jews) celebrate their annual Independence Day, the Palestinians (and increasingly the Arab citizens of Israel) observe Nakba, or Catastrophe Day. Jewish liberals in Israel say, of course, Arabs have every right to these observances and even to use government funds for them; Jews on the right condemn them and say that even as voting citizens, the Arab minority will never relinquish that part of their history and integrate themselves into the country. And of course the Jews have their competing narrative of suffering in the Holocaust, after the longer history of victimization the Jews can point to, going back more than two millennia. These competing narratives relentlessly feed a ravenous mimetic rivalry.

On the positive side, we can consider someone like Gerry Adams, who used to be a terrorist and a very violent man, and who today is a widely accepted political leader who led most of his militant followers to decommission weapons, laying down their arms. This was surely a difficult process for Catholic pride and security and required Protestants to relinquish a part of their history of suffering at the hands of men like Adams. Surely many Protestants alive today did really suffer from IRA militancy, yet they are learning to live without taking revenge. This can happen with some leaders in the Palestinian community who are considered terrorists, but it will take time. Derick Wilson's observation that Northern Ireland is still in a period between conflict and reconciliation—that it's not over yet—emphasizes how much psychic work has to be done to emerge from the deep well of grief that fuels mimetic rivalry.

The temptation toward ongoing tit-for-tat, revenge for revenge, operates very strongly in the Middle East. But the tit-for-tat game can be played both ways; you can cooperate and get cooperation in return, just as you can take revenge and get vengeance in return. Game theorists and modelers have shown that there are conditions in which, if you play the game over and over again, you can get a steady state of cooperation.

Wilson has argued that people have to do reconciliation with their head, their heart, and their gut. That is consistent with everything I know about human behavioral biology. And yet, as he notes, we have seen the Queen of the UK visiting and honoring the graves of IRA members who fought and sometimes killed her own soldiers. This was a "first," and surely a step forward.

Will a Jewish leader in Israel someday visit the graves of Hamas militants? Will Hamas leaders honor not only the victims of the Holocaust but the soldiers of Israel who died while trying to kill them? The difficulty of imagining either of these outcomes shows how far the resolution of the Middle East conflict lags behind that of the Troubles in Northern Ireland.

Girardian theory holds that an arbitrarily chosen sacrificial victim can provisionally put an end to mimetic rivalry through the shedding of innocent blood, directing violence instead toward the victim. But consider this variant scenario: at the end of *Romeo and Juliet,* the Montagues and the Capulets appear to lay down their swords because of the huge loss each side has suffered in the tightly linked deaths of their innocent children. "All are punished," proclaims the prince. One might add, all are in a less violent mood. Grief, which has so often led these two families to vendetta, appears now to lead to resolution.

Could the star-crossed lovers be in effect sacrificial victims? And could the linked victims of any conflict—not lovers, but twin brothers under the skin—serve a similar purpose through joint, mirrored grieving, leading the surviving rivals not to more violence but to reconciliation, or, at a minimum, to a kind of grief-stricken quietude?

One of my Jewish friends in Israel is a combat veteran of the 1973 war—she was a trauma officer at the front, having been trained as a disaster psychologist. Her husband was a helicopter pilot in the same war. We stood in a room of her home and she pointed and said, "See that tree? That will be Palestine," an outcome she strongly favors. I asked, "Aren't you worried that you will be in danger here?" And she said, "French people live on the German border today. Are they worried?"

Yet there are millions alive on both sides who remember the losses of World War II, millions who to this day still grieve, and for them the reconciliation is ongoing after seven decades. But the French and the Germans, like the Montagues and the Capulets, have ended by in effect grieving together over their losses, creating a Europe determined never again to shed rivers of blood. Perhaps in the modern world such losses can take the place of the sacrificial victim in Girardian theory, and be effective in defusing the explosive confrontation that makes mimetic rivalry so destructive—in Northern Ireland, in the Middle East, and throughout the world.

However, in fairness to the complexity of Girard, he does *not* see any such easy "survivalist" solution. As early as *Violence and the Sacred,* he wrote,

> We have managed to extricate ourselves from the sacred somewhat more successfully than other societies . . . to the point of losing all memory of generative violence, but we are now about to rediscover it. . . . The essential violence returns to us in a spectacular manner. . . . This crisis invites us . . . to expose to the light of reason the role played by violence in human society. (Girard 1977)

In his latest work, such as *Battling to the End,* he has emphasized the "escalation to extremes" that he considers ever-present and dangerous in the current world as it is.

I don't think it's a contradiction to believe, as I do, that the world is gradually becoming a less violent place—that we *can* survive and even transcend our origins, and at the same time be alert for dramatic and unexpected explosions of violence such as those we have seen many times in the past century. Even while preparing for the worst, and being vigilant against its possibilities, we can hope for and work toward peace.

South Africa: Positive Mimesis and the Turn toward Peace

Leon Marincowitz

When a "transcendent" social order collapses, nations and communities usually dissolve into anarchic violence (Praeg 2007). We have seen notable examples of this in recent years: Iraq after the collapse of Saddam Hussein's regime; Yugoslavia, which erupted into violent ethnic, racial, and religious violence with the lifting of the Communist state at the end of the Cold War. Rwanda, following the shooting down of the plane carrying its Hutu president, lurched into ethnic genocide, which spread like wildfire.

South Africa, in this company, is an anomalous case: it is one of the few countries that remained intact as it migrated from one order to another. Moving from the polarizing policy of Apartheid to a democratic regime in the 1990s, South Africa escaped the widespread violence that generally occurs when the established sacral underpinning of a unifying social order (to speak in Girardian terms) is removed.

How did Apartheid function as a modern equivalent of the "archaic sacred" founded by emissary victimization? How did it subsist for so long, despite constituting a massive anomaly within the human rights–conscious world that emerged from the Second World War? How was it anomalous within the history of South Africa itself? Against this historical background, it will be possible to read the reconciliation undertaken by Nelson Mandela as an example of positive mimesis. The enigma of how South Africa managed to move from one social order to another without disruptive and anarchic violence has, in other words, a Girardian resolution.

Apartheid as a Modern Ideological Form of the Archaic Sacred

In the Girardian model, the surrogate victimage mechanism operates when orderly violence is used to vanquish disorderly violence by discharging itself upon an innocent victim (Girard 1977). The archaic sacred is a byproduct of this process: a transcendental order is created as peace returns to a community after the expulsion of this scapegoat victim. Girard considers that in the modern world, the victimage mechanism has degenerated in potency because it has become impossible to eliminate violence through violence. However, the archaic sacred can still be found wherever the transcendental order in place attempts to maintain itself through ever greater repressive violence; indeed, we can consider that this ratcheting up of institutionalized violence is the function and role of ideology in its modern conception.

Ideology-led analysis makes a conceptual error, Girard thinks, which is to reason within categories of "difference" when the root of all conflicts is rather "competition"—mimetic rivalry between persons, countries, cultures (Girard 2010). Attempting to define the differences between participants in a conflict or competition is futile, as each participant, irrespective of his/her "differences," is in fact *imitating* their opponent. Categorical mis-reasoning of just this type is evident in South Africa's official policy of Apartheid between 1948 and 1990, which put the category of race at the center of its entire analysis of politics and society.

The most—treacherously—"obvious" of differences between human beings, that of race, thus produced a policy of segregation that represented one of the most extreme forms of institutional racism ever seen. It divided South Africa into white and black populaces, thus creating an absolute dichotomy and a pure rivalry of mimetically self-renewing resentment-and-fear. The underlying claim of Apartheid was that the differences between the races exist as *inherent realities* and are a *cause* of conflict (Verwoerd 1958). Its opponents saw, or felt, that "differences" were being understood rather as a pretext for excluding people, and in order to justify the use of violence in so doing.

Secondly, ideologies promise and pre-trace some utopia. The ideological utopia is, then, necessarily the absence of difference, because according to this categorical reasoning, it is difference that causes conflict in the first place. Mythic-ideological peace envisages a peace of unanimity, because the victim has been expelled—which is why ideologies are, in Girard's submission, the "mythical happy endings to our histories of persecution" (Girard 2007, 237). The utopian ending to these grand narratives conceals the list of persecuted or scapegoated victims, whose exclusion makes "unanimous" peace possible. However, the ideological utopia remains fictional because it is impossible to fully implement it in practice. The sheer number of victims needed results in massacres that cannot establish order and peace.

Apartheid is precisely a case in point. Its utopian promise was the peaceful and harmonious development of the races separately, according to their own traditions, customs, decisions . . . and ability (Verwoerd 1958). It promised peace between and within the racial groups; and although large-scale massacres were relatively few in number, many were killed, most were actively oppressed, all were alienated in one or another sense; and the result was still the tyranny of one group ("white people") over another ("black people").

Categorical mis-differentiation and mythic utopias count as dimensions of the archaic sacred, and they qualify Apartheid as a modern ideology. Yet it is the concern for victims, something pervading all modern thinking, according to Girard, that shows us why ideologies are inherently short-lived; and why the tendency to differentiate arbitrarily, and then exclude, usually through self-justificatory violence, is no longer tenable.

In the period post–World War II, South Africa with its institutionalized, race-based ideology was, however, a *subsistent anomaly* in an international world pervaded by the ethos of human rights and universal democracy. The reason why the Apartheid government was tolerated by the international community for so long was because of the larger ideological rivalry represented by the Cold War. Within the framework of that larger rivalry, South Africa positioned itself strategically on the "right side," thereby reinforcing the broader transcendental order, and the rivalry generated by it. Apartheid South Africa was tolerated because the country aligned itself with the "Capitalist," "Democratic," and "Christian Western" world, as opposed to the "Communist," "Totalitarian" and "Atheist" East. These differences were used to scapegoat the "Other within," and to entrench further the internal "order of sacrifice" in which they operated. As the West and the East both shared the same inherent paradoxes of scapegoating the Other, Apartheid mirrored, and fitted easily within, this second, overarching sacrificial order.

Conversely, it is important to recognize that Apartheid's collapse occurred amidst the apparent "victory" of the West over the East. When Soviet Russia collapsed, so did the mimetic rivalry at the heart of a form of archaic sacrality that enfolded the world. International rivalry was generated, in fact, by an ideology-based analysis that arbitrarily divided the world. Its end also exposed Apartheid's hypocritical categories of difference and hastened its downfall.

Historical Patterns of "Sacrificial" Violence

Having located the Apartheid ideology as a continuation of the archaic sacred in the twentieth century, it is possible to turn to the "transcendental" order created within South Africa, and to see how the various patterns of sacrificial scapegoating occurred there. Apartheid, as we have said, created a socialized order premised on the scapegoating of black people, excluded by white power from white society. This exclusion makes that internal frontier the fascinating stake in a rivalry of mimetic reciprocity between "black" and "white" peoples. Meanwhile, the act of scapegoating postulates an illusory homogeneity in both excluders and excluded.

Within the "racial" category, there is no single majority group but instead a multitude of overlapping ethnic or linguistic groupings that make up South Africa. For instance, among "white people," there are the Afrikaners who are descendants of the Dutch/French Huguenots, and German and Malay immigrants who speak Afrikaans. Then there are the "English," who as British colonialists might be descendants of either Irish, Scots, Welsh, or the English themselves (Giliomee 2003). Among "black people" there are nine recognized tribal ethnicities (isiXhosa, IsiZulu, SePedi, SeSotho, SeTswana, siSwati, Xitsonga, isiNdebele, Tshivenda). The assumed homogeneity results purely from the polarity created as a result of the focus on the categorical differences set up in a situation of mimetic rivalry. What Apartheid did was conceal the existence of past rivalries between ethnic and linguistic collectives within a broader yet even more destructive dichotomy of race rivalry. Within postcolonial contexts such as South Africa, it is becoming critical to revisit the preexisting transcendental order(s) that *also* came about as a result of ethnic and linguistic victimage.

Two examples, each showing the already existing rivalries, violence, and scapegoating *within* the "races," will reveal the claims of racial homogeneity as false. The first is the period of South African history characterized as the *difaqane/mefecane* (Giliomee and Mbenga 2007, 127). This was a period in the late eighteenth century characterized by intertribal wars, migration, and forced assimilation. The Zulu Kingdom's imperialism is best known in this regard, but more recently, scholars show that most of the tribes or ethnic groupings participated. Campaigns of violence directed against external sacrificial victims created the internal social cohesion of the perpetrators. It seems that these ongoing battles, solidifying the ethnic identities concerned, have experienced a revival in recent years.

The second example is that of the Afrikaners' humiliation at the hands of the British in the Anglo-Boer War at the turn of the nineteenth century. The profound effect of this defeat lay in the Boer nationalism it stoked up: a movement looking, firstly, toward independence from the British; and secondly, to the establishment of Apartheid (Giliomee 2003). In both examples, external victims were found to placate tensions by redirecting the violence upon an immediate and convenient internal scapegoat.

In the process, a scarcity of resources was also caused, for a number of ethnic collectives, by neighboring tribes; so that several decades of violent battles swept across South Africa. The exclusion of the English from politics and, gradually, from the commanding heights of economy was not sufficient to reestablish Afrikaner identity (Van der Westhuizen 2007); and so further victims were required. In both examples, scapegoats are found to "explain" the lack of external resources or the internal dissension within a community.

Common to both examples is the archaic sacred, born of the exclusion of a scapegoat, and premised upon categorical reasoning. Sacrificial violence is done to victims "not for what they did, but for who they were" (Giliomee 2003, 254). The archaic sacred enables the persecutor to deny his own violence while simultaneously motioning in self-justification toward his own victimary status. Where this happens, history itself (i.e., the authorized narrative of "us and them") becomes an object of contest. There is a failure to reflect critically and responsibly upon history, accepting the faults and violence of both oneself and others. Such an abuse of memory and of history only results in further persecution and in a continuation of the victimage process (Ricoeur 2004).

The result of these historical interactions premised upon emissary victimization is that mimetic interaction is locked into a negative or "diabolic" mode, always taking the Other as an enemy to be striven with, expelled, or killed. When the Other is seen in this light, the momentum of crescendo toward paroxysm is certainly engaged. How then did South Africa escape this baleful conclusion implicit in the logic of its own violence?

From Negative to Positive Mimesis through Forgiveness and Reconciliation

The answer to this question, and the reason why South Africa is today lauded for its democratic and rights-based social contract, is linked to the transition leading away from Apartheid. For the first time in South African history, the change of social and political epochs did not result in the creation of a new category of scapegoats.

Within the newly instituted sociopolitical order, the former perpetrators of Apartheid did not become victims. By refusing the obvious tendency to think and act in differential categories, "arbitrarily" scapegoating the Other, a new public space was created in which it was possible for people from all ethnic groups to participate. The polarity of the various rivalries lessened as the transition process set about creating a politics without discrimination, not defined by categorical differences. It was to all intents and purposes a "victimless" transition. This was in no small part due to the political prisoner who became the first democratically elected president, Nelson Mandela.

The hatred and thirst for revenge that existed between rivals collapsed before Mandela's magnanimous example. Having accepted great violence done to his own person and overcoming it in a spirit of reconciliation, he revealed that all rivalry was futile, all revenge perilous. One could say he capitalized on the vacuum created by the collapse of the archaic-sacral order with its institutions of categorical differentiation-by-race; he "addressed their hearts" (Carlin 2008, 145).

In preaching forgiveness and reconciliation, Mandela withdrew from negative mimetic and rivalrous interactions and was able to draw all South

Africans around him into a program of reconciliation that was non-sacrificial (at least in the archaic-sacral sense). Mandela stood above the fray of negative reciprocity at the very moment when all expected him to lead the charge of revenge. The real individual for Girard is the "one who goes against the crowd for reasons that aren't rooted in the negative aspects of mimetic desire" (Girard 2007, 239).

We recall his symbolic gestures: by meeting the wife of the former architect of Apartheid, Betsie Verwoerd (Van Zyl Slabbert 2003, 316), and by wearing the "white" man's green jersey at the Rugby World Cup in 1995—an event memorably represented in the film *Invictus*—Mandela undermined racial categorization by showing the "white populace" that he was neither rivalrous, nor vengeful; and that true unity as a nation of people irrespective of race, ethnicity, and language was possible.

Conclusion

It was not the first time that individuals in South African history had gone against their own group identity,[1] but this was the defining moment, forestalling by very little the paroxysm of a runaway dynamic of mimetic reciprocity, the moment that ensured the transition to a peaceful and non-sacrificial order. "We have to think of reconciliation, not as a consequence, but as the reversal of the escalation to extremes" (Girard 2010, 46). Mandela understood that, and began to act accordingly.

There is a romantic notion that the struggle against unfair discrimination has resulted in democracy and reconciliation. This is a confusion. The truth is rather that Mandela's example of forgiveness and reconciliation provided the opportunity to establish a stable and workable democracy—without which negative mimesis resulting in heightened group polarities would have made peaceful discussions impossible and in the process destroyed South Africa in a maelstrom of racial and ethnic violence. Morrow is correct in saying that without a sufficient degree of reconciliation, democracy as a "ritual for resolving conflict" will fail (it can exacerbate and further polarize existing rivalries).

Currently, eighteen years into our democracy, South Africa is no longer in transition. All Apartheid laws have been rescinded, and the mundane details of life have again taken precedence. Adherence to the constitution is growing, yet the document itself remains contentious, as if constructed in another era. South Africa is no longer in transition, but it is far from stable.

The hoped-for reconciliation of Mandela's "rainbow nation" has dimmed somewhat, in part because reconciliation is still approached from within a negative mimetic model—perhaps in part because the goal of "development" has too quickly displaced and replaced that of "reconciliation." The TRC (Truth and Reconciliation Commission) created a public space for reconciliation, but its stock has since diminished somewhat, with the perception that such reconciliation as it has achieved functions, in fact, at a political level, useful to the new order, rather than in spiritual reality, with real persuasion at grassroots level.

Just like Northern Ireland, South Africa, despite huge progress, remains in a place of fascination with, and resentment against, the Other—tired, and suspicious, of violence, yet not entirely willing to embrace the "perfect offering" that reconciliation requires: admitting one's own filiation to violence, while recognizing the victimhood of others and accepting the Other as gift, not as rival.

Notes

1. Other examples include the last Apartheid president, F. W. De Klerk, who after realizing the implications of the collapse of the Cold War, "took the gap" (Van Zyl Slabbert 2006, 36), unbanned the ANC, and freed Mandela. Another is Archbishop Desmond Tutu, who chaired the Truth and Reconciliation Commission; he provided an alternative model with a non-sacrificial narrative of personal forgiveness and reconciliation in face-to-face encounters between perpetrators and victims (Tutu 1999, 78).

Cited Texts and Further Reading

Allen, J. 2008. *Desmond Tutu: Rabble-Rouser for Peace: The Authorised Biography.* Johannesburg: Lawrence Hill Books.

Carlin, J. 2008. *Playing the Enemy: Nelson Mandela and the Game That Made a Nation.* London: Atlantic Books.

De Klerk, F. W. 2000. *The Last Trek—A New Beginning: The Autobiography.* Johannesburg: Pan.

Giliomee, H. 2003. *The Afrikaners: Biography of a People.* Cape Town: Tafelberg.

Giliomee, H., and B. Mbenga. 2007. *New History of South Africa.* Cape Town: Tafelberg.

Girard, R. 1977. *Violence and the Sacred.* Translated by Patrick Gregory. New York: Continuum.

———. 1986. *The Scapegoat.* Translated by Yvonne Freccero. Baltimore: Johns Hopkins University Press.

————. 2001. *I See Satan Fall Like Lightning.* Maryknoll, NY: Orbis Books.

————. 2007. *Evolution and Conversion: Dialogues on the Origins of Culture.* With Pierpaolo Antonello and João Cezar de Castro Rocha. London: Continuum.

————. 2010. *Battling to the End: Conversations with Benoît Chantre.* Translated by Mary Baker. East Lansing: Michigan State University Press.

Mandela, N. 1995. *Long Walk to Freedom: The Autobiography of Nelson Mandela.* London: Abacus.

Praeg, L. 2007. *The Geometry of Violence. Africa, Girard, Modernity.* Stellenbosch: Sun Press.

Ricoeur, P. 2004. *Memory, History, Forgetting.* Translated by Kathleen Blamey and David Pellauer. Chicago: University of Chicago Press.

Tutu, D. 1999. *No Future without Forgiveness.* Johannesburg: Rider Books.

Van Der Westhuizen, C. 2007. *White Power and the Rise of the National Party.* Cape Town: Zebra Press.

Van Zyl Slabbert, F. 2003. "Reconciliation: Negotiating Reconciliation." In *Nelson Mandela: From Freedom to the Future: Tributes and Speeches,* ed. Kadar Asmal, David Chidester, and Wilmot James. Johannesburg: Jonathan Ball Publishers.

————. 2006. *The Other Side of History: An Anecdotal Reflection on Political Transition in South Africa.* Johannesburg: Jonathan Ball Publishers.

Verwoerd, H. F. 1958. *Aparte ontwikkeling, die positiewe aspekte.* Pretoria: Dept. van Naturellesake, RSA.

Peace-Making in Practice and Theory

An Encounter with René Girard

Scott Atran

I much enjoyed all the texts in this section; and, of course, I heartily endorse Mel Konner's vibrant salute to those who put in the "hard yards" for peace.

Without being a Girardian or even knowing Girard's theory intimately, I've often found my paths crossing with his. I'll try and say how I see the pattern of our encounters from the two points of view that interest me: as a consultant in "hands-on" peace-making, and as an academic anthropologist of violence and the sacred, based at the French CNRS (I also have American and British University connections).

Northern Ireland: Diagnosis and Resolution

Morrow's diagnosis of origins of the Irish conflict was enlightening: its roots in the Reformation and Counter-Reformation; its embeddedness in the story of British relations with the Continent and the struggle for empire. We always need a contextual understanding, referring to the play of geopolitical factors. The amalgam of religious-and-political identity struggles, with their reciprocities of mimetic rivalry, and the embedding, within this complex of historic forces, of rising Nationalist sentiment have conspired to give the Irish conflict the long-lasting and seemingly intractable character it held right up until the 1990s.

I would perhaps want to add something more on the period 1815–1930. Partly because it's my basis for understanding how that knot of tensions comes undone in the subsequent period, our own lifetime; and partly because it provides some basis for generalizing from the Irish conflict to the conflicts of the other contemporary hot spots envisaged here.

The post-Napoleonic period introduced Europe to universal values through the French Revolution, relayed by its aftershocks of 1830 and 1848. These generated a current of popular fervor and ideas *very much like the "Arab Spring" of today.* "The Revolutionary idea" failed everywhere in Europe at that time; but it led to the real formation of nations as tribal entities based on blood (i.e., genetic kinship) and on cultural narratives of "imagined kinship." It thus created ethnic or multi-ethnic national "identities" demanding their consecration in statehood. Monarchs also realized they were going to have to incorporate the lower orders into the nation, which made the same call on narratives, symbols, and rituals. The result was to ratchet up "nationalism" everywhere, Ireland included—especially so in the wake of the famine, where British landlords had treated the Irish with harsh contempt, while brutal laissez-faire economic theories in London had restrained the sending of corn in relief. In this context of crisis, the amalgam of blood, nation, and religion provided a powerful salvational antidote—a Way Out.

I find Morrow even more compelling when he lays out the reasons why the conflict proved ultimately amenable to a loosening of the knot of determinants. The defeat of Nazi Germany was very important, as was the quasi-federalization of Europe in the creation of the EU. Here was an entity that would protect "our" values, and, at the same time, wasn't British and wasn't Irish. It allowed all protagonists to imagine their own national boundaries as dissolving away. The thought was this: "We'll keep intact at least some parts of our ethnic-and-religious identity, but we don't need to sacralize the nation-state, its territory, or its boundaries, as an overarching principle of identity."

The Nation-State, as a sacred value, had been discredited in many popular and political circles by the blood sacrifice of the Great War, itself caused by the play of mimetic rivalries between Europe's great nation-states;

but it was the Second World War that destroyed the very idea of the *essence-based* nation. Consider here Girard's definition in *Clausewitz:* the object of war, like that of a duel, is to compel the enemy to accept your will—or else exterminate him, to annihilate the adverse identity. Nazism tried, quite literally, to equate war with its principle—to wage war *absolutely.* Its defeat, taken together with the British retreat from the practice and the mentality of empire, and with the creation of the European Union, opened up a new space of possibility.

You have to risk vulnerability, creatively, in order to do this. I have from John Alderdice,[1] one of the principal architects of the Good Friday Agreement, the following account of the "tipping point" in the Irish process.

At that time, in the aftermath of the 1985 Anglo-Irish Agreement, there was little or no contact between the parties, and Alderdice spent the next few years trying to get the warring Northern Ireland politicians to engage in informal talks. Early on he met the Irish Taosieach, Charles Haughey, and British Prime Minister Margaret Thatcher, and stressed to them the necessity of an initiative to engage the Northern Irish parties. The message to the British and Irish governments was: "You guys need to get on with it. Within appropriate boundary conditions (e.g., the UK was not going to give up sovereignty without the consent of the people of Northern Ireland, and the Irish would not abandon the aspiration of making Northern Ireland fully a part of an independent Irish Republic; and both wanted to ensure that no violence spilled over their respective borders). The two governments were clear: "We're not going to force any outcome; but we'll help and we'll fund." So the big players worked together as the engine for the process. They did not force a particular outcome; but together they became the honest brokers that they could not have been separately. This helped create *conditions of trust:* it became possible for each side to begin to risk something, since the two sponsors were giving each some protections—though neither side in the North necessarily believed this all of the time.

It wasn't quick—eleven years, in fact. While John Hume (the leader of the Nationalist SDLP) focused on engaging with Sinn Fein, Alderdice spent the next three years moving back and forth among the two governments and the non-paramilitary parties in talks about talks. It looked like a dialogue of the deaf, with no positive outcome at all, except that the antagonists were getting used to (and getting their people used to) the idea that there would eventually be engagement. Meeting (and often refusing to meet) each other in television and radio studios, they were talking about what could and could not happen, and engaging with intermediaries. Talks began in 1991, initially between the so-called constitutional parties (i.e., those without clear para-military attachments), but after eighteen months they broke down because of Unionists' suspicion about what they regarded as Hume's excessive focus on Sinn Fein, which was inextricably linked to the IRA. The violence continued, but so did the unrelenting search for a way through.

In 1993 the two governments spelled out in the Downing Street Declaration the parameters within which they believed a settlement might now be possible; and then in 1994, U.S. President Bill Clinton made a dramatic intervention. He allowed Sinn Fein President Gerry Adams a brief visit to New York. Alderdice and Hume went too, but the Unionists refused and were outraged. Alderdice used the opportunity on a *Larry King Live* show to challenge Adams to stop the violence so that talks could begin. Within months the IRA declared a "complete cessation of military operations," and the loyalist paramilitaries followed suit a few weeks later. Alderdice led his party into the Forum for Peace and Reconciliation organized by the Irish government in Dublin Castle—the only non-Nationalist party there, because it was boycotted by all the Unionist parties.

Another two years were spent with Unionists and Nationalists yelling at one another across the airwaves. There were litanies of victimization: no one recognizes their own violence, only at first the violence of "the Other" and the injury done to one's own community or tribe. But then they got *hoarse*—if not literally, then metaphorically. There were more contacts, and an agreement to have an election in 1996 for representatives to possible peace talks. Despite the ceasefires, the bombings and killings were returning, and it took until 1997 to get a renewal of the ceasefire and a serious engagement with talks under the chairmanship of U.S. Senator George Mitchell.

The adversaries began to see the roots of their own violence and prejudice, and to open up to recognition of "the Other." The courtesy and patience of George Mitchell began to have an effect. Fighting and screaming Irishmen had to be *polite:* "Gentlemen, if you wish to be heard, you must be prepared to listen to 'the Other'—even at great length." A final push was needed. An agreed deadline emerged, and with George Mitchell and Bill Clinton in place as overarching "Holders of the Ring," the two governments and the historic adversaries were then able to *agree not to agree*—and to figure out *what to do in the meantime.*

If it hadn't been for the containing relationship of the British and Irish governments (partners since 1973 within the EU), nothing would have happened. Without the informal encounters (some of them in the U.S. Consulate in Belfast), it would have been difficult for the formal process of the peace talks to gain traction. The major players, little by little, agreed to take the "national question"—focus of rivalry, conflict, and violence—out of the equation. Not permanently—this question was not *resolved*—but its resolution was suspended, and, in a sense, *transcended.* The key was to persuade all concerned that it was only acceptable, and in the interests of both sides of the community, to pursue political ambitions solely through peaceful democratic processes. What was perhaps new was not just the realization that they had fought to a stalemate where neither could be defeated, but neither could win. It was also the fact that together they had created joint institutions in which all sides of the community had a stake and an opportunity for participation at the highest level.

Taking away the constitutional feud as a *live issue right now* created space in which to address issues of institutional inequity and discrimination within the society (ceasefires, political structures, social practices, institutional functions such as policing, etc.), and to promote an adjustment of relationships and a healing of memory—a process that is still ongoing more than a decade later.

I think Americans can understand this maturation or modulation of perspectives, and this slow reframing of memory, reinterpreting history, even when it comes to celebrating a Victory (as the Lambeg drums still do, divisively, commemorating the Battle of the Boyne in 1690)[2] or a continuity of Struggle (a specialty of all IRA funerals). The American North once celebrated Gettysburg in that way, for umpteen years. But now, the commemoration of that battle means something different. It means: "we both sacrificed and lost."

In South Africa, the tipping point came, within the changing context described by Leon Marincowitz, with Mandela. His example was quite crucial, because he absorbed injury done to his people, to himself in person, without retaliation—indeed, with a great generosity of outreach. He managed to hold the allegiance of whites and blacks (at the price of profound tension with the left wing of the ANC). Today, he's a secular world saint, the more impressive for being so simple, humorous, and transparently honest. I'm surprised and pleased at the large-scale structural conversion nonviolently achieved; delighted to see how much has improved in South Africa. But, looking at the limits of the truth and reconciliation process, and at the corruption of parts of the ANC, I wonder how well the post-Apartheid settlement will evolve without Mandela.

The Truly Intractable Conflict

Now look at the case of the truly intractable conflict of Israel-Palestine—a conflict so knotted, as Konner intimates, as to stand as a symbol of *all* human conflict.

I don't see in any of the papers grouped here the least immediate possibility of hope for the Middle East. In fact I think the situation there is fast going backwards. Peace seemed much more possible in the early 1990s. The seeds were there, with the same sort of stories emerging as Wilson recounts; the same nascent or inchoate attempts to bridge the moral gap. But then a number of things happened internally. There was the assassination of Rabin by his own people; the settler Goldstein killed twenty-nine Muslims in the mosque at Hebron; Hamas took advantage to launch its suicide attack program. We saw the impotence of Shimon Peres to do anything but respond with retaliatory repression, which became less and less discriminating through the early Sharon years. (An architect of Sharon's targeted assassination program later conceded that "we were wrong to adopt a scattergun approach"). Hardliners on both sides came to occupy the political ground. To the point where UN Secretary General Ban Ki-moon declared recently that the level of building in support of Israeli settlement in the Occupied Territories is now so invasive as to make even a "two-state solution"—Israel and Palestine existing autonomously side by side—increasingly unthinkable.

And then the contextual environment has seen an *inverse evolution* to that which unloosened the knot of the Irish problem. In the Middle East, there has been a remorseless tightening of geopolitical tensions. Iran, which had nothing to do with Israel, and has indeed had reasonably good relations with Jews for 2,700 years, all of a sudden began arguing for the extermination of Israel as a state—questioning even whether Jews should exist in that part of the world, since they are "cancerous." That brings back the whole Holocaust memory (which has a very different resonance among Arabs, precisely because they weren't part of European anti-Semitism). So they don't understand Israeli reactions ("Look, we've been through this madness once, we're not going to tolerate it again"). In turn, Arab regimes fail to understand Western reactions to holocaust-talk and the imminence of Iranian nuclear weapons ("There the West goes again; they're telling us what to do; they defend Israel because Israel defends their interests"). If Iran goes nuclear, Egypt, Turkey, and Saudi Arabia would likely attempt to "nuke up" too—not an inviting prospect within the most volatile region of the world.

Of course, the Israel-Palestine problem is embedded in the wider, and very complex, phenomenon of Arab awakening, in turn related to the phenomenon of a—frequently reluctant or ambiguous—relinquishing of historic Western hegemonies in the region. In its early- and mid-twentieth-century stirrings, Arab awakening was a matter of adopting Western political models and values, inspired by mainly Christian intellectuals. But the deeper convulsions of the end of the twentieth century brought a more radical recourse to the unifying authority, the identity-guarantee and moral compass of Islam. By a spectacular own-goal, this factor was declared, in 1964, by leading Western expert on the Middle East Bernard Lewis to be a spent force, henceforth irrelevant. He was proved dead wrong by the rise of radical Islam, then of al-Qaeda. This in turn elicited misjudgment, and an outsized U.S. response: this included the introduction of torture under the Orwellian concept of "enhanced interrogation" and even now the extrajudicial warrant to kill American citizens, the prolonged de facto occupation of Afghanistan, and, particularly, the invasion of Iraq (a core Arab country). Saddam Hussein was indeed a Creep, but he was *their* Creep.

In one sense, the Israel-Palestine dispute is a highly charged symbol; it has little or nothing, directly, to do with any of this. The first Jewish settlers in modern Palestine were poor Jews from the Pale who were suffering from the pogroms in Russia. They were seeking a life where they wouldn't have to suffer any more. Palestinians didn't have a title to any of the land; that was owned by bankers of the former Ottoman Empire, like the Sursuk family in Lebanon. The Jews came with titles that they paid their last *kopek* to acquire—some having walked 2,000 miles to get there. The Arab peasant

said: "I don't understand what this means; my ancestors have always cultivated this land." So what happens? Both parties internalize themselves as
victims, rather than face the problems. The Other became the *"cause"* of their
victimhood.

Isaac Deutscher has a parable describing this. Right after the Six Day
War of 1967, writing in the *New Left Review,* he compared the core situation
to that of a man in a burning house. He's only got one window left to escape
from. He looks out, sees a man walking below him, but jumps anyway—and
falls on the man, breaking his legs and arms. The jumping man had no choice;
yet to the man with the broken limbs, he was the cause of his misfortune.

Both are right. But rather than deal with that situation by taking into
consideration one another's history and motives, the injured man blames the
other for his misery and swears to make him pay. The other one, afraid of the
injured man's revenge and soon confusing him with those who started the
fire, kicks the injured man to keep him down. So you have the Israelis, with
their holocaust obsession, projecting Nazi intentions onto the Palestinians,
when Palestinians had originally nothing to do with it. And you have Palestinians projecting imperialist ambitions on Jews, soon putting in an anti-
Semitic frame like the *Protocols of the Elders of Zion,* when Jews originally
wished only to be safe in a home of their own.

The Middle East doesn't actually have the deep-rooted historic anti-
Semitism of Europe. Yet the language of anti-Semitism is now creeping in
there, virally: into Egypt and throughout the Middle East. And then you
have Iran trying to do what Saudi Arabia failed to do (and what al-Qaeda
has, thankfully, also—to date!—failed to do): present itself as the *vanguard
of Islam.* The Palestinian issue is seen as their issue; it's the only one they've
got to achieve hearing and influence in the region. If they can co-opt the
Arab world on this point (rather than on Afghanistan), then they've won a
clear advantage in the game.

So: in this geopolitical context, all the negative factors that seemed
dormant or moribund in the past are now being revived to exacerbate and
re-envenomate the conflict. Israelis and Palestinians are increasingly inter-
nalizing the worst of their anti-Other rhetoric, in a mimetic reciprocity of
mistrust, resentment, and rage. The two-state solution is disappearing. And
whereas the whole of Europe supported the Irish settlement, and America
came in there as actual fairy godmother, almost everyone is against an

Israel-Palestine settlement: from the Israeli Right and the 70 to 80 million strong fundamentalists of America (far more powerful politically than the Jewish lobby with which they often make common cause) to militant Islamists (who see Israel as America's proxy in the region), and to loose cannon Iran, with its acolyte militias currently wreaking havoc in Syria, Iraq, and Lebanon. In this context and climate, there are not too many chinks for the light to get in.

Is there, nevertheless, some hope, potentially, in the current "Arab Spring"? Do we see emerging potential sponsors of a process of detoxification and trust-building parallel to the Irish one? That's exactly why, as I write this piece,[3] I'm thinking that the White House should be sounding out the Muslim Brotherhood leadership and talking again to reelected and now "tenderized" Israeli Prime Minister Netanyahu. The Muslim Brothers have an immense following, more "people power" clout than any of the Arab regimes ever had. Do they see the possibility of peaceful coexistence? Can they be persuaded, with America, to sponsor a peace process?

If the United States and Muslim Brothers can create the conditions of regular and reliable exchanges of the kind that we saw bridging the gap in Ireland, and then of creating a *relational space* for looking at the consequences of one's own violence, one's own prejudices, then the game is on. The Israeli extremists can, I think, be contained. Even Netanyahu, who has Zionist antecedents and who thinks it's time for Israel to win in the struggle of two emergent nationalisms, once ventured the opinion, in a moment of human confidence, that if ever he saw anti-Semitic references excised from Palestinian textbooks, then he would be prepared to take Israel back to its pre-1967 frontiers.

My latest trip to Cairo in October 2012, however, does not give me grounds for optimism. Muslim Brother leaders there told me that they had no intention of ever trying to engage Israel directly; some told me they hoped to march into Jerusalem someday to liberate it for the Arab people (and also to liberate Jordan, Saudi Arabia, and the rest of the Arab world from rulers they hope to replace); and some even professed the need for an Egyptian nuke to balance Israeli and American power in order to "create a level playing field that will allow Islam to triumph in the hearts and minds of men everywhere in the world." Of course, the responsibilities of governance could well moderate ambitions, but the Israelis cannot bet their life on it.

From Practice to Theory

So much for concrete and practical peace-making. What of its theoretical elucidation and of Girardian theory as a mapping of the ground? How well does it contribute to a science of diagnosing conflicted and violent situations, and as a prognosis for peace-making?

The existing science (such as it is) of conflict negotiation is mainly based on the "rational-actor" model. This model says: "Look, we can both be better off if we cooperate. That will mean you giving up a little bit of your self-interest and me a little bit of mine. But in the end we're both going to be better off." That's fine for business, and within groups that share the same moral framework. But when you have conflicting moral frames, they become very salient—just as food is not important as long as you have it. If you don't, it becomes *asymptotic* in the hold it has over your values and preoccupations. Sacred values are a bit like that. They cover the whole range of human relationships to the group: from separatist hermits and misogynists to the *complete fusion* of identities characteristic of extremists (like suicide bombers). They are the group, the group is them; and they empower one another, making them feel invincible, but also blinding them to compromises, alternatives, exit strategies. Peace-making is unlocking that irrationally—but comprehensibly!—locked door.

Empirically speaking, I find that in this task, a Girardian analysis often fits well. It's a very useful tool to have around. Its concepts, categories, and themes are often mine. When I find myself thinking, "The Americans shafted the Russians in Afghanistan as the Soviets had done to them in Vietnam," I'm talking mimetic rivalry: the age-old tit-for-tat that Girard develops so powerfully to explain all conflict and its multiplier effect in human beings (its "ratcheting-up," as I frequently find myself saying). When I speak of the Palestinians as "the sacrificial lamb," both of Israeli intransigence and of the politicking of impotent Arab states, who cultivate their plight (e.g., by failing to give them passports so as to exploit them as a political symbol), I'm using a Girardian language of sacrifice, and accepting the Hebrew scriptures and the Christian gospels as cultural hinterland.

It's the structural reciprocities and the qualitative relationalities of human conflict we need to come to grips with; and the notions of mimetic rivalry, emissary victimization, and sacrifice do indeed go to the heart of this matter. When I quote Isaac Deutscher's parable of the man-who-jumps, I know I'm dealing also with "blame-transfer" and "double victimization," Girard's scapegoating mechanism operating in the second degree. And when I speak of the Holocaust of European Jews as "a parable of the modern world," I imagine Girard himself will have seen and said precisely that (even if our agreement at this point, in respect of the contemporary world, doesn't mean that I'm really persuaded of his founding scenario of scapegoat murder in the evolutionary process of "hominization"; my instinct is to see that as a gospel-based myth).

So I can broadly endorse an analysis predicated on negative and positive mimesis. All conflicted situations and societies illustrate the first. The peace process gains traction in Ireland and loses it in the case of Israel-Palestine because the conditions exist—or do not yet exist—for converting the first valency into the second. I have already cited Mandela as a capital force for positive mimesis in South Africa. I'm sympathetic to Girard's analysis of the modern eagerness to claim victim status, even to the point of developing a rivalrous fascination for the victimary position, seen these days as advantageous and attractive. We both see Christianity as the ultimate cause of this, since it declares the victim innocent, even worthy of respect, awe, and love. Girard would presumably say that what sets up the conditions of this phenomenon and the contemporary cult of victim status are two different things (he would probably tend to refer the modern cult of victimhood, rather, to an Enlightenment discourse of "rights").

We might discuss the way the term "black" has been internalized, turned around, and adopted in America, as a title to dignity and a claim to consideration . . . And we might then go on to discuss Martin Luther King and his creation of the narrative of the civil rights movement. King believed (as Girard does) in a Gandhi-like Christianity as the way of salvation, and the way of peace—a way of throwing back their own violence at the perpetrators of violence (which, so I'm told, is the way Girard explains the crucifixion of Jesus). By contrast, look at the Hamas leadership now. "Why don't you use Gandhi and Martin Luther King?" I ask them. "That's fine for Indians and for American blacks," they say. "Not for us." They explain: "The Jews are exclusive; they will not allow us to exist" (the Israelis have exactly the same response: "they want to annihilate us"). That's a case study in mimesis . . . but here, mimetic reciprocity relates to the offloading-and-transfer of blame; and rivalry consists in vying for self-justification—which describes the "locked" or "blocked" character of situations of conflict.

My empirical convergence with Girard extends out from this central core of overlap, toward a concern with identity politics and social group dynamics, though here I often find myself diverging significantly. The question that keeps my discussion with Girardians rebounding, often in quite sparky and revealing ways, is to know how far our divergent "takes" are *complementary*, and how far they are mutually *exclusive* responses.

We're both hugely interested in ritual as a means of social bonding. I recently wrote an article in *Science* magazine, exploring how the rise of large-scale societies in human cultural development is a function of shared ritual and beliefs (the latter explicating the former). The more outlandish, proprietary, costly, and generally "crazy" they are, the more these ritual practices (together with their justifying ideological or religious belief systems) give the assurance of trustworthy belonging; trust being the operative functional requirement since it ensures the cohesion and viability of loosely knit—and geographically extended—social networks, which can no longer be bound together or managed by tightly knit family or ethnic ties. The creation and spread, in the history of human development, of large-scale societies is explicable as a function of the identification between cooperators; and ritual (with its attendant ideology) is the key to this.

I don't doubt that Girard would subscribe substantially to this basic thesis. He is, after all, a fellow Durkheimian, who sees religion as the matrix of all social being (ritual, institutions, moral codes, and myths). God is group: *vox populi, vox dei.* That puts him on my side when I object to fellow "four horsemen" (Dawkins, Hitchens, Harris, and Dennett)[4] that religion isn't reducible to propositional utterance, verifiable or not; that it is *ritual practice,* with an identity-bonding function. I also tell them that suicide bombers are not *incomprehensible monsters.* When you investigate their backgrounds they turn out to be extreme, exceptionally "sacrificial" participants in the sacred values of their ritually bonded communities. We would certainly agree about the sacralizing function of ritual practice.

Sacred values are the things that make life meaningful and possible in a social context. That's why you can't *change* sacred values, or *set them aside;* you can only (given favorable circumstances) reframe them in an open-textured, reconfiguring sort of way—up to a point. And to achieve even that, there has to be a change of social relationships—a change of ideas won't do it (that's too superficial, not intimate enough). To create a different moral system, you have to create that sense of symbiotic relationships and dependencies. It's the web of personal relationships that actually best does the trick (as we saw in Northern Ireland). That's what can make people "sacrifice"—in the sense of costly solidarity and self-giving—for one another . . . and for peace.

Girardians tell me additional—complementary?—things that I find more difficult to accept. For instance that outlandish craziness or "excess" belongs to created nature before it characterizes human behavior; that the "sacred" is a manmade category, secreted and cultivated to "regulate" and "contain" violence; and that it is made "archaic," in principle, by Christianity . . . And that what I envisage as a *framing and enabling trust* is to be envisaged as a feature of bonding in *both* horizontal (human-human) *and* vertical (divine-human) dimensions of interaction. I use "sacred values" as a descriptive or neutral term; whereas I'm aware that Girard thinks of the "archaic sacred" as something *convertible* into "holiness" or "sanctity."

Girardians and I agree that the most general formula of our basic divergence is the difference between a "survivalist" and a "salvational" perspective. My main objection, when I first read all, or nearly all, these peace-making texts, was that I found them to be *ultimately religious and salvational.* The background assumption is that humans should unite. Unite on the basis of what they regard not as imagined kinship, but as the inevitable way humans will go if they can overcome ritualized violence and group separation. Like all religious-salvational stances, that strikes me as idealistic, teleological, essentialist. I tend to consider all the ideologies that made the modern world, as salvational constructs off-printed in some manner from Christendom. Religions, particularly Christian monotheism, allow even atheism to come into being as a salvational idea, even a salvational political ideology. The idea of salvational ideologies is religious at its core. We see this in their ritual expressions: liturgies and symbols, ceremonies, parades, and anthems—think of Hitler's Nuremburg rallies.

Both Northern Irish contributors argue as if, when you do away with the centrifugal forces, new bondings will come into being. For example: Derick Wilson talks about undoing the false sacred and ritualized values that keep conflict going. For my part, I'm not sure there *is* anything that can be called "false" sacralization. Whatever is sacred is part of who you are. It's "false" once you've made this jump of Girardian "conversion." But making this jump is the problem. You can't really *throw away* those—supposedly "archaic"— sacred values, any more than you can negotiate away a piece of yourself; you can only *reframe* them.

The survival/salvation dividing line is where most Girardians and I agree to disagree. I have tried, though, to explore with them how we come, respectively, to that point of divergence and what is at stake in our disagreement.

It's partly a matter of the way Girardians, or some of them anyway, appeal to Christianity. I agree with those who think Girard's theory is not to be extracted or abstracted from its Christian matrix. But that is a problem for me. The underlying assumption is that Christianity, real Christianity—not the way Catholics and Protestants have played with their "false sacralizations" in Ireland—is at its heart and core a peaceful salvational framework for humankind, to rid it of violence. That seems to me subject to caution: once you believe you have a set of ideas or beliefs that are *the* Way, the true and only right way (as with Dick Cheney and Mahmoud Ahmadinejad!)— whether you like it or not, you create the conditions of violence.

My own anthropology of Christian origins goes like this: The way Christianity took over the Roman Empire is that during the first hundred years following the expulsion of the majority of the population from Judaea, most Christians lived on the periphery of Jewish communities throughout the empire. Then they began tending the second-class citizens of the empire: slaves, women, strangers, and so forth. What really brought people in was that, for example, during plague, Christians would give the victims water while the Roman relatives would run away. Just giving water significantly upped the possibility of survival. But it exposed the Christians themselves to the sickness. Wow, these people are willing to put themselves at risk to help us; why are they doing this? We don't really understand, but it's good. There was about 4 percent growth of enlistment to the faith every year; so that by the time of Constantine, Christians were already a majority in the Roman Empire.

Then ritual identification kicks in, and it becomes an organic thing. The more proprietary, ritualized, and costly the ideas become from the point of view of the outside, the more successful in bringing the group—or, from Constantine's viewpoint, the empire—together. But this increased the gap with other groups, who found the proprietary practices bizarre and threatening. So that mistrust is increased. The paradox is this: as these groups became bigger and bigger and formed themselves into proprietary groups based on rituals and ideas, they increased antagonism with other groups. On top of which, universal ideas were coming into play: monotheisms, starting with Christianity, merging Greek and Jewish ideas, etc., offering a salvation based on a remediation of violence, and on an all-inclusive unity of human brotherhood.

Christianity universalizes the message of love, so that the group is no longer the ethnic unit, but humanity itself. However, those who are recalcitrant toward this message, or impede or persecute it, get it in the neck even worse—look at the biblical Book of Revelation.

I would also cite different readings of the evolutionary frame. I register the Girardian account of hominization, and the critical role played in it by the need to manage human violence, so much more apocalyptic—already *then* and increasingly so *today*—than animal conflict. I can see how evolutionary self-programming could run deep, how its default mechanisms would be long-lasting—and might explain the patterns of emissary victimization still extant everywhere today. Particularly, of course, our paradigmatic twentieth-century recapitulation of human violence in the Holocaust. I can even glimpse how it might begin to make sense of the undoubted and troubling fact that "religion" contains *both* the best *and* the worst of humanity—that's a fair offer, worth any amount of discussion. My view of evolution, however, allows no nodal or originary place for this paradigm in the account of the threshold emergence of *Homo sapiens.*

I subscribe to a post-Enlightenment (cognitivist) picture of human origins, somewhat of the Jared Diamond type: the real determinants of adaptive advantage and selectivity are biomedical, geo-environmental, and technological (mainly the technologies of sewing, and food and weapons production). With these determinants, we can explain, differentially, how *Homo sapiens* became smart and, progressively, civilized. And if, digging previously and deeper into the order of causalities, we need to explain what permits the actual quantum leap of hominization and triggers the acceleration of history everyone agrees on, then, civilizationally speaking, the answer must lie in language and in *group cooperation*—as also in our ability to envisage the mental worlds of other cospecifics, hence also "other worlds" of human possibility. Perhaps the voice box, not the victim, is the thing?

◆ ◆ ◆

My Enlightenment background is important in shaping my views. It connotes a—preferably scientific—cognitivism (as opposed to some teleology, essentialism, or idealism). I prefer a material-functional form of rationality (at the cost of appearing "reductionist"). The same imprint implies—rather than moral optimism in relation to human nature—a sense of justice, or rather a desire to relieve injustice, providing this doesn't simply displace the burden of victimhood.

I also have Jewish antecedents. Judaism is a very historical religion, in which a belief in God is often almost ancillary to a sense of ethnic-and-spiritual identity traversing and transcending history through narrative (I have an almost visceral sense, in walking the fields of Shiloh,⁵ of treading where Saul and Jonathan trod). On top of which, I'm a professional anthropologist, former assistant to Margaret Mead, and a post-critical, post-death-of-God modern critical theorist.

Malraux echoes my basic "take" on human existence when he writes: "The greatest mystery is not that we are thrown here by chance, between the profusion of atoms and that of the stars. It is that, in this prison, we should draw out of ourselves images powerful enough to negate our nothingness" (Malraux 1972, 44). Radical contingency, existential freedom, tragic humanism, yes; but, along with this grandiloquent *réplique* to Pascal, Malraux defines the one mystery I find convincing at gut level.

I don't see any Sponsor for the "vertical" peace operation; no cosmic-metaphysical Trust-bearer or Trust-broker to humankind. So I do what I can.

Notes

1. John (now Lord) Alderdice was leader of Northern Ireland's nonsectarian Alliance Party (1987–98). He resigned this post and became the first Speaker of the Northern Ireland Assembly after the Good Friday Agreement. He is currently Convener of the Liberal Democrat Parliamentary Party in the House of Lords.

2. Fought on the banks of the river Boyne (near Drogheda) between the Protestant monarch William III ("William of Orange") and James II, pretender of the deposed Catholic line to the thrones of England, Scotland, and Ireland, this battle ensured the Anglo-Irish ascendancy and is commemorated by Protestants in Northern Ireland as foundational for their identity and for the British connection.

3. This paper was written before the election of President Hassan Rouhani in Iran (August 2013) and before the coup displacing Egyptian President Mohammed Morsi (July 2013). (Ed.)

4. In 2007, I was invited to Beijing, along with these "new atheist" thinkers, to give a talk on religion

co-sponsored by the Chinese government Commission on Atheism. I told them equating religion with superstition was naive; this got sponsored applause . . . I jumped ship.

5. Shiloh, site (in Tennessee) of a major battle of the American Civil War, is named after an ancient city mentioned in the Hebrew Bible. The ancient city's site is at modern Khirbet Seilun, south of ancient Tirzah and ten miles north of the Israeli settlement of Beth El in the West Bank.

Cited Texts and Further Reading

Anderson, Benedict. 1983. *Imagined Communities: Reflections on the Origin and Spread of Nationalism.* New York: Verso.

Atran, Scott. 2002. *In Gods We Trust: The Evolutionary Landscape of Religion.* New York: Oxford University Press.

———. 2006. "Is Hamas Ready to Deal?" *New York Times,* August 17.

———. 2010a. "Pathways to and from Political Violence": Testimony to the Senate Armed Forces Subcommittee on Emerging Threats and Capabilities. March 10. Http://www.jjay.cuny.edu/ US_Senate_Hearing_on_Violent_Extremism.pdf.

———. 2010b. *Talking to the Enemy: Violent Extremism, Sacred Values, and What It Means to Be Human.* New York: HarperCollins; London: Penguin.

Atran, Scott, and Jeremy Ginges. 2012. "Religious and Sacred Imperatives in Human Conflict." *Science* 386: 855–57.

Atran, Scott, Robert Axelrod, and Richard Davis. 2007. "Sacred Barriers to Conflict Resolution." *Science* 317: 1039–40.

Deutscher, Isaac. 1967. "On the Israeli-Arab War." *New Left Review* 1, no. 44 (July-August).

Diamond, Jared. 1997. *Guns, Germs, and Steel: The Fate of Human Societies.* New York: W.W. Norton.

Durkheim, Émile. [1912] 1995. *The Elementary Forms of Religious Life.* New York: Macmillan.

Lewis, Bernard. 1964. *The Middle East and the West.* New York: Harper and Row.

Malraux, André. 1972. *Antimémoires.* Paris: Gallimard "Folio."

Rappaport, Roy. 1999. *Ritual and Religion in the Making of Humanity.* New York: Cambridge University Press.

Stark, Rodney. 1997. *The Rise of Christianity: How the Obscure, Marginal Jesus Movement Became the Dominant Force in the Western World in a Few Centuries.* New York: HarperCollins.

Young, Dudley. 1992. *Origins of the Sacred: The Ecstasies of Love and War.* New York: HarperPerennial.

PART FOUR

Between Progress and Abyss: Our Modernity

Nuclear Apocalypse

The Balance of Terror and Girardian "Misrecognition"

Jean-Pierre Dupuy

In the section of *Des choses cachées depuis la fondation du monde* entitled "Science et apocalypse" (Girard 1978, 276–85), René Girard makes important observations on what we might take to be an improbable oxymoron: that of "nuclear peace." This expression, he says, shows clearly that we are already living under a spell of Apocalypse. The Bomb has become like the "Sovereign of this world"; we exist under Her protection, even if we also know that Her destructive power derives from and expresses our own, purely human, powers.

In this key work, Girard writes: "In a world that is ever more desacralized, only the permanent threat of total and immediate annihilation stops human beings from destroying one another. As always, violence is that which prevents the unleashing of violence" (279). Remarkably enough, Girard feels the need to underline the fact that such a nuclear peace is *not* the sign that the Kingdom of God is already with us (281). Yet he also says that "in certain respects, the destructive power of the bomb functions in a way similar to the logic of the archaic sacred."

The demonstration that the modern world still borrows its notions of apocalypse and the sacred from the originating culture-matrix that, in evolutionary terms, launched humanity into the adventure of survival and salvation, is of course capital. Yet I hope to push the analysis running through this agreed diagnosis further. More precisely, I hope, on the basis of this Girardian example of the threat of nuclear apocalypse, to open a contestatory dialogue with Girard on one key element of his theory, a matter of fundamental importance engaging our common survival and/or salvation: namely, the question of "misrecognition."

If, as René Girard and I both agree, the nuclear peace is a new and contemporary form of the archaic sacred, and yet is informed by some understanding that its power of destruction is self-generated; and if, as we further agree, this paradoxical protection against that tragic End derives not from God, but from ourselves, then our question must be: what manner of sacred is involved? Is it compatible—not just with what Girard himself regards as the modern erosion of "misrecognition," but compatible even with the disappearance from human history of any properly transcendent sacrality, any metaphysical hope? And where does *that*—exact, secular, and post-Enlightenment—*recognition* take us?

Girard sees the complexity of the issue, but seems to be satisfied with the remark that "We are dealing here with a situation that is intermediary and complex" (281). Unfortunately, he does not try to go further in the clarification of the "intermediary" status of our situation. That is what I will now endeavor to do.[1]

The Atomic Bomb, Our New Sacred

In January 2000, President Clinton paid a visit to President Putin. Clinton's paradoxical task was to convince his partner that the anti-missile shield that the United States was planning on setting up would not prevent Russia from being able to destroy American society if it had to. The shield, Clinton explained to Putin by way of placating his concerns, would be *thick* enough to stop ballistic missiles launched by rogue states, but *thin* enough to be easily penetrated by Russian missiles. This shows up in a glaring light the fact that nuclear deterrence, in the form that has fittingly been called MAD (for "Mutually Assured Destruction"), entails the abandonment of the military defense of one's nation: the policy of deterrence does not contemplate doing anything to defend the homeland. In fact, it positively requires that each side leave its population open to attack, and makes no serious effort to protect it. The logic of this weird paradox is that *our safety can be only as great as is the terror.* If the terror were to be diminished—by, for example, building bomb shelters that protected some significant part of the population—then safety from the nuclear threat would be diminished, too, because the thus-protected side might be tempted to launch a preemptive strike, in the belief that it could "win" the hostilities thus begun. In the logic of MAD, "mutual destruction" must, perversely, be *assured,* as though our aim were to destroy, and not to save, humankind.

All these features of MAD run so consistently counter to the far simpler, more familiar, and emotionally more comprehensible logic of traditional military thinking (not to mention instinct and plain common sense) that the doctrine of deterrence through a balance of terror—at least, at the time when it was being applied integrally, during the Cold War—was constantly under challenge from the traditional doctrine. The hard-won gains of deterrence were repeatedly contested by a recrudescence of the old desire for victory, for national defense in the old sense, and for military superiority: all marking the failure to register clearly the historic phase change that René Girard underlines in pointing to the *utter untenability,* henceforth, of Clausewitz's dictum that "war is the continuation of diplomacy by other means" (Girard 2007).

For a long time, strategic thinking had it that nuclear deterrence rested on an *intention:* the threat that, were the adversary to take any transgressive step forward, "we" would blow up the whole world, precipitating its apocalyptic End. There were many problems with the internal consistency of this theory, not least its blatant immorality: is not the readiness to envisage killing billions of innocent people frighteningly close to killing them for real?

Another of the major problems had to do with the credibility of the threat itself. As Jonathan Schell puts it:

> Since in nuclear deterrence theory the whole purpose of having a retaliatory capacity is to deter a first strike, one must ask what reason would remain to launch the retaliation once the first strike had actually arrived. It seems that the logic of the deterrence strategy is dissolved by the very event—the first strike—that it is meant to prevent. Once the action begins, the whole doctrine is *self-cancelling.* It would seem that the doctrine is based on a monumental logical mistake: one cannot credibly deter a first strike with

a second strike whose *raison d'être* dissolves the moment the first strike arrives. (1982, 307)

The solution to this dilemma came with a name: "*existential* deterrence." If our threatened retaliation, launching a counterattack that will lead to the Apocalypse, is problematic, then let us bracket the category of intention altogether. As two major philosophers put it: "The existence of a nuclear retaliatory capability suffices for deterrence, regardless of a nation's will, intentions, or pronouncements about nuclear weapons use" (Kavka 1987, 48); "It is our military capacities that matter, not our intentions or incentives or declarations" (Lewis 1989, 67).

If deterrence is at bottom an "existential" notion, this is because the very existence of the weapons is what deters; and, more secretly, because the fundamental category being invoked is that of our *survival*—in evolutionary terms, the original and only existential stake. Deterrence is inherent in the weapons themselves because "the danger of unlimited escalation is inescapable," as Bernard Brodie put it in 1973. He explains:

> It is a curious paradox of our time that one of the foremost factors making deterrence really work and work well is the lurking fear that, in some massive confrontation crisis, it may fail. Under these circumstances *one does not tempt fate.* If we were absolutely certain that nuclear deterrence would be 100 percent effective against nuclear attack, then it would cease to have much if any deterrence value against non-nuclear wars. (1973, 430–31)

The kind of rationality at work here is not a calculating rationality, but rather the kind of rationality in which the agent contemplates the abyss and simply decides never to get too close to the edge. As David Lewis puts it: "You don't tangle with tigers—it's that simple" (1989, 68). The probability of error is what makes deterrence effective. But error, failure, or mistake, here, is not strategic. It has nothing to do with the notion that a nation, by irrationally running unacceptable risks, can limit the extent of a war or the number of armed conflicts and achieve military or political advantage by inducing restraint in the opponent. Thomas Schelling popularized this idea, which has since been known as the "rationality of irrationality" theory, in his landmark *The Strategy of Conflict* (1960). Here, by contrast, the key notion is "Fate."

The error is inscribed into the future. In other words, the game is no longer played out between two adversaries. It takes on an altogether different form. Neither is in a position to deter the other in a credible way.

However, both want and need to be deterred. The way out of this impasse is a brilliant *trouvaille*. The antagonists and potential enemies become complicit in creating jointly a fictitious entity that will deter both of them at the same time. The game is now played between one actor, humankind, whose *survival* is at stake, *and its double*, i.e., its own violence externalized, sacralized, and hypostasized in the form of "fate." If we are impressed by this devious invention, it is only fair to point out that it is also the oldest under the sun, since it corresponds exactly, if we have followed Girard, to the first-and-original creation of the "archaic sacred" (save that humankind is now not just the sole Author—but perforce also the potential Victim of this specular and speculative pharmacology). The mythic-sacral "Tiger" we had better not tangle with is nothing other than the violence that is in us: something that we project—such is perhaps the dreamlike logic of "misrecognition"?—outside ourselves. It is as if we were threatened by an exceedingly dangerous entity, external to us, whose intentions toward us are not evil, but whose power of destruction is infinitely superior to all the earthquakes or tsunamis that Nature has in store for us.

Heidegger famously said, "Nur noch ein Gott kann uns retten" [Only a God can still save us]. In the nuclear age, this (false) God, fashioned by our own social psyche, is the self-externalizing "projection" of human violence, engendering a shadow of nuclear holocaust that we inscribe mythically into the future, as both accident and destiny. This is what the mythic-sacral Tiger stands for symbolically, and what, in sober fact, it signifies. This is, indeed, one more chapter in humankind's ancient and devious game, consistently diagnosed as such by Girard, of exorcising violently our own violent shadow.

◆　◆　◆

Robert McNamara asserts that thirty-odd times during the Cold War we were "that close" to a total nuclear self-annihilation of humankind (McNamara and Blight 2001). Does this mean that deterrence was ineffective? Quite the contrary: it was the constant "playing with fire" that kept us permanently on our guard. Those "near misses" were the very possibility condition of the efficient functioning of the system of nuclear deterrence.

For deterrence to be effective at all, we had to be at the right distance from the black hole of humankind's self-annihilation: not too close, lest we be in very fact consumed by the Holocaust; but not too far away either, lest we should forget the existence of the Threat. That structure is *exactly* that of the archaic Sacred envisaged by Girard. We are not speaking here of an analogy: this is the very selfsame thing. We must not be too close to the sacred, because it would release the violence that it keeps in check, like a Pandora's Box; we must not be too far from the sacred, because it protects us from our own violence. The sacred *contains* violence, therefore, in the classic twofold meaning of the word.

There is a fundamental difference, however, between the sacred as newly embodied in nuclear deterrence, and the former, properly "archaic" sacred. We Moderns know that the Tiger is a myth, an artful stratagem, a devious human projection. We pretend to believe that it is real in the same way that we pretend to believe that the story we are being told or shown is true. This "suspension of disbelief" is essential for fiction to bring about real effects in us and the world.

Nuclear deterrence in its "existential" interpretation appears to be a self-reflexive, self-organized, self-externalized social system—neither a blind, spontaneous collective phenomenon, nor yet a formal, carefully crafted set of procedures, as in a concerted ritual such as archaic sacrifice. It is indeed, as Girard wrote, an "intermediary case." At the very least, it shows that the mechanisms of the sacred are perfectly compatible with a good measure of *"connaissance"*—i.e., of "recognition" based on self-knowledge. This is where my own contestatory dialogue with Girard begins.

Is Misrecognition a Necessary Condition?

As early as 1981, Henri Atlan and I questioned in a joint paper the validity of a central postulate in René Girard's mimetic and sacrificial theory (MST), namely, that the misrecognition of sacrificial mechanisms is a necessary condition for their functioning (Atlan and Dupuy 1981). Three years later, in June 1983, I took up the same topic in my contribution to the international symposium that Paul Dumouchel and I organized in France, at the Centre Culturel International de Cerisy-la-Salle, in tribute to René's work, with his active participation (Dupuy 1988). Later, Paul Dumouchel wrote an important essay on the role of misrecognition in social processes in general. In that essay he proposed a typology of the effects on its own functioning that the self-knowledge of a social system can bring about (Dumouchel 1992). And that is about all. In thirty years, to the best of my knowledge, no further reflection has been devoted to this fundamental issue. That is why I rejoice over the possibility that we have today of taking up again the discussion initiated such a long time ago. The misrecognition issue is one of the major keystones in the magnificent edifice of theory built up by René.

Henri Atlan, for his part, denies that the misrecognition of mechanisms is a necessary condition for their functioning. Observing at two different levels the social system of which they are a part, the actors can very well see, from the "exterior," the arbitrariness of the process of social differentiation brought about by the "choice" of the victim, while still giving it meaning from the "interior." He writes:

> In ancient societies, drawing lots was a way to question the oracle and make the divine reveal hidden things. This means that one can perfectly well know that the victim is chosen at random and nevertheless believe in the efficacy of the process. In order to prevent the contagious violence, conscious scapegoating is possible. And if we want to prevent the additional violence against the victim, we must find a way to channel it to a different kind of victim, as in an animal sacrifice or even with no victim at all as in a ritual playing it symbolically. Drawing lots to choose between two animals was essential in the biblical ritual of the scapegoat. The post-biblical ritual with no more sacrifices has kept until today the detailed narration of the whole procedure as its central part. Thus, after replacing the human sacrifices with animals and then with their plain narratives, what is left is the conscious role of randomness in the process. (Atlan 2011, n.p.)

It is worth noting that in his critique, Atlan considers only the case of sacrifice as ritual. A ritual is a social construction, a carefully thought-out set of procedures, designed in order to pursue a goal. It is indeed hard to deny that there is a good measure of consciousness and intentionality in the design. A lot of knowledge is already embodied in the setting up of ritual.

But let us be more specific and address the sacrificial case. As Mark Anspach (2011) clearly explains: "Girard distinguishes *sacrifice* as a ritual-ized institution from the spontaneous episodes of 'generative' or 'founding' violence that gave rise to the institution. A lynching is not a sacrifice, even though it may provide the template for sacrifice." Anspach hastens to add that the term "founding violence" coined by Girard "is potentially mislead-ing because it could suggest that the event already possessed an institutional character. Unlike 'foundation sacrifices,' truly founding violence in Girard's sense is not carried out with the deliberate intent of founding anything; it is only in retrospect that it may be recognized as having unwittingly laid the foundation for what came later." Anspach then goes on to suggest that

> the context in which ritual sacrifice takes place is not the same [as in the case of the spontaneous occurrence] because differences still exist and must be maintained and reinforced as a barrier against the spread of violence. *The sacrificial victim must therefore satisfy conflicting criteria:* it must be similar enough to serve as a recognizable substitute, but not so similar that the killing of the victim too closely resembles the murder of a member of the community, for that would carry the risk of provoking new violence. Ritual victims therefore tend to have marginal status—slaves, children, livestock; they must display both continuity and discontinuity. (Anspach 2011, 129–55)

The ritual victim must be carefully chosen, as must be the means of its physi-cal elimination, in order to satisfy this double bind: the ritual sacrifice must echo the primordial lynching, without triggering an uncontrollable chain of reprisals. No way to do that without resorting to ruse, stratagem, artifice, which requires a deep knowledge of what is at stake. At the acme of its bloody performance, a sacrificial ritual very often looks like an enterprise of collective bad faith, a deception that everyone engages in vis-à-vis everyone else—whose meaning is: "This is not violence!" Or the setting is such that no one can be said to have dealt the fatal blow, and the victim, conspicuously chosen at random, can only be said to bear any guilt through a "suspension of disbelief" in the fiction that is being collectively crafted and staged. There is manifestly so much wisdom and thoughtfulness in those acts that the Revela-tion that seems to speak in that suspended interval may appear to simply state the obvious.

How about the spontaneous mechanism itself—the primordial lynching? I Have read again for the umpteenth time *Things Hidden since the Foundation of the World* for the sake of this discussion, and I can say the following: whenever in that book Girard mentions the increasing loss in efficiency of sacrificial mechanisms, either he refers explicitly to the ritual or he makes no distinction between the ritual and the primordial spontaneous event.[2] Let us ask ourselves, then, what might be the effect of the knowledge that the "surrogate victim"[3] is innocent on the dynamism of the crisis. If the members of a lynch mob are told that they are persecuting a person who has done no evil, will that stop them from stoning her? The natural evolution of a process of collective hatred makes that doubtful. At the culmination of a collective victimage, it seems that the moral notions of guilt and innocence lose all relevance.

Our Choice: Nuclear Apocalypse with and without the Christian Gospel

My disagreement with René Girard thus turns on the notion of misrecognition; but beyond that, it engages the entire question of how we ourselves may recognize and repair the plight of mimetic humanity under the threat of nuclear apocalypse—and on the possibility or otherwise of a *conversion of the heart* as envisaged by the Christian gospels and by Girard.

Girard's "hypothesis," as he calls it himself, asserts that the sacred is produced by a mechanism of self-externalization that, in transforming violence into ritual practices and systems of rules, prohibitions, and obligations, allows human violence to limit or contain itself, i.e., to *survive.* If we follow this view, the sacred is to be identified with a "good" form of institutionalized violence that holds in check a "bad," i.e., anarchic, ruinous, and apocalyptic kind of violence. Whereas the desacralization of the world that modernity has brought about is driven by a kind of knowledge—or *suspicion,* at least?—that has gradually insinuated itself into human thinking: could it be that good and bad violence are not opposites, but actually the same thing; that, at bottom, there is *no difference* between them?

There is no doubt that we now know that *Satan casts out Satan,* as the Bible says; we know that evil is capable of self-transcendence, and, by virtue of just this, capable of containing itself within limits—and so, too, of avert-ing total destruction. The most striking illustration is to be found in the history of the decades that made up the Cold War. Throughout this period it was as though the bomb protected us from the bomb—an astonishing paradox that some of the most brilliant minds have sought to explain, with only mixed success. The very existence of nuclear weapons, it would appear, has prevented the world from disappearing in a nuclear holocaust. That evil can *contain* evil (in both senses of the term) is therefore clearly possible, but plainly it is not necessarily so, as the nuclear situation today shows us with unsurpassable clarity. The question is no longer: why has an atomic war not taken place since 1945? Now the question has become: when will it take place in the future?

Remove "misrecognition" from Girard and from mimetic theory, and much of the theory of cultural development post-Revelation—and with it, the entire Girardian reading of modernity—is in serious danger of collaps-ing. *Ante apocalypsis* (i.e., before Christian revelation), according to René's theory, the participants in the collective victimage "know not what they do"—which may indeed be the reason why they should be "forgiven." They *do not know* their victim for what he is: the unlucky focus of an arbitrary process of convergent animosities; nor do they know the meaning of his victimization, i.e., they do not *understand* the functional expedient of emis-sary collective violence, operating *unjustly, cruelly,* and *absurdly* in respect of the real origin and cause of conflict, yet "rationally" still, at least insofar as this process discharges "pharmacologically" the charge of conflict-generating violence that accumulates within and between human communities—and to the extent that emissary victimization "exorcises" the ever-returning specter of the apocalypse.

Girardian misrecognition is not an accidental phenomenon, therefore: it is an essential part of the mechanism, necessary to its proper functioning. The convergence of all-against-one rests on the common conviction that this Victim carries ultimate responsibility for ongoing violence. The peace that follows the victim's death confirms everyone in this prior belief.

If Christianity can be said to be "the religion of the end of religion" (Gauchet 1999), is this not, for Girard, precisely because the Christian message slowly corrodes sacrificial institutions and progressively gives rise to a radically different type of society? The mechanism for manufacturing sacredness in the world, Girard thinks, has been irreparably disabled by the body of knowledge constituted by Christianity. Instead, it produces more and more violence—a violence that is losing the ability to self-externalize and contain itself. This is how I interpret Jesus's enigmatic words: "Do not think that I have come to bring peace on earth; I have not come to bring peace, but a sword" (Matt. 10:34). The Christian *revelation* here appears to be a snare, and the knowledge it carries a kind of trap—since it deprives humanity of the only means it previously had of keeping its own self-generated violence in check.

It is probably owing to the influence of Christianity, moreover, that evil has come to be most commonly associated with the intentions of those who commit it. And yet the evil of nuclear deterrence, in its existential form, is an evil disconnected from any human intention, just as the "sacrament" of the bomb is a sacrament without a god.

Where does this leave us in respect of the threat of nuclear apocalypse? The strategy of deterrence through a balance of terror, if we accept the "existential" interpretation of it, appears, as I have said, to be a self-reflexive, self-organized, self-externalized social system; and, indeed, as Girard notes, an "intermediary case." In my own work, I have proposed to extend the lessons to be drawn from this case to the whole gamut of threats that today put the survival of our species in jeopardy (Dupuy 2002).

Under the name of "Enlightened Doomsaying," I have set out to rehabilitate the figure and the role of the "prophet of doom" within civil society. It is only, paradoxically enough, as we *take those threats to be fatalities and not risks* that we have a chance of being spared from their actually coming to pass. And it is, paradoxically again, only if we *pretend to believe* that our destiny is the self-annihilation of humankind that we shall have a chance to avert it. We have to recover what Paul Valéry calls the creativity of the human power to think and act "*as if.*"

Is enlightened doomsaying a heartening prospect and an encouraging role? Not necessarily. It leaves deeply unsatisfied basic spiritual requirements intrinsic to our defining sense of the human. In 1958, for instance, another such prophet, Günther Anders, went to Hiroshima and Nagasaki to take part in the Fourth World Conference against Atomic and Hydrogen Bombs. After many exchanges with survivors of the catastrophe, he noted in his diary: "Their steadfast resolve not to speak of those who were to blame, not to say that the event had been caused by human beings; *not to harbor the least resentment, even though they were the victims of the greatest of crimes*—this really is too much for me, it passes all understanding." And he adds: "They constantly speak of the catastrophe as if it were an earthquake or a tidal wave. They use the Japanese word, *tsunami*" (Anders 1995).

The evil that inhabits the "nuclear peace" is not the product of any malign intention. It is the inspiration for passages of terrifying insight in Anders's book *Hiroshima Is Everywhere,* words that send a chill down the spine:

> The fantastic character of the situation quite simply takes one's breath away. At the very moment when the world *becomes apocalyptic,* and this owing to our own fault, it presents the image ... of a paradise inhabited by murderers without malice and victims without hatred. Nowhere is there any trace of malice, there is only rubble. There is no call to hate. But in this context no *worse news* than the imminent end of hatred and resentment can be imagined. (1995, 87)

And Anders prophesies: "No war in history will have been more devoid of hatred than the war by tele-murder that is to come. . . . This absence of hatred will be the most inhuman absence of hatred that has ever existed; absence of hatred and absence of scruples will henceforth be one and the same" (1995, 114). Violence without hatred is so inhuman that it amounts to a transcendence of sorts—perhaps the only transcendence still left to us.

Yet politics in its noblest moments is able to resort to fiction or make-believe in order to change the world.[4] It has to be said and repeated that Girard's theory leads inevitably to political relativism and even political nihilism. If only to defend itself against this grave accusation, if my conclusions are correct, we see that it needs to jettison one of its key postulates—namely, the incompatibility between the sacred and self-knowledge. *Is the price too high?*

We need to ponder that question urgently in the coming years.

Notes

1. I draw here from chapter 6, "The Nuclear Menace. A New Sacrament for Humanity", *The Mark of the Sacred,* Stanford University Press, 2013.

2. See, for instance, under the signature of Guy Lefort, but clearly endorsed by Girard, page 281 of *Des choses cachées depuis la fondation du monde* (1978): "La violence étant vraiment révélée, les *mécanismes victimaires* ont cessé de fonctionner" [Violence being truly revealed, *victimary*

mechanisms are no longer functioning]; and page 277, under Girard's own signature: "L'histoire du christianisme historique consiste . . . en un desserrement graduel des contraintes légales, à mesure que diminue l'efficacité des *mécanismes rituels*." [The evolution of historic Christianity realizes a progressive loosening of legal constraints, in keeping with the diminishing efficiency of *ritual mechanisms*.]

3. A phrase used by Girard at the beginning of his work to designate the victim of a spontaneous collective victimage.

4. "Fiction" comes from Latin *fingere:* to make up, to make believe, to invent, to feign—to act *as if* . . . (and not from *facere:* to make, which gives us "*fact*").

Cited Texts and Further Reading

Anders, G. 1995. *Hiroshima ist über all.* Munich: C.H. Beck.

Anspach, M. 2011. "Imitation and Violence: Empirical Evidence and the Mimetic Model." In *Mimesis and Science: Empirical Research on Imitation and the Mimetic Theory of Culture and Religion,* ed. S. Garrels. East Lansing: Michigan State University Press.

Atlan, H. 2010. *The Sparks of Randomness.* Vol. 1. Stanford, CA: Stanford University Press.

———. 2011. "Biological and Cultural Evolution. Relevance of Girard's Mimetic Theory." Http:// www.imitatio.org/thinkingthehuman/Papers_files/Atlandraft.pdf.

Atlan, H., and J.-P. Dupuy. 1981. "Mimesis and Social Morphogenesis: Violence and the Sacred from a Systems Analysis Viewpoint." In *Applied Systems and Cybernetics,* vol. 3, ed. G. E. Lasker. New York: Pergamon Press.

Brodie, B. 1973. *War and Politics.* New York: Macmillan.

Dumouchel, P. 1992. "Systèmes sociaux et cognition." In *Introduction aux sciences cognitives,* ed. D. Andler, 472–88. Paris: Gallimard.

———. 2011. *Le sacrifice inutile: Essai sur la violence politique.* Paris: Flammarion.

Dupuy, J.-P. 1988. "Totalization and Misrecognition." In *Violence and Truth: On the Work of René Girard,* ed. P. Dumouchel, 75–100. London: Athlone Press.

———. 2002. *Pour un catastrophisme éclairé.* Paris: Seuil.

———. 2005. *Petite métaphysique des tsunamis.* Paris: Seuil.

———. 2009. "The Precautionary Principle and Enlightened Doomsaying: Rational Choice before the Apocalypse." *Occasion: Interdisciplinary Studies in the Humanities* 1. Http://occasion.stanford. edu/node/28.

———. 2011. *La marque du sacré.* Paris: Flammarion.

Gauchet, M. 1999. *The Disenchantment of the World.* Princeton, NJ: Princeton University Press.

Girard, R. 1978. *Des choses cachées depuis la fondation du monde.* Paris: Grasset. (Ed. quoted by PD and PG, Le Livre de Poche "Essais," 1989).

———. 2007. *Achever Clausewitz: Entretiens avec Benoît Chantre* (Paris: Éditions Nord, 2007). Translated by M. Baker, *Battling to the End: Conversations with Benoît Chantre.* East Lansing: Michigan State University Press. 2010.

Kavka, G. 1987. *Moral Paradoxes of Nuclear Deterrence.* Cambridge: Cambridge University Press.

Lee, Steven P. 1993. *Morality, Prudence, and Nuclear Weapons.* New York: Cambridge University Press.

Lewis, D. K. 1984. "Devil's Bargains and the Real World." In *The Security Gamble: Deterrence Dilemmas in the Nuclear Age,* ed. D. MacLean. Totowa, NJ: Rowman and Allanheld.

———. 1989. "Finite Counterforce." In *Nuclear Deterrence and Moral Restraint,* ed. Henry Shue. Cambridge: Cambridge University Press.

McNamara, R., and J. G. Blight. 2001. *Wilson's Ghost: Reducing the Risk of Conflict, Killing, and Catastrophe in the 21st Century.* New York: Public Affairs.

Schell, J. 1982. *The Fate of Earth.* New York: Random House.

Schelling, T. 1960. *The Strategy of Conflict.* Cambridge, MA: Harvard University Press.

Responses to
Jean-Pierre Dupuy

The "Intermediary" Case

Margo Boenig-Liptsin

From *Things Hidden since the Foundation of the World* to *Battling to the End*, René Girard describes our contemporary historical-cultural situation as a hybrid one, in which people have some awareness of the sacrificial mechanism while the mechanism continues to function. The type of explanation he seems to envisage is that the cultural osmosis of Christian values advances slowly and without uniformity; and that it has achieved no absolute ascendancy over the logic established, originally and to ongoing effect, within the social psyche at large by the economy of the archaic sacred.

Girard does not very fully analyze the nature of this hybrid and intermediary situation. In *Battling to the End,* he admits specifically that he cannot explain how the archaic program persists in a more "diabolical" variant: "I have a lot of trouble formulating the intuition that I feel is nonetheless very important," he writes. "Once unbridled, the principle of reciprocity no longer plays the unconscious role it used to play. Do we not now destroy simply to destroy? Violence now seems deliberate and the escalation to extremes is served by science and politics" (Girard 2010, 20). We know that we stand in an "apocalyptic" logic of escalation to extremes; and, knowingly, we still "go with it." But *why?* How can we be both demystified and unreformed, still complicit in our own violence?[1]

Jean-Pierre Dupuy, it seems to me, therefore, touches on a very strategic issue by focusing on what Girard, already in 1978, called the "intermediary and complex situation" of nuclear weapons. According to Dupuy, nuclear weapons and the strategies of their operational use (e.g., mutual assured destruction, or MAD) constitute a form of the sacred that challenges the normal functioning of the sacrificial mechanism in Girard's theory. Sacrificial mechanisms are said by RG to work only when their human actors are in a state of "misrecognition" (*méconnaissance*). Dupuy argues that the nuclear sacred has been able to contain violence effectively (in the sense of keeping it in check) even in the presence of knowledge by the actors about how the system works: so that the sacred, he thinks, can coexist with a certain "self-knowledge."

Does that "self-knowledge" meet the criteria of "recognition" as defined by Girard? The latter defines recognition as the "knowledge of the [sacrificial] mechanism" (Girard 1987, 128). What is recognized here is that the sacred is nothing other than the externalization of our own violence. It isn't simply "knowing" in a factual sense; it is crediting that knowledge in a way that transforms how we see the rest of the world; it is "seeing by" the light of that knowledge.

We might think here of C. S. Lewis's description of his Christian belief. "I believe in Christianity as I believe that the sun has risen," said Lewis, "not only because I see it, but because by it I see everything else" (Lewis 1980, 92). He is evoking an epistemic shift in how we see the world—a change in underlying conditions upon which our knowledge rests that enables that knowledge to become actionable, not just a shift in *what* or *how much* we see. "Recognition" thus entails a *conversion*—a radical and complete supplanting of one state (misrecognition) by another state (recognition).

If we were to believe these epistemological pointers alone, Girard's world, is or ought to be, a binary one, not admitting any "intermediary" cases. One is converted and "recognizes"—or unconverted and in misrecognition. Despite this formal epistemological impossibility, Girard is suggesting that the existential (time-bound) and practical (accident-linked) challenge of our contemporary situation is that we inhabit precisely such an intermediary state. We live in an "in-between time" or hybrid culture-zone where recognition is partial and patchy. Intermediary cases, like the one of nuclear weapons, are characteristic of a certain time in cultural evolution in which the osmosis of Christian "seeing" into general (secular) culture prevents entire ignorance of the sacrificial in our collective acts and choices—without, however, securing "conversion" in the sense that Lewis implies and Girard looks for.

Dupuy's notion of "self-knowledge" seems to be far removed from Girard's take on "recognition." People may know that human beings make the weapons and develop paradoxical unofficial agreements like MAD, but it is still possible to interpret this information according to a "misrecognition" episteme: that is, as a kind of calculation of risks versus benefits with the ultimate goal of ensuring national security. To exhibit true "recognition" in the Girardian sense would mean recognizing the total existential and ethical import of this situation in such a way that our recognition renders impossible any recourse to these weapons—either as tools of destruction or as a "default" means of securing an uneasy peace. If we attend to contemporary political discourse surrounding nuclear weapons, it seems clear that we indeed do, so far, lack this kind of active, society-wide "recognition."

But even if he does not work with "recognition" in the Girardian sense, Dupuy is perhaps right to suggest that the knowledge we do have about the nuclear sacred amounts to something important. It is "self-knowledge," he suggests, that characterizes the intermediary case. *Self-knowledge" is based upon the formal knowledge of socio-technical systems by the people who help to make them and live with them.* Formal knowledge of socio-technical systems sheds light on the functioning of the sacrificial mechanism at the same time as it obscures it: it *sheds light* because, clearly, we are aware of being the creators of technological artifacts; it *obscures* it because of the nature of our relationship to these artifacts.

Observers of science and technology frequently report that even engineers do not believe that they have complete knowledge about how the technologies they created "work," and do not feel that they have complete control over them, in the social as well as technical sense. Instead of confidently asserting our mastery over nature and society by means of technology, as Heidegger thought to be the human inclination, we tend to describe technologies deterministically, suggesting that technology effects social change of its own accord. Einstein himself did so when he evoked "the ghostlike character" of the process of building up the nuclear arsenal, something that lay, he suggested, "in its apparently compulsory trend. Every step appears as the unavoidable consequence of the preceding one" (Einstein 1950, 71).

The development and use of technologies appears here to involve an agency obscurely intrinsic to the process itself—a phenomenon due, however, to the coproduction of the technical (epistemic) and the social (normative) order in which any given technology is embedded and whose functioning it sustains (Jasanoff 2004). Technologies can also appear autonomous and outside human control because of the tremendous power of destruction, with all its consequences, that they can unleash. These consequences can operate in temporal and spatial scales beyond what human beings can readily experience or even imagine. This is especially the case with nuclear technology, which is frequently described as "uncanny," in the sense that it is a transcendent value escaping human senses and rationality (Masco 2006).

Nuclear peace, consequently, provides an excellent example of a sacred that human beings know they have themselves engendered ("self-knowledge"), yet without this knowledge causing the necessary and adequate spark of "recognition" in the Girardian sense. Such "self-knowledge," founded upon formal understanding of the technical systems, enables the nuclear weapons and the protocols governing their use to acquire a mythical status. What David K. Lewis refers to as "not tangling with the nuclear tiger" should, logically, mean that one does not come close to using nuclear weapons, just as one does not deliberately put oneself in harm's way with tigers, because of the extreme danger that they represent.

Dupuy argues here that our reluctance to risk a nuclear holocaust by launching a preemptive strike invokes the Tiger *in order to protect us* from our own destructive violence—thus functioning as a form of the archaic sacred as described by RG. The tiger analogy invests nuclear weapons with a beastly intentionality; and the existential threat to humans, apparently against human will and outside of human control, secretes an intentionality that is "divine" in the archaic-sacral sense. Our very "self-knowledge" functions within this process to ensure that we *know* that we *cannot be sure* that accidents do *not* happen: that nuclear weapons never fall into the wrong hands, never deteriorate and leak radiation, despite our best efforts to contain them in underground storage (etc.). We are also fascinated by what terrifies us, and pretend that *sacrificing* to it *protects* us; and we do so for want of being able to walk away or kill the tiger (i.e., by nuclear disarmament). As our self-knowledge grows, so indeed does the size of the Tiger—and our appeasing of the Tiger-god. One could argue, therefore, that "self-knowledge" is itself an *impediment* to "recognition"; and the later Girard does indeed seem to be arguing thus.[2]

In this intermediary—and confusing—situation, Dupuy argues that to preserve peace we must keep the Tiger in view, keep her around, sacrifice to her. He is, of course, careful to characterize our attitude as "pretending to believe" in the Tiger. He writes:

> We Moderns know that the Tiger is a myth, an artful stratagem, a devious human projection. We *pretend to believe* that it is real in the same way that we *pretend to believe* that the story we are being told or shown is true. This "suspension of disbelief" is essential for fiction to bring about real effects in us and the world. [my italics]

Dupuy uses "pretending to believe" as a synonym of "suspending disbelief," "engaging in make-believe," "acting as if"—an attitude related to the activities of "fiction" and "projection." This is the possibility opened by our self-knowledge of our creations, be they works of fiction (i.e., imaginative constructs in language) or socio-technical systems (imaginary constructs in matter or in process). A person "pretending to believe" is aware of the separation between the world where one is and the world of "make-believe." In artistic fictions, this separation can be effected physically by a frame of the painting, a cover of a book, the stage-frame of the theater. This physical or metaphysical boundary ensures that there is a distance established from the events at stake in "pretending to believe"—a distance that, significantly, does not exist in "believing."

Dupuy implies that only an attitude of "pretending to believe" can enable a self-aware sacralization to function as a form of the archaic sacred and contain violence. He writes paradoxically: "only if we *pretend to believe* that our destiny is the self-annihilation of humankind that we shall have a chance to avert it." The logic of this argument comes from his earlier work on "enlightened doomsaying" and the alternative metaphysics of time that he developed following Henri Bergson, Ivan Illich, and Hans Jonas (Dupuy

2002). In this work, Dupuy proposes that "pretending to believe" is a solution to the problem of catastrophic violence in human society. As he hints in the current essay,[3] he does not appear to believe in the possibility of a fully salvational Girardian "recognition," *reversing* the escalation to extremes of human violence. The alternative to conversion, according to Dupuy, is to continue to "pretend to believe": as long as we do so, the "intermediary" situation is stabilized and we can forestall apocalypse.

Do we believe in "pretending to believe"? That is, then, the question. The contemporary world tends to reduce or obscure the difference between "pretending to believe" and actually "believing." We tend to subsume "make-believe" itself under the category of the real (Baudrillard 1994). Today theater spills onto the street; cinema is made about the lives—and with the participation—of everyday people. Engineers insist upon technological transparency as a design value and seek to conceal as much as possible the functioning of technological mediation. Speaking to someone in person can seem equivalent to speaking to them by video conference; we are immersed in the "realism" of the feathers of a digitally animated bird, impressed by tele-war operations as much as by actual combat. One might argue that, on the contrary, instead of *celebrating the real,* electronic simulations plunge us into a world of permanent fiction and *erode our hold on any reality* that could lead us to situate it as such. But however one looks at it, the consequence of the all-mediating simulacrum is the erosion of the possibility of "pretending to believe"—this very specific attitude requiring *elaborate and fragile mediations* between the world in which one pretends and the real world one hopes to influence or transform.

In relation specifically to nuclear weapons, the loss of our capacity to make-believe is exemplified by the undermining of MAD since the end of the Cold War. Today it seems that people purely and simply *believe* in the menace of the Nuclear Tiger. The uncanny nature of nuclear weapons—the unimaginable and apocalyptic power of destruction that elicits sacralization in the first place—is experienced only in part, and only by the relatively small number of people who have the misfortune to live in the vicinity of polluted land or who are victims of a nuclear disaster. For the majority, nuclear weapons are banal (banalized by the familiar *images* of the nuclear mushroom cloud). The contemporary peril is that they will be used banally, as traditional weapons by a rogue state or by terrorists. Dupuy is perhaps right to suggest we need a salutary terror; but wrong to imply that this will of itself protect us.

His contribution is to highlight the intermediary case and our hybrid cultural situation that produces it. Acting "as if" may not ensure a once-and-for-all resolution; but it may, more modestly, constitute a step forward in problematizing the peril we face and provide a way to live with it. Only by explicitly pointing out the actor's *mask,* and exaggerating the actor's *playing,* can we actively draw attention to the boundary between the world onstage—the world of make-believe—and the real world; only so can we remobilize the resources of creativity needed.

"Enlightened doomsaying," that is, has its place, even if this version of it is not one that René Girard himself—and many others, Girardians or not—will find heartening. Outside of a true *conversion of the heart,* it may be our only choice.

Misrecognition of "Misrecognition"

Paul Dumouchel

According to Jean-Pierre Dupuy, "misrecognition" poses a difficulty that may require a major revision of the mimetic theory of culture. However, I am quite sure that many of us who are also interested in mimetic theory—among them certainly I, for one—disagree profoundly.

First, concerning Henri Atlan's criticism, Dupuy, in response to Atlan, rightly remarks that René Girard distinguishes between the *victimary mechanism,* which puts an end to the mimetic crisis, and *sacrifice,* together with the other institutions that emerge from it. This distinction is fundamental. Misrecognition, according to Girard, is at the heart of *spontaneous* events of collective victimage; it gives them their form and their efficacy, which leads in turn to the creation of the sacred, of sacrifice, and of rituals in general. This same misrecognition is, so to speak, carried over into these institutions. However, according to Girard, ritual and the sacred constitute a *schooling* of humanity ("rites had slowly educated them"; 2007, 10 [2010, x]). The evolution of human institutions corresponds to a progressive discovery and understanding, a greater knowledge of the originary mechanism and of the role of violence. The presence of this knowledge, and even of quite extensive knowledge of the mechanism in later institutions, does not in itself, therefore, constitute a *counter-example* to the theory, or even an *anomaly;* it is one of its *normal predictions.* What Girard claims is that this knowledge will always be partial, incomplete; as he often says, misrecognition *increases* with the growth of knowledge. In particular what, in spite of our greater knowledge of violence and of the origin of culture, we fail to understand is that we cannot have a complete and rational control of our violence—more precisely of the complex phenomena to which our violent exchanges give rise.

To this objection, Henri Atlan can respond that he is not talking just about any form of knowledge of the victimary mechanism, but about a form of knowledge that, according to Girard, should not be there—a form of knowledge that, if Girard is right, should make impossible the proper functioning of the mechanism, and yet which, Atlan argues, it does not: namely, the arbitrary nature of the victim. Atlan gives examples of rituals where the designation of the victim is chosen by lot. "In ancient societies," he says, "drawing lots was a way to question the oracle and make the divine reveal things hidden." This means that one can perfectly well know that the victim is chosen at random and nevertheless believe in the efficacy of the process. Yet already in *Violence and the Sacred* (1977 [1972]) Girard drew our attention to the many rituals where drawing lots plays a central role in the designation of the victim; but he drew a different conclusion from these examples. He argued that because participants in those rituals believed that, through the lots cast, the divine revealed "things hidden," therefore they did not perceive the arbitrary character of the designation of the victim, but rather were convinced of the victim's guilt or of its "destiny" to be sacrificed (Girard 1977, 311–15). Girard also argued that our modern idea of randomness, as a concept of things that happen without any reason, was progressively constructed out of reflection on these ritual practices and the discovery that the "gods were silent."

Atlan further claims that Girard never analyzes or justifies his claim that the mechanism of resolution of the crisis can only work if it remains unknown to those who affect it; and that as soon as the actors understand the mechanism, it fails to reconcile the community. I do not think that this is correct. However, I can sympathize with Henri Atlan's claims for at least two reasons. First, Girard extensively analyzes the role of misrecognition in two different chapters of *Violence and the Sacred,* while the claim that an exact knowledge of the mechanism would prevent it from functioning constitutes a central element of another book, *Things Hidden since the Foundation of the World* (1987); and at that point Girard does not refer to his previous analysis, so that the statement does seem unjustified.[4] Second, when Girard analyzes social phenomena in the world of the sacred, he usually gives more importance to what people *do* than to what they *think.* For example, in the analysis of the resolution of the sacrificial crisis, it is not because people believe that the victim is guilty that he or she is collectively immolated; it is, on the contrary, because the victim's collective immolation has the desired effect that its persecutors believe that he or she is guilty. More precisely, according to Girard the two dimensions of the phenomenon are inseparable. However, when he turns to Christian revelation, Girard centers his analyses on texts only, which creates the unreliable impression that in order to calm a raging crowd lynching an innocent, it is enough to draw their attention to the fact that the victim is innocent. That indeed would be magic, but, as I have tried to show elsewhere, this is not what Girard has in mind (Dumouchel 2011, 225–33).

Dupuy bases his conclusion on his original analysis of nuclear deterrence. His goal is to show us that in the case of nuclear deterrence, knowledge of the fact that violence is protecting us against violence is compatible with a stable institution; or perhaps it is to show us that the externalizing projection of violence into a kind of sacred is compatible with men knowing that it is their very violence that protects them from violence.[5] Further, he adds, this institution and solution can be stable. He concludes:

> Nuclear deterrence in its existential interpretation appears to be a self-reflexive, self-organized, self-externalized social system—neither a blind, spontaneous collective phenomenon, nor a formal, carefully crafted set of procedures as in a ritual . . . it shows that the mechanisms of the sacred are perfectly compatible with a good measure of *connaissance*—i.e., self-knowledge.

Let us grant for the sake of argument that the first part of this quotation corresponds to an exact description of nuclear deterrence. Then two questions arise. First, who has this knowledge? Answer: a few authors and university professors, the participants in this conference, and a few others. Did President Clinton have this knowledge? I don't think so. He may have had a very partial access to some of it, but certainly not to all. Did the numerous historical actors (President Eisenhower, Joseph Stalin, and all the others, generals, scientists, and politicians) whose numerous decisions progressively made this "intermediary reality" and who constructed this system, have this knowledge? Clearly, they did not. They simply reacted to what they saw as emergencies that needed to be dealt with, or as opportunities for their nations. This "well-crafted system" is the result of their blind actions and decisions, and in relation to the choices they made in the heat of the moment, we are rather like anthropologists reflecting on the cultural practices of native peoples.

The second question is: when did this knowledge become available? Answer: once the system was already in place, once it had taken form and the world had found its peace under the threat of total annihilation. Moreover, this "stable institution" did not long survive the knowledge it gained of itself. Nuclear deterrence is unraveling before our very eyes, or rather, it is already *passé*. Today, as Dupuy is the first to know, the weapons we accumulated when stockpiling nuclear warheads was the road to peace, constitute the greatest danger that now threatens us, because they provide a justification for proliferation and an occasion for the private appropriation of weapons of mass destruction.

Nuclear deterrence *does not work anymore* because the world of violence of which it was part and parcel has changed. If tomorrow a "martyr" carrying a nuclear bomb blows himself up in downtown New York, what will our reaction be? Should we drop a hydrogen bomb over Waziristan where leaders of al-Qaeda roam free, or should we "take out" most of Pakistan since our secret services will inform us that terrorists could never have had access to such a weapon without the help of Pakistani secret services? (We do know, do we not, since 9/11, that the secret services of Western countries are *never* wrong? So clearly we would be *justified* in retaliating!) The fact is that simply stating these alternatives shows how ludicrous and utterly useless, in many circumstances, has become a nuclear response to a nuclear threat. There is today a radical *imbalance* of terror. Terrorist networks do not have any fixed address. You cannot fry the house of a homeless bum. Nuclear deterrence requires assured mutual destruction; and that only works with targets that are clearly identifiable and separated in space.

Nuclear deterrence *as an institution* is gone, therefore. What it has left behind has become a source of danger greater than ever before. The weapons are still with us, but they have lost their ability to protect us; they have been reduced exclusively to their enormous capacity to destroy. According to Girard, the central illusion at the heart of misrecognition, the illusion that drives the mimetic crisis to its resolution, is the *belief that we can rationally master violence.* The claim that we can, and that we have given ourselves political institutions that can rationally contain our violence, *en toute connaissance de cause,* is, I believe, vastly premature.

If we look at the evolution of the forms of the institutions that aim at protecting us from our own violence—from ritual sacrifice to nuclear deterrence!—and if we look at today's political terrorism, we find an interesting continuity. The sacrificial principle—well summarized by Caiaphas—is: "Let one man die that the nation may live." Its strength and cultural efficacy lie in the *economy* of violence it provides. However, in nuclear deterrence *one for all* has been replaced by *all for all.* In order that all may live, all must be under the threat of total destruction. Terrorist martyrs, for their part, ask to die so that others may die.

This evolution, described in this way, does give exactly the impression Girard suggests: namely, that sacrificial mechanisms are becoming less and less effective, less and less capable of renewing themselves . . . Yet this ever-diminishing containment of violence, and this ever-greater violence, is, as Girard argues in *Battling to the End,* inseparable from the belief that we can rationally master and control our own violence and its consequences (Girard 2010).

Personally, my feeling is, therefore, that misrecognition is not an endangered species. The growing inefficacy of cultural institutions at protecting us from our own violence is not the consequence solely of the growth of knowledge concerning the origin and function of violence in human society; it stems also from the parallel *increase* of misrecognition. Girard writes: "There is, I repeat, no absolute knowledge possible; we are obliged to remain at the heart if history-in-the-making, in the bosom of violence, because we understand the mechanisms of it ever better. Does that mean we can undo them? I doubt it" (Girard 2007, 80 [2010, 35]).

Most fundamentally, we need, in the discussion Dupuy so urgently calls for, to see what "misrecognition" ("méconnaissance") means and entails.

Misrecognition is not just any kind of inadequate knowledge or inappropriate relation to what we know. It can be argued that, according to Girard, "méconnaissance" precedes "connaissance," that "mis-knowledge" comes before "knowledge"; which is a way of saying that knowledge always constitutes a gain over an original ignorance—an ignorance that is not only a passive failure to know, but also an active form of "not-knowing." The reduction of "méconnaissance"—cognitive progress, in fact—corresponds more to the reorganization of our knowledge than to the addition of new elements. That is why Girard often compares this experience to a religious conversion—a conversion that does not consist so much in discovering new knowledge as of suddenly seeing everything in a new light or from a different point. According to him, it is precisely those shifts in our outlook on the world that allow our knowledge to expand and make us able to progress into new domains of enquiry.

"Méconnaissance" essentially concerns our relation to others, and that is why it affects and colors all that we know. Not only because most of what we know we learn from others, but mainly because what we do not realize or do not want to recognize is the role that others play in the determination of our "true and justified beliefs." What we ignore is the extent to which others, by their mere presence, act upon us; determine our beliefs, our desires, our choices and preferences. The point of *méconnaissance* is precisely that we ignore it, not necessarily that we do not know it. So *méconnaissance,* like *mauvaise foi* according to Sartre, who clearly influenced Girard on this, implies of kind of "lying to oneself."

When we lie to others, we seek to manipulate the information that they have about the world, but we want the world to remain as it is. When one lies to oneself—at least in one way: there may be other forms of lying to oneself—the intention and the conditions for the lie to be successful are quite different. Suppose that I am finding more and more indications that my wife is having an affair, and that I do not want to recognize that this may be the case. I deny flatly the relevance of the growing evidence. Others observing my behavior may say that I am lying to myself; that I know, but that I refuse to believe what I know. Note, however, that when I say that my wife is not having an affair, I want this statement to be true. I want the world to be as I say that it is; which is not the case when I lie to others—here, I want the world not to be as I say that it is. This difference is crucial; lying to oneself is guided by a different intention than lying to others. This fundamental intention is to change the world; it is to make the world as we say that it is.

In this particular case, this intention is doomed to failure, if it actually is the case that my wife is having an affair. But, our intention to change the world is not always doomed to failure. This intention, the desire to make the world as we want it to be, is the reason for the close relationship between violence and lying to oneself; for violence also aims at changing the world. It often aims, precisely, at making "true" the lies we have been telling ourselves.

Misrecognition is a form of action, not simply a lack of knowledge which some additional information could remedy. This is why the danger that threatens us does not come from the disappearance of *méconnaissance,* but from its omnipresence in the world in which we live.

Survival without Salvation?

Paul Gifford

Jean-Pierre Dupuy has one very good, entirely Girardian idea: that the balance of terror is a contemporary expression of the archaic sacred (or its evolutionary legacy); and that it represents a half-lucid attempt at containing the immanent "god" of our own violence. He has a series of less good ideas: he thinks that this case is somehow at odds with the Girardian doctrine of misrecognition; that it demonstrates a strategic and fatal flaw within it; and that the concept of misrecognition should, therefore, be excised from the theory, lest the flawed theory give rise to accusations of moral indifferentism and nihilism. Finally, he has a highly questionable idea: that the nearest thing we can manage to salvation is to follow just this model of half-lucid, game-playing make-believe, while telling ourselves it could be a formula for human survival in apocalyptic times.

Margo Boenig-Liptsin and Paul Dumouchel have already performed the key task of showing Dupuy's *mis*recognition of *méconnaissance:* its range of reference, its place, tenor, and significance in Girardian theory. Girard is not naturally a system-builder; there are gaps, missing correlations, flaws of cross-referencing and consolidation in his immensely suggestive body of work (he might very well echo another very strategic, but dispersed and fragmentary

French thinker, Paul Valéry: "I need a German to finish off my ideas!"). Yet this is by no means the same thing as saying that the edifice is without strategic coherence and consistency; or that it is built on structurally unsound ideas, even on perilous ones.

The contrary impression results from a simplifying schematism of understanding, predicated at bottom on a false working hypothesis: namely, that Girard's theory *should* be dealing with a simple, rationally functioning "mechanism" that operates uniformly in time and cultural space and is decipherable mechanically in all its expressions.

Both respondents already point to the flaws in this approach: the mechanism is, on the contrary, diverse and multiform; it evolves in cultural time and space. Mimetic theory itself points to a dawning recognition, operating by ritual first, then institutions, then through religious traditions, then, decisively, though the pivotal advent of Christianity, which sets running a deeply subversive principle of anthropological *demystification—of waking up to ourselves.* Girardian *méconnaissance* always-already implies some form of hybrid consciousness, some *clair-obscur* of partial understanding and self-knowledge. (How else, in Genesis, could there be such a clear description of mimetic blame-transfer? Adam, questioned by the Lord, blames "the woman Thou gavest me"; who is, in turn, already blaming the Serpent; who began the scenario of *Homo sapiens* by blaming the repressive order of moral prohibition, supposedly referable to *God*). The notion of *méconnaissance,* in other words, has a *thickness* quite unsuspected by Dupuy. It extends far beyond rational judgment and objective third-person knowledge, since it engages the entire submerged volume of the iceberg of intentionality, including the entire dynamics of desire-led "group intelligence" in humans.

What, exactly, is being "misrecognized"? Dupuy and like–minded critics seem to believe that it is simply the arbitrary nature of victim selection, or the juridical innocence of the victim—i.e., some limited and localizable defect of factual knowledge or rational cognizance. At most, they envisage marginally that what is being misrecognized is some element of moral complicity in the consequences of emissary victimization, some degree of agency or participation in individual or collective violence. But they miss what appears with tremendous force of evidence in the course of cultural evolution and of human history, and is so often commented on by Girard: not so much the elementary default mechanisms of veiling or mystification as first programmed into us, at the threshold of hominization, by evolution; but, over the longer term, our human *deficiency of self-awareness,* our human *desire-led partiality,* and our human *moral obliquity.*

Dupuy's own chosen example illustrates memorably the recesses of human moral *inconscience* and its hypocritical subtleties of blame-*transfer.* The game of nuclear terror, he tells us, is no longer being played between two adversaries. It is defined by the fact that neither rival is truly in a position to deter the other from violence; whereas each wants and needs to be deterred. The way out of this common dilemma is to invent a fictitious entity that will deter both at the same time. The game being played, therefore, is that between one actor, humankind, whose survival is at stake, and its double—namely, its own violence projectively externalized as Fate.

It is as though we had tacitly agreed to pretend that we are, in common, threatened by an exceedingly dangerous enemy whose power of destruction surpasses all the earthquakes and tsunamis nature could throw at us. Our real adversary is a false god whom we sacralize darkly, out of fear of ourselves, and whom we worship expensively, at our own peril. *Knowing and not knowing* what we do, we walk, as at the threshold of hominization—but now more ambiguously and more perilously—between Progress and Abyss.

And yet Robert McNamara, in Dupuy's understanding, commends effective nuclear deterrence, defining effectiveness as what sets us at the right distance from the black hole of self-destruction. Not too close, lest we be swallowed up in the vortex or consumed in the holocaust. But not too far either, lest we forget the threat and its salutary terror. That is exactly what Girard has in mind by the archaic sacred "containing" violence in the double sense of that word, and by its resorting to a "make-believe" of bad faith (replacing a more primitive and innocent unknowing) in the vain hope of changing the world.

Do we not already know the epitaphs of such sophisticated modern *misrecognition?* "Science sans conscience n'est que ruine de l'âme" (Rabelais). "Et pendant une éternité, il ne cessait de connaître et ne pas comprendre" (Paul Valéry).[6] "Father, forgive them; for they know not what they do" (Jesus, in Luke's gospel [Lk. 23:34]).

The pivotal point of misunderstanding in this chapter appears to me to lie, precisely, in the mismatch between the place accorded respectively by Girard, on the one hand, and by Dupuy (but also by Atlan and Anspach), on the other, to Christian revelation. It is pivotal because Girard insists: "Mimetic theory is essentially a Christian theory" (Girard 2007, 203 [2010, 113]); and that "the Passion is modelled around the 'folds' and 'tricks' of the founding murder, showing us all its workings; what was misrecognition has become revelation" (215 [120]).

If the gospels show the scapegoat mechanism operating at full tilt, and yet failing to disarm the mimetic crisis gathering around first-century Israel, this is because of the powerful light of critique shed upon it by the Victim, who says and shows that the victimizers "know not what they do."[7] And if "misrecognition" is always a fundamental condition of the efficacy of emissary victimization as a symbolico-ritual means of managing social violence, this is because, as we observe clearly in this paradigmatic case, without the sanction of the sacrality it creates, emissary victimization is *without potency* in the symbolic order; and though we may still act in the logic and image of archaic sacrifice, we can no longer quite believe in the magic containment of violence by this means; and, for want of that entire, unanimous, and sacralizing credence, our "sacrifices" henceforth *work less and less well.*

But the "revelation" that actively dissipates misrecognition, by the same token, is not to be equated solely with new information acting objectively, uniformly, or immediately. It is a paradigm-switching and progressive conversion of the heart that makes its way unpredictably in the thickness of individual persons and, more slowly still, in the cultural and social psyche of human collectivities—leaving behind it, precisely, the hybrid and intermediate cases envisaged in this discussion: knowing and not knowing; knowing and not understanding; knowing and not doing; lying to oneself; making-believe instead of doing, etc. (If Girard sometimes gives the impression of subscribing to "saving illumination," it may be that as an intellectual of Cartesian antecedence and prompt imagination, he tends to simplify this process and marvel unduly at its slow progression!)

In the contemporary world, at all events, we are indeed in a transitional zone of patchy half-light and half-protection. We *know,* in principle; but we behave *as if we did not know* and as if we still placed credence in the archaic god: exactly the ambiguity just noted in Dupuy's example.

And Dupuy's own understanding of the gospel? "Remarkably enough"—he declares—"Girard feels the need to underline the fact that such a nuclear peace is *not* the sign that the Kingdom of God is already with us." Misconstruing the Kingdom as a vague synonym for "utopia,"[8] he thinks Girard is here laboring the obvious. Not so: Girard is stating something that quite escapes Dupuy: namely, that the Kingdom is a *novel* and *radically antithetical* account of transcendence and the sacred. Here, for Girard, is the *pertinent and adequate antidote* to the lie of archaic religion, with its self-mystifications, its misty misrecognitions, and its contained violence. Here is the dawn that dispels the night:

> In the tender compassion of our God
> the dawn from on high shall break upon us,
> to shine on those who dwell in darkness and the shadow of
> death,
> and to guide our feet into the way of peace (Lk. 1:76–79)

The real apocalypse, if we take the gospels seriously, is not the holocaust that looms in the balance of nuclear terror (this belongs very much still to the haunted dreams of the night); it is the advent among men, in the person of Jesus, of all the good that is God—come, coming, and still to come. The real apocalypse *is* the Kingdom.

Dupuy claims that in the gospel reference to "Satan casting out Satan" (see Mk. 3: 20–28), we have a mythic restatement of a truism of mimetic theory: namely, that the "bad" violence of disorder, anarchy, and social implosion is contained by the "good violence" of social norms, codes, and institutions. But this paraphrase applies Girardian theory mechanically. Jesus, in Mark's gospel, is referring to his miracles of healing; and he challenges the spokesmen of the archaic sacred within Judaism to say whence comes the inspiration and the enabling power to overthrow the evil of human suffering within God's creation. Since Jesus is their rival and threatens their authority, the religious experts wish to reply: "from Satan." But Jesus's point is that Satan, precisely, *cannot* be the power destroying Satan. If he were, we should not see what we do in fact see: namely, evil and suffering *subsisting* in the world around us; nor should we see, in these miracles of healing, the released power of God transforming the house Satan has appropriated.

"Satan's house," for Girard, is the construction of the archaic sacred, with its violence-led demonology, edified in concealment of the Founding murder. What Jesus sees and brings is not the repetition and reinforcement of this construct, therefore, but the *end* of it—a real transcendence replacing a false one by a revelation of the true likeness of God, and a conversion of the heart.

For want of entering into this antipodally different gospel logic, Dupuy *discounts* Christianity: it represents the first part of Girardian theory to be jettisoned. Christianity is then seen no longer as Girard sees it—as the salvation of mimetic humanity, its healing light of truth, peace, and grace from above—but as a *diminished and treacherous reworking of the archaic sacred.* "The Christian revelation appears to be a snare, the knowledge it carries a kind of trap, since it deprives humanity of the only means it had to keep its violence in check. As Girard puts it . . ." (etc.).

In fact, the way Girard increasingly puts it, as self-declared Christian apologist, leaves Dupuy in uncomfortable divergence from him—trying to pull the blanket of theory in another direction and cutting the cloth to his appropriated figure of sense, while attempting, simultaneously, to pull some crucial existential chestnuts out of the fire.

Can we see his own proposal on nuclear weapons as other than a policy of "whistling in the dark" pursued on the edge of the vortex of unlimited modern violence? And is this essay then, perhaps, a good case study in the difference between "survival" and "salvation"; genuinely *good* . . . in its pertinent focusing of the unresolved tension between two considerable, if divergent, exponents of "apocalypse thinking"?

Notes

1. For Girard, this confounding enigma is linked to another: "What astonishes and fascinates me, is the formidable resistance encountered by this [New Testament] message [that we must destroy each other or love each other]. Resistance is even stronger, now that Hegel's star has dimmed, now that [the] identity [between enemy brothers and of all men] will soon be manifest to all, and we can no longer delay it" (Girard 2007, 102 [2010, 49].

2. See, in particular, the whole section entitled "An Impossible Reconciliation" (Girard 2010, 43–51).

3. This is how I interpret his expression: "My disagreement with René Girard . . . engages the entire question of how we ourselves may recognize and repair the plight of mimetic humanity under the threat of nuclear apocalypse; and on the possibility or otherwise of a *conversion of the heart* as envisaged by the Christian gospels and by Girard" (original emphasis).

4. The claim that knowledge of the arbitrary character of the designation of the victim would endanger the proper functioning of the mechanism already appears toward the end of *Violence and the Sacred* (Girard 1977, 311).

5. Note that Girard in *Things Hidden* provides a similar analysis of nuclear deterrence but reaches a completely different conclusion. According to him, in nuclear deterrence everything is revealed, in the sense that "the hidden infra-structure of all religions and cultures is disclosing itself" and because we are in "an objectively apocalyptic situation"; and yet most people still fail to recognize it (Girard 1978, 366, 372).

6. "Knowledge without gathered understanding is but ruin of soul"; "And for a whole eternity, he knew and yet did not understand."

7. Dupuy suggests this plea applies only to the immediate victimizers of Jesus; and that all subsequent times and places fall outside its pertinence. Another French agnostic, Paul Valéry, reflects more accurately Girard's own view when he describes this prayer of Jesus as a "supreme and august word, the deepest, simplest and truest ever spoken on the human species, and therefore on its politics, its progress, its doctrines, its conflicts" (*Oevres,* ed. J. Hytier, tome 1 [Paris: Gallimard, Bibliothèque de la Pléiade, 1957], 530; my translation).

8. Girard himself refers this mis-persuasion to Ernest Renan (Girard 1978, 370).

Cited Texts and Further Reading

Anders, G. 1995. *Hiroshima ist über all.* Munich: C.H. Beck.

Anscombe, G.E.M. 1981. "Mr. Truman's Degree." In *Collected Philosophical Papers,* vol. 3, *Ethics, Religion, and Politics,* 62–71. Minneapolis: University of Minnesota Press.

Anspach, M. 2011. "Imitation and Violence: Empirical Evidence and the Mimetic Model." In *Mimesis and Science: Empirical Research on Imitation and the Mimetic Theory of Culture and Religion,* ed. S. Garrels. East Lansing: Michigan State University Press.

Atlan, H. 2010. *The Sparks of Randomness.* Vol. 1. Stanford, CA: Stanford University Press.

Atlan, H., and J.-P. Dupuy. 1981. "Mimesis and Social Morphogenesis: Violence and the Sacred from a Systems Analysis Viewpoint." In *Applied Systems and Cybernetics,* vol. 3, ed. G. E. Lasker. New York: Pergamon Press.

Baudrillard, Jean. 1994. *Simulacra and Simulation.* Ann Arbor: University of Michigan Press.

Brodie, B. 1973. *War and Politics.* New York: Macmillan.

Dumouchel, P. 1992. "Systèmes sociaux et cognition." In *Introduction aux sciences cognitives,* ed. D. Andler, 472–88. Paris: Gallimard.

———. 2011. *Le sacrifice inutile: Essai sur la violence politique.* Paris: Flammarion.

Dupuy, J.-P. 1988. "Totalization and Misrecognition." In *Violence and Truth: On the Work of René Girard,* ed. P. Dumouchel, 75–100. London: Athlone Press.

———. 2002. *Pour un catastrophisme éclairé.* Paris: Seuil.

———. 2005. *Petite métaphysique des tsunamis.* Paris: Seuil.

———. 2009. "The Precautionary Principle and Enlightened Doomsaying: Rational Choice before the Apocalypse." *Occasion: Interdisciplinary Studies in the Humanities* 1. At http://occasion.stanford.edu/node/28.

———. 2011. *La marque du sacré.* Paris: Flammarion.

Einstein, A. 1950. "Arms Can Bring No Security." *Bulletin of the Atomic Scientists.* VI (3), 71.

Gauchet, M. 1999. *The Disenchantment of the World.* Princeton, NJ: Princeton University Press.

Girard, R., 1977. *Violence and the Sacred.* Translated by P. Gregory. Baltimore: Johns Hopkins University Press. Original edition, *La violence et le sacré* (Paris: Grasset, 1972).

———. 1987. *Things Hidden since the Foundation of the World.* Translated by Stephen Bann and Michael Metteer. Stanford, CA: Stanford University Press. Original edition, *Des choses cachées depuis la fondation du monde* (Paris: Grasset, 1978).

———. 2007. *Achever Clausewitz: Entretiens avec Benoît Chantre* (Paris: Éditions Nord, 2007). Translated by M. Baker, *Battling to the End: Conversations with Benoît Chantre.* Michigan State University Press. 2010.

Jasanoff, S. 2004. *States of Knowledge: The Co-Production of Science and Social Order.* New York: Routledge.Kavka, G. 1987. *Moral Paradoxes of Nuclear Deterrence.* Cambridge: Cambridge University Press.

Lee, Steven P. 1993. *Morality, Prudence, and Nuclear Weapons.* New York: Cambridge University Press.

Lewis, Clive Staples. [1941] 1980. "Is Theology Poetry?" In *The Weight of Glory, and Other Addresses.* Revised and expanded ed., with introduction by Walter Hooper. London: Collins.

Lewis, D. K. 1984. "Devil's Bargains and the Real World." In *The Security Gamble: Deterrence Dilemmas in the Nuclear Age,* ed. D. MacLean. Totowa, NJ: Rowman and Allanheld.

———. 1989. "Finite Counterforce." In *Nuclear Deterrence and Moral Restraint,* ed. Henry Shue. Cambridge: Cambridge University Press.

Masco, J. 2006. *The Nuclear Borderlands: The Manhattan Project in Post–Cold War New Mexico.* Princeton, NJ: Princeton University Press.

McNamara, R., and J. G. Blight. 2001. *Wilson's Ghost: Reducing the Risk of Conflict, Killing, and Catastrophe in the 21st Century.* New York: Public Affairs.

Schell, J. 1982. *The Fate of Earth.* New York: Random House.

Schelling, T. 1960. *The Strategy of Conflict.* Cambridge, MA: Harvard University Press.

Wieseltier, L. 1983. *Nuclear War, Nuclear Peace.* New York: Holt, Rinehart, Winston.

Girard, Climate Change, and Apocalypse

Michael Northcott

In his latest book, *Battling to the End,* René Girard undertakes a series of culture-readings centered on an account of the end-game of modernity and its potential apocalypse. The book represents the culmination of the thesis, maturing throughout his work, about mimetic violence, rivalry, and the sacred. He suggests that the twentieth-century trend toward total war, including borderless wars such as the "war on terror," and borderless economic competition to access the remaining natural resources of the planet, represented a phase change in the history of the age-old problem of human attempts to control and manage the threat of mimetic rivalry and violence.

According to Girard, the mechanism that deflects the perils of collective violence also confers sacral authority on the apparatus of moral codes, social institutions, and ritual practices designed to protect the social community against its own negative reciprocities. By the twentieth century of the Common Era, however, that same cloud cover had, he thinks, been burned away as never before by secular reason, technological power, and other forces and processes of modernity—all set in train, structurally speaking, by the secularizing tendencies immanent in Christianity (Berger 1967).

Modern violence may be still "sacrificial" and "victimizing," and it may still generate self-justifying sacralities; but, for Girard, moderns do not believe in these new forms of the sacred implicitly enough or unanimously enough for them to have either much repressive-protective force or, certainly, any salvific virtue in respect of the runaway dynamic of negative reciprocity that first elicits and secretly drives them. The consequence is that rivalry and violence are becoming increasingly global in reach with weakening mediating codes, institutions, and practices between individuals and families and the social forces of competition and coercion. For example, there is growing and direct economic rivalry between corporations and peasants for farmland in Africa, and growing rivalry for water supplies within and between nations. This reflects the increasingly borderless character of global economistic competition for natural resources and profit, and the economistic refusal that the human economy is earthbound, on a finite planet, in a universe that is otherwise a hostile and death-dealing vacuum outside of the fragile envelope of the earth's atmosphere (Northcott 2014). Girard argues that the contemporary escalation of mimetic rivalry into global economic competition for the remaining land and water resources of the planet, and for planetary sinks for human waste including the atmosphere, involves a growing level of planetary "sacrifice," increasingly unlimited in its scale and effects (Girard 2010). These effects include the growing extinction of species, the emptying of the oceans of most of their fish stocks, and most recently, the growth of extreme weather events fueled by anthropogenic climate change. The gravity of this phase change is registered overall in the fact that the "innocent victim" is now, for the first time, our nurturing and sustaining mother-earth, the very basis and condition of the survival of all biological life.

The modern Prometheus, as Girard situates him, is consequently "apocalyptic": that is, he is delivered up to the law of his own intrinsic dynamic, as it is expressed in the model of the "mimetic crisis"—Girard's famous "montée aux extrêmes." Often translated as "the trend towards extremes," this expression is, as we shall have occasion to observe, better and more tellingly translated in most contexts of application as a "crescendo towards paroxysm."

Girard usually expounds the apocalyptic context and climate of our times by referring to the "mini-apocalypses" (as they are sometimes called) of the synoptic gospels. These are prophetic, in his view, of the fact that human violence interacts, as never before, with the natural world, engaging cosmic nature in its own spirit-driven crescendo toward a destructive paroxysm, and suffering in return the effects of a human disordering of cosmic nature:

> Violence is today unleashed at a global and planetary level, bringing about
> something heralded by the gospel texts on this theme: a fusing of natu-
> ral and man-made disasters, a confusion of the natural and the artificial
> orders: global warming and the rising of oceans are today no longer just
> metaphors [of human violence]. The violence which once generated the
> sacred, no longer produces anything but itself. (Girard 2007, 11 [2010, x])

This "ultra-modern theme of the contamination of nature by the works of
man" (205 [114]) is described by a number of natural scientists as a "second
Copernican revolution" (Schellnhuber 1999) and a new geological era,
known as the Anthropocene (Crutzen 2006). The Anthropocene is the first
era in which human mimetic rivalry has extended in power to such an extent
that human agency has overtaken other geologic and geospatial forces in
determining its climate and the future direction of evolution. The declaration of this new height of human agency over the earth is visibly close to the
nerve of "that apocalyptic feeling" in Girard. But he insists:

> This is not me repeating myself, but reality catching up with a truth not of
> my invention, since it was declared two thousand years ago. Our unhealthy
> obsession with contradiction and innovation will not and cannot hear this.
> But the paradox is that, drawing ever closer to the alpha point, we are mak-
> ing our way ever closer to point omega. As we understand better and better
> where we have come from, we realize a little better each day that this origin
> is coming towards us: the bolt holding in the founding murder has been
> drawn back by the Passion, and is today letting loose a planetary violence;
> and there is no way of closing the stable door. (Girard 2007, 12 [2010, x–xi]

It is from this observational standpoint that Girard speaks to the troubled
and troubling contemporary debate on anthropogenic climate change, i.e.,
the ecologically motivated concern to explore the nature and effects, direct
and collateral, of human action in relation to our planetary environment
and its ecosystems. What follows here is an attempt to discern and assess his
contribution to understanding in this field.

Apocalyptic Scenarios of Anthropogenic
Climate Change

Apocalyptic language and scenarios in relation to "anthropogenic" (human-induced) climate change (ACC) are instantly recognizable as a feature of popular and media representations of this phenomenon. Two films illustrate particularly powerfully this form of modern apocalypticism.

The first film, *The Day After Tomorrow,* envisages a catastrophic and extremely sudden cooling of the Northeast Atlantic as the Gulf Stream, which draws heat from the tropics into the North and East Atlantic, ceases to function. The extreme cooling and winter storm that then engulfs the U.S. Eastern Seaboard is unscientific, as is the sudden turning off of the Gulf Stream. Nonetheless the Gulf Stream is currently weakening because of the extent of ice melt from a warming Arctic. Together with related changes in the Atlantic Jet Stream polar ice melt was responsible for the "polar vortex" that engulfed the Midwestern United States and Canada in the winter of 2013–14, and for the weeks-long blanketing of the UK in ice and snow in the winter of 2009–10. The power of the film, however, is to turn ACC into a sudden life-threatening apocalyptic scenario that reduces life in the center of one of the world's largest and richest cities—New York—into a desperate and violent struggle for survival against the elements.

The second film, *Age of Stupid,* depicts a man in early old age who is ensconced on a technological Noah's Ark somewhere in the ice-free Arctic Ocean on an earth in which much of the formerly settled land area, including coastal cities, energy generating facilities and ports, is under water. He takes the viewer back through a series of flashbacks on a transparent screen on which he manipulates video clips that depict the prehistory of the "end of history," including climate protest marches, failed international conferences, wars for the remaining fossil fuels under the earth's crust, and growing extreme weather events that ultimately see the seas rise as the polar icecaps melt and engulf the land and the cities whose metropolitan elites had brought the earth to this final cataclysm.

The language of scientific discourse on ACC and its likely future effects is generally more measured. However, a number of recent examples of science writing by established climate scientists reveal a similar apocalyptic turn. James Hansen, NASA's foremost climate scientist, has written *Storms of My Grandchildren*. James Lovelock, the inventor of the Gaia hypothesis, and who discovered the ozone hole over the Antarctic, entitled his penultimate book *The Revenge of Gaia*. Two Australian scientists entitled their collaborative book *Climate Code Red*. Each title indicates a different apocalyptic theme. The first points to growing natural catastrophes affecting our children and children's children. The second indicates that the earth itself manifests, in the extreme conditions brought on by future climate change, the same cycle of violent retaliation that for Girard is the universal pattern of human interaction across cultures. The third adopts a technological metaphor for the earth as a machine—analogous to a nuclear power station that is about to go critical and into meltdown.

Marshall Burke et al. (2009, 20670–74) demonstrate a link between climate change and increasing human conflict in Africa, something that is not a rhetorical device but a statistical fact. They find that a single degree Centigrade of warming in Africa correlates, over the last thirty years, with an increase of 49 percent in the incidence of civil war in the continent, as compared to years when the temperature returns to pre-crisis norms.

They account for this dramatic result by the fact that the economic welfare of the majority of African households is directly related to agricultural crop production. Temperature increases create heightened water stress for crops while reducing the rate of crop growth. Together these effects result in declines in yields of 10 to 30 percent. And because "economic welfare is the single factor most consistently associated with conflict incidence," they conclude that "it appears likely that the variation in agriculture performance is the central mechanism linking warming to conflict in Africa" (Ragnhild and Gleditsch 2007, 627–38). Others have also observed a link between climate change and violence in the Middle East, where conflict and civil war were sparked by food price rises in Tunisia, Egypt, and Libya in 2009–10, and by drought and declining water sources in Mali, Syria, and elsewhere (Hendrix and Salehyan 2012).

The link between climate change and conflict is also made in a range of reports emanating from the United States military and from institutes of strategic studies. One such report cites Admiral Lopez, the former NATO commander from Bosnia, as follows:

> Climate change will provide the conditions that will extend the war on
> terror. You have very real changes in natural systems that are most likely to
> happen in regions of the world that are already fertile ground for extrem-
> ism. Droughts, violent weather, ruined agricultural lands—those are the
> kinds of stresses we'll see more of under climate change.

The result of such changes, the general continues, will be more poverty, more
forced migrations, higher unemployment. These conditions are ripe for
extremists and terrorists (Sullivan et al. 2007).

The link between climate change and violent conflict may be readily
observed also in the media and political rhetoric generated around the science of climate change in the United States and beyond. For many years,
media in the United States have given prominence to the small number of
physical scientists, and the much larger number of political commentators,
who express skepticism concerning the claims that present changes in the
earth's climate are human-induced. Boykoff shows that journalistic norms
and standards require the imposition of the frame of conflict on their report-
ing of climate science, even though the scientific community itself is largely
of one mind on the matter, as evidenced by contributions to peer-reviewed
journals on ACC (Boykoff 2007, 477–89). This frame of conflict arises ironically from the idea that responsible public media have a duty to represent
a balance of views. Although the number of physical scientists who take a
contrarian stance on ACC is very small relative to the mainstream scientific
view, journalistic norms require that this very small minority of "contrarians"
be given equal prominence. In the public mind, the view therefore emerges
that there is no scientific consensus about ACC, and no basis for collective
action in response to the problem.

The framing of disagreement around ACC in the United States and
beyond has itself turned increasingly violent in the context of the "Climategate" allegations arising from media interpretations of a set of e-mails stolen
from the University of East Anglia's Climate Research Unit. Individual
scientists caught up in the story—such as Michael Mann and Phil Jones—
received hate e-mails and even death threats. This turn to violent rhetoric on
the part of believers in climate-change denialism reveals a growing tendency
to treat scientific claims as reflecting personal commitments and worldviews,
rather than the collective process of data collection and analysis and peer

review that represents scientific judgment. Thus it is now common in discourse about climate change to hear it said that scientists promote ACC because ACC provides the funding for their research, and that ACC is a set of false claims that are adopted by those whose principal intent is to grow the power of the State over the individual.[1]

Another and potentially far more grievous occasion of conflict is that the nations of the earth are unable to agree to restrain fossil fuel extraction and burning so as to prevent dangerous climate change (Northcott 2014, 143–44). The atmosphere is a commons that cannot be easily divided according to territory, since greenhouse gases emitted in one terrain infect all other terrains through atmospheric circulation. Therefore, absent an agreement to limit the extraction of the resource that is toxic to the atmosphere, nations simply burn what they will in pursuit of fossil-fueled growth. In so doing, they endanger the terrains of other nations by the kinds of destabilizing climatic effects observed in the papers and reports cited above on climate-related conflicts.

The inability of the nations to agree to restrain climate damaging fossil fuel extraction and use through an effective international legal treaty is a classic Hobbesian dilemma. The capacity of the atmosphere to absorb emissions from fossil-fueled economic activity, without change to the historic heat-exchange relationship between the earth and the sun, is limited. Conflict between nations arises because they all want greater access to the limited object of atmospheric "sinks" for fossil-fuel emissions. This is a classic example of what Girard characterizes as the egocentric and object-centered nature of desire, turbocharged by its accompanying quality of Other-referred mimetism.

Defenders of their "right to pollute" the atmosphere resist the need either to limit energy consumption or to reduce other kinds of consumption in order to pay for the costs of moving energy sources from cheap fossil fuels such as coal and gas to more technically complex and expensive renewables such as solar and wind (Northcott 2014, 173–76). Defenders of the status quo of excessive fossil-fueled consumption in the United States, Australia, and other developed countries scapegoat climate scientists as the inventors of a false scenario, and hence the legitimate objects of hate, persecution, and violence.

Others who deny that the science is wrong, but also deny that there are limits to consumption, turn to the rhetoric of failed states, political extremism, mass migration, and terrorism to indicate the way in which the coming climate crisis will turn out (Smith 2007). On this account, the cause of climate-change-related conflict is not excessive consumption by the rich, but the existence of resource-poor or poorly governed nations located in areas that will experience greater climate threats from ACC. Such scapegoating rhetoric justifies attempts by the United States—and now Europe—to prevent environmental refugees from crossing international borders (Feng, Krueger, and Oppenheimer 2010). And it justifies military interventions, using drones, or other "sub-formal war" interventions, in countries where climate change and extreme weather may be destabilizing, including Pakistan and Yemen.

The context and ethos of the debate around ACC has, it will be seen, gathered all the classic makings of mimetic crisis—albeit a crisis at a now globalized level, interactive-with-nature and for unlimited stakes. And so far, we have only envisaged the question of human agency in the changes proceeding; we have hardly considered the disputes occasioned by mimetic rivalry over the resources themselves that are being put at risk (e.g., minerals and oil in the polar regions, tropical forests in Central Africa and Southeast Asia, or water sources in Turkey and Syria). We have, if anything, understated therefore the conformity of this ethos and context with the Girardian analysis.

Apocalyptic Sacralities: A Late-Modern Return of the Religious?

As Brigitte Nerlich notes, one of the more striking effects of the Climategate controversy was to reveal that beliefs about climate change—whether mainstream or contrarian—have acquired the status of myth. Opponents of ACC propose that its proponents are "believers" in a set of mythic beliefs: that the climate is changing in a way unparalleled in history; that fossil fuels are the cause; that fossil-fueled growth needs to be limited if meltdown is to be avoided. These beliefs are held to represent not a legitimate scientific interpretation of hard data, but a quasi-religious worldview that some dub "climate creationism"—the view that human beings create the climate. These beliefs, skeptics argue, are sustained by personal and political commitments of scientists, and by professional norms and practices rather than "hard science" (Nerlich 2010, 419–42).

Nerlich offers a table extracted from a review of a month's blogs in 2009 around Climategate that reveals the extensive use of religious rhetoric among climate-change skeptics. She registers in this way the troubled and troubling liturgy of sacralization involved:

- Science (is): "cult," "fear-mongering," "climate-change faith-system."
- Scientific theories (are): "dogma," "myth," "gospel," "bible."
- Scientific consensus (is): "orthodoxy," "collectivism and Godism," "canon," "singing from the same hymn sheet."
- Scientists (are): "messiah," (confirmed, true) "believers," "zealots," "prophets," "apostles," "wizards and warlocks," "gurus," "false priests," "high priests," "unchallengeable priesthood," "clerics," "acolytes," "adherents," "evangelists," "the converted, man-made global warming *illuminati*."
- Scientific dissemination (is): "crusade," "preaching."
- Scientific confidence (is): "belief, "religious conviction," "almost religious type beliefs," "devotion," "worship."
- Scientific predictions (are): "prophecies," "doomsday prophecies."
- Scientists interacting with skeptics (is): "cult in which nay-sayers must be crushed," and where skeptics are "heretics," "witches" (Nerlich 2010, 429–30).

Girard would recognize the telltale signs of the archaic sacred at work— albeit, in this hybrid era of our modernity, now integrated into adversarial *critique*.

The release of the CRU e-mails during the Copenhagen Climate Conference by parties unknown was clearly designed to unsettle public opinion on ACC. And it had the desired effect. Belief in ACC declined markedly in the months in which Climategate was reported, and remained lower two years later, despite investigations by scientific panels of the CRU and of other scientists accused of manipulating climate data and suppressing contrary evidence, public opinion, and the opinion of key public informants, such as meteorologists, on ACC reveals notably higher levels of skepticism. Climategate also undermined belief in global warming among many American TV meteorologists (Maibach et al. 2011, 31–40). But most crucially, the Copenhagen Conference during which the e-mails were released was mired in controversy, and it failed to produce a successor international climate treaty to the Kyoto Protocol.

The increasing turn to apocalyptic and religious language in relation to ACC indicates, we might think, a particular case of the larger phenomenon of the late-modern "return to the sacred" observed in many different cultural and political discourses and settings around the turn of the millennium. But the Girardian "take" is, as we shall see, somewhat different and more strategic, in accordance with his evolutionary purview.

The mobilization of sacred discourses and symbols has been particularly prominent among fundamentalist religious groups in the United States, the Middle East, South and Southeast Asia in the last twenty years. And with the rise in fundamentalisms there has been a growth in religiously inspired violence, of which the best known were the terrorist attacks on the United States now known as 9/11 (Ebaugh 2002, 385–95). The late-modern return of religion brings into question at some level the traditional post-Enlightenment secularization thesis: the thesis that economically and scientifically advanced societies experience a demise in awareness of God, and in the influence of religious institutions and practices as scientific explanations and procedures replace magical thinking about human-nature relations.

Girard is not alone in arguing that secularization in the Christian West is not so much the enemy, as the fruit of Christianity in modernity. But what he adds to that proposal is the claim that the demise of the archaic sacred in the modern West is the proper outcome of the influence of Christianity, since traditional religions of all kinds manifest a universal mimetic structure of scapegoating, victimage, and sacrificial violence. Christianity for Girard is the only religion that has the potential to subvert what he identifies as a universal cultural tendency. But it does this *only* when the meaning of Christian revelation is understood as essentially to do with the *end* of sacrifice (in its archaic acceptance) and the *end* of scapegoating, violence and retaliation— in short, when Christian revelation is seen as the end the "old religion."

If, on the other hand, Christians interpret the death of Christ as a sacrifice that is salvific *principally* because it atones human sins to God—as in many seminal texts in Western Christianity such as Anselm's *Cur Deus Homo* and Bach's *St. Matthew Passion*—then Christianity is at risk of underwriting rather than repairing the same law of mimetic violence and archaic sacrality that accrues to "the sacred" in other religious traditions (Northcott 2005). In Girardian language, such a salvific emphasis in Christianity would return the Christian religion to "default" patterns programmed by evolution at the threshold of hominization. Hence the infection of climate-change dis-course and politics by apocalyptic language and by religious discourses of blame and victimage, in which scientists in particular are threatened with a witch-hunt and victimized. This phenomenon is indicative not so much of a return of Christianity in American culture (and beyond its boundaries) but of an assertion of the older logic of the archaic sacred, as evolutionary default mechanism for resolving mimetic rivalry and violence. It also points to a tragic loss in relation to the distinctive truth of Christianity as the reli-gion that alone offers the repair to mimetic violence, thus ending forever the societal need for a sacrificial system to channel and express such violence. That much of the violent rhetoric around climate change originates in the United States appears, at this point, as deeply ironic, given that the United States sustains higher levels of Christian activity and belief than other devel-oped nations, and is the clearest exception to, if not a sufficient falsification of, the theory of secularization. This just underlines the extent to which the culture of Christianity in the United States, with its unbalanced emphasis on substitutionary atonement, is far from the end of its cult of sacrifice and victimhood, and despite the hopes of the Pilgrim Fathers and Mothers, now stands in tragic opposition to the kingdom of peace and non-retaliation that Christ inaugurated. (This is very much the thesis of Pahl and Wellman else-where in this volume.)

I have elsewhere argued that this problem of the contradiction between aspects of the culture of the United States—and in particular its adulation of violence and war—and the peaceable ontology of Christianity as interpreted not only by Girard but by Augustine and many others, is in part explicable by the continuing mythic status of the wars of violence on which the United States was founded. These aspects include the genocidal destruction of Native Americans, the Revolutionary War against England, the wars against France and Mexico, and the American Civil War (Northcott 2004). As Marvin and Ingle (1999) argue, these wars established blood sacrifice as the fundamental identity-making ritual of the American nation-state in which the soldier and the enemy function respectively as heroic and anti-heroic scapegoats.[2]

It is for this reason that from the Second World War onwards, the United States frames its relations with the outside world—and its internal policing and "security" policies—around war, from the Cold War to the War on Terror and the growing "war," for the present primarily expressed in terms of military interventions in Central Asia, with China, and in the broader use of drones against putative "enemies" (Northcott 2014, 231–32). Efforts in particular to link ACC with the War on Terror just underline this thesis. U.S. Christianity is deeply implicated in the cult of blood sacrifice, as the flag in the sanctuary and the extent of Christian involvement in the military both indicate.

Unsustainable Consumerism and the "Apocalypse"

A Girardian perspective on ACC offers another crucial insight into the problem of ACC in relation to the dominant cult of consumerism in the United States and beyond—a cult that, it seems to suggest, is unsustainable.

This cult is essentially driven by mimetic desire, which the advertising, marketing, and public-relations industries clearly indicate, since they so frequently link the sale of products to mimetic desires and to rivalry for material status objects and sexual attraction. But until ACC, the link between this cult and blood sacrifice and scapegoating was obscure. ACC reveals that the cult of consumerism also requires blood sacrifice; but in this case it is not the lives of American soldiers that are sacrificed, but the lives of the victims of ACC, linked as they are to water shortages, raised temperatures, and strengthened floods, droughts, and storms.

The first hint of this victimage mechanism in relation to ACC was manifest in the failure of the U.S. federal government, or the military, to intervene in a properly humanitarian way in New Orleans during Hurricane Katrina. The first encounter many black victims of the flooding in New Orleans had with federal and state agencies in the aftermath of the collapsed levees was their arrest—and in some cases lethal shooting—by state troopers and police as "looters," when in reality they were taking bottled water, powdered milk, and other foodstuffs from flooded stores to flood victims assembled in the city's stadium. Neither state nor federal authorities provided food or clean water to the flood victims in the first days of the disaster, but when the victims themselves attempted to do so, they were treated not as innocent victims but as criminals.

In the light of Katrina, the victims of raised sea levels in the Maldives, or of flooding in Bangladesh, or of rising food prices and declining crop production in Africa and the Arab world, are victims who will "merit" violent restraint and criminalization should they seek to escape rising waters and spreading deserts by relocating to other nations. Their victimage does not provide a motive for mitigating the practices of fossil-fuel burning and excessive material consumption and mobility that drive ACC. They are instead the scapegoats of ACC who, along with the victimized scientists, provide an enemy that can be mobilized to unite the dominant powers—oil and coal companies, the governments of the United States, Saudi Arabia, Russia and so on—against the claim made by the United Nations Intergovernmental Panel on Climate Change, and most physical and social scientists, that reduced use of fossil fuels is an urgent and necessary response to ACC.

It now seems likely that the refusal of the United States and China, the two largest national climate polluters, together with the principal non-national corporate climate polluters, to ration fossil-fuel supply to the absorptive capacities of the atmosphere will tip the planet into a warming episode from which no about-turn is possible. The Arctic is on course for the complete disappearance of summer ice by 2020. After that, all bets are off as to the warming implications since there is no historic proxy evidence available from fossilized tree rings or ice cores of such a sudden melting in any previous era in Planet Earth's history; such evidence as there is indicates that an event of this speed never happened before. The likelihood after this is that the conservative projections of gradual warming and sea level rise of the IPCC will be far exceeded even by the mid-twenty-first century, and that runaway global warming will then be unstoppable.

In *Evolution and Conversion,* Girard brings his account of mimetic desire and redemption into a consideration of the material and psychological roots of the ecological crisis. Human beings have appetites that are mediated, as Augustine also recognized, through their desires. People desire food and water when they are hungry or thirsty. In modernity most eating and drinking is not so much shaped by physical appetite because of the abundance of cheap food in industrial societies. Instead, desires for food, drink, and other objects for consumption are mimetically shaped by behavioral models that, though seeming to express personal preferences, are socially mediated through such media as advertising, entertainment, and films, as well as on the street, in homes, and in workplaces.

Girard does not deny that material struggles, including poverty and hunger, endure in consumer societies. But mimesis acquires a strong acquisitive and status-led dimension in consumer societies that arises paradoxically from the abundance of consumer objects. While they seem to reduce the need for rivalry, in fact the surplus of objects produces a situation where objects are weakened in their capacity to diffuse and siphon off the distorted desire of envy and rivalry. Hence, as Veblen earlier argued, it is the very success of the consumer society in generating an abundance of available objects that necessitates the constant creation of new objects (Veblen 1902). As everyone becomes the possessor of a fridge or a television, the capacity of consumer objects to diffuse rivalry is devalued, and people lose interest in the "universally available" objects.

This process of devaluing requires that new objects—*designer* fridges, *smart* phones, *luxury* cars—are created. This constant need for reinvention, also undergirded by designed obsolescence, is the motive power that drives the market society into "devouring the earth's resources, just as primitive society devoured its victims" (Girard 2008, 79). This creates an inflation of objects, the consequence of which is that one now has an array of objects that go directly from the shop to the bin, with hardly a stop in between. One buys objects with one hand, and throws them away with the other—in a world where half of the human population goes hungry (Girard 2008, 54). The eventual outcome of this increased consumption and destruction of objects is analogous to the primitive potlatch. The consumer society becomes "a system of exchange of signs, rather than actual objects," and as conspicuous consumption loses its appeal, it becomes fashionable to look emaciated or to be anorexic. Potentially this process "turns us into mystics in the sense that it shows us that objects will never satisfy our desires."

The cult of consumerism is not just sustained by the commercial requirement of the modern business enterprise to sell more and more to sustain profits and wealth accumulation. Instead the cult is essentially driven by mimetic desire, which the advertising, marketing, and public-relations industries clearly indicate since they link the sale of products so frequently to mimetic desire and rivalry for material objects as status signifiers whose possession provokes sexual attraction.

This adds a significant dimension to the analysis of the role of advertising in the etiology of the ecological and climate crisis. It is not only that advertisers have found ways to manipulate human desire through depth psychology, and to attach to objects a quasi-mystical "desire of desire" (McIntosh 2008;

Wannenwetsch 2007, 315–30). Girard's analysis *reveals the link between the cult of consumerism and the sacrifice of the earth:* the earth itself becomes the victim, the necessary oblation and scapegoat, without which rivalry in the age of fossil-fueled material abundance is always at risk of turning violent. This cult is also, as Wendell Berry suggests, a "cult of the future" in which progress in consumption of technologically "advanced" objects is associated with progress in the human condition (Berry 1978).

For Marx, the original alienation between land and labor, consumption and production, that preceded the consumerist fetishism of objects represented a necessary tendency to victimhood on the way to ultimate revolutionary emancipation. Violent, coercive removal of peasants from land and the corralling of peasants and their children in urban slums and workhouses were the means through which the product of the earth was accumulated into fewer hands and the masses prevented from making their own living. For Marx, this process created the conditions for class conflict that would ultimately provoke revolutionary transformation. But most of the revolutions of the twentieth century did not produce less materialistic or more just communistic societies. While worker organizations restrained life-shortening factory conditions and inequalities in capitalist societies until the late twentieth century, in the outsourced global economy of the twenty-first century, where workers in Brazil, China, India, or Mexico toil in similarly life-shortening conditions, class war between capital owners and the rest has resumed, especially in the United States, the UK, and mainland Europe where "austerity economics" and rising inequality and under-employment produce an accelerating social crisis of rising household debt, homelessness, and hunger.

Absent a greater willingness by the rich and capital owners for a just distribution of existing wealth, ACC indicates that an acceleration of mass consumption and material prosperity—and hence economic growth—in these new domains will only improve the material conditions of working people at the cost of destabilizing the earth's climate and diminishing material prospects for future generations. Hence the cycle of victimage involved in the origination of the industrial revolution is not simply reproduced mimetically around the world in newly triggered processes of industrialization, but "cycles" also across the generations. Future people whose homes and habitats are at risk of being drowned or desertified through climate change will become the victims of a cult driven by mimetic desire, whose objects, while they may turn away local blood sacrifice, nonetheless still rest upon a modern avatar of blood sacrifice, expressed now within the framework of a global human community.

Is "Apocalypse" the Right Word?

The question then arises whether the frame of apocalypse for such an eventuality remains a legitimate one. For Girard the Old Testament view of apocalypse as a violent, wrathful judgment by God is announced as having come to an end in the New Testament. To the extent that apocalyptic thinking remains in the New Testament, it serves a different function and purpose than it does in the Old. But what is this function? Chris Rowland and Richard Bauckham argue that in the New Testament, the inherited Hebrew apocalyptic form is taken up with a new purpose, not to prophesy the coming violence of divine judgment, but to announce that the shedding of the blood of the innocent "lamb of God" has brought violence to an end.

Apocalypse also serves another function in the New Testament—that of unconcealing the true state of things and of opening the way for a reversal of the present order (Bauckham 1993; Rowland 2002). Hence what the last book of the New Testament, the Apocalypse of St. John of Patmos, points to is not that the world will end in a violent conflagration, but rather that the violence of the imperial power of Rome will ultimately be undermined by the innocent suffering of those Christians who remain faithful witnesses to the divinity and lordship of Christ as the lamb of God, and the one who now reigns at the right hand of God.

The *millennial* reign of the saints that is forecast in the Book of Revelation is the antidote and outcome of the fall of Rome, which is—as Augustine percipiently argued in *City of God*—founded on the mythic violence of Romulus and Remus. With the end of Rome, a new reign of peace ensues, which, Augustine argues, is already present as the heavenly city—or what Girard calls the Kingdom—within human history.

If we follow this reading, ACC presents an ultimate contest between the two cities with two possible outcomes. In the one ending, the nations of the world recognize that the victims of ACC are innocent of having caused it. Africans, Bangladeshis, black residents of the Mississippi Delta, Pacific Islanders, and others in the front line of extreme weather events are seen as innocent victims of the excessive use by rich consumers, corporations, and government agencies of fossil fuels, polluting the atmosphere. When their lands, deltas, and islands become uninhabitable from sea-level rise or spreading deserts, they are then admitted into residence in those countries whose lands are still habitable.

At the same time, the witness of the "small island states" and other climate-challenged nations at international forums such as the United Nations and the Conferences of the Parties persuades the other nations—and especially the large polluters—that they have an urgent moral duty to reduce their emissions of greenhouse gases by de-energizing their activities and fueling the rest with genuinely renewable sources, which do not include such dubious fossil-fuel substitutes as biomass burning, biofuel, and hydraulically fractured gas, whose atmospheric footprints are in reality no better than oil or even coal.

In this case, we might say that the influence of Christianity as read by Girard—and before him, of course, by Leo Tolstoy, Mahatma Gandhi, and Martin Luther King Jr.—as a non-retaliatory and nonviolent religion has proven to be a political force within history.

However, this outcome looks at time of writing increasingly unlikely within immediate horizons. At a conference on the ethics of climate change, in Cambridge in 2011, the present author had the opportunity of an informal discussion with Anthony Giddens about the possible contribution of a Christian moral frame to the climate-change arena. In that discussion, I proposed to Giddens that the core teaching of Christ concerning non-retaliation and turning the other cheek was a vital one for international negotiations over climate change. Until some nations take exemplary action and abandon the game of tit for tat in international relations, no breakthrough can be imagined in these negotiations; but such an approach—a non-retaliatory approach—has the only real prospect of breaking through the logjam. He dismissed this idea, however, as unrealistic. Pragmatic attempts to establish carbon-emissions markets were for him the only game in town, though evidence is piling up that they do not work to restrain fossil fuel use and that they are highly prone to corruption, as are other markets in financial derivatives (Northcott 2014, 122–28). International relations are intrinsically retaliatory and self-interested. And we cannot expect an alternative moral frame to influence it, even when the innocent victims of the failure so to do might include most future human inhabitants of the planet.

Here, then, we arrive at a point where Girard's reading of Christian apocalypse has very interesting resonances with our present predicament. For Girard the apocalyptic discourses in the New Testament are not only concerned to eviscerate the wrath of God, and the idea that God or the gods require human sacrifices to appease them—for they do indeed predict violent events at the end of history of an apocalyptic nature. They also have the intent of predicting that before the Second Coming of Christ, it is entirely possible that humans will nonetheless bring such a violent end upon themselves. For Girard this violent end now seems increasingly likely. The twentieth century has been so dramatically marred by such world-encompassing events as the two world wars and the invention of the atomic bomb that it becomes clear that despite the liberating promise of Christ's teaching to enable humanity after his resurrection to establish a peaceable Kingdom, the apocalyptic nature of the present age and its headlong rush to a violent end of history indicates that Christianity has failed in this historic mission:

> Christianity is the only religion that has foreseen its own failure. This prescience is known as the apocalypse. Indeed, it is in the apocalyptic texts that the word of God is most forceful, repudiating mistakes that are entirely the fault of humans, who are less and less inclined to acknowledge the mechanisms of their violence. The longer we persist in our error, the stronger God's voice will emerge from the devastation. This is why no one wants to read the apocalyptic texts that abound in the synoptic gospels and Pauline epistles. This is also why no one wants to recognize that these texts rise up before us because we have disregarded the Book of Revelation. Once in our history the *truth about the identity of all humans was spoken,* and no one wanted to hear it; instead we hang on ever more frantically to our false differences. (Girard 2007, 10–11 [2010, x])

In the passion of Christ, human beings once and for all were released from the bindings that, from the murder of Abel by Cain onwards, had shackled them to the iron law of mimetic violence and sacrificial scapegoating. But—and here is the twist that Girard adds to an otherwise relatively orthodox and even Augustinian reading of Christian history:

> The incredible paradox that no-one is willing to accept is that Passion turned violence loose at the same time that it set holiness free. The modern form of the sacred is thus not a [simple] return to some archaic form. It is a sacred that has been satanized by the awareness we have of it, and it indicates, through its excesses, the imminence of the Second Coming. (Girard 2007, 12 [2010, xi])

Girard argues that human beings now have the means to destroy the world. For Girard the means are primarily those of total war, as he indicates in *Battling to the End* and in the conclusion to an article in *First Things* (2009). Total war is the new condition of warfare first identified, Girard claims, by von Clausewitz in the nineteenth century in the course of the Napoleonic wars; these set the stage for the totalizing claims of the German state in the twentieth century, and the blitzkrieg that the Third Reich ultimately unleashed on Europe, but they also usher in, more obliquely, the era of ecological crisis.

"Apocalypse," in the sense of a total catastrophe comparable to some divine liquidation of all things, is thus the logical outcome of the trend to total war that Clausewitz first identified. But Christ's nonviolent teaching and his willingness to suffer innocently and be the ultimate scapegoat creates hope even in the face of potential annihilation, since seeing the possibility of apocalypse reverses the claims of modernity that the world of nature as a world of objects lacks subjectivity and therefore lacks meaning intrinsic to itself.

Here Girard is at one with Rowland and Bauckham and, indeed, William Blake. The recognition of the potential of apocalypse at the end of modernity unmasks the claims of science and technology to redeem the human condition through industrialism. The antidote to these salvific claims is to recognize that the sacrifices imposed on workers in grim factories where they must work without days off for weeks at a time and the sacrifices of soldiers in wars putatively "against terror" in regions where the great game for oil and gas continues represent the attempted revival of the archaic-sacrificial sweep of the old religions that Christ's death and resurrection was supposed to have swept away.

The hope remains that even in the midst of this attempted revival, there is a virtuous Christian way that Christ has already exemplified; and that

Christians are still called to live as if it were true, even as the true meaning of the subjection of the present civilization to the false religion becomes ever more evident:

> To make the revelation wholly good and not threatening at all, humans have only to adopt the behavior recommended by Christ: abstain completely from retaliation and renounce the escalation to extremes. For if that escalation continues, it will lead straight to the extinction of all life on the planet. (Girard 2007, 18 [2010, 14])

And at this point, Girard sounds perhaps more theological than in any previous place in his writings. For the destiny of those who renounce violence in a world in which violence threatens even the extinction of life on earth is participation in the divine kingdom that reaches beyond space and time:

> Christ came to reveal that his kingdom was not of this world but that humans, once they have understood the mechanisms of their own violence, can have an accurate intuition of the divinity beyond it. We can all participate in the divinity of Christ so long as we renounce our own violence. (Girard 2007, 19 [2010, xv–xvi])

The imminent catastrophe envisioned by our own contemporary era appears, in the retrospect of this perspective, to amount to a secular reversal of the gospel-proclaimed apocalypse of the Second Coming. Instead of a truly holy end to history,[3] in the return of Christ to rule the earth, technologically enabled humanity has acquired such technological prowess, and such power over nature, that humans now have the means to destroy the world through total war. "Ye shall be as gods, knowing good and evil": the mirific promise of the Serpent of Genesis has never been writ larger than in the era first identified by Clausewitz during the Napoleonic wars as the era of total war—the era that conceived in turn the specter of nuclear annihilation and ecological apocalypse that now shapes the twenty-first century.

Yet we can see that the very notion of apocalypse, in its proper—Christian—sense, has here been immanentized and reappropriated by the various discourses of technological dominion and of the all-too-human variations on the theme of "godlikeness." For this new form of "secular apocalypse" declares, if we follow a carefully considered Girardian reading, its ambiguous filiation, in keeping with what Girard calls our time of transition. On the one hand it is secretly related to the old forms of the archaic sacred, ever-predicated on the "catastrophic" significance of the mimetic crisis, with its crescendo toward paroxysm; and, on the other hand, contrastively, it calls to the nonviolence of Christ, and his willingness to suffer innocently and be the ultimate scapegoat.

Seen in this second aspect, modern catastrophism or secular apocalypticism (as we may henceforth prefer to term it) creates the opportunity for a antipodally different kind of mimesis by the followers of Christ who, in imitating Christ's nonviolence and his willingness to suffer innocently on behalf of others, sustain hope even in the face of potential annihilation.

Conclusion

In this perspective, the apocalyptic pronouncements of military strategists, and even of some scientists, about the imminent threat of climate meltdown represent at best a pale imitation of the apocalypse of the New Testament, for they give no grounds for hope that extinction is not the end, or that ultimately non-retaliation and peace will be revealed as the true meaning of history.

This also helps to explain why investigations into climate-change discourse indicate that the tendency of scientists and others to paint apocalyptic scenarios of the extreme consequences of climate change are disabling and fail to promote the more hopeful scenario in which nations, corporations, and consumers reduce their demands on the planet and its atmospheric "sinks" and accept the simpler and de-energized way of life that the crisis demands.

Even though we may, with Clausewitz, know that humans will refuse to renounce violence, yet the gospel of nonviolence and the Peaceable Kingdom that is not of this world sustain Christians in the hope that beyond the end of history, beyond even the extinction of life itself, there is a divine Beyond, which is the destiny and the present justification of those who refuse to participate in the *spiritual violence* of "crescendo towards paroxysm."

Notes

1. "Seeing No Evil on Climate-gate," *Investors Business Daily,* February 12, 2009.

2. See also the analogous message of Pahl and Wellman in "Empire of Sacrifice: Violence and the Sacred in American Culture" in the present volume.

3. Girard specializes the use of the word "sacred" anthropologically, so that it applies only to the darker or more demonic numinous intuitions, grasped "from below."

Cited Texts and Further Reading

Bauckham, Richard. 1993. *The Theology of the Book of Revelation.* Cambridge: Cambridge University Press.

Berger, Peter. 1967. *The Sacred Canopy.* Harmondsworth, UK: Penguin.

Berry, Wendell. 1978. "Living in the Future: The Modern Agricultural Ideal." In *The Unsettling of America,* ed. W. Berry. San Francisco: Sierra Club Books.

Boykoff, Maxwell T. 2007. "From Convergence to Contention: United States Mass Media Representations of Anthropogenic Climate Change Science." *Transactions of the Institute of British Geographers* 32.

Burke, Marshall B., Edward Miguel, Shanker Satyanath, John A. Dykema, and David B. Lobell. 2009. "Warming Increases the Risk of Civil War in Africa." *Proceedings of the National Academy of Sciences* 106 (December): 20670–74.

Crutzen, Paul. 2006. "The Anthropocene." In *Earth System Science in the Anthropocene: Emerging Issues and Problems,* ed. Eckart Ehlers and Thomas Krafft. New York: Springer.

Ebaugh, Helen Rose. 2002. "Presidential Address 2001: Return of the Sacred: Reintegrating Religion and the Social Sciences." *Journal for the Scientific Study of Religion* 41.

Feng, Shuaizhang, Alan B. Krueger, and Michael Oppenheimer. 2010. "Linkages among Climate Change, Crop Yields and Mexico-US Cross-Border Migration." *PNAS* 107: 14257–62.

Girard, René. 2008. *Evolution and Conversion.* With Pierpaolo Antonello and João Cezar de Castro Rocha. New York: Continuum.

———. 2009. "On War and Apocalypse." *First Things* (August/September). Http://www.firstthings.com/article/2009/07/apocalypse-now.

———. 2010. *Battling to the End: Conversations with Benoît Chantre.* Translated by M. Baker. East Lansing: Michigan State University Press.

Hendrix, Cullen S., and Idean Salehyan. 2012. "Climate Change, Rainfall, and Social Conflict in Africa." *Journal of Peace Research* 49: 35–50.

Maibach, E., J. Witte, and K. Wilson. 2011. "'Climategate': Undermined Belief in Global Warming among Many American TV Meteorologists." *Bulletin of the American Meteorological Society* 92.

Marvin, C., and D. W. Ingle. 1999. *Blood Sacrifice and the Nation: Totem Rituals and the American Flag.* Cambridge: Cambridge University Press.

McIntosh, Alastair. 2008. *Hell and High Water: Climate Change, Hope and the Human Condition.* Edinburgh: Birlinn.

Nerlich, Brigitte. 2010. "'Climategate': Paradoxical Metaphors and Political Paralysis." *Environmental Values* 19.

Northcott, Michael. 2004. *An Angel Directs the Storm: Apocalyptic Religion and American Empire.* London: I. B. Tauris.

———. 2005. "Atonement, Violence, and Modern Imperial Order." In *Consuming Passion: Why the Killing of Jesus Really Matters,* ed. Simon Barrow and Jonathan Bartley. London: Darton, Longman and Todd, 89–98.

———. 2014. *A Political Theology of Climate Change.* London: SPCK.

Ragnhild, Nordas, and Nils Peter Gleditsch. 2007. "Climate Change and Conflict." *Political Conflict* 26.

Rowland, Christopher C. 2002. *The Open Heaven: A Study of Apocalyptic in Judaism and Early Christianity.* Eugene, OR: Wipf and Stock.

Schellnhuber, H. J. 1999. "'Earth System' Analysis and the Second Copernican Revolution." *Nature* 402: C19–23.

Smith, Paul. 2007. "Climate Change, Mass Migration and the Military Response." *Orbis* 51: 617–33.

Sullivan, Gordon R., Frank Bowman, Lawrence P. Farrell, et al. 2007. *National Security and the Threat of Climate Change.* Alexandria, VA: CNA Corporation.

Veblen, Thorstein. 1902. *The Theory of the Leisure Class: An Economic Study of Institutions.* New York: Macmillan.

Wannenwetsch, Bernd. 2007. "The Desire of Desire: Commandment and Idolatry in Late Capitalist Societies." In *Idolatry: False Worship in the Bible, Early Judaism, and Christianity,* ed. Stephen Barton. London: T&T Clark.

A New Heaven and a New Earth

Apocalypticism and Its Alternatives

Michael Kirwan

G irard's engagement with "the apocalyptic theme" would appear to be more recent than his classic preoccupation with "sacrifice," spun out over the last forty years. Commentators have discerned an "apocalyptic turn" in his writings since 2001. The atrocity of 9/11 and the conflicts generated by it are for Girard one signal marker of a phase change ushering in the era of a newly unbridled "escalation to extremes," a globalized relaunching of the age-old dynamic of violence between nations and groups.

This phenomenon, he thinks, is something that we can no longer hope to keep under control by "sacrificial" means, such as the traditional institution of "limited" warfare, i.e., warfare in which the supposition of limitability (in respect of its restricted and local theater of conflict, of the weapons and tactics employed, and of the actors put at risk by the contagion of violence) *still holds,* as was the case in Europe up until the First World War. Girard's riposte to the nineteenth-century Prussian theorist Carl von Clausewitz is that warfare can today *no longer* be considered the "continuation of diplomacy by other means."

According to this view, our situation is unprecedented and immensely serious; only the language and conceptuality of "apocalypse" approaches adequacy in helping us to comprehend it; and adequate understanding is, even then, to be achieved at the price of a strenuous clarification of this complex and ambiguous notion. These are the tasks I propose to undertake here.

With this more recent theme, therefore, and for the second time, Girard articulates a key theological-anthropological discovery by means of a powerful but problematic religious concept—the difference between these two cases being that whereas he argued for a *rejection* of "sacrificial" thinking and practice in the name of the Christian revelation (a stance he was later to revise markedly), he now argues—albeit again, in the name of Christian truth—in *favor* of "apocalypse" as an essential hermeneutical key for the contemporary epoch of human culture.

Why does Girard stake his intellectual credibility at all on such a charged, freighted, and easily misunderstood notion? How is his use of this term different from that of the frenzied soothsayers of the "Left Behind" mentality—a resentful remnant awaiting their rapturous summons to heaven, whence they can watch with satisfaction the destruction of evildoers? As indicated above, an answer to these questions demands attention to the journey of transvaluation that this concept undergoes from our evolutionary beginnings.

The present investigation demands that we combine three strands of thinking, not all of which will be represented equally here. Firstly, it requires an evolutionary psycho-poetics of the apocalyptic imagination; we are, it increasingly seems, "hard-wired" by our evolutionary origins to experience the world as tending toward the paroxysm of some quasi-mimetic crisis. More exactly, we are conditioned by the *logic of evolutionary survival* to anticipate and react to disaster; and so we tend to decipher world process anthropomorphically, through the category-lens of threat-rising-to-paroxysm, hence in terms of terminal crisis. The crisis we fear is always a crisis of undifferentiation, involving the effacement of important distinguishing markers between individuals and groups. The "apocalypticist" identification of good and bad parties in a cosmic struggle, for instance, makes functionally rational sense in this perspective, as a visceral attempt to shore up imperiled categories of difference. We aspire also to a global catharsis, liberating us from metaphysical struggle, as from social disorder and violence, etc. In dealing with the ambiguities of apocalypse, it will be well to remind ourselves that there is an evolution-programmed, "survivalist" *first logic* to this term.[1]

Secondly, there is a historical thesis open to pursuit and worth pursuing within this same logic: that the origins of our current crisis are to be found in the French Revolution and its Napoleonic aftermath, in which the first mass mobilization for warfare constituted a fateful escalation of the conflict between Germany and France, foreshadowing the era of violence unlimited; this, responding to Clausewitz, is Girard's thesis in *Battling to the End* (2007 [2010]).

Thirdly, there is a biblical-theological strand: in the gospels, in the Book of Revelation, and in other scriptural apocalyptic texts, we discover a reworking of the entire *first logic* of the archaic sacred, centering precisely on the notion of apocalypse (literally: "unveiling," "revelation"), and offering instead a radically *alternative consummation* in "a new heaven and a new earth." This alternative imagining is the eschatological realization of the strictly nonviolent coming of the Kingdom of God (an alternative that is conveyed effectively by James Alison's theological distinction between the "apocalyptic" and "eschatological" imagination [Alison 2010, 125]). We enter here a second logic of discourse, which might be termed "salvific," as distinct from "survivalist."

My own argument here, woven from these strands, will unfold in four stages. Firstly, we will note the ambiguity within theological tradition, but also within the biblical texts themselves, regarding apocalyptic ways of thinking. Secondly, the alleged "apocalyptic turn" in MT (mimetic theory) will be examined, in Girard's *Battling to the End* and other texts. Thirdly, the suggested parallelism between "sacrifice" and "apocalyptic" will be explicated in terms of René Girard's settled position on the former, which is most profitably rendered as an "exodus from sacrifice" (Keenan's useful shorthand term; Keenan 2003). Finally, some concluding remarks will attempt to clarify the overall argument of Girard's *Battling to the End* with reference to its fifth chapter (on "Hölderlin's Sorrow"), and to themes advanced in the preceding chapters of this section.

Apocalyptic Affirmation and the Counter-persuasion of Gospel "Reticence"

We need to begin this exploration from a serviceable definition of "apocalypse," functioning at three levels. It has to help us to distinguish the secular, and popular, sense, such as we find in sensationalist predictions ("The End of the World is Nigh," etc.) from two more specialized, academic usages: firstly, that of contemporary philosophy, where arguments are deployed in favor of and against an apocalyptic hermeneutic; and secondly, the more technical discussions conducted within biblical scholarship (without ever implying, or even aspiring to, any definite and defining consensus among the army of exegetes who have addressed this theme). Insofar as Girard, and MT after him, engage with apocalyptic thought, they do so to some extent on all three levels.

Slavoj Žižek's *Living in the End Times* (Žižek 2010) analyzes the end of the world at the hands of the "four riders of the apocalypse": the world-wide ecological crisis; economic imbalances; the biogenetic revolution; and exploding social divisions and ruptures. He suggests that our collective responses to this onslaught correspond to the classic stages of grief, including denial, anger, and depression. On the other hand, Jacques Derrida (1982, 1984), in his cry "No Apocalypse, Not Now," famously warns against the new apocalyptic tone in philosophy, while Carlo Martini's response to Umberto Eco plays down the significance of the "new apocalyptic" (Eco and Martini 2000).

There is indeed biblical warrant for resisting such "fascination." In Mark 13, Jesus describes how many people will lay claim to apocalyptic insight:

> And if anyone says to you then, "Look, here is the Christ" or "Look, he is there," do not believe it; for false Christs and false prophets will arise and produce signs and portents to deceive the elect, if that were possible. You therefore must be on your guard. (Mk. 13:21–23)
> They will say to you, "Look there!" or, "Look here!" Make no move; do not set off in pursuit. (Lk. 17:23)

The same ambiguity is noted by Józef Niewiadomski, in a chapter of *Politics and Apocalypse* (2007) entitled "'Denial of the Apocalypse' versus 'Fascination with the Final Days.'" The early Christian belief in further apocalyptic convulsions, despite their firm conviction of Christ's eschatological victory and of Christ's Lordship over the cosmos, might appear something of a puzzle . . . at least until we recall the "apocalyptic times," the potent persuasion of the evolution-programmed human imagination, already alluded to, and the long and tortuous subsequent history of Christian exegesis in separating out "salvific" gospel truth from popular or "survivalist" apocalypticism. Aligning the expectation of ongoing struggle in the ordinary time of this world's history with the radically novel christological *once-and-for-all* in "vertical" time cannot have been an easy task. The more dramatic the theological perspective, the more "the analogies and differences between legitimate Christian apocalyptic expectations and the undifferentiated fascination with apocalyptic scenarios become apparent" (Niewiadomski 2007, 60). Jesus explicitly rejected the apocalyptic expectations of his environment; and, by disavowing any knowledge of dates and times, he enabled a new, "personalist" confidence in the power of God, as subject and prime actor of history to traverse and inflect human time, while allowing it to emerge culturally as a received perspective of faith.

This scripturally warranted *reticence* with regard to apocalyptic thinking is not adduced here as a counterargument to the "apocalyptic turn" in MT, but very much as a dimension of it and a tool for understanding it. As we shall argue below, the ambivalence of "apocalypse" is structurally parallel to that of "sacrifice" in MT, an ambivalence we are seeking to explicate by means of "survivalist" and "salvific" understandings of apocalypse.

It seems appropriate, therefore, to begin with a broad definition that does not in fact foreground the question of violence:

> "Apocalypse" is a genre of revelatory literature with a narrative framework, in which a revelation is mediated by an otherworldly being to a human recipient, disclosing a transcendent reality. (Collins 1979, 9: see introduction)

The essential feature of the genre "apocalypse" is therefore the *unveiling of divine mysteries,* also and even referring to visions of God himself. In this sense, the theophanies in chapters 4–5 of Revelation, and in Ezekiel chapter 1, are "apocalyptic," as is the experience of Paul in being "caught up into paradise" (2 Cor. 12:1–10). From a purely definitional point of view, there is no apparent intrinsic connection between apocalyptic and violence in the second or "revised" logic of Christian revelation. Robert Hamerton-Kelly is able to make such a connection by virtue of the first, "survivalist" logic when he defines apocalypse as "an interpretation of politics in the form of a coded narrative" (Hamerton-Kelly 2007, 5). "Something is being revealed

about our world order, whether by divine grace or human reason." This
revelation not only documents the threat to order, but is itself a cause of
the instability.

James Alison, drawing on Wayne Meeks (Alison 2010, 124), similarly
draws attention to the binary oppositions in the apocalyptic genre, and in
the apocalyptic imagination that gives rise to it: cosmic (heaven and earth);
temporal (now and the age to come); social (division between righteous and
unrighteous). The apocalyptic imagination is partial, because it is the imagining of God's eschatological vengeance on behalf of the persecuted righteous;
it is stuck within the notion of a violent God. For this reason, Jesus's discourse
about the end time, insofar as it eschews these dualities, is to be understood
as a *subversion from within* of the apocalyptic imagination, using its language
and imagery to say something different. This practice Alison refers to as the
"eschatological imagination" (125).

The above-mentioned dualities are not deconstructed by Alison for
the sake of it, but so that social bonds may be redefined and reestablished
around the person of the victim: the marginalized sufferers in Matthew 25,
or the stricken traveler in Luke 10. The status of the victim takes precedence
over all other identifying markers, especially those of religious or national
belonging. Above all, by dissolving the distinction between righteous and
wicked (cf. the Matthean parables of the wheat and tares, and the catch of
fish), it becomes impossible to maintain the apocalyptic imagination, understood as "the increasingly fear-laden and violent dualistic way of thinking in
which God and the violence of our world are confused together" (Alison
2010, 203). Such a mindset is subverted by the eschatological imagination:
something fixed on God, and which is entirely without violence, and which
Jesus taught and teaches us.

The "Apocalyptic Turn" in Mimetic Theory (MT)

In his postface to the second edition of *Raising Abel,* James Alison emphasizes
the importance of *Battling to the End* in crystallizing for him the enormous
difference between these two imaginations. Girard offers us, says Alison,
"the possibility of the first genuinely post-Hegelian account of Christian
eschatology and apocalyptic" (2010, 204)—an account, in other words, that

impels us to confront, without facile optimism, and without any overarching event-narrative, the true state of affairs in which we find ourselves.

Alison's preferred strategy for describing the semantic transvaluation is therefore to introduce an absolute distinction between "apocalypse" and "eschatology." Other commentators variously render this passage as a transition from "bad" to "good" apocalyptic, or else to "ironic" apocalypse. Despite Alison's firm renunciation of the term "apocalyptic," it may be expedient here, therefore, not to overemphasize the terminology itself, since the process being variously described looks much the same under differing labels.

According to Robert Hamerton-Kelly, the attacks of 9/11 and their aftermath in creating a "globalized civil war" have created a heightened sense of history and its convulsions. These in turn have initiated a significant change in Girard's mimetic theory, an "apocalyptic turn" (2007, 5) that Hamerton-Kelly has proposed as constituting a fourth phase in Girard's intellectual career: a historical-apocalyptical analysis, following on his earlier engagements with literature, comparative anthropology, and biblical theology.

This interpretation is formally inscribed in an apocalyptic framework in a collection of essays, *Politics and Apocalypse* (Hamerton-Kelly 2007). Girard himself further articulates the apocalyptic theme in an interview with Robert Doran (Girard 2008) and in *Achever Clausewitz* (*Battling to the End*). The 2008 *Colloquium on Violence and Religion* met in Riverside, California, under the banner of "Politics and Apocalypse." Finally, the Innsbruck theologians committed to the "dramatic theology" have made specific contributions: as well as Józef Niewiadomski's essay in the 2007 volume cited above, we have Karin Peter's dramatic-critical study of the Book of Revelation (Peter 2011). The same year sees a reissue of James Alison's book on eschatology, which we have considered above, with a postface updating the argument since the original edition in 1996.

With the exception of Alison, who eschews the term, these authors regard Girard's mimetic theory as "a form of apocalypse," albeit with a twist:

> Mimetic theory is ironically apocalyptic, because it is the opposite of what normally passes for that genre. It is nonviolent, while the vulgar apocalypse is violent, it decodes while the vulgar encodes, nevertheless, it is apocalyptic because it deals with universal history and human nature and assumes that historiography is possible and the human story is not "a tale told by an

idiot." It is apocalyptic because it decodes the encryption of violence in the vulgar apocalypse, in symbols such as the divine judgment and the torture of the guilty. (Hamerton-Kelly 2007, 15)

Hamerton-Kelly insists that MT was an "apocalyptic theory" from the outset. In his first book, *Deceit, Desire, and the Novel*, Girard has a chapter entitled "The Dostoyevskian Apocalypse," while in his other main works, Girard has developed "an apocalyptic anthropology" that unveils the sacred structure of "this world." In Girard's account of human desire and its inherent instability, we have, *in nuce*, the "escalation to extremes" that Girard later comes to describe in historical-apocalyptic terms.

René Girard declares, "I am a Darwinist; I believe in natural selection" (Girard 2011, 41); he laments, nevertheless, the crucial failure of evolutionary theory to recognize the importance of the mimetic insight. Our evolutionary origins required of us the construction of a behavioral mechanism that will enable us to forestall, and therefore survive, the negative effects of acquisitive mimesis and competition. Such a mechanism proceeds apotropaically, by creation of its own mini-cataclysms; there is an inherent apocalypticism in humanity, therefore. In the last analysis, it is of theological significance: the instability caused by desire for possession denotes a more fundamental lack of being, which is ultimately the dreadful realization that we are not gods.

This is the background to understanding our present crisis, including its religious elements. Girard reaffirms his view that 9/11 is a continuation and intensification of mimetic conflict (Girard 2008, 20), expressing a concern that, seven years on, people are becoming forgetful of 9/11. Of course, the temptation to "consecrate" Ground Zero as a place of spectacular, cathartic grief (leading to violent mobilization) needs to be resisted. Nevertheless, 9/11 represents a unique and seminal event, "a strange return of the archaic within the secularism of our time" (25). The globalized threat is more powerful even than communism, because of its religious dimension. "We must be willing to think in a wider context, and in my view this wider context is the apocalyptic dimension of Christianity" (25).

Apocalyptic language is essential for describing this situation, provided we do not equate it with pessimism. Our situation is, rather, a mixture of good and bad (Girard quotes Maritain, to the effect that "there is more good and more bad in the world all the time"). Nor may we forget that apocalyptic

violence is the violence not of God, but strictly of God's creatures, and sig-
nally of human beings. The threats that now face us are entirely real, and
entirely comprehensible according to biblical apocalyptic. However, this is a
very different set of claims from those of fundamentalists who see ultimate
violence as coming from God, not humanity.

The difference is stated by S. Mark Heim, who considers "two kinds of
apocalypse" (Heim 2006). Apocalypse is a genre of violence, oriented toward
the final resolution of world history and the fate of human community. Texts
such as Revelation offer absolutely contrasting alternatives—the reign of God
and that of the anti-Christ—which can nevertheless look identical. Apocalypses describe the increased violence that may stem from the unmasking of
violence: like the increased dosage of a medicine that is no longer working,
"the sacrificial solution is applied with redoubled, even frenzied effort, but
with diminishing success" (Heim 2006, 264).

Like Alison, Heim articulates apocalyptic in terms of polarities: predic-
tion of violence/God requiring violence; violence resulting from human fac-
tionalism/cosmic warfare; God's wrathful anger against violence/righteous
exercise of violence. "Biblical apocalyptic texts combine these features in
different proportions," though it is in the gospels that we find a preponder-
ance of the first element of each polarity ("good" apocalypse). The "little
apocalypses" of Mark 13 and Luke 17 do not speak of a cosmic battle, but of
an entirely human conflict, "just as it was in the days of Noah." By contrast,
the Book of Revelation tells of the wrath of God, exercised on behalf of the
slain martyrs who cry for justice from the altar of holocausts.

The final book of the Bible seems, therefore, to mirror the sacrificial
violence that is being overcome. Nevertheless, as Heim points out, the *true*
ending of the Bible is neither the self-destruction of the world, nor a climactic battle. It is, rather, "a new creation into which people are adopted," the
New Jerusalem coming down from heaven. For Heim, this ironic, subversive quality is more evident in the Synoptic passages (specifically Mark 13)
than in Revelation, in which more traditional patterns of violence (God's
punishment, cosmic war) predominate. By contrast, Hamerton-Kelly sees a
cumulative witness in the various texts, including the Synoptic Gospel and
the Book of Revelation.

The Book of Revelation would appear to be what Girard would refer to
as a "mixed text," or a text "in travail." Walter Brueggemann speaks of texts

that are to be read from "within the fray" and "above the fray"; this one is written, surely, by and for people who are struggling *within the vortex of mimetic contagion,* rather than from a position of serene detachment above it. Particularly problematic passages would include the cries for vengeance from the martyrs (Rev. 6:9–10), and the extraordinary "mythologizing" events of chapter 11:3–13, in which the two unnamed corpses are resuscitated and a retributionary earthquake kills seven thousand people.

Once again we may note the theological insistence that it is the gospels that interpret the last book of the Bible, not the other way round. Revelation's narratives of righteous devastation and full-scale cosmic war are situated in the middle of the book; they are by no means climactic. We must not let ourselves be duped into according this strange book a definitive authority, simply because it occurs at the end of the Bible: "[These texts] need to be interpreted from the centre of the Passion narratives and the Gospels rather than the other way round" (Heim 2006, 268).

Apocalypse and Sacrifice: The Girardian "Exodus" from Each

Józef Niewiadomski (2007) concurs with the general argument of this chapter when he notes that Girard's use of "apocalyptic" is best understood in the light of Girard's engagement with "sacrifice." Just as MT rests upon a hard-won but clearly articulated distinction between two kinds of "sacrificial" mentality, so the present phase of MT draws attention to two ways in which we might make sense of the language of apocalypse. Girard's mature position on sacrifice coincides with what the French theologian Louis-Marie Chauvet describes as an "anti-sacrificial" position, more vividly understood as an "exodus from sacrifice." If the parallel holds, we may speak of an "exodus from apocalypse," a *"taking leave" of the popular understanding of apocalypse as divinely sanctioned violence.*

The position of Girard, and of mimetic theory, on the question of sacrifice should by now be a question resolved and closed; though for some reason Girard continues to be misrepresented by his critics as a "straw man" advocate of the exclusion of sacrificial categories from Christian discourse. Nevertheless, Girard's "repentance," and his acknowledgment that his earlier polemic on sacrifice was mistaken, is by now very fully established, in an interview with Rebecca Adams (Girard and Adams 1993; partly reproduced in *The Girard Reader* 1996), and in his subsequent writings.

Adams asks Girard whether in *Things Hidden* he had fixed on the Epistle to the Hebrews as the sacrificial "bad father" (Girard and Adams 1993, 28). He concedes that he did indeed "scapegoat" the book of Hebrews, as well as the word "sacrifice," expecting the author to use the same vocabulary as himself. Hebrews's description of Christ as the "last sacrifice" is in fact perfectly compatible with Girard's own theory: there is "no serious problem." Girard refers us to the end of *Things Hidden*, where he declares that "the changes in the meaning of the word 'sacrifice' contain a whole history, a religious history, of mankind" (1987, 29). He also softens his opposition to the term "self-sacrifice," to which he had previously objected because of a psychoanalytical "phobia" with regard to all sacrificial language. The importance is noted of the biblical story of the Judgment of Solomon for liberating him from this phobia: the story records "good" and "bad" sacrificial practice, in which the life-giving sacrifice of the "real" mother is entirely free of masochism.

Girard has given at least two other accounts of why he "scapegoated sacrifice," which interestingly contrast with one another. In the *Festschrift* for Raymund Schwager's sixtieth birthday (Niewiadomski and Wandinger 2003), he congratulates Schwager for his boldness when Girard himself was hesitant, for apologetic reasons, to blur what he saw as the crucial difference between the Christian revelation and other religions:

> I believed that the overriding significance of the mimetic theory had to be in directing all apologetic efforts against religious relativism. It was to expose its weaknesses. I wanted nothing other than to make even more precise the clarity of this position, which pressed upon me almost like a proof. A recourse to the concept of sacrifice, which already designated the rite of archaic religions, as a description of the Passion of Jesus, stood in the way of me and my program. I was afraid that the traditional definition of the Passion in terms of the concept of sacrifice would supply so many additional arguments for assimilating Christianity to the category of archaic religion. For this reason I have for a long time considered this usage to be degenerate. (Niewiadomski and Palaver 1995, 24 [trans. MK])

Girard sought a "non-sacrificial" understanding of the Judeo-Christian revelation, a quest he now recognized as mistaken: firstly, because the separation for which he so ardently tried to argue is in no way necessary; secondly, because recourse to the same word to describe different types of sacrifice is in fact a testimony to the paradoxical unity of all religions in actual human history. Interestingly, in the interview with Robert Doran, fourteen years later, Girard's apologia is slightly different:

> Christianity has always been sacrificial. It's true I gave the non-sacrificial interpretation [in *Things Hidden*] too much importance—in order to be heretical. That is what was left of the avant-gardist attitude in me. I had to be against the Church in some way. The attitude was instinctive, since my whole intellectual training came out of surrealism, existentialism and so forth, which were all anti-Christian. (2008, 30)

Girard's mature position on sacrifice is identical to the "anti-sacrificial" approach defined by Louis-Marie Chauvet. Chauvet notes that a text such as the Letter to the Hebrews is a transmutation or subversion of the Old Testament cult, whereby the priesthood of Jesus (descending, kenotic, in solidarity with human beings) is expressed in terms directly opposite to those of the latter (Israelite) priesthood (ascending, separatist). Jesus's priesthood and sacrifice were exercised "existentially and not ritually" (Chauvet 1995, 299).

Chauvet proposes a third option, "anti-sacrifice," between the Girardian dichotomy of sacrifice and non-sacrifice. These distinctions may become clearer if we turn to Dennis Keenan, a philosopher. Keenan notes that we have plenty of reasons for giving up on the concept of sacrifice altogether, given the systematically distorting structural features, such as economics, sexism, and Christo-centric evolutionism. However, such an abandonment would be

> a sacrifice of sacrifice, which, if performed naively (i.e., without dwelling with the question of sacrifice), would unwittingly preserve some form of sacrifice. One would be duped into believing that one could be done with sacrifice, which could then return (relatively unchanged) in far more subtle and pernicious forms ... one is called to remain attentive to the irreducible ambiguity of the sacrifice of sacrifice. (Keenan 2005, 14)

Keenan speaks of an "exodus from sacrifice," which would avoid the "gnostic" denial of the sacrificial pattern within each of us (the mistake of the Pharisees who assure Jesus that scapegoating was something their ancestors did, and not they themselves). There is, instead, the never-ending task of conversion.

Chauvet, once again: "The anti-sacrificial regimen to which the gospel calls us *rests upon* the sacrificial, but it does so to turn it around and thereby to redirect ritual practice; it is in ethical practice where the ritual practice is verified" (Chauvet 1995, 307). The evidence points to "an undeniable anti-sacrificial and anti-priestly subversion. . . . From now on . . . the sacred work, the cult, the sacrifice that is pleasing to God, is the confession of faith lived in the *agape* of sharing in service to the poorest, of reconciliation and of mercy" (Chauvet 1995, 260). An "exodus from sacrifice" implies, therefore, not an abandonment of the concept altogether, but a recognition of its transformation and subversion as, simply, "a religious history of humanity." The term is also a reminder of the dangers of regression to archaic sacrifice; just as the Israelites' annual ritual celebration of the Exodus was an important way of acknowledging, and thereby preserving, their status as a free people.

Can the same move be made for "apocalyptic"? To abandon the concept altogether, because of its unsavory association with resentful violence, is to hazard a "return of the repressed." The same applies to the appropriate treatment of apocalyptic texts, such as the Book of Revelation. The impression of a structural symmetry between the place of sacrifice in mimetic theory and that of apocalypse is reinforced when we consider that not a few scholars would like to see the Book of Revelation removed from the canon, just as Girard himself sought to "expel" the Letter to the Hebrews, in each case because of their regression to sacralized violence. D. H. Lawrence puts the case bluntly:

> No, we can understand that the Fathers of the Church in the East wanted Apocalypse left out of the New Testament. But like Judas among the disciples, it was inevitable that it should be included. The Apocalypse is the feet of clay to the grand Christian image. And down crashes the image, on the weakness of those very feet. There is Jesus—but there is also John the Divine. There is Christian love—and there is Christian envy. The former would "save" the world—the latter will never be satisfied till it has

destroyed the world. They are two sides of the same medal. (Lawrence
1931, 144)

How then is a "scapegoating" of the Book of Revelation to be avoided?
Some form of what exegetes describe as canonical "kenneling" seems to be
required, such as we find in Mark Heim and others, that "[These apocalyptic
texts] need to be interpreted from the center of the Passion narratives and
the Gospels rather than the other way round" (Heim 2006, 268). It is hard to
avoid the conclusion that its location as the last book of the Christian testament has given Revelation a spurious climactic authority, whereas in fact it
is a "mixed text," struggling to free itself from the fray of sacred resentment.

"Come, Lord Jesus": From Divine Promiscuity to Divine Presence

This chapter has articulated the salient aspects of "Girardian apocalyptic" by
means of a suggested isomorphic relation to "Girardian sacrifice." It is in this
light that we can turn once again to the preceding chapters, which read the
nuclear arms race and the ecological crisis respectively in terms of mimetic
theory and apocalypse.

Jean-Pierre Dupuy judges us to be in a transitional zone of "patchy half-
light and half-protection" in which our theoretical knowledge of the failure
of this archaic god is not enough to alter our behavior toward it. What distance we have from the "classical" Cold War up to 1989 allows us to see the
sacrificial dimension of the logic of "Mutually Assured Destruction," which
required whole populations on either side of the Iron Curtain to be left
unprotected from annihilation. According to Dupuy, the truth is even more
disturbing: what the various political memoirs and archival records from this
period make clear is that the determining factor was not the rational calculation between two adversaries, but their mutual deference to a fictitious
entity: Fate, humanity's double, its own violence externalized, was entrusted
with enforcing the deterrence of which each side was incapable.

While this aspect of the arms race has affinities to the archaic sacred,
Girard has been at pains to stress that what countered the threat, in part
at least, was the fact that both sides operated within a humanistic logic,

recognizable from a gospel perspective. Khrushchev in 1962 "turns the other cheek" as the resolution of the Cuban missile crisis. Girard's current anxiety stems from the fact that in a struggle against fundamentalist combatants engaged in cosmic warfare, such a humanistic background can no longer be taken for granted.

It might also be alleged that the recession of Cold War angst with the fall of the Communist bloc in 1989 has allowed something of a "remission" of the escalation to extremes, such that it is possible still for world leaders to prolong the illusion of a salvific violence. The military campaigns in Afghanistan and Iraq witness to our persistent dream of a consummative, revolutionary act of violence, at once wholly modern and fully apocalyptic; "perfect" in the double sense of morally justified but also definitive and complete.

Dupuy regards the Cold War as one act of homage to our externalized violence, a "false god" as implacable as the most destructive forces of nature. For Michael Northcott, the crisis of anthropogenic climate change is that of an "end of history," which could not be more different from the immanentist triumphs envisaged by Hegel and Fukuyama. Here it is "the new religion of capitalism," rather than the arms race, that functions "sacrificially": its irrevocable destruction of the earth's resources constitutes a "crescendo towards paroxysm," destined to escalate in the struggle for global economic domination between the United States and China. This paroxysm is structurally similar to that of the Cold War, and is likewise to be read in terms of a Clausewitzian escalation of violence with no logical limit. Earth's "backlash," in terms of extreme and catastrophic weather conditions, clearly invites a Girardian reading of classic "signs" of apocalyptic disintegration: natural disorder aligned with divine wrath.

In each case, we stand on the edge of the abyss.

If Girard's analysis is correct, and if a disastrous propulsion over the edge is to be avoided, then we require nothing less than a "rewiring" of our evolutionary circuitry. The "apocalyptic" surge that has enabled us thus far to "survive our origins," by the restoration and maintenance of differentiation through practices and myths of sacral violence, will no longer serve. "Apocalyptic" must now be subverted, transvalued—something MT has already achieved in relation to the notion of "sacrifice."

There are several ways of describing this process. An absolute distinction between apocalypse and eschatology is one option (Alison); Heim speaks of "good and bad apocalypse," while Hamerton-Kelly describes mimetic theory as "ironically apocalyptic," in contrast to "vulgar apocalypse." We may choose to speak of "descriptive" and "normative" senses of the apocalyptic (by analogy with Robert Daly's discussion of sacrifice); or we may decide that MT adopts an "anti-apocalyptic" position—an "exodus from apocalypse," which nevertheless does not pretend to a "gnostic" renunciation that merely invites a return of the repressed.

"Apocalyptic" covers a huge semantic and conceptual field; the question remains why René Girard chooses the more difficult path of adopting a language and conceptuality that will almost certainly lead, once again, to misunderstanding and distortion. The important answer is that Girard sincerely believes that only this concept, with all its ambiguous biblical, philosophical, and everyday resonances, is adequate to the task. It may also be noted, more generally, that MT relies upon categories—desire, sacrifice—that allow for a broad explanatory reach rather than precisely detailed analysis, and "apocalypse" appears to be one more such category-term.

The lack of precision with each of these terms, which from one angle looks like the Achilles' heel of MT, is perhaps unavoidable if the theory is to do justice to the ambivalence of our situation. It is this ambivalence which Girard finds affirmed in the opening verse of Hölderlin's "Patmos" (2004):

> Near is
> And difficult to grasp, the God.
> But where danger threatens
> That which saves from it also grows.

Friedrich Hölderlin's presence in chapter five of *Battling to the End* is significant. Girard's autobiographical references, in which he expresses deep empathy with Hölderlin's hyper-mimetic struggle, merit close attention. Also, it is in this chapter, rather than in his "conversation" with Clausewitz, that Girard articulates a christological hope, as the only response to mimetic catastrophe. For the poet finally to realize the futility of his project of a "new mythology," a "monotheism of reason and the heart," a "polytheism of imagination and art," he needed to renounce what Girard calls "divine promiscuity" (Girard 2010, 125–26). Only a deepening commitment to Christ, the "Only One," during his years of recuperation, enabled a renunciation of the fevered mimetic imagination that had overwhelmed him: "The *presence* of the divine grows as the divine withdraws: it is the withdrawal that saves, not the promiscuity" (Girard 2010, 122).

Hölderlin's withdrawal replicates Christ's imitation of the Father's withdrawal. By his being handed over to death on the Cross, and then, on the morning of the Resurrection, by "breaking his solar scepter," Christ *withdraws*—at the very moment when he could exercise dominion. There is a mode of divine presence therefore, which is not to be equated with proximity:

> But Christ gives himself up.
> Hercules is like the princes.
> Bacchus is the spirit of the community.
> But Christ is the end.
> The presence
> Which the heavenly beings lack, which
> They cannot give to others,
> Christ gives.

Here, too, is the only possible criterion for judging the adequacy of our apocalyptic thinking: to what extent is it aligned on the Cross of Christ? For Girard, only Christian revelation brings about the immense anthropological reversal required: the subversion from within of the practice of sacrifice, and of an apocalyptic ordering of the universe, which, as we can perhaps now see, are two sides of the same coin. It is interesting to note that while Girard was persuaded by his theological interlocutors to change his mind on sacrifice, when it comes to the subversion of apocalyptic, his strategy is more deliberate—almost as if he is compensating for his earlier reticence. While he accuses himself of timidity with regard to his earlier treatment of "sacrifice," in his forthright assertion of an "apocalyptic hermeneutic" Girard is just the opposite.

This insistence on "Christ, the Only One" raises the vexed question of an alleged Christian exclusivism in Girard's work. While there is no space to address the topic adequately here, it is worth noting a subtle change of emphasis in *Battling to the End*. Girard had previously declared himself to be "anti-Nietzsche," insofar as he sided with Christ "against" Dionysus, while

Nietzsche did the opposite. Girard now argues instead that the Christian revelation has transformed and incorporated the pagan sacred, not simply replaced or superseded it. While he previously opposed religions-and-mythologies to the demystifying antidote they found in Christianity, Girard, in *Battling to the End,* insists that Christianity brings out "what is true in all religions" (2007, 20 [2010, xvi]).

But his insistence that the "hermeneutical key" is the Person of Christ remains unequivocal. It is this christological insistence that enables, finally, a strategy with regard to "apocalyptic" texts. The exegetes offer two possibilities: one is to emphasize the root meaning of apocalypse as "unveiling," and to group together so-called apocalyptic texts as theophanies (Ezekiel, 1 Corinthians, Revelation 4–5), which of themselves do not hint at resentment-fueled violence. Even so, the nettle has to be grasped; and the second option is to make some attempt to "kennel" problematic readings, including the "mythological" passages from the Book of Revelation. Such a procedure requires that the problematic passages be read in the light of the gospel narratives (particularly the Passion accounts), and not vice-versa.

From the perspective of mimetic theory, these approaches are complementary. At the heart of the theory is, precisely, a theophany that is also an "anthropophany." God's self-revelation in the act of withdrawal is simultaneously an exposure of the false sacred, which presents itself as a rivalrous proximity. Christ's mode of presence, however, has nothing to do with the proximity of the false sacred, the effervescent social "other." In John's gospel, and in the Synoptic tradition also, the face of the deity is revealed precisely at the moment of the sacral victim's expulsion, or in the person of the marginalized (Matthew 25). Finally, the enthronement of the Lamb in Revelation is both the apotheosis of the crucified victim and the revelation of the genuine Other, which only such an apotheosis makes possible.

Only when these are kept together can we draw the sting from the ambiguity of these potentially dangerous texts. If the apocalypse does not unveil "the monstrosity of Christ" (Žižek and Milbank 2009), or if the "sacrifice" deciphered is other than the nonviolent and loving sacrifice of Calvary Mount, then neither our apocalyptical thinking nor our sacrificial practices will be of any avail.

It is not too large a simplification to claim that the work of René Girard, as presented in this chapter and in this volume as a whole, can be regarded as an extended meditation upon two important biblical and religious concepts: firstly, sacrifice and then apocalypse. A properly theological elucidation reveals their inner connection in the context of Girard's mimetic theory, and reveals something of the "method" in what otherwise seems to be disturbed and obsessional thinking. The reader of this volume is thus returned to the decision to which Girard continually provokes us, but especially in *Battling to the End:* do we dismiss his insights as the ramblings of a disillusioned sage, or do we recognize in their prophetic vehemence a strategic understanding of the in-between time of our "modernity," precariously advancing between Progress and Abyss?

At least we now have an informed basis for decision.

Notes

1. On this theme, see, in this volume the chapter by Robert Hamerton-Kelly, which nuances considerably the position adopted in the editor's introductory essay of *Politics and Apocalypse* (2007).

Cited Texts and Further Reading

Alison, James. 2010. *Raising Abel.* 2nd ed. London: SPCK.

Astell, Ann, and Sandor Goodhart. 2011. *Sacrifice, Scripture, and Substitution: Readings in Ancient Judaism and Christianity.* Notre Dame, IN: University of Notre Dame Press.

Bauckham, Richard, and Trevor Hart. [1999] 2004. *Hope against Hope: Christian Eschatology in Contemporary Context.* London: Darton, Longmann and Todd.

Chauvet, Louis-Marie. 1995. *Symbol and Sacrament: A Sacramental Reinterpretation of Christian Existence.* Collegeville, MN: Collegeville Liturgical Press.

Collins, John J. 1979. "Apocalypse: The Morphology of a Genre." *Semeia* 14.

Daly, Robert. 1978. *The Origins of the Christian Doctrine of Sacrifice.* Philadelphia: Fortress Press.

———. 2009. *Sacrifice Unveiled: The True Meaning of Christian Sacrifice.* New York: T&T Clark International.

Derrida, Jacques. 1982. "Of an Apocalyptic Tone Recently Adopted in Philosophy." *Semeia* 23: 63–97.

———. 1984. "No Apocalypse, Not Now (full speed ahead, seven missiles, seven missives)." *Diacritics* 14, no. 2: 20–31.

Eco, Umberto, and Cardinal Carlo Martini. [1996] 2000. *Belief or Nonbelief? A Confrontation.* New York: Arcade Publishers.

Finamore, Stephen. 2009. *God, Order, and Chaos: René Girard and the Apocalypse.* Eugene, OR: Wipf and Stock.

Girard, René. 2007. "The Evangelical Subversion of Myth." In *Politics and Apocalypse,* ed. Robert Hamerton-Kelly, 29–49. East Lansing: Michigan State University Press.

———. 2008. "'Apocalyptic Thinking after 9/11': Interview with Robert Doran." *SubStance* 115 (vol. 37, no. 1): 20–32.

———. 2010. *Battling to the End: Conversations with Benoît Chantre.* East Lansing: Michigan State University Press.

———. 2011. "Mimesis, Sacrifice, and the Bible: A Conversation with Sandor Goodhart." In *Sacrifice, Scripture, and Substitution: Readings in Ancient Judaism and Christianity,* ed. Ann Astell and Sandor Goodhart, 39–69. Notre Dame, IN: University of Notre Dame Press.

Girard, René, and Rebecca Adams. 1993. "Violence, Difference, Sacrifice: A Conversation with René Girard." *Religion and Literature* 25, no. 2: 9–33.

Hamerton-Kelly, Robert. 2007. "An Introductory Essay." In *Politics and Apocalypse,* ed. R. Hamerton-Kelly, 1–28. East Lansing: Michigan State University Press.

Heim, S. Mark. 2006. *Saved from Sacrifice: A Theology of the Cross.* Grand Rapids, MI: Eerdmans.

Hölderlin, Friedrich. 2004. *Poems and Fragments.* 4th ed. Translated by Michael Hamburger. London: Anvil Press.

Keenan, Dennis King. 2003. "The Sacrifice of the Eucharist." *Heythrop Journal* 44, no. 2: 182–204.

———. 2005. *The Question of Sacrifice.* Bloomington: Indiana University Press.

Kirwan, Michael. 2007. "Eucharist and Sacrifice." *New Blackfriars* 88, no. 1014 (March 2): 213–27.

———. 2012. "A Candle in Sunshine: Desire and Apocalypse in Blake and Hölderlin." *Contagion: Journal of Violence, Mimesis, and Culture* 19: 179–204.

Lawrence, D. H. 1931. *Apocalypse.* London: Penguin Books.

Niewiadomski, Józef. 2007. "'Denial of the Apocalypse' versus 'Fascination with the Final Days': Current Theological Discussion of Apocalyptic Thinking in the Perspective of Mimetic Theory." In *Politics and Apocalypse,* ed. Robert Hamerton-Kelly, 51–67. East Lansing: Michigan State University Press.

Niewiadomski, Józef, and Nikolaus Wandinger, eds. 2003. *Dramatische Theologie im Gespräch: Symposium/Gastmahl zum 65. Geburtstag von Raymund Schwager. Beiträge zur mimetischen Theorie.* Münster: LIT.

Peter, Karen. 2011. *Apokalyptische Schrifttexte: Gewalt schürend oder transformierend? Ein Beitrag zu einer dramatisch-kritischen Lesart der Offenbarung des Johannes.* Vienna: Lit Verlag.

Wright, N. T. 2011. *Revelation for Everyone.* London: SPCK.

Žižek, Slavoj. 2010. *Living in the End Times.* London and New York: Verso Books.

Žižek, Slavoj, and John Milbank. 2009. *The Monstrosity of Christ: Paradox or Dialectic?* ed. Creston Davis. Cambridge, MA: MIT Press.

About the Authors

PIERPAOLO ANTONELLO is Reader in Italian Literature and Culture at the University of Cambridge, and Fellow of St John's College. He has worked extensively on mimetic theory. With João Cezar de Castro Rocha he published a long interview with René Girard, *Evolution and Conversion: Dialogues on the Origins of Culture* (2008), which has been translated into nine languages. He has also edited several collections of essays and books by Girard, including his dialogue with Gianni Vattimo, *Christianity, Truth and Weakening Faith* (2010). He is a member of the Research and Publications Committee of Imitatio.

SCOTT ATRAN is Research Director in Anthropology at the CNRS (Paris); Visiting Professor of Social Anthropology at both the City University, New York and the University of Michigan; Senior Research Fellow at Harris Manchester College, University of Oxford; and Research Director at ARTIS International. His publications include *Cognitive Foundations of Natural History: Towards an Anthropology of Science* (1993); *In Gods We Trust: The Evolutionary Landscape of Religion* (2002); *The Native Mind and the Cultural Construction of Nature* (2010); and *Talking to the Enemy: Violent Extremism, Sacred Values, and What It Means to Be Human* (2011).

MARGO BOENIG-LIPTSIN is Research Associate in the Case Study Team, and Doctoral Candidate in the History of Science and Technology at Harvard University.

PAUL DUMOUCHEL is Professor in the Graduate School of Core Ethics and Frontier Sciences at Ritsumeikan University, Kyoto (Japan). His interests lie in the field of the philosophy of biological and social sciences. His publications, often encountering the work of René Girard, include *L'enfer des choses: René Girard et la logique de l'économie* (1979); *Emotions: Les empêcheurs de tourner en rond* (1999); *Le sacrifice inutile* (2011); and *The Ambivalence of Scarcity and Other Essays* (2014).

JEAN-PIERRE DUPUY is Professor of Political Science at Stanford University. He is a member of the French Academy of Technology, and head of the ethics commission of the French High Authority on Nuclear Safety and Security. He is cofounder of the Imitatio foundation and current Director of its research program. His publications include *Le sacrifice et l'envie* (1992); *Pour un catastrophisme éclairé* (2004); *La marque du sacré* (2009); *On the Origins of Cognitive Science* (2010); *The Mark of the Sacred* (2013); and *Economy and the Future* (2014).

PAUL GIFFORD is Buchanan Professor of French (Emeritus) at the University of St Andrews, where he directed the Institute of European Cultural Identity Studies. His publications in the field of culture, identity, and religion include his French state thesis *Paul Valéry: Le dialogue des choses divines* (1989); the coedited *2000 Years and Beyond: Faith, Culture and Identity in the Common Era* (2002), which includes contributions by René Girard, Paul Ricoeur, Jürgen Moltmann; and his study of *Love, Desire and Transcendence in French Literature: Deciphering Eros* (2006). He is a member of the French CNRS (ITEM), was in 2007–08 a Visiting Scholar at Stanford University, and is sometime Visiting Research Fellow with the Stanford-based Girardian foundation Imitatio.

ROBERT G. HAMERTON-KELLY was former Senior Research Scholar at the Center for International Security and Arms Control (now the Center for International Security and Cooperation), Stanford University, where he was also Dean of Chapel. He was a founding member of the two most significant Girardian organizations: the standing Colloquium on Violence and Religion, and Imitatio (of which he was Chairman Emeritus until his death in 2013). Books include *Violent Origins: Walter Burkert, René Girard, and Jonathan Z. Smith on Ritual Killing and Cultural Formation* (Editor, 1987); *Sacred Violence: Paul's Hermeneutic of the Cross* (1992); and *The Gospel and the Sacred: The Poetics of Violence in Mark* (1994).

MICHAEL KIRWAN, SJ, is Head of Theology at Heythrop College, London; regular guest lecturer at the Institute of Ecumenical Studies in Prague; and a member of the standing interdisciplinary and international Girardian studies association "Colloquium on Violence and Religion." Among his publications in the field are *Discovering Girard* (2004); *Political Theology: A New Introduction* (2008); and *Girard and Theology* (2009).

MEL KONNER is Samuel Candler Dobbs Professor in the Department of Anthropology at Emory University, currently working with the Neuroscience and Behavioral Biology Program. He taught at Harvard for six years and has been a Fellow with the Center for Advanced Study in the Behavioral Sciences at Stanford University, a member of the Social Science Research Council, and Fellow of the American Association for the Advancement of Science. He is the author of *The Tangled Wing: Biological Constraints on the Human Spirit* (2nd ed. 2002); *Unsettled: An Anthropology of the Jews* (2003); and *The Evolution of Childhood: Relationships, Emotion, Mind* (2010).

LEON MARINCOWITZ is a graduate of the University of Johannesburg, and currently lectures on philosophy and international studies at Monash University (South Africa). He is interested in applying the social thought of René Girard's mimetic theory to violence, post-conflict resolution, and transitional justice and forgiveness in Africa. He has papers and publications on child and youth development, anthropology, political science, international relations, and philosophy.

DUNCAN MORROW is the Chief Executive of the Northern Ireland Community Relations Council, the government-appointed body promoting change toward community reconciliation in the wake of the Good Friday

Agreement. He is also Northern Ireland Sentence Review Commissioner, implementing the early release of paramilitary prisoners under the Agreement. As Lecturer in Politics at the University of Ulster, and later, as cofounder of that university's Future Ways Programme, he developed a framework for learning and training courses on issues of diversity, trust-building, and equity. He is coauthor of *A Worthwhile Venture? Practically Investing in Equity, Diversity and Inter-dependence in N. Ireland* (1997).

MICHAEL NORTHCOTT is Professor of Ethics in the School of Divinity at the University of Edinburgh. His research focuses on the interface between religious ethics and ecology. His published works include *The Environment and Christian Ethics* (1996), *A Moral Climate: The Ethics of Global Warming* (2007); *Theology after Darwin* (2009), edited with R. J. Berry; *Diversity and Dominion: Dialogues in Ecology, Ethics, and Theology* (2010), edited with Kyle S Vanhoutan; *A Political Theology of Climate Change* (2014); *Climate Change and Systematic Theology* (2014), edited with Peter Scott; and *Place, Ecology and the Sacred* (2015).

JON PAHL is the Peter Paul and Elizabeth Hagan Professor of History and Director of MA Programs in The Lutheran Theological Seminary at Philadelphia. He is the author, most recently, of *Empire of Sacrifice: The Religious Origins of American Violence* (2012), and he is working on a sequel entitled "A Coming Religious Peace" that explores the history and potential of American religious peacebuilding. Dr. Pahl is also conducting ongoing research on the global Hizmet ("service") movement associated with the Turkish imam Fethullah Gülen.

WOLFGANG PALAVER is the Dean of the School of Catholic Theology of the University of Innsbruck. He was also President of the Colloquium on Violence and Religion, and Chair of the "Politics-Religion-Violence" working group of the Austrian Research Association; from 1991–1992, he was Visiting Fellow at the Center for International Security and Arms Control at Stanford University. Palaver is Editor in chief of the "Edition Weltordnung-Religion-Gewalt" series. He has published extensively on René Girard's mimetic theory of religion and violence, most recently *René Girard's Mimetic Theory* (2013).

JAMES WELLMAN is Professor and Chair of Comparative Religion at the Jackson School of International Studies, University of Washington. His field is American religious culture, history, and politics. Publications include *The Power of Religious Publics: Staking Claims in American Society* (1999); *Belief and Bloodshed: Religion and Violence across Time and Tradition* (2007); and *Religion and Human Security: A Global Perspective* (2012).

ROWAN WILLIAMS was born in South Wales and studied in Cambridge and Oxford. After seventeen years of teaching theology, he became Bishop of Monmouth in 1992, Archbishop of Wales in 1999, and Archbishop of Canterbury in 2002. He is now Master of Magdalene College, Cambridge. He has written numerous books of poetry, literary criticism, ethics, and theology, including *Dostoevsky: Language, Faith and Fiction* (2008), in which he first encountered the work of René Girard, and *The Edge of Words* (2014), based on his widely followed Gifford lectures, given in 2013 at Edinburgh University.

DERICK WILSON, MBE is Reader in Education (Emeritus) at the University of Ulster, specializing in Community Relations and Restorative Practices in a six-country EU research program, "ALTERNATIVE." As Director of the Corrymeela Reconciliation Centre (1978–85) he developed an extensive practical Girard Study Programme. He has also been an Academic Associate of the Victims and Survivors Forum; Northern Ireland Equality Commissioner (2002–07); and Research Fellow with the Centre for the Study of Conflict (1985–91), University of Ulster. With Duncan Morrow, he cofounded "Future Ways," a university based community research, teaching, and learning program for Northern Ireland (1989–2006).

HARALD WYDRA is a Fellow of St Catharine's College, Cambridge. He previously taught political science at Regensburg and has held visiting fellowships at the École des hautes études en sciences sociales (Paris), and the National University of Australia (Canberra) and was Visiting Professor at the University of *Paris Ouest Nanterre-La Défense*. He is founding Editor of the journal *International Political Anthropology*. Wydra's books include *Communism and the Emergence of Democracy* (2007), *Democracy and Myth in Russia and Eastern Europe* (2008), *Politics and the Sacred* (2015), and *Breaking Boundaries: Varieties of Liminality* (2015).

Index

A

abjection, 40, 45n5, 60

ACC (anthropogenic climate change). *See* climate change

Adams, Gerry, 221, 236

Adams, Rebecca, 321

Aeschylus, 100, 101

Age of Stupid, 290

Ahmadinejad, Mahmoud, 246

Alderdice, John, 235–36, 248n1

Alison, James, 313, 316–17, 319, 325

al-Qaeda, 63, 239, 240, 276

altruism, parochial, 97–99, 101–3, 108, 112; universal, xl, 247. *See also* Christianity: universalism and; universalism

Anders, Günther, 263–64

animals: altruism and cooperation among, 5–7, 9–10, 15; animal-human interface, xxxii; competition and conflict, 5–7, 9–17, 22nn9–11; ritualized behavior of, 32; as sacrificial victims, 37, 57, 119, 157, 259; sociality of, 8–10, 21n3, 22n7, 51; violence between, xv, xxxix, 3–17, 19–21, 22n13

Anselm, 296

Anspach, Mark, 260, 281

Anthropocene era, 289

anthropology, xxi, xxviii, xxx, xxxix, 26, 28, 52, 55, 62, 98, 116–18, 129–30. *See also* Girard, René: as anthropologist

Antigone. See Sophocles

anti-Semitism, 60, 104, 130, 239–40

Antonello, Pierpaolo, 73

Apartheid. *See* South Africa

apocalypticism (apocalypse), xx, xxi–xxiii, xxv–xxvi, xxviii, xxxii, xxxvi–xxxviii, xl, 58, 98, 107–8, 137, 143–44, 155; alternatives within, 311–29; in American history, 73; apocalyptic age, 90, 289; climate change and, 287–91, 296–97; and consumerism, 298–302; gospel reticence in respect of, 313–316; in New Testament, 125, 132, 162, 283–84, 302, 304, 307, 313, 314–15, 319–20, 323–24, 328; nuclear, 253–58, 261–64, 268, 324; psychopoetics of apocalyptic imagination, 146–51, 312, 316; semantic ambiguity and, 302–7, 311–12, 326

Appleby, Scott, 85

Arendt, Hannah, 81

Aristotle, 17

atheists, xx, xxii, xxxvii–xxxviii, 79, 85, 90n7, 135, 244, 248n4

Atlan, Henri, 258, 273–74, 281

337

PIEPAOLO ANTONELLO is Reader in modern Italian literature and culture at the University of Cambridge and Fellow of St John's College. He is coeditor of the series Italian Modernities for Peter Lang, Oxford, and he is a member of the Research and Publications committees of Imitatio.

PAUL GIFFORD is Buchanan Professor of French emeritus at the University of St Andrews, where he also was Departmental Chair for seven years and directed the Institute of European Cultural Identity Studies for ten years. He is one of the very few non-French academics to hold the most prestigious of France's many doctorates, the Doctorat d'État ès Lettres.